THE
MOST HATED MAN
IN AMERICA

Jerry Sandusky
and the Rush to Judgment

MARK PENDERGRAST

Mechanicsburg, PA USA

Published by Sunbury Press, Inc.
Mechanicsburg, Pennsylvania

SUNBURY

www.sunburypress.com

For information about special discounts for bulk purchases, please contact Sunbury Press Orders Dept. at (855) 338-8359 or orders@sunburypress.com.

To request one of our authors for speaking engagements or book signings, please contact Sunbury Press Publicity Dept. at publicity@sunburypress.com.

ISBN: 978-1-62006-765-9 (Trade paperback)
ISBN: 978-1-62006-766-6 (Mobipocket)

Library of Congress Control Number: 2017959083

FIRST SUNBURY PRESS EDITION: October 2017

Product of the United States of America
0 1 1 2 3 5 8 13 21 34 55

Set in Bookman Old Style
Designed by Crystal Devine
Cover by Lawrence Knorr
Cover photos from Getty Images
Edited by Janice Rhayem

Continue the Enlightenment!

To Dottie Sandusky, for her steadfast courage

For I am become as it were a monster unto many:
But thou art my sure trust....
Cast me not off in the time of age:
Forsake me not when my strength faileth.

—Psalm 71: 7-9, Geneva Bible (1599)

— TABLE OF CONTENTS —

— FOREWORD —

By Gary Gray, Visiting Professor of Finance,
Penn State Smeal College of Business

T HE MOST Hated Man in America raises important questions about the Jerry Sandusky case. I am a Penn State professor of finance, so I lived through the shock, grief, and outrage that occurred on this campus, in this state, and in this country in the wake of the Jerry Sandusky scandal.

But for me, it was even worse, because I thought I had known Jerry Sandusky as a true hometown hero. I went to Penn State on a football scholarship and was a linebacker during the 1968-72 seasons. Then I was Jerry Sandusky's graduate assistant (assistant coach) in 1975 and 1976, as he was planning to start the Second Mile program. When word of molestation allegations leaked out, I didn't believe them, and I wrote a letter to the editor supporting my old mentor. In part, I wrote:

> He (Jerry Sandusky) is straightforward, honest and caring—a person that I have always admired. I have never known him to take an alcoholic drink, never heard him utter a cuss word (and he could have legitimately cursed at me on many occasions), or tell a lie. I remember well when the Second Mile was just his dream. He talked often about it and worked tirelessly to raise funds to start that charity (disclosure—I am a contributor) and he made it wildly successful. I do not believe the allegations against Jerry.

But then the horrific multiple charges against Jerry became public with the Grand Jury Presentment in November 2011, much worse than I could have imagined, and I backed away from him. Everyone did. He was toxic. He had become a monster. I was completely confused. I felt betrayed. I couldn't believe it, but with all those allegations, it *had* to be true.

Still, part of me never could accept it, and now that I have read Pendergrast's thoroughly researched, well-documented book, I believe that my old friend and mentor, Jerry Sandusky, is almost certainly an innocent man, the victim of a tragic miscarriage of justice.

You may or may not conclude the same thing, but I challenge you to read this book with an open mind and judge for yourselves.

Sandusky, the Monster Story

How easy it was to erase a man's past and to construct a new version of him, an overwhelming version, against which it seemed impossible to fight. —Salman Rushdie, *Joseph Anton: A Memoir*[1]

J ERRY SANDUSKY, former defensive coordinator of the Penn State football team and now convicted of serial child molestation, is perhaps the most hated man in America. Everyone now knows him as the pedophile who was discovered sodomizing a ten-year-old boy in the shower. Sandusky allegedly got away with his sick predatory behavior with children for years. In 1977, he started the Second Mile program, supposedly to help troubled youth, but really as a kind of juvenile candy shop where he could find fresh, vulnerable boys to groom and molest, as the abuse narrative has it.

In 1998, the first alarm bell went off when the mother of a Second Mile boy learned that Sandusky had showered naked with her child. She turned him in to the police, but they couldn't prove that he had done anything illegal and let him go. Just three years later, grad student Mike McQueary (who had played quarterback at Penn State and would go on to be an assistant coach there) walked into a Penn State locker room and heard wet slapping sounds that he interpreted as sexual. It was Sandusky with a boy. McQueary alerted Penn State officials, who didn't inform the police, but merely prohibited Sandusky from working out with boys in Penn State facilities.

Finally, in November 2008, a shy fifteen-year-old boy named Aaron Fisher blew the whistle on Sandusky, telling high school officials that he had been touched inappropriately. Psychologist Mike

Gillum, under contract with Clinton County Children and Youth Services (CYS), encouraged the traumatized Fisher to tell him the worst—Sandusky had forced oral sex on him—and Gillum and CYS told the cops. Still, Sandusky wasn't arrested until three years later, in November 2011, after the Grand Jury Presentment was issued. After the trial, Fisher, his mother, and Gillum described these events in their book, *Silent No More*.[2]

Crusading local reporter Sara Ganim had first revealed the Sandusky investigation on March 31, 2011, eight months before.[3] But it was only after the Grand Jury Presentment was made public that the media exploded with the sensational story. "The number one priority has to be protecting our kids," pronounced President Barack Obama, who suggested that the allegations leveled against Jerry Sandusky should move the entire nation to do "some soul-searching."[4] Penn State board members searched their souls and quickly fired both legendary Head Coach Joe Paterno and University President Graham Spanier.[5] Just before they voted to do so, Pennsylvania Governor Tom Corbett told the Penn State board via speakerphone, "Remember that little boy in the shower."[6] The following Saturday, during the Nebraska-Penn State football game, Paterno was diagnosed with lung cancer. He died two months later, his reputation in ruins.

More self-proclaimed Sandusky victims came forward. There were ten official alleged victims by the time the trial began in June 2012, though two remained unidentified. In the middle of the trial, one of Sandusky's adopted sons, Matt (who had previously supported his father and testified for him in front of the grand jury), went to the police and revealed that he, too, had been abused.

After Sandusky, then sixty-eight, was convicted on forty-five counts of child sexual abuse, more men came forward to say that Sandusky had molested them as well. Penn State University set aside $60 million to pay the alleged victims, but that was just the start. So far, there have been thirty-three confirmed settlements for a total of $93 million, yielding an average of $2.8 million per alleged victim, though the individual amounts and names of all recipients have not been made public. The fallout from the Sandusky scandal continued, with former Penn State University President Graham Spanier, former Vice President Gary Schultz, and former Athletic Director Tim Curley prosecuted for allegedly covering up complaints against Sandusky and failing to notify the police, NCAA sanctions against Penn State, federal Clery Act fines, a multi-million-dollar whistleblower lawsuit, and more.[7]

The overwhelming loathing that the name Jerry Sandusky now evokes was captured in an editorial by former policeman Peter Bella, who wrote a column headlined, "Jerry Sandusky More Than a Monster," in the days following Sandusky's conviction:

> *Sandusky was a pillar of the community, a local celebrity and a man of stature. People looked up to him. He was good-looking, personable, charming, and dressed well. He was the perfect example of upper middle class success and achievement.*
>
> *Sandusky lived a horrible dark secret life. He terrorized and sexually abused children. Children who trusted him. Children whom he carefully selected. Children who had behavioral, emotional, and social problems that made them vulnerable.*
>
> *These children sought or were brought to Second Mile, the charity Sandusky established and ran. He used the charity to troll for victims then prey upon them.*[8]

* * *

But what if this compelling story, which has appalled virtually everyone in America, isn't true? What if Jerry Sandusky was, in fact, what he originally appeared to be—a decent man who tried to help thousands of children? After extensive research and interviews with Jerry Sandusky himself (in two prison visits and extensive correspondence), Sandusky's family members, former colleagues, Second Mile alums, accusers, psychologists, sports figures, and others, I have come to the startling conclusion that Sandusky may indeed be innocent. In the pages that follow, I will argue that his conviction as a serial child molester was a rush to judgment unparalleled in the history of the American media and justice system.

Like virtually all Americans, I deplore the sexual abuse of children, which occurs far too frequently in our society. But I also deplore false allegations and false convictions, and these occur far too frequently as well, especially when horrific allegations pile atop one another in a media-fueled frenzy.

What follows will emphasize that memory is a crucial factor in the Sandusky case. Not only is memory fallible, but it can be reshaped by influential authority figures and prevailing opinions. Even if Sandusky did not molest anyone, this does not necessarily mean that all his accusers were consciously lying. They may have envisioned abuse scenarios which, over time, have become all too real for them.

The American public assumes that the multiple allegations against Jerry Sandusky must have been irrefutable—how else could he have been convicted? Yet no one outside the prosecution has provided a detailed analysis of the case, and the actual facts may surprise you. Contrary to inaccurate media reports and how these shaped public perception of Sandusky, there were no credible eyewitnesses to molestation, and this includes the alleged sodomy in the shower. Sandusky had no pornography on his computer or anywhere else, nor was there any other physical evidence. If he was in fact a pedophile, he apparently showed no signs of his sexual attraction to children until his fifties, whereas pedophiles usually are in their late teens when they begin trying to seduce children.*

Of the hundreds of former Second Mile kids interrogated by the police, just over one percent eventually agreed that Sandusky abused them (some with help from psychotherapists in enhancing their memories). Many of the other Second Mile alums not only refused to accuse Jerry Sandusky but, as one policeman complained in an email, "We have recently been interviewing kids who don't believe the allegations as published and believe Sandusky is a great role model for them and others to emulate."[9]

It is impossible to prove a negative, and no one can *prove* that Sandusky didn't molest any children. But there are clearly many problems with the way the allegations came about, and there is a reasonable case to be made for Sandusky's innocence. It is a matter of weighing the evidence, and then readers can reach their own conclusions.

The idea of a serial child molester getting away with his crimes for years is compelling, shocking, and makes for great press. If true, it *should* be shocking. But the converse is equally true. It would be shocking if an innocent man has been sent to prison in such a high-profile, emotional case. Yet in the current climate, few have dared to express any doubts, let alone suggest that Sandusky may not be a pedophile, and those who question the conventional monster narrative have been ignored or shunned, as demonstrated by the case of lone crusader John Ziegler, covered here in Chapter 19. The real story needs to be told.

---

* Anonymous accusers later came forward (after Sandusky's conviction) to claim abuse as far back as 1966, when Sandusky was twenty-two, but the claims are highly questionable, especially since millions of dollars were at stake, and they involve stereotypical claims of rapes in basements and the like.

This book is part psychological thriller, part detective story, and part cautionary tale about how moral panics can be created by our media, public perception, and legal system. The Jerry Sandusky saga has condemned not only the accused former coach, who will spend the rest of his life in prison (unless he is granted a new trial), but also the legendary Joe Paterno, former University President Graham Spanier, two other accused administrators, the entire Second Mile program for helping troubled youth, Penn State University as a whole, and members of the Sandusky family who still support him. It has also damaged the alleged victims, if they have come to envision and believe in traumatic events that never occurred.

The case has thus far probably cost over $1 billion in legal fees, remuneration, spin-off investigations and studies, related lawsuits, and time.[10]

This book explains why Jerry Sandusky could be innocent. It also presents historical examples of cases in which people convicted of equally heinous crimes were later exonerated and explains how such cases were the result of moral panics. These include the Salem Witch Trials and the false convictions of care workers in Welsh facilities who allegedly molested troubled adolescents.

Ultimately, *The Most Hated Man in America* is not simply a book about the Jerry Sandusky case. It is about how easily our memories can be revised to suit the wishes of authority figures and prevailing opinions, and how moral panics can make it reprehensible to even suggest examining the facts more carefully.

The key to understanding what took place in the Sandusky case is to look closely at the role of psychotherapy in convincing young men that they were abused. At issue is the search for "repressed memories," a fad in psychotherapy that peaked in the late 1980s and 1990s before it was thoroughly discredited by memory scientists, investigative reporters, and multi-million-dollar judgments against offending therapists. But such therapy did not disappear and continues to destroy lives and families—the subject of my 2017 books, *Memory Warp* and *The Repressed Memory Epidemic*. This type of discredited therapy played a starring, though hidden, role in the Sandusky case.

Through such suggestive influences, the original alleged victims kept changing and modifying their stories; none of these accusers spontaneously came forward to say that Sandusky abused them. It was only after their parents, the police, lawyers, and therapists became involved that the abuse narrative grew. Likewise, Mike McQueary kept changing his testimony. Despite widespread and inaccurate media reporting to the contrary, he did *not* see San-dusky sodomizing a child in the shower. He overhead slapping sounds from the shower that he interpreted as sexual, when it was (according to the young man who later identified himself as that boy in the shower) Sandusky and a thirteen-year-old boy snapping towels at one another.

Once it became clear that Penn State was going to dispense mil-lions of dollars in reparations to alleged victims, repressed memory therapy became less important. Financial incentives and lawyers became the drivers for allegations at that point, though counsel-ing may also have played a role in enhancing the certainty of the "memories" of abuse.

A word on the organization of *The Most Hated Man in America*. The first section, "Creating Victims," delves into the specific allega-tions, who made them, and why they may be false. The second sec-tion, "The Rush to Judgment," reviews the events from the time the Grand Jury Presentment was made public on November 4, 2011, which introduced the myth of the shower sodomy and eight origi-nal "victims," through the June 2012 trial and its aftermath. The third section, "The Real Jerry Sandusky," explores who Sandusky really was, before he was turned into a Monster and imprisoned, including what he, his wife, and children have to say, as well as Second Mile alums and former colleagues who continue to support him. This section includes a portrait of Sandusky's life in prison, where he is kept in solitary confinement. His wife, Dottie, drives several hours each week to visit him. She is not allowed to hug or even touch him. A final chapter reviews the evidence and draws conclusions.

One of the first things I did when I began this investigation was to interview Sandusky's children. All six children were adopted. The Sanduskys couldn't have their own biological children, because Jerry Sandusky's testosterone levels were too low. I thought that if Sandusky were a serial child molester, a compulsive pedophile, surely he would have abused his adopted children, who were not even biologically related. And, indeed, his last adopted son, Matt, after vociferously defending Sandusky at the grand jury proceed-ings in 2011, turned on him in the middle of the 2012 trial, alleg-ing that Sandusky had abused him after all. (Matt's saga, which includes repressed memories, is covered in Chapter 10.)

Yet the other five children—four men and one woman—told a very different story. Their father had never molested them, they told me, and they didn't believe that he had touched Matt either.

Nor did they think that Jerry Sandusky was a pedophile. He had been a loving father, perhaps naïve about the ways of the world, but a genuinely kind, concerned man. Yet when I interviewed them in 2013, they wouldn't go public with what they told me, because (for understandable reasons) none of them trusted the media. Also, they feared that amidst the hysteria and anger, their careers might be ruined, their families hurt, their children traumatized. So they remained silent, with their lack of public support for their father perceived as another indication that Jerry Sandusky was indeed guilty.

When I approached them again near press time in 2017, several finally agreed to go on the record. Here is what Jon Sandusky, now a football scout, told me:

> Dad never abused me, and I can't imagine that he abused anyone else. I always thought the Second Mile kids—mostly young adolescents—Dad brought into the house were like extended family. He treated them the same as us, wrestling, or whatever with them. He thought of them as being his sons, which is where this whole boundary issue thing comes into play. Others couldn't grasp that concept.

> His whole picture of the world was stuck in the 1950s and 1960s, with no concept of what was politically correct or what is taboo nowadays. He's living in an era where taking communal showers at the Y was fine. To him, horsing around in the shower, snapping towels or throwing soap wasn't out of the realm of normality, especially through the lens of a father/son relationship. But people's view of the world is different now, and you have to be much more careful, even if you don't think you are doing anything wrong. I don't think he really understood that.

> My parents gave me morals. They taught me how to live my life, with a work ethic but mixing in pleasure, too, with trips to bowl games, kickball games in the back yard, trips to the lake. They were well-rounded parents. They modeled things I'm striving to be as a parent myself. Church was a big deal on Sunday. Dad would go into his office before we'd leave for church, then we'd have lunch together, then back to his office because Sunday and Monday were big game planning days. He was either with us, helping a Second Mile kid, or back to football.

He was there every night for dinner at 6 p.m. It was a big deal to him, eating dinner as a family. I tell my friends that now, and they say, "What are you talking about?" We lived in an era of hard work, family growth and discipline.

I need my vacations, my TV time. But Dad didn't need that stuff, the material things, the vacations. He was passionate about helping people. If he didn't help someone, he felt it was a bad day. It's how he grew up, his parents were that way. There are times I feel guilty I'm not more that way.

I also interviewed Second Mile kids who did *not* accuse Jerry Sandusky of abuse.* They didn't find lawyers, didn't look for money, didn't go to therapists who helped them seek abuse memories. Some of them are quoted later in this book. A few didn't want their names used either. They were afraid for their own jobs and families. Here's a typical interview excerpt:

Jerry would make sure I got to picnics at their house. I would go on trips with him and his family. Jerry would take me to sports banquets. He was always there for me. Jerry really helped me get through school. He has done so much for me. He made me who I am today. I used to tell him all the time how much he means to me. This just doesn't add up or make any sense, all these accusations. Jerry would go so far out of his way to pick up kids that needed rides. As I grew up, I appreciated him even more. A lot of kids really took advantage of him. They didn't even say thank you. All his dedication and time went to helping kids who needed help. I was totally devastated by this. He called me to tell me these things were happening, that he was being accused of things that just were not true. He was always up front and honest with me.

Finally, I will try to explain who Jerry Sandusky was and is. He grew up in a recreation center run by his parents, a world of innocent sports and easy camaraderie, of good sportsmanship, pickup games, and, yes, shared showers for boys and men. Sandusky matured into a kind of "big kid" who became a successful college

---

* I attempted to interview those who claimed that Sandusky had abused them but was able to interview only one of them, Dustin Struble. Otherwise I relied on their police interviews, courtroom testimony, or public documents.

football coach and a mentor for troubled youth. He was also ignorant beyond belief in terms of culturally sanctioned views about "boundaries" and what could be misinterpreted as grooming for sexual abuse. He sometimes showered with boys after exercise. He squeezed their knees when he was driving. He wrestled with them, threw them in the swimming pool, cracked their backs, tickled them, kissed them goodnight. It is clear that he enjoyed their company. But none of these affectionate gestures means that he sexually abused them.

Besides, it seems unlikely that a pedophile would call his autobiography *Touched*, as Sandusky did when he published it in 2000, or form a singing group called the Great Pretenders (named after the 1950s song by the Platters, and a self-deprecatory reference to their terrible singing) at Second Mile camps with another football coach and staff. Of course, such observations are in no way "proof" of his innocence. Sandusky may have been an incredibly bold or stupid pedophile.

Still, it's hard to imagine that he would off-handedly write so many things that could be taken wrong. In *Touched*, Sandusky commented on what he meant by being a "pretender," which would later be quoted as evidence of his guilt. "I live a good part of my life in a make-believe world. I enjoyed pretending as a kid, and I love doing the same as an adult with these kids. Pretending has always been a part of me. I've loved trying to do the right things to hopefully make a difference in kids' lives and maybe make things better off for them. . . . I enjoy the life that I have had, and I'll never regret being called a 'great' pretender."[11]

Those ellipses in the quote above (as it was used in a book assuming Sandusky's guilt) left out two important qualifying sentences: "I am tough and competitive with the kids, but the one thing that has never been pretend or make-believe about me is my genuine love and care for the kids. I've always wanted to be accountable and trustworthy to them." Earlier in his book, Sandusky also made it clear that his "pretending" as a child involved his acting out all the parts in a baseball game.[12]

In another passage that could easily be read in a sinister light, he wrote: "Wherever I went, it seemed like trouble was sure to follow. Not the kind of trouble that would land me in jail. Just the mischievous kind of trouble. The kind that might leave me with a bloodied nose or a reprimand from a teacher. . . . I thrived on testing the limits of others, and I enjoyed taking chances in danger."

Finally, if you had been molesting children in the family basement, it is hard to imagine that you would write this passage:

> One time, there were some Second Mile kids at our house, and Dottie [my wife] was concerned that they might be misbehaving in the basement. She asked me to check on the source of the noise down there . . . I descended the stairs, and as I turned the corner, there came one of the dogs flying over the sofa. I barely had time to turn my head when next came one of the kids hurtling over the same sofa . . . I rolled my eyes, threw my hands in the air, and went back upstairs. "Everything's fine," I said to Dottie. "Just another typical, normal evening in the Sandusky household." And that really was a common way of life for us. Kids sometimes turning the place upside down, and I was often the biggest kid in attendance.[13]

— SECTION I —

CREATING VICTIMS

— CHAPTER 1 —

What Did Mike McQueary Hear and See?

ECAUSE THERE are so many alleged Sandusky victims, many of whom remain anonymous, it's important to look at how the first allegations against Sandusky developed. Let's look first at the infamous sodomy-in-the-shower scene, since that is usually regarded as the most compelling, horrifying evidence. I know that's what convinced me that Sandusky was guilty when I first heard about the case.

The Sandusky Grand Jury Presentment of November 5, 2011, a summary of secret grand jury testimony, stated that, on March 1, 2002, a Penn State graduate assistant (later identified as Mike McQueary) had gone to the Lasch Football Building at Penn State around 9:30 p.m. As he entered the locker room, he heard "rhythmic, slapping sounds" that sounded sexual to him. "He looked in the shower. He saw a naked boy, Victim 2, whose age he estimated to be ten years old, with his hands up against the wall, being subjected to anal intercourse by a naked Sandusky."[1]

Because grand jury testimony is supposed to be secret, there is no available public transcript to show exactly what Mike McQueary said there, but it is clear from everything else he said about this incident, including his subsequent courtroom testimony, that he did *not* witness sodomy or any other form of sexual abuse that day in the Lasch locker room. His version of events morphed over time, but none of the narratives included witnessing overt sexual abuse.

Here's what appears to have happened. On a Friday night, December 29, 2000, over a year earlier than the inaccurate date in the grand jury presentment, Jerry Sandusky was indeed taking a shower with a Second Mile boy in the locker room of the Lasch

11

Football Building.*[2] Sandusky took it for granted that boys and men showered together after exercise. It was part of the way he was raised, an accepted part of the sports world. Though he had retired as a Penn State coach two years before, he could still use the facilities, and he sometimes brought the troubled Second Mile boys there for a workout, followed by a shower.

As he often did, Sandusky, whom everyone considered "a big kid" himself, was goofing around with the boy. They were snapping towels at each other, or perhaps slap boxing, according to both Sandusky and the boy in the shower. Mike McQueary, then twenty-six, who had been a Penn State quarterback as an undergraduate, was halfway through his post-graduate education, while working as an assistant football coach. This Friday evening, he came to the Lasch building to retrieve tapes of possible recruits. On the way, he figured he might as well put his new shoes away in the locker room.[3]

Before he opened the door to the locker room, McQueary heard slapping sounds. He thought they sounded sexual. As McQueary later put it when describing the scene, "Visualizations come to your head."[4] By the time he got to his locker at the near end of the wall, it had quieted down. Curious, he looked obliquely into the shower room through a mirror across the room and caught a glimpse of a boy in the shower. Then an arm reached out and pulled the boy back. Horrified, he assumed that he had just overheard the sounds of child sexual abuse. After closing his locker, he saw Jerry Sandusky walk out of the shower. *Was his former coach a pedophile?*

McQueary quickly left the building and called his father, John McQueary, and told him his suspicions. His father advised him to come right over to talk about it. Then John McQueary called his employer and friend, Dr. Jonathan Dranov, a nephrologist, asking him to come over and help them sort out Mike's disturbing experience.

---

* This shower date is a best approximation. Because Mike McQueary went to see Joe Paterno about the incident on Feb. 10, 2001, most commentators have assumed that the shower must have taken place the previous day. But investigator John Ziegler makes a powerful case that it actually occurred on December 29, 2000, after Jerry Sandusky had done a book signing for his book, *Touched*, and just before he discovered that he was not being offered the head coaching job at the University of Virginia. Sandusky confirms this hypothesis. Ten years later, McQueary recalled that the shower took place during spring break, but in fact it was Christmas break, during which the campus really was nearly deserted, as he recalled, whereas there were various events taking place nearby on Feb. 9, including a hockey game and rock concert.

Dranov attempted, using the diagnostic and interviewing skills that he used with patients, to get a clear description of the scene that had so upset his friend's son. Dranov was unable to get Mike McQueary to put into words anything sexual he had seen, in spite of asking several times, "But what did you *see*?" McQueary explained that he had seen a boy in the shower, and that an arm had then reached out to pull him back. Dranov asked if the boy had looked scared or upset. No. Did Mike actually see any sexual act? No. McQueary kept returning to the "sexual" sounds.[5]

Upon the advice of his father and Dr. Dranov, Mike McQueary eventually took his concerns to legendary head coach Joe Paterno at his home. Apparently because McQueary did not actually witness anything sexual, they did not suggest he contact the police, nor did they feel called upon to do so.

If the date of December 29, 2000, is correct for the shower, then Mike McQueary went to see Joe Paterno over five weeks later, on Saturday, February 10, 2001. Why did it take him so long? The simplest explanation is that he calmed down and thought that maybe the sounds he overheard weren't worth making a big fuss about. And he may have decided to see Paterno partly as an excuse to ask about a job as a wide receiver coach, since Kenny Jackson, who held that position, had just announced on Febuary 8 that he was taking a job with the Pittsburgh Steelers. (McQueary did get that position at Penn State, but that was three years later.)

This was the only initiative McQueary ever took connected with the shower incident. Paterno subsequently told his immediate supervisor, Athletic Director Tim Curley, about it, who told Vice President Gary Schultz and University President Graham Spanier. Curley and Schultz met with McQueary to hear what he had seen and heard.[6] From that conversation, they concluded that Sandusky had been "horsing around" with a kid and that, while it was not sexual abuse, it wasn't a good idea, particularly because they remembered that a parent had complained back in 1998 about Sandusky showering with her child (details on that incident shortly). So Curley told Sandusky that as a result of someone (he didn't name McQueary) complaining about the shower incident, he should stop working out with Second Mile kids on campus, and there the matter was left, case closed.

McQueary apparently accepted that he may have overreacted and that perhaps Sandusky *had* just been "horsing around." He remained at least overtly friendly with Jerry Sandusky over the following years. He signed up for the Sandusky Celebrity Golf Event in the fall of 2001, less than a year after the shower incident, then took part in other Sandusky charity-related events, such as flag football fundraisers coached by Sandusky in March 2002 and April 2004 and another golf event in 2003.[7]

By the time the police questioned McQueary about the shower incident in late 2010, he couldn't remember exactly when it occurred, and he said that it happened during spring break of 2002, more than a year after the actual date. At the time, McQueary was a 6'4", 220-pound twenty-six-year-old. Some critics would later question why, if he had witnessed horrifying child sexual abuse, he would not have rushed in to put a stop to the behavior.

McQueary's story changed several times after the police told him that they *knew* Sandusky was a pedophile, as we will see in Chapter 12. In response to the police telling him that Sandusky was a child molester, McQueary searched his decade-old memory and now "remembered" seeing something that he had not reported back in 2000 or 2001—that he had seen Sandusky with his hips moving against a boy's backside in the shower.

In short, Mike McQueary did not witness Jerry Sandusky sodomizing a ten-year-old boy in the shower, although he later came to believe that he had. At the time of the incident, he overheard slapping sounds and interpreted them as being sexual.

We know a great deal more about this incident because we know the identity of that boy, a Second Miler named Allan Myers, who was nearly fourteen years old at the time, not ten, and who remained friends with Sandusky until after the allegations created a public furor in November 2011. Sandusky later recalled that shower with Myers. "He [Allan] turned on every shower [and] he was like wild, he put soap on himself and was sliding, he was seeing how far he could slide. I remember that. Then we may have been like slapping towels, slap boxing, doing something like that." He laughed, remembering that "he (Allan) always, no matter what, he'd always get the last lick in."*[8]

Recalling his relationship with Allan Myers, Sandusky said, "He was like family. We did all kinds of things together. We studied. We tutored. We worked out. He went to California with my wife and me twice. He spoke for the Second Mile numerous times." This all took place after the December 2000 shower incident. "He asked me to speak at his high school graduation, and I did. He stayed with

---

* This quote is from a long taped prison interview that John Ziegler conducted with Sandusky in February 2013. See Chapter 19.

us the summer after his high school graduation, worked part-time jobs with classes. He would go home on weekends. We went to his wedding."[9]

Indeed, Myers, a Marine who had recently received an honorable discharge at the time the allegations broke, came forward to defend Sandusky, telling Sandusky's lawyer and his investigator, Curtis Everhart, what had actually happened. Myers, born on February 28, 1987, had endured his parents' volatile marriage, in which he witnessed his father threatening his mother with a gun. His guidance counselor suggested Myers for the Second Mile program, which he attended as a fourth and fifth grader, getting to know Jerry Sandusky the second year. Myers said that Sandusky was a "father figure" associated with "many positive events" in his life. On "Senior Night" at a West Branch High School football game, Myers asked Sandusky to walk out onto the field with his mother, as the loudspeaker announced, "Father, Jerry Sandusky," along with his mother's name.

About the McQueary shower incident, Myers said, "This particular night is very clear in my mind." In the shower after a workout, he and Sandusky "were slapping towels at each other, trying to sting each other. I would slap the walls and would slide on the shower floor, which I am sure you could have heard from the wooden locker area."[10] Myers said that he recalled hearing a locker slam but he never saw who closed it. Although McQueary would later claim that both Sandusky and Myers saw him, neither of them had any idea he was there that night.[11]

Myers repeatedly and emphatically denied that Jerry Sandusky had ever sexually abused him. "Never, ever, did anything like that occur." Yes, Sandusky had put his hand on his left knee while he was driving, but that didn't bother him. "I often would stay at Jerry's home overnight," he said. "Jerry never violated me while I was at his home or anywhere else. On many occasions there were numerous people at his home. I felt very safe and at ease at his home, whether alone with Jerry or with others present."

The only thing that made Myers feel uncomfortable and violated was his September 2011 interview with Pennsylvania State Police officers. "They would try to put words in my mouth, take my statement out of context. The PSP investigators were clearly angry and upset when I would not say what they wanted to hear. My final words to the PSP were, 'I will never have anything bad to say about Jerry.'"[12]

Allan Myers also wrote a letter to the newspaper and the Pennsylvania attorney general and submitted a sworn statement to both the Pennsylvania State Police and a private investigator to the effect that he was not abused that night or any other time by Jerry Sandusky.

"I am one of those many Second Mile kids who became a part of Jerry's 'family.' He has been a best friend, tutor, workout mentor and more," Myers wrote to the attorney general. "We've worked together, competed together, traveled together and laughed together. I lived with Jerry and Dottie for three months. Jerry's been there for me for 13 years; and stood beside me at my senior parent's football night. I drove twelve hours to attend his mom's funeral. I don't know what I would have done without him."[13]

Myers wrote that letter on May 1, 2011. But like so many Second Milers, Myers subsequently found a lawyer, Andrew Shubin, and joined the throng of those seeking millions of dollars in compensation for alleged abuse. He did not testify at the trial, however. Both prosecution and defense lawyers knew that Allan Myers was the boy in the 2001 McQueary shower incident, but for their own strategic reasons, neither chose to identify him, so that the jury never learned that Myers was in fact the anonymous "Victim Number 2."[14]

The McQueary story of the alleged sodomy-in-the-shower became the linchpin of the entire case against Sandusky, lighting a fire under the investigation and creating a media firestorm, and it is what led to the firing of Penn State University President Graham Spanier and football coach Joe Paterno, as well as subsequent lawsuits against Spanier and former Penn State administrators Gary Schultz and Tim Curley. Ironically, the sodomy charge of "involuntary deviate sexual intercourse" in the McQueary incident was among the few for which the jury found Sandusky not guilty, since the witness did not say that he had literally seen penetration. The jury did find Sandusky guilty of four other McQueary-related charges: "indecent assault, unlawful contact with a minor, corruption of minors and endangering a child's welfare."[15]

CHAPTER 2

The 1998 Shower Incident

O NE REASON that Curley, Schultz, and Spanier decided to tell Jerry Sandusky not to bring kids to the Penn State showers again, after the McQueary incident in 2001, was due to a previous complaint.

In 1998, Debra McCord became alarmed when her son, eleven-year-old Zachary Konstas, returned home after being with Sandusky and mentioned that they had showered together. A single parent, she wanted to make sure her children were okay. Like most of the children whom Sandusky mentored, Konstas was a Second Mile kid, and Sandusky was particularly concerned about him because of the childhood cancer from which Konstas had suffered. Sandusky often expressed compassion for those who were disabled or otherwise challenged in some way.

On this Sunday evening, May 3, 1998, Sandusky had picked Konstas up at his home to go to the Penn State sports facilities. Konstas later recalled that he got to see the players' gear, he was given a pair of socks, they played "Polish soccer" in the hall (a game using a makeshift ball made from a folded towel), and then spent about twenty minutes in the training room learning to use the equipment. Afterwards, Sandusky indicated that a shower was in order. When they were in the shower, they began to roughhouse, and Konstas recalled that Sandusky grabbed him playfully from behind, saying, "I'm going to squeeze your guts out." Sandusky also lifted him up closer to the showerhead to help him get soap out of his hair.

After this outing, Sandusky took Konstas back to his home. On the way to his room Zach Konstas remarked to his mother, "We took a shower, just in case you're wondering why my hair's wet."

Debra McCord became concerned and asked more questions, to which he responded, "I knew you'd make a big deal of it."[1]

The following morning McCord called her son's therapist, Alycia Chambers, whom he had been seeing for behavioral issues. Chambers advised her to proceed with her plans to involve the police.

By 11:25 a.m. that Monday of May 4, 1998, the mother and son were speaking to Penn State Police Investigator Ronald Schreffler, whose name had been provided to McCord by the wife of a police officer she knew. Around noon John Miller of Centre County Children and Youth Services had been informed of the incident. At 3:00 in the afternoon Zachary Konstas met with Alycia Chambers at her office, where she asked him about Sunday's events. At 8:10 p.m., Detective Schreffler and John Miller interviewed Brendan Kempton, one of Zach's friends, who had also showered once with Sandusky, and who told the police that nothing sexual had occurred. Finally, at 9:45 p.m., Schreffler and Miller interviewed Zachary Konstas officially, tape-recording the session.

During a therapy session that Monday, Chambers probed Zachary for the details of the outing with Jerry. He told her about the Polish soccer, the work-out, the bear hug, and being lifted up under the shower. He told Chambers that he was concerned about making trouble for Sandusky. Chambers thought that Konstas seemed to be getting irritated, so she directed him to do some "release" work. In her notes, she expressed her satisfaction with the good job he did whacking the chair with a tennis racket. She explained how to make a homemade punching bag so that he could release his anger safely at home. His anger may have been directed at figures of authority such as his mother and the police rather than Sandusky, however. Alycia Chambers later shared details of this session with Detective Schreffler.

Miller and Schreffler questioned Zachary Konstas closely about exactly what had happened in the shower. During this interrogation, which took place only about twenty-four hours after the visit with Sandusky, Konstas described his experience once again. The report describes Konstas as "talkative and laid back." Debra McCord, who was allowed to be present during the interview, is described as "agitated."[2] Protocol for good interviewing technique in suspected sex abuse cases forbids others to be present who might contaminate or influence the interview, so the boy's mother should not have been present.[3]

Portions of this interview were revealed during the trial, with John Miller of Children and Youth Services asking the questions:

Miller: Did he try to shampoo your hair or anything?

Konstas: No. He just gave me the bottle of shampoo and I shampooed my hair and everything.

Miller: Okay. At any time in the shower did Jerry's penis look like it was erect?

Konstas: No, no.

Miller: Not at all?

Konstas: No.

Miller: Okay. At what point did Jerry then—you explained to me—what did he do to you then?

Konstas: First—first thing, like he was pretending to try to squeeze my guts out. He, like—after that he was, like, just trying to get the shamp—the soap out of my hair, and he lifted me up. But he lifted me up pretty high so, like, my feet were just around his waist. My back was touching his chest.

Miller: Are you telling me that he never touched you any place that was inappropriate?

Konstas: No, he did not.

Miller: Did he ever ask you to touch him in any place inappropriate?

Konstas: No.

Miller: Okay. Do you know what a good touch is and a bad touch is?

Konstas: Yes, I do.

Miller: What is a good touch?

Konstas: A good touch is like shaking your hand or something, and a hug, and a bad touch is like touching something that you are not supposed to touch.

Miller: Okay, and I'm going to ask you—you know that this is real important—but you tell me, did Jerry ever touch you in a place that was inappropriate?

Konstas: No, he did not.

Miller: Okay. This is the last time I'm going to say this. Okay. And I want you to know that it is very important—it is very important. See, we don't want to get anybody that doesn't deserve to be in trouble—do you feel that Jerry touched you in an inappropriate way when he lifted you up?

Konstas: No, I don't think so.

Miller: Did he ever touch you on your private parts?

Konstas: No.

Miller: Did he ever ask you to touch his private parts?

Konstas: Definitely no. I wouldn't have done it anyways.

Miller: Okay. One last time. Are you sort of not telling us everything to protect—I just—look at something here. Okay. Let me just look at something here. All right.

Konstas: Well, I am just remembering this now, like, the locker room, like, when we were doing on the machine. I think I just remembered this now, like he—like when I was done the first time, when I was, like done on the machines and everything, he just said good job and everything and then I like—I could sort of feel like—he, like, kissed me once or twice on the head, like you would kiss your child, like, on the head. You know what I mean?[4]

Note that Miller used extremely poor interviewing technique. Instead of asking open-ended questions, he began by focusing on Jerry Sandusky's penis and whether it was erect. Unhappy with the answer he got, he asked the same question again. He was never satisfied with Konstas's denial that anything even remotely sexual had taken place. He asked six separate times whether any kind of inappropriate touch had taken place, in addition to focusing on good touch/bad touch. It was very clear to Zachary Konstas that Miller wanted him to come up with *something* incriminating, but the best the eleven-year-old could do was to conjure up an image of Sandusky kissing him on the top of the head during their workout. It sounds as if Konstas may not actually have remembered this kissing on the head, and it may be that even this harmless incident did not occur.

The following day, Children and Youth Services (CYS) of Centre County held a meeting. Because Sandusky was associated with Second Mile, which was an "agent" of CYS, the case was bumped up to the Pennsylvania Department of Public Welfare (DPW). That afternoon Jerry Lauro from DPW informed the police that he was assigned to the case.

Within a few days of the shower incident, a plan was hatched to observe Jerry Sandusky's interaction with Debra McCord, Zachary's mother, from hidden locations in her apartment. McCord phoned Sandusky with a request for him to pick Zach up. Before he arrived, Ronald Schreffler and Ralph Ralston, another Penn State police detective, hid in a bathroom and bedroom in order to take notes. During the conversation, McCord told Sandusky that she didn't approve of him being naked in the shower with her son and that Zach was having trouble sleeping recently. She said that he just hadn't been the same since Sunday. Sandusky asked her if she wanted him to talk to Zach. He was puzzled, because Zach seemed very upbeat when he last saw him. Sandusky asked several times if she wanted him to speak to Zach about it, but McCord said she didn't think that was appropriate. Sandusky then left, not knowing that he was being observed.

Ronald Schreffler reported this unsuccessful attempt to obtain incriminating evidence to the District Attorney's office, and it was decided to arrange another sting effort. McCord was given instructions, and again the ruse was that Sandusky was supposed to pick up Zachary Konstas. When Sandusky arrived, McCord confronted him at the door and blamed him for her son's sudden weird behavior. Sandusky seemed to be prolonging his departure as he tried to resolve the difficulty. From his hidden location, Ronald Schreffler allegedly heard the words, "I would ask forgiveness. I know I will not get it from you. I wish I were dead."

No tape recording was made, so this is hearsay. Sandusky denied that he said this, since he would never have said, "I wish I were dead."[5] During a prison interview, he asserted, "I never said that to anybody. It just wouldn't have come out that way." He did say, however, "I felt bad, though, I did feel bad, because the mother said that she wasn't sure if Zach was going to be allowed to go to football games any more, or things like that, things he wanted to do."[6]

In other words, according to Sandusky, saying "I wish I were dead" just wasn't in his vocabulary or thought process. He felt bad because perhaps Zachary Konstas would be unable to enjoy going to football games or other activities with him. He may have asked for her forgiveness for doing anything that upset her or her son, but he would not have been referring to anything sexual, because nothing sexual had taken place, according to both Zachary Konstas and Jerry Sandusky.

On Thursday, May 8, five days after the shower incident, John Seasock, a psychologist who served as a consultant for Centre County Mental Health and Children and Youth Services, interviewed Zachary Konstas for an hour, as well as talking to a few football coaches, then informed the various agencies of his determination. He could find no indication of child abuse:

> The behavior exhibited by Mr. Sandusky is directly consistent with what can be seen as an expected daily routine of being a football coach. This evaluator spoke to various coaches from high school and college football teams and asked about their locker room behavior. Through verbal reports from these coaches it is not

uncommon for them to shower with players. This appears to be a widespread, acceptable situation, and it appears that Mr. Sandusky followed through with patterning that he has probably done without thought for many years.

Seasock also said that he had never heard of a fifty-two-year-old man suddenly becoming a pedophile, and since no one had ever accused Sandusky in the past, he doubted that the coach had transformed at that age into a child predator. He said that Sandusky didn't "fit the profile of a pedophile," though he didn't explain how he came to that conclusion, and he had not interviewed Sandusky. It is possible that Seasock already knew Sandusky through the coach's work at the Second Mile program, because the psychologist later told Debra McCord that it was customary for someone from the Second Mile to call kids once a week to see how they were doing, in response to her complaints about Sandusky calling her son.[7]

Several weeks later, on June 1, 1998, Jerry Lauro and Detective Schreffler visited the locker room at Penn State, where they interrogated Jerry Sandusky, who explained his routine when he worked out with youth. Schreffler apparently advised him not to shower with any more children, though Sandusky heard only that he was not to shower with Konstas again.[8] A few days later, Sandusky received a notice saying the investigation had concluded and that the concern about possible sexual abuse was unfounded. As far as Sandusky was concerned, the entire affair had been nothing but a neurotic mother misconstruing a perfectly harmless shower after exercise. He didn't learn about the elaborate sting operations, with people hiding in McCord's house, until his trial in 2012.

And there the matter should have ended for all time, according to Pennsylvania state law, which ordered that the unfounded report be "expunged" by the end of 1999. It was indeed deleted from the Department of Public Welfare, but both the Penn State Police and the State College Police departments failed to expunge their records of the closed sex abuse investigation.[9]

Despite Debra McCord's serious effort to incriminate Jerry Sandusky for the 1998 shower incident, over the next dozen years she allowed Zach to spend a great deal of time with the Sanduskys. The following year, when Zachary Konstas did not receive a ticket to the last home game that Jerry Sandusky would coach, she waved Sandusky down on the street, pleading with him to get her son into the stadium, which Sandusky managed to do.

Konstas continued to attend games with Sandusky and other Second Mile kids after Sandusky's 1999 retirement from coaching. Konstas visited the Sandusky home many times after he left the State College area and was treated as if he were a family member, eating meals with them. In 2010 he asked for and received a donation to support his mission trip to Mexico with his church. Konstas borrowed a car from the Sanduskys in the summer of 2011, six months after Konstas had been contacted by the police about the allegations. He and Allan Myers even shared a restaurant meal with Jerry and Dottie Sandusky in July 2011. Myers at that time was still planning to testify for the defense.[10]

Over the years, Konstas expressed his admiration and gratitude to Jerry Sandusky for his role in his life through notes and greeting cards. In 2009, as a twenty-three-year-old, Konstas wrote: "Hey Jerry just want 2 wish u a Happy Fathers Day! Greater things are yet 2 come!" Later that year he wrote: "Happy Thanksgiving bro! I'm glad God has placed U in my life. Ur an awesome friend! Love ya!"[11]

But Zachary Konstas's perceptions were to be altered drastically between the fall of 2010 and June 2012. As Allan Myers did, Konstas got a lawyer. He never did accuse Sandusky of sexually abusing him, but he made it sound as though the coach had wanted to, that Sandusky had been "grooming" him for abuse. He also implied that perhaps Sandusky *had* abused him, but that he, Konstas, had forgotten it. Konstas may have come to believe that he had "repressed" the memories. He had asked another accuser "if [he] remembered anything more, if counseling was helping," and Konstas himself was clearly undergoing psychotherapy. At Sandusky's sentencing hearing, he said, "I have been left with deep, painful wounds that you caused and had been buried in the garden of my heart for many years."[12]

At age eleven, less than a day after the shower, Konstas clearly stated that Sandusky did not have an erection. Thirteen years later, after therapy and discussions with his civil attorney, Konstas, now labeled as "Victim Number 6," repeatedly said that he was afraid to look and implied that Sandusky might well have been aroused. He told the jury that he couldn't remember anything after being lifted to the showerhead because it was "blacked out," implying that something may have happened but had been repressed. He went into great detail about being lathered up with soap, unlike his original testimony, when he told the officers that Sandusky just handed him the shampoo.[13]

Konstas's attorney, Howard Janet, explained in an interview how Konstas and the other alleged victims could "create a bit of a Chinese wall in their minds. They bury these events that were so painful to them deep in their subconscious."[14]

Zachary Konstas may not have recovered specific memories of abuse, but his reinterpretation of his past, along with implications that he may have repressed the memories, were enough for the jury to find Sandusky guilty of *planning* to abuse him. Other alleged victims were far more successful in coming to believe that they had repressed memories of abuse, including oral sex and attempted sodomy. The theory that people can repress traumatic memories of sexual abuse is key to understanding how the allegations against Sandusky were developed.

CHAPTER 3

The Repressed Memory Myth

KNOW THE damage that a belief in such mythical "repressed memories" can do. As a science writer, I am the author of three books on the subject: *Memory Warp* (2017), *The Repressed Memory Epidemic* (2017), and *Victims of Memory* (1996, 2d ed.). My research on human memory and suggestibility has been comprehensive, recognized as such by *Scientific American, Journal of the American Medical Association, Psychological Reports, American Scientist, New York Review of Books*, and many of the world's leading memory experts and psychologists.[1] My work, along with other critical books and studies by psychological scientists and memory researchers, demonstrates that the theory of repressed memories—first put forward in the late-nineteenth century by Sigmund Freud—is pure pseudoscience. The rest of this chapter is a brief tutorial on the subject, but I urge you to read *Memory Warp*, my book that thoroughly explicates the issue, as well as books and articles by Elizabeth Loftus, Richard McNally, Julia Shaw, Paul McHugh, Harrison Pope Jr, Richard Ofshe, Frederick Crews, Paul Simpson, C. J. Brainerd, and others who have come to the same conclusions.[2]

People do not forget years of traumatic events. They remember them all too well. Yet, under the influence of misguided therapy, they can come to "remember" horrifying events with great detail and emotion, even though they are not true.*[3] As memory expert

---

* There is a variant on repressed memory theory, the concept of dissociation, which allegedly produces multiple personality disorder, an iatrogenic "disorder" that is produced by misguided therapy and books. This purported disorder, still mistakenly enshrined in the *Diagnostic and Statistical Manual of Mental Disorders* as "dissociative identity disorder," has it that severe childhood trauma can be completely forgotten because an "alter" (alternate personality) develops to cope with the trauma outside the consciousness of the "host" personality. I debunked this theory in my repressed memory books, as have other science writers. It doesn't matter whether you call the mechanism "repression" or "dissociation"—people do not completely forget years of traumatic childhood abuse.

Elizabeth Loftus observed in a Sandusky hearing, "People can be very emotional and detailed and confident about [memories] even when they're false."[4] Not only that, many studies have shown that false memories can be "largely indistinguishable from true memories in both emotional content and brain activation," as researchers concluded in a 2015 summary article.[5]

Several alleged Sandusky victims apparently underwent such therapy, even though, by the time of the Sandusky trial, it had been thoroughly discredited in the scientific community, which is why the lawyers did not trumpet the way that some abuse "memories" in the Sandusky case had been created during suggestive therapy. Repressed memory therapy became a hidden, secret weapon of sorts in the Sandusky case. The term was never used by the prosecution, but the concepts of repression (or dissociation, which amounts to the same thing) informed not only the therapists who treated the alleged victims, but the police and prosecutors.

Even normal memory is subject to distortion and bias, particularly as time passes, which is why several Sandusky trial witnesses who did not go to therapy to seek "repressed memories" came to alter their recall of events and to embellish them towards recalling Sandusky as a child abuser. Most of us think of our brains as being similar to computers or file drawers. We believe that we "store" memories in specific mental compartments, and that with the appropriate mental keystroke, they can be retrieved intact. But that's not how memory works. Our brains are in fact mini-lightning storms of tiny electrical currents snapping over billions of synapses awash in a sea of hormones. We do not record the past in neat, computer-like bits and bytes.

Our memories are stored in fragments all over our brains, and every time we recall something, we have to reassemble it. We literally "re-member," patching together the puzzle bits of our past. The human species has evolved a brain that is adaptable, nimble, versatile, and imaginative, but not always accurate. In fact, our memories are never full representations of what really happened, though they are usually fairly close. Yet the further back in time we stretch to recall, the less accurate we tend to be, and the more subject to distortion to match our current attitudes and prejudices.

We also forget a good deal more than we remember. Moreover, our versions of the personal past are highly colored by our own emotions, family myths, and opinions. Most of us recognize that our siblings tend to recall the same events from different perspectives.

We are quite capable of projecting emotions and reinterpretations backward through time, and of creating absolutely clear memories of events that never occurred. This phenomenon is shocking to many people, because it threatens our cherished sense of self. Who should know better than *we* what *we* have experienced? Yet, as pioneering memory scientist Frederic Bartlett wrote in his classic 1932 book, *Remembering: A Study in Experimental and Social Psychology*, we engage in an "effort after meaning," rewriting our pasts to make them match our current opinions. Our memories "display invention, condensation, elaboration, simplification and all the other alterations which my experiments constantly illustrated."[6]

Bartlett did not, of course, assert that memories bore no relationship to real events of the past. He posited that we can indeed recall specific details, particularly through words and visual images, but we weave those bits into a reconstructed narrative. It is, as Bartlett put it, "the struggle to get somewhere, . . . and the eventual building up of the complete story accompanied by the more and more confident advance in a certain direction."[7] The problem is that this confidence can be misplaced.

When we struggle to remember events from our lives, we begin with a general attitude or framework, then fill in the gaps with probable dialogue and detail. Or, as psychologist Stephen Crites put it: "To the extent that a coherent identity is achievable at all, the thing must be made, a story-like production with many pitfalls, and it is constantly being revised, sometimes from beginning to end."[8]

Similarly, we can summon up fragmentary visual images and edit them into an internal movie of our lives. "The immediate return of certain details is common enough," Bartlett wrote, "and it certainly looks very much like the direct re-excitation of certain traces." Once these images pop up, "the need to remember becomes active, an attitude is set up."[9] From these beginnings, a visual scenario develops, the psychic camera rolls, and the imagination—whose root word, after all, is "image"—takes over. We become expert actors in the internal drama of our own lives. At first, these memories may seem tentative, but with repeated visualization, or the verbal repetition of the stories, they become more real. Memory, then, is largely a product of rehearsal.

Experimental psychologist Elizabeth Loftus, arguably the preeminent memory researcher of our times, wrote a book about the fallibility of eyewitness testimony called *Witness for the Defense*, before she became involved in repressed memory issues. In that book, she wrote:

Eyewitness identification is the most damning of all evidence that can be used against a defendant. When an eyewitness points a finger at a defendant and says, "I saw him do it," the case is "cast-iron, brass-bound, copper-riveted, and airtight," as one prosecutor proclaimed. For how can we disbelieve the sworn testimony of eye-witnesses to a crime when the witnesses are absolutely convinced that they are telling the truth? Why, after all, would they lie?

Ah, there's the word – lie. That's the word that gets us off the track. You see, eyewitnesses who point their finger at innocent defendants are not liars, for they *genuinely believe in the truth of their testimony.* The face that they see before them is the face of the attacker. The face of innocence has become the face of guilt. *That's the frightening part—the truly horrifying idea that our memories can be changed, inextricably altered, and that what we think we know, what we believe with all our hearts, is not necessarily the truth.*[10]

Loftus was writing here about eyewitness testimony and its problems, which certainly applies to Mike McQueary's shower story, as we shall see. But Loftus went on to investigate repressed memory cases, in which people also came to believe sincerely in extensive childhood abuse that never occurred. In her lost-in-the-mall study, she demonstrated that many people could "remember" in great detail the trauma of being lost in a shopping mall as a young child, when such an event did not happen. Since then, she and her colleagues have persuaded people to "remember" many false memories, such as spilling punch on the mother of the bride at a wedding or even committing a crime. Loftus went on to write *The Myth of Repressed Memory.*

Loftus's work has been replicated and extended by many other experimental psychologists, including Julia Shaw, whose book, *The Memory Illusion,* was published in 2016. Shaw concluded: "Any event, no matter how important, emotional or traumatic it may seem, can be forgotten, misremembered, or even be entirely fictitious. . . . All of us can come to confidently and vividly remember entire events that never actually took place." Shaw also appeared on *The Memory Hackers,* an informative 2016 Nova show on public television.[11]

Thus, even if they were not telling the truth, most of Sandusky's alleged victims were probably not consciously lying. Some had real memories of hugs, swimming-pool frolics, locker-room showers, wrestling, or hands on the knee in cars—all of which may have been well-intentioned actions that years later could have been reinterpreted as sexual abuse. Others came to visualize scenes that probably never occurred, often through suggestive memory therapy. And it is also possible that some were intentionally lying in order to please authorities and reap financial rewards, especially after the media onslaught created a moral panic in which even the most implausible allegations were readily accepted. Finally, of course, it is possible that they were telling the truth, even though most initially denied they were abused and their stories changed substantially over time.

Our memories are, then, infinitely more suggestible and malleable than we would like to believe. With this background on how normal memory functions, let us examine how the myth of repressed sexual abuse memories arose. From approximately 1895 to 1897, Sigmund Freud believed in what he called his "seduction theory," which explained that a number of his "hysterical" patients' problems stemmed from forgotten, "repressed" childhood sexual abuse. The idea was that the sexual abuse (usually incest) had been so traumatizing that it had to be banished from memory, but that it remained buried in the unconscious mind, where it festered like an abscess or an overfull cesspool. Only by delving into these nether mental realms and retrieving the memories to consciousness would the abscess be lanced, the hysteria cured.

It is quite clear from Freud's own writings that his patients were not spontaneously recalling true abuse memories, but were merely complying with Freud's demands to conform to his theory. "We must not believe what they say [when they deny having memories], we must always assume, and tell them, too, that they have kept something back."[12] Freud explained that "these patients never repeat these stories spontaneously, nor do they ever in the course of a treatment suddenly present the physician with the complete recollection of a scene of this kind. One only succeeds in awakening the psychical trace of a precocious sexual event under the most energetic pressure of the analytic procedure, and against an enormous resistance."[13]

Freud soon abandoned the seduction theory, though he never admitted that he himself was the source of the so-called "memories." Instead, he invented the theory of the Oedipus Complex, saying that his patients were really *fantasizing* about having sex with their parents—another bit of pseudoscience that led many analysts to dismiss claims of *real* sexual abuse that had never been forgotten.[14]

The theory of repressed memories was resurrected in the 1970s and 1980s. It gained mainstream acceptance in the psychotherapeutic community and in the media after the publication of a book called *The Courage to Heal*, by Ellen Bass and Laura Davis, in 1988. This best-seller spawned a cottage industry of other books about how to unearth repressed memories.

"*Forgetting* is one of the most effective ways children deal with sexual abuse," wrote Bass and Davis. "The human mind has tremendous powers of repression. Many children are able to forget about the abuse, *even as it is happening to them.*" They continued: "You may think you don't have memories, but often as you begin to talk about what you do remember, there emerges a constellation of feelings, reactions, and recollections that add up. . . . To say, 'I was abused,' you don't need the kind of recall that would stand up in a court of law." Unfortunately, repressed memories *did* enter courtrooms, helping to convict quite a few innocent people until most judges finally began to throw out evidence based on so-called repressed memories.

"Often the knowledge that you were abused starts with a tiny feeling, an intuition," wrote Bass and Davis. "It's important to trust that inner voice and work from there. Assume your feelings are valid." They asserted that this was the beginning of an inevitable progression. "So far, no one we've talked to thought she might have been abused, and then later discovered that she hadn't been. The progression always goes the other way, from suspicion to confirmation. If you think you were abused and your life shows the symptoms, then you were." And those symptoms could be any problem someone had, including eating disorders, depression, marital problems, general unhappiness, work conflicts, or sexual dysfunction.[15]

The Courage to Heal inspired a whole slew of similar books, such as *Repressed Memories*, by Renee Fredrickson (1992), and *Secret Survivors*, by E. Sue Blume (1990).[16] Other books, such as *Dancing with Daddy*, by Betsy Petersen (1991), offered dramatic first-person accounts of alleged incest survivors who had recovered memories of abuse. Let me quote from Petersen's book to illustrate exactly how this process could work. During therapy, she became obsessed with the idea, "*I'm afraid my father did something to me.*" She had a "sense of urgency," wanting to *know* for sure. Consequently, she decided to make it up.

"I had no memory of what my father had done to me, so I tried to reconstruct it. I put all my skill—as reporter, novelist, scholar—to work making that reconstruction as accurate and vivid as possible. I used the memories I had to get to the memories I didn't have." Using what she already knew about her father—a calm, didactic physician who wore steel-rimmed glasses—she wrote a short story called "Surgeon's Hands," set in 1945, in which she imagined him abusing her in her crib when she was three years old:

> I lie there with his fingers crawling over me. I keep jerking, I can't help it, jerking under his fingers. I think it hurts, but I'm not sure. My flesh is so soft down there, so different from the firm skin all over the rest of me. He rubs against the bars of the crib and his eyes cross and roll up behind his glasses. Suddenly he groans and slumps over the bars. His finger stops moving. Is he dead?

Re-reading what she had written, Petersen "began to scream and curse and cry. I cried so hard I wet my pants." She took this self-generated horror to be evidence that her imagined scenario was true. "The feelings that came up for me were so intense I felt they must be grounded in some reality." Her therapist encouraged her. "I wanted to believe it: I wanted not to be crazy," Petersen explains. Subsequently, "wanted or not, memories came" in the form of daydreams as she lay in the sun on a couch. "I sink into the welter of images, and there is a moment when one of them sharpens, and I can see it clearly. Then it drifts out of focus again and disappears."[17]

Frederic Bartlett would have understood Petersen's description, because he observed that visual images tend to appear as isolated fragments. "The course of description, when images abound, is apt to be more exciting, more varied, more rich, more jerky," he noted. "There is an image, and meaning has to be tacked on to that, or, perhaps more accurately, has to flow out of it, or emerge from it, before words can carry the process further." This method of reconstruction has the evolutionary advantage of surmounting mere chronological logic. It permits intuition, inspiration, and poetry. "A man can take out of its setting something that happened a year ago, reinstate it with much if not all of its individuality unimpaired, combine it with something that happened yesterday, and use them both to help him to solve a problem with which he is confronted today." Unfortunately, when that "problem" involves a suspicion of sexual abuse, its "solution" can be devastating and misleading. As Bartlett explained, "The device of images has several defects that are the price of its peculiar excellences."[18]

Most of the repressed memory books of the early 1990s featured women remembering abuse, but there were also books such as *Abused Boys: The Neglected Victims of Sexual Abuse*, by Mic Hunter (1990), which included testimonials. Greg, for instance, sought counseling, depressed because of a job demotion. "My memories of the incest only started to surface after I had been in therapy for a while," he wrote. "Even now my memories are few and sketchy."

Sonny Hall had been in therapy for fourteen years, but "it is only in the last year that I have known that I am recovering from incest." Allen, another male survivor, lay on his bed one night trying to find his memories. "I laid there trying to listen to my body, my spirit." He worked himself up into a panicky state until he began gagging. "It was then I knew the awful truth: I was getting in touch with recalling the abuse I had suffered at my father's hands." His father, he thought, had stuck his finger in his rectum while choking him. "So many questions answered: why I hated turtleneck sweaters, neckties; anything on my throat brought me back at some level to my father choking me."[19]

It is difficult for most people to understand how someone who had a perfectly normal childhood, without any sexual abuse, could come to believe that they had undergone horrific rapes for years, and that the rapist had been a formerly trusted and loved person— a family member, teacher, coach, or babysitter. But that is exactly what happened during the height of the repressed memory epidemic in the early 1990s.

In my books about repressed memory therapy, I compare the belief in repressed memories to a seed planted in the brain. *Could this be true? No! Not Mom or Dad, they didn't molest me. I would remember.* But then people had to know: *Was this really true? Does it explain why I am depressed? Why I take drugs? Why I can't keep a job?* When you seek therapy, you are looking for answers. By definition, you are at a vulnerable time in your life, and you look to the therapist, a figure of authority, for answers.

All too many therapists—poorly trained in how memory actually works—have assured their clients that they probably have repressed memories of sexual abuse, which explains all of their problems, and only by remembering the abuse will they get better. This provides a powerful motivation to recover these memories and to believe in them. Once the idea of possible molestation is planted, most people become obsessed with knowing whether it is true or not. Have they been abused? How would they find out?

Their therapists have helped them to "remember" abuse in several ways. They could use various forms of hypnosis, including so-called guided imagery, visualization, or, in the case of certain Christian therapists, telling people to pray to Jesus or God to reveal their abuse memories to them. During hypnotic guided imagery sessions, people are told to envision a "safe place" and then to venture into abuse memory recovery. Like much of the sanctimonious Orwellian vocabulary of the sex abuse industry, "safe" meant the opposite, just as the promise of "healing" often means falling apart.

All of the foregoing methods put people into a trance state of high suggestibility, in which they are led to visualize abuse, as if they are playing a movie inside their heads. With rehearsal, these false memories can become quite real to people, with all the emotions that would accompany the memory of real traumatic abuse.

Another method that is now known to create illusory memories is dream interpretation. Therapists tell their clients that their memories might come back in dreams. Since all of us tend to dream about what we are worried about, this became a self-fulfilling prophecy. People worry over whether they may have been abused and then will dream about it, and that is taken as proof that it is true.

Others become convinced that they have "body memories" of abuse. This pseudoscientific theory holds that "the body remembers what the mind forgets," and clients are encouraged to pay close attention to any twinges or pains and to interpret them as evidence that they have been raped or sodomized. Another convincing method is to bring clients into such a high state of anxiety that it induces panic attacks that are then interpreted as flashbacks to abuse. Some are told to be alert to "triggers"—going to the house where it may have occurred, or seeing someone or something that reminds them of the suspected abuse.

Others might be encouraged to look at childhood photos to look for subtle signs of abuse. They are given "homework" to try to remember abuse, which might come in a fleeting glimpse or image while they are driving or lying in bed. Others are told to write anything that comes into their heads, perhaps using their left hands, or to draw an imagined abuse scene that then becomes real to them.

It doesn't really matter what method is used. Some people never actually remember anything specific, but they are still convinced that they must be sex-abuse victims. Once the idea is planted, its growth is almost inevitable, especially if a patient is highly motivated and comes to believe in the theory. For some, that motivation includes a hunger for sympathy and attention, along with the comforting thought that nothing they did was their fault—it can all be blamed on having been abused.

The process of recovering memories usually starts with therapists asking their patients to recall their childhoods. Therapists thus build rapport, getting to know their clients, and then they begin to reshape and recast these *real* memories. Many come to believe that the love their parents or other caretakers had for them was "toxic," a form of "emotional incest" that was just as bad as actual incest. Frequent hugs become evidence of abuse, and generosity is interpreted as a way to manipulate affection.

Many such therapists explain that abuse memories are likely to come back in bits and pieces, little flashes, which accounts for the growth of more and more abuse memories over time in these cases, which are then woven into a coherent abuse narrative. One characteristic of illusory recovered memories is that they tend to morph over time. They might initially be based on something that really happened—a camping trip, playing in the pool, stories at bedtime—but they then grow through visualizations of what must have happened during the camping trip, or in the pool, or at bedtime. Often these "memories" incorporate convincing elements of real memories, such as the smell of Daddy's aftershave lotion.[20]

Once such illusory memories are rehearsed and believed (often outside counseling sessions), the therapists encourage clients to express *rage* at the parents or caregivers they formerly loved. They have been *betrayed* by the very people who were supposed to love and care for them! Thus, millions of people have come to believe, through suggestive therapy or reading books or attending groups, that they were victims of profoundly disturbing sexual abuse, which has led to false accusations, ruptured families, and sometimes lawsuits, both civil and criminal.

There are semi-apologists for repressed memories who say that there is a "middle ground" to this issue. Yes, they say, some misguided therapists help people create false memories of abuse, but other repressed memories are real. Yet I have never been able to find even one convincing case of "massive repression"—cases in which people were severely sexually abused for years of their childhood and completely forgot it, only to recall it in adulthood. This theory runs counter to everything we know about how human memory works. People might not remember every abuse incident in detail if it happened over and over—in fact, they probably wouldn't—but they would certainly know they were abused for years and would never forget it. They might not talk about it, but they don't forget it, unless they have organic brain injury, and in that case, they couldn't ever remember it. If people could experience complete repression following prolonged trauma—whether in childhood or as adults—then many Holocaust survivors would have walked out of Dachau and Auschwitz with no memory of what had happened to them.

It is certainly possible for people to forget an incident of sexual abuse—or any other unpleasant experience, such as going to the hospital or being in an accident—especially if they never talk about it afterward. They might recall that incident many years later, often when triggered by something familiar, in the same way we start recalling high-school memories we thought long gone when we are at a reunion. Sometimes a shocking early experience can be recalled in or out of therapy, and in *Memory Warp* I give examples. But in these cases, it's not that the memories were "repressed." Rather, they were not rehearsed or discussed, and so they faded from recall, only to reappear with a retrieval cue. Such experiences may be forgotten simply because we did not perceive them as traumatic at the time, just confusing or annoying. Once we recall them in adulthood, we might reassess that memory and decide the early experience was traumatic after all. These instances are simply examples of normal forgetting and remembering, not repression.[21*22]

Elizabeth Loftus agreed in *The Myth of Repressed Memory*: "If you define repression as a process in which the mind selectively picks and chooses certain memories to hide away in a separate, hidden compartment of the mind and decades later return in pristine form," then no, she had seen no evidence of such a mental mechanism. There is, Loftus testified at a Sandusky hearing in 2017, "no credible scientific support for the idea of massive repression."[23]

Richard McNally, a renowned professor of clinical psychology at Harvard, came to the same conclusion in his meticulously researched 2003 book, *Remembering Trauma*. "Events that trigger overwhelming terror are memorable, unless they occur in the first year or two of life or the victim suffers brain damage. The notion that the mind protects itself by repressing or dissociating memories of trauma," McNally wrote, "is a piece of psychiatric folklore devoid of convincing empirical support." His conclusions were essentially confirmed in *The Science of False Memory*, a 2005 book by experimental psychologists Charles Brainerd and Valerie Reyna.[24]

People tend to recall the worst and best things that happen to them the most clearly, which makes sense from an evolutionary standpoint. We can then avoid the worst experiences and seek out

---

* One such case is that of Brown University Professor Ross Cheit, who recalled being fondled as an adolescent by a camp counselor, and he subsequently came to believe that the abuse had been more extensive. Cheit became a crusader for a belief in the theory of massive repression and assembled an array of allegedly "corroborated" cases. But none appear to stand up to close scrutiny, relying on plea bargains or other circumstantial evidence. Some apparently did not involve repressed memories. Others may be examples of simple recall or claims of repression to avoid statutes of limitation.

the best in the future. As Paul McHugh, long-time director of the Department of Psychiatry at Johns Hopkins University School of Medicine, put it in *Try to Remember*: "Mountains of evidence have demonstrated that shocking and frightening traumatic experiences are difficult to forget rather than difficult to remember." McHugh concluded: "The recovered memory movement represented a form of social madness." [25]

Yet it's a madness that has unfortunately become embedded in our culture, in spite of the lack of compelling evidence. It is impossible to prove a negative. You can't prove that ghosts do not exist. Nor can anyone "prove" that repressed memories don't exist. But they are highly unlikely to be true. Nevertheless, many people just "know" that traumatic memories can be repressed.

As the epidemic of false memories was recognized in the mid-1990s, most professional associations issued cautionary statements, such as this 1994 conclusion from the American Medical Association: "The AMA considers recovered memories of childhood sexual abuse to be of uncertain authenticity, which should be subject to external verification." [26] As a consequence of scientific books and articles by psychologists and sociologists such as Elizabeth Loftus, Harrison Pope Jr., Paul McHugh, Richard Ofshe, and others—plus successful million-dollar lawsuits against therapists who were sued by former patients after they realized that they had been misled into false beliefs—the height of the repressed memory epidemic had passed by the turn of the century, and repressed memories were no longer admissible in most courtrooms.

But repressed memories did not disappear. Indeed, the idea that people could completely forget years of childhood sexual abuse and then remember it later has become enshrined in the popular imagination. In a 2014 survey in the United States, psychology professor Lawrence Patihis and colleagues found that 83.9% of the general public thought that traumatic memories are often repressed. Even more alarming, the vast majority of practicing psychotherapists thought so, too—60.3% of clinical psychologists, 69.1% of psychoanalysts, and, for "alternative" therapists who practiced hypnotherapy or believed in internal personalities, the consensus on repressed memory validity went up to 84%. [27]

Repressed memory cases continue to occur in robust numbers, despite the "memory wars" that many thought had ended the repressed memory fad. According to a 2017 survey of over two thousand people, which Lawrence Patihis and I conducted, in the current decade, beginning in 2010, eight percent of all those seeking therapy in the United States came to believe that they were abused as children, without any previous memories.[28]

One such case was, ironically, wending its way through the Pennsylvania courts at the same time as the Sandusky case. On June 8, 2012, just three days before the opening statements in the Sandusky trial, a twenty-two-year-old woman testified at a preliminary hearing that her father, known as TJW Jr. in court documents, had raped her orally, vaginally, and anally from the time she was four years old until she was seventeen, but that she had repressed the memories until she was nineteen, though she claimed she always remembered one incident in a shower when she was four. She had recovered these alleged abuse memories in therapy. It was a classic case of purported massive repression, and the courts eventually dismissed it without a trial.[29]

As journalist Emily Yoffe pointed out in a September 2017 *Atlantic* article, "The Bad Science Behind Campus Response to Sexual Assault," another variety of repressed memory has infiltrated the investigation of alleged rapes, with the idea that trauma induces "tonic immobility" (being "frozen" and unable to move or think) and fragmented memories that must be pieced together to remember sexual abuse. Under the influence of alcohol, many such sexual experiences are indeed poorly remembered, but Elizabeth Loftus warned that trying to reconstruct these assumed abuse memories made them "very vulnerable to post-event suggestion."[30]

So the theory of repressed memory has not gone away. It has just morphed and gone underground. Most therapists who specialize in trauma continue to believe in the theory of repression, and many continue to encourage clients to recall mythical abuse memories in order to get better. But in general they don't write about it or brag about it, and lawyers who use such "memories" in court do not advertise their origins.

— CHAPTER 4 —

Aaron Fisher: Victim Number One

J ERRY SANDUSKY would probably be a free man today if fifteen-year-old Aaron Fisher had not begun to have frequent counseling sessions with Pennsylvania psychotherapist Mike Gillum. Fisher was the son of Dawn (Fisher) Daniels, who was impregnated early in 1993 when she was seventeen by her boyfriend Michael. Aaron was born on November 9, 1993, and his biological father saw him only a couple of times, then disappeared completely by the time he was one year old. His mother consequently gave him her maiden name, Fisher, as his last name.*[1]

Dawn then met Cliff when she was eighteen and lived with him, unmarried, until Aaron was nearly five. Then she married Eric Daniels, a relationship that lasted five years. "He began to abuse me when Katie was a baby," she later asserted. "Eric turned out to be very controlling and he was emotionally *and* physically abusive."**[2] Katie, Aaron's younger sister, was later diagnosed as bipolar. Dawn's three children each had different fathers.

Clearly, young Aaron Fisher had an unstable childhood. His mother apparently enjoyed frequenting bars, getting drunk, and flirting with strangers. In 2008, when Fisher was fourteen, the same year that the abuse claims arose, his mother posted photos of herself in a saloon, bragging of her extreme intoxication, on her MySpace page. She had a glazed, happy look on her face, with

---

* These facts come from *Silent No More: Victim 1's Fight for Justice Against Jerry Sandusky* (Ballantine Books, 2012), written in the names of Aaron Fisher, his mother Dawn Daniels, and his psychotherapist, Michael Gillum, though it was in fact ghost-written by a professional writer, Stephanie Gertler, who interviewed the three "authors" in depth. This section quotes repeatedly from the book.

** In December 2013, Eric Daniels, then forty-four, was arrested in his RV trailer along with his wife April, twenty-six, on charges of child pornography and exploitation of children. Two girls, five and fifteen years old, were taken from the trailer, and Daniels pled guilty to one hundred counts.

me at the saloon..who knows who that guy is...lol

Dawn Daniels's 2014 post on her MySpace page.

explanatory captions: "Drunk as hell . . . lol; me at the saloon . . . who knows who that guy is . . . lol," and a photo of her posterior, showing the top of scanty underwear, explaining "my thong, tha thong, thong, thong . . . look at that ass."

A neighbor said that "Dawn Daniels would regularly try to ship her kids off every weekend so that she could go out and party and drink at the local bars."[3]

The summer after fourth grade, a counselor sponsored Aaron Fisher for Second Mile, the program for troubled youth that Jerry Sandusky had started in 1977. Fisher loved the program, calling it "awesome," and his mother thought that Sandusky was "some sort of an angel." She thought he "acted like a big kid. . . . I just took him to be a real dumb jock with a heart of gold."[4]

As he did with many Second Mile kids, Sandusky took Aaron Fisher under his wing, taking him to football games, and playing various physical, rough-and-tumble games with him and other children. It is difficult to tell exactly how Fisher felt about him, because what he came to believe was colored by prolonged, intense psychotherapy with Mike Gillum, who assumed from the beginning that Fisher had been terribly abused.[5]

Sandusky recalls him as a very needy boy. "Aaron was always attention-seeking. When he visited, it wasn't unusual for him to put his arm around me or jump in my lap. . . . It was clear he hadn't had a father around." Fisher also tried to impress friends by telling stories. "Some of them seemed weird," Sandusky said. "I passed them off as his way of getting more attention." At one point, "Aaron used my cell phone, without permission, to create a video in my car. He alleged he was being kept captive and being fed scraps. He was a storyteller."[6]

The abuse claims arose in November 2008, when Fisher was about to turn fifteen. By that time, wanting to spend more time with his friends and girls, he had broken off contact with Sandusky, who remained quite worried about him. At the same time, Fisher was acting out and misbehaving with his mother as well. Sandusky continued to reach out, calling Aaron numerous times to try to re-establish contact.

Some of Aaron's reported memories about Sandusky seem to be essentially accurate. "One day at the pool, when there were about four of us boys there, I got my first sort of funny feeling. Jerry was roughhousing with all of us in the water, but when he picked me up—you know, to toss me in the air and then I'd come down with a splash—I felt like he was holding on to my crotch just a little too long." Another time, Sandusky put his hand on Fisher's leg while he was driving, "and it creeped me out a little." Sandusky would also crack Fisher's back sometimes.[7]

Sandusky does not deny those basic facts, though he denies any sexual intention. Yes, he roughhoused and threw kids in the air at the pool. Yes, he might put his hand on a kid's leg while driving, or crack his back. He was the kind of guy who hugged, wrestled, and threw kids in swimming pools. He grew up in a rec center owned by his parents, where rough-and-tumble games and males showering together were the norm. His father kept a sign in his office, "Don't give up on a bad boy, because he might turn out to be a great young man," and Sandusky claimed to live by that credo.[8]

Yet Aaron Fisher apparently felt increasingly uncomfortable, and he had been exposed to the idea that sex offenders were lurking. It was part of his schooling and part of his mother's concerns. "I had taken a class in which they told us about websites where you can look up sex offenders," said Fisher. "I'd also heard about those websites on TV, and I knew that Mom checked them out, because one time she looked up this creepy guy who was hanging around the playground, and sure enough, she found his picture on one of those websites and called the police."[9]

In November 2008, according to his story in *Silent No More*, Fisher sat down in front of a computer in his apartment.* "I asked Mom what the website was where she read about people who did bad things to kids—you know, like people who are sexual weirdos." His mother, who reported later that she was there with her friend Kathy, asked who he wanted to look up. "I said I wanted to see if Jerry was on there. . . . She asked me if I was saying that he's a sex offender, and I said I wasn't saying that. I was just saying that he's weird, that's all. Then I got mad and shoved the keyboard and went outside to hang out with my friends."[10]

"After my little brother and sister went to sleep that night, Mom came into my room. I told her that I was just upset because Jerry was coming to the school and pulling me out of classes so he could talk to me about stuff. . . . At that point, she did ask me if Jerry had done anything to me that was sexual and I just said no."[11] (Sandusky denies pulling Fisher out of class, saying that he once asked to see him during a school assembly, but that's all.)

Dawn Daniels, Aaron Fisher's mother, became very disturbed after he asked her about looking up Jerry Sandusky on a sex offender website. "I sat there with Kathy and started thinking back; things were flashing in my mind. I was thinking, *Oh my God*. I started thinking about the relationship between Aaron and Jerry, and as I talked to Kathy, she said, 'You're going to have to grill Aaron when he gets home.'"[12]

But when she did ask him about it that night, "he said that Jerry was taking him out of classes and teachers hated him now at school and the kids hated him because he wasn't in class a lot because of Jerry. . . . He repeated again that the teachers and kids were giving him attitude, thinking maybe he was some kind of troublemaker. . . . Then I asked him, for sure, if that was all this was about, and he said yes, and please let's not talk about it anymore; he was beginning to get irritated. I dropped it. I still didn't know what was going on, but at that point I had a sense that there was more to what Aaron had told me. I was up all night that night, going over everything in my mind . . . I was going nuts thinking about why he wanted to look up 'sex weirdos.'"[13]

---

* In fact, according to next-door neighbor Josh Fravel, Fisher's mother had no Internet connection in her apartment at that time. See Chapter 19.

Joshua Fravel, at that time a next-door neighbor, provides a far more unsavory interpretation of Dawn Daniels's motivation for claiming that Sandusky had molested her son. "I'm going to get a lawyer and make a million dollars off Jerry Sandusky," she allegedly told him. "This will be my ticket out of the neighborhood." Aaron Fisher later allegedly told Fravel that he planned to buy a big house in the country for his mother and family, where he could have as many dogs as he wanted, since the development where they lived restricted them to one dog.[14]

Regardless of the motivation for the abuse claims, things quickly escalated. The next day, Wednesday, November 19, Dawn Daniels called the principal and guidance counselor at Central Mountain High School in Mill Hall, PA, and said she feared that Jerry Sandusky might have molested Aaron. It is unclear what happened when the principal, Karen Probst, and the guidance counselor, Mrs. Smith, summoned Fisher. Here is Fisher's account in *Silent No More*:

> They asked me if I knew why I was there. I said I didn't. They said that my mom had some concerns about me, that she was worried something was going on with me. They asked me if everything was okay at home. And I said it was. Then they asked me again if I was sure that everything was all right. And I kept saying that everything was okay. Then they said they were going to ask me a question, and I had to try to answer it as honestly as I could: Did someone do something to you? Is anyone hurting you? That was when I just couldn't take it anymore. I broke down and cried and said yes. Then they asked if someone was hurting me sexually and I said yes. When they asked me who it was . . . I told them that it was Jerry Sandusky. . . . I wouldn't give them any details.[15]

Apparently, Probst and Smith kept notes on the meeting, but they may have destroyed them. At any rate, they have not been made public. Two years later, Karen Probst told investigator Gerald Moulton, "A. F. (Aaron Fisher) did not describe overtly sexual conduct by Sandusky, and said he did not know whether Sandusky was sexually aroused." According to Probst, Fisher described "repeated incidents of Sandusky getting into bed with him and rolling A. F. on top of him, so that the two of them were lying face to face. These incidents occurred either in Sandusky's home or in hotel rooms when the two traveled together. Occasionally, Sandusky would 'crack' A. F.'s back, pulling A. F. in even closer."[16]

Sandusky admitted that he would indeed wrestle around with Fisher on a bed, because it provided better protection from scrapes than a rug, but he emphasized that there was a big difference between being *in* bed and *on* a bed. He would allow Fisher to "pin" him by pushing his shoulders down on the mattress, and sometimes he would then crack his back by squeezing his spine.* All of this occurred when both were fully clothed. Sandusky denied any sexual intent.[17]

Karen Probst called Dawn Daniels and told her to come right away to the school. Since Fisher's and his mother's accounts were written with the intent of implicating Sandusky, they must be accepted with some caution, but here is Daniels's account from *Silent No More*:

"Aaron was sitting there with his backpack at his feet and he was in tears, just staring down at the floor." She demanded, "He did something to you, didn't he?" The principal said that "Aaron had something he needed to tell me. She said he had told them some things, but he had to tell me, too. . . . I asked him if Jerry was doing sexual stuff to him and he said yes."[18]

That is as specific as the initial allegations were, and it is not even clear whether Dawn Daniels actually asked about "sexual stuff." A year before *Silent No More* was published, she told a reporter that the principal had said that Aaron Fisher "thought something inappropriate might have happened with Jerry." That is a far cry from allegations of overt sexual abuse. At that point, Daniels merely recalled saying, "Look how upset he is! Something happened."[19]

Aaron Fisher was emotional and distraught. Obviously, that could have been because he really had been molested by Sandusky. But it could have been due to a variety of other reasons, including being singled out for such questioning. Either way, he was extremely vague and very upset. The school principal, Karen Probst, apparently suggested that they "sleep on it," since there were no clear allegations. She and the school counselor were mandated by law to report child sex abuse, but clearly, they did not feel at that point that there was sufficient reasonable cause to do so.

His mother began to scream, "We are calling the fucking police right now!"[20] Instead, however, Daniels called Erin Rutt, a Clinton County Child and Youth Services employee who was the CYS

---

* Some people, including children and teens, relieve tension by stretching and twisting their backs, or having others do so, which makes a popping sound as the vertebrae realign. It isn't clear why they crack, but it feels good and does not appear to do any harm.

coordinator for the Big Brother/Sister program and Second Mile. Daniels and Rutt had become friends through Fisher's involvement in both programs.

In *Silent No More*, Daniels recalled that she met Rutt at her home and that Rutt then volunteered to drive them both to Clinton County Children and Youth Services in Lock Haven, Pennsylvania, but in fact that occurred the following afternoon, Thursday, November 20, 2008. That same Thursday, after consulting with her school superintendent, Karen Probst called CYS to report the incident. According to the CYS employee who took the call, Probst explained that Fisher and his mother would be coming to make allegations, but that they should "consider the source," implying that Aaron Fisher was known for telling lies. Probst later denied making such a remark.[21]

When Fisher and his mother arrived at CYS, Aaron Fisher was interviewed by two caseworkers, Matt Allegretto, a long-time employee, and twenty-six-year-old Jessica Dershem. The director of the agency, Gerry Rosamilia, told them that they were to investigate alleged inappropriate sexual behavior between Aaron Fisher and Jerry Sandusky. The taped interview lasted an hour.

During that hour, Fisher told them that Jerry Sandusky had cracked his back when they were both fully clothed over thirty times, ten in a hotel setting. This back cracking occurred over the past three years, until he was around fourteen years old. Fisher said that Sandusky would hold him close for ten to fifteen minutes at a time.[22] Sandusky later said that when he allowed Fisher to "pin" him by lying on Sandusky to hold his shoulders down, they would maintain this position for only a minute or so.[23]

Fisher tried to explain to Dershem the reasons he responded the way he did at the high school. "I disclosed to the principal and the guidance counselor when I was sitting in their office because my mom felt that maybe Jerry was getting a little too weird. . . . and him getting a little too close for comfort. I mean, not sexually close."

The young teenager also described his mother's motivations for the office visit that day by saying, "Because I kept getting, my mom kept getting, phone calls from Jerry asking where I was, and I tried to do the avoidance thing where . . . my mom would tell him I'm not there, or I'm sleeping. . . . And my mom started to get a little creeped out by it, so she set up a thing with the guidance counselor."[24]

Disappointed with the insufficient details and no actual sex abuse allegations, Dershem called her supervisor, Gerry Rosamilia, and complained that she had an uncooperative fifteen-year-old in her office who was not disclosing sex abuse. She later said that she "sensed he was holding back." Rosamilia told her to send him to Mike Gillum, a psychologist who had a part-time contract with Clinton County CYS, and who conveniently occupied an office upstairs in the same building.[25*26]

When Gillum came down to the CYS office to get Aaron Fisher, he got this first impression: "He had on a pair of raggedy jeans and some beat-up sneakers. His blond hair was scruffy and on the longer side, and he just looked disheveled, but it wasn't the way he was dressed that stunned me. He was so extremely anxious, and moving around a lot, pacing the floor, in a really tight area in the lobby outside Jessica's office, but looking down at the floor. His agitation was so high that he was wringing his hands."[27]

Fisher was obviously feeling pressured. He later recalled: "The truth is, I only agreed to go to his office because I wanted Jessica to stop asking me questions, and she said that Mike was the alternative, since I wasn't answering her."[28] Mike Gillum escorted Fisher into his office, where he began to reassure and disarm his young client, building the foundation for a trusting relationship that might enable future disclosure of sex abuse. Gillum rescheduled his other clients and spent the rest of the day focusing entirely on Aaron Fisher. Gillum wrote up a report for Jessica Dershem based on this initial confidential counseling session, which she apparently used as the ghost-written CY-104 form that she sent to the police the next day.[**29]

The police subsequently set up an interview on December 12, 2008, with Aaron Fisher, Jessica Dershem, and state troopers Joseph Cavanaugh and Joseph Akers. Most of this interview was not tape-recorded because Cavanaugh prohibited it, observing that "taped interviews help out defense lawyers."[30] During the three weeks leading up to that interview, Fisher saw Gillum almost daily, but Dershem's report indicated that nothing additional was disclosed to her during that time.[31]

Fisher never told his mother exactly what was supposed to have happened to him. "Even now, these years later, he hasn't told me

---

* Mike Gillum's contract with Children and Youth Services of Clinton County was terminated in 2013, apparently because of his promotion of *Silent No More*, which was perceived as a conflict of interest.

** During the trial, Jessica Dershem said that she didn't have enough information to "indicate" sexual abuse after Aaron Fisher's first interview, but that a second interview provided sufficient information. This is confusing, since she apparently never conducted a second interview. She was probably referring to the report Gillum gave her after his first counseling session, or to the December meeting with the two policemen.

any details," Daniels wrote. "Knowing what little I know, I can only imagine. And it makes me shudder."[32]

At first, Fisher was equally uncommunicative with Mike Gillum, but Gillum immediately assumed that the teenager really had been sexually abused. "Look, I know that something terrible happened to you," he said. "I really think I know what you must be going through even though you won't tell me. I've been doing this for a long time. You know . . . if someone touched you in your private parts, well, that's really embarrassing and hard to talk about because you're probably very scared. . . . It's my job and purpose to protect you and help you."[33]

Gillum apparently believed that memories too painful to recall lie buried in the unconscious, causing mental illness of all kinds— among them, anxiety, depression, schizophrenia, bipolar disorder, and alcoholism. "They (abuse victims) just want to numb themselves and push away the unpleasant memories," Gillum believed.[34] His duty as a counselor was to entice clients whom he suspected had been subjected to abuse to reveal this abuse or to raise buried memories to the surface, where healing could begin. Fisher's agitated behavior during his first meeting was a red flag and a certain indicator of child sexual abuse in Gillum's mind. "He looked at me straight in the eye, and you could see the pain in his eyes, you could see how uncomfortable he was, he was physically shaking at times, his voice was cracking."[35]

Later, in 2014, when I interviewed Mike Gillum in his office, he denied that Fisher had repressed memories, though Gillum admitted that he believed in the Freudian theory and had helped other adult clients recall previously "repressed" abuse memories. *The Courage to Heal*, the "bible" of the recovered memory movement, was prominently displayed on his bookshelf. In Fisher's case, however, he said that it was more a matter of "peeling back the onion," and that "Aaron did what a lot of people do during abuse. He would dissociate with his body. Aaron would freeze up and stare into space so that he wasn't even there. Many rape victims report the same thing. They kind of pretend it's not happening."

I was impressed by Gillum's sincerity during our interview. He certainly had no intention of encouraging false allegations. He truly wanted to help his clients, and he clearly *had* helped many of them who really had been abused. Yet it was also clear that his presumptions and methods, especially in the case of Aaron Fisher and other alleged Sandusky victims, might lead to well-rehearsed but illusory memories. Like many other repressed memory therapists I have interviewed, Gillum emphasized that he took care not to lead his clients, even though that was precisely what he was doing. "You have to be careful not to put words in their mouth," he said. "You try to take your time to get through the layers of information."[36]

Before he began seeing Mike Gillum, Fisher did not think of himself as a victim of sexual abuse. In *Silent No More,* Gillum wrote, "It didn't even hit him that he was a victim until he was fifteen."[37] Fisher verified this, writing, "It really wasn't until I was fifteen and started seeing Mike that I realized the horror."[38] Although Fisher showed signs of mental distress that got more serious over the course of his therapy, Gillum did not question himself or his therapeutic approach. Instead, he blamed it all on the supposed abuse and the uncertainty over whether the allegations were going to result in an arrest.

Gillum explained in *Silent No More* how he cued and prodded reluctant clients such as Aaron Fisher. "If I'm lucky, they just acknowledge spontaneously without too much prodding." But otherwise, he asked many *yes* or *no* questions. "It's like that old kids' game of Hide the Button, where the kids say yes when you get closer and no when you're just on a cold trail." This is classically bad technique for interviewing those suspected of being abused. It is highly suggestive, and it is often clear from the inflection of voice or body language (leaning forward expectantly, etc.) what answer is expected. And when *no* isn't acceptable, the interrogator just keeps asking until he or she gets a *yes.* "Although they give me information," Gillum said, "they don't feel held accountable because I'm guessing, but my guesses are educated."[39] Gillum compared delving into the unconscious to "peeling back the layers of an onion," and he knew what he would find at its rotten heart.[40]

To Gillum, Aaron Fisher seemed immature, scared, and not very bright. "Aaron was beginning to open up, not in words, but his body language relaxed some. Though I knew he was fifteen, I couldn't get over how young he looked—and his mental function and maturity appeared to be that of a twelve-year-old as well." Finally, Gillum got him to answer *yes* to his more and more specific questions. "He finally admitted that the man had touched his genitals and kissed him on the mouth, and he was painfully uncomfortable as he told me."[41]

Gillum kept at it for three hours that first day with Aaron Fisher. "The whole time I was with him, I wasn't really taking notes, even during that first session. I wrote my notes up afterward. I did write down some trigger words, though." After two hours, Gillum claimed that Fisher "told me that oral sex had occurred. Even then he didn't tell me on his own; I asked him and he said it had. . . . I was very blunt with him when I asked questions but gave him the ability to answer with a yes or a no, that relieved him of a lot of burden." In a later interview, however, Gillum said that it took him six months to get Fisher to say that he was subjected to oral sex.[42]

After that first counseling session, Mike Gillum took it upon himself to call Karen Probst, the principal of Central Mountain High School. "I told her who I was," he wrote in *Silent No More*, and stated that Jerry Sandusky was now under investigation for child abuse. "I then stated in no uncertain terms that he could not be on the campus of her school." Gillum was a contract worker, not a full-time employee of Children and Youth Services, but he did not consult with anyone at CYS, nor had Sandusky's case yet been "indicated," in the bureaucratic jargon, so that he was not yet officially labeled a likely sex abuser. Nonetheless, Probst summoned Sandusky and told him that he would no longer be permitted onto the school grounds.[43]

Aaron Fisher confirmed that he said very little during his initial counseling sessions. "As long as I told him that something happened, I didn't need to go into any detail. I just needed to tell him if something sexual happened, like touching or oral sex, and he would ask me so all I had to do was say yes or no. . . . Mike just kept saying that Jerry was the exact profile of a predator. When it finally sank in, I felt angry." Gillum helped Fisher reinterpret Sandusky's previous acts of kindness and support in a sinister light. "I've explained this process of grooming many times over his three years in therapy sessions," Gillum wrote.[44]

This was the beginning of the process of turning Jerry Sandusky into a monster in Aaron Fisher's mind, a process all too familiar to those who know about repressed memory therapy. Indeed, one of the books about the process, by Richard Ofshe and Ethan Watters, is called *Making Monsters*.[45]

Three years later, Mike Gillum would join the board of an organization called Let Go Let Peace Come In, whose website is filled with repressed memory references and assumptions, and he would go on to counsel four other alleged Sandusky victims.[46] But until then, Gillum spent the next three years reinforcing Fisher's abuse narrative. At that point, the theory of repression had been denounced as a fiction by memory scientists for nearly two decades. Nevertheless, Michael Gillum was convinced that Fisher had buried memories that must be exhumed, like peeling back the layers of an onion, and he explained it all to him, though he apparently avoided using the term "repressed memories." Instead, he talked about "compartmentalizing" memories.

After this tutelage, Fisher asserted that "I was good at pushing it (memories of abuse) all away . . . Once the weekends [with Jerry] were over, I managed to lock it all deep inside my mind somehow. That was how I dealt with it until next time. Mike has explained a lot to me since this all happened. He said that what I was doing is called compartmentalizing. . . . I was in such denial about everything."[47]

And for once Aaron Fisher had someone who believed him no matter what. Once Fisher entered therapy with Gillum, nothing he said would be doubted or scrutinized for its historical truth. The chair in Gillum's office would become Fisher's sanctuary. For an adolescent who had a widespread reputation among classmates, neighbors, and teachers for deceit, this was a welcome change. "Aaron would consistently lie and scam," his history teacher Scott Baker told an investigator. Another teacher, Ryan Veltri, said that "Aaron was untruthful, conniving, and would blame other kids to save himself."[48] Next-door neighbor Joshua Fravel claimed that Aaron Fisher was "a conniver and always made up stories. He lied about everything. He would say just about anything if it got him what he wanted."[49]

Even after Sandusky's conviction for multiple counts of abuse, many people in his hometown continued to disbelieve Fisher. "There are . . . people in my community [who] said I was a liar," he complained in 2014. "They never apologized and still say I'm a liar." Fisher said that the hardest thing for him was not the alleged abuse by Sandusky, but "the failure of almost everyone in his community to believe him," as he told a reporter.[50]

Gillum saw himself as Fisher's savior and protector. "At the end of that day I promised Aaron that I would be with him throughout this whole ordeal. I said I would see him through from beginning to end and meet with him every day if that's what it would take to make him whole again." Indeed, as Fisher said, "I saw Mike every day for weeks, and I called his cell whenever I needed him. I still see him every week, and he's still always at the other end of the phone."[51]

Again, this is classically bad therapy, encouraging an over-dependence on the therapist. I have written about this kind of therapy at length in my books about memory, most recently in *Memory Warp* (2017). The therapist becomes the most important person in the client's life, and the client will go to great lengths to please the therapist. The relationship develops into an unhealthy pattern where, in order to continue to elicit sympathy and attention, the client must produce more and worse memories of abuse.

From then on, Gillum was the main driver behind the abuse allegations. When Aaron first spoke to the police, on December 12, 2008, Gillum was upset because they wouldn't let him sit in on the interview. At that point, he had been seeing Fisher every day for three weeks. "I had prepared Aaron as best I could for this interview," he explained. "Aaron was scared and didn't want to tell his story, but we had talked about it extensively and he knew this was something he had to do."[52]

Gillum was absolutely certain that Jerry Sandusky was a sexual predator who had abused his client, and that it was his job to pressure Fisher into giving a detailed account of the abuse. Gillum never talked to Sandusky, but that probably would not have made any difference. It clearly never occurred to Gillum that he might be pressuring a troubled, vulnerable, young teenager into making false allegations. Jessica Dershem, the CYS caseworker who was present during this first police interview, told Gillum that during the interview, "Aaron was reticent." Still, he was now talking about fondling and kissing on the mouth, which he had not alleged initially. Fisher denied that oral sex had occurred. "They could have asked him the proper questions in the right way to ascertain the extent of the abuse," Gillum complained.[53]

Fisher's statements about what occurred between himself and Jerry Sandusky were to change dramatically from November of 2008 until June of 2011. Indeed, his own conception of his experiences would be altered permanently as well. When first interrogated, he told the authorities that Sandusky cracked his back. His clothes were always on. He denied that Sandusky ever went below his waistline, even though he was asked multiple times throughout the interview. He told them that nothing else occurred.

By December 12, 2008, Fisher had been questioned three times by authorities (the school, child protective services, and the police), yet he told them that nothing had happened that could be considered criminal. He told the state troopers that Sandusky had never touched his genitals, and when asked if oral sex occurred, he denied it. But he was never going to be questioned by the authorities alone again. Michael Gillum would be constantly by his side.

Jerry Sandusky was first called in for questioning on January 15, 2009. Oddly, Jessica Dershem and a CYS lawyer conducted the interview without police involvement. As Gillum wrote in *Silent No More*, Sandusky denied that he had sexually abused Aaron Fisher, though he admitted hugging and "horseplay":

> [Sandusky] admitted that he cracked Aaron's back; he hugged him and kissed his forehead in the way that you would a son or grandson. He said there was horseplay, for sure . . . but the notion that anything sexual occurred was ridiculous. He not only denied the fondling and kissing Aaron on the mouth, but he dismissed it categorically. [He] assume[d] a sympathetic bent to Aaron, saying that the charges were all trumped up and that Aaron was angry at him, although he didn't know why, since he'd done so much for the boy. He was disheartened that Aaron was making these false claims since they had enjoyed such a great relationship. Sandusky suggested that perhaps Aaron was angry and sullen because he, Sandusky, had started doing things and going places with other boys and maybe Aaron was jealous. All in all, Sandusky acted as though he was totally mystified by the entire situation . . . . Basically, he just said that Aaron was a screwed-up kid, and rather than act angry the way other perpetrators do when faced with these kinds of allegations, he . . . seem[ed] almost sorry for Aaron and this fantasy he had evidently created.[54]

According to Jessica Dershem's notes from that meeting, Sandusky admitted that Fisher would sometimes lie on top of him and that he would rub and crack his back, with his hands underneath his shirt. When asked whether the back rubs extended to Fisher's buttocks, Sandusky said, "I can't honestly answer if my hands were below his pants."[55] If Sandusky were a child molester who had cleverly hidden his guilt for years, this kind of painful attempt at honesty seems remarkably inept. "He admitted to everything except the sexual contact," Dershem recalled later. "To me, that meant it was all true."[56] Her logic is difficult to follow.

Nonetheless, the wheels had been set in motion. On January 16, 2009, Dershem submitted the allegations as "founded" to state trooper Joseph Cavanaugh. During that time period, Cavanaugh also interviewed four young men identified by Central Mountain High School assistant principal and football coach Steve Turchetta as having been mentored by Sandusky. All four denied any sexual contact with Sandusky.[57]

After the Fisher allegations were "founded," Mike Gillum observed with satisfaction, "I was now permitted to sit in on all the interviews, though I still wasn't allowed to speak for Aaron." He could, however, influence him. "The more time we had, the better," Gillum thought. "Maybe as time went by, Aaron would be more forthcoming. . . . They needed more details and information [and hopefully] Aaron would not only have revealed more details to me but would be more comfortable revealing them to someone else as well."[58]

Gillum virtually became a member of the prosecution's team, although it ran counter to professional ethical standards for him to work closely with the police. He was thrilled when he got a call from Jonelle Eshbach of the state attorney general's office. *Holy crap,* he thought, *this is even bigger than I thought.*[59]

Seven months went by. After daily and weekly therapy sessions, Fisher had finally answered again with a "yes" to a suggestive question from Gillum about oral sex. As Fisher explained it, "As long as I told him that something happened, I didn't need to go into any detail. . . . He was real straightforward. When I said yes, that oral sex happened, Mike just said that I didn't have to talk about it more right now, but at some point, when I was ready, I could talk to him more."[60]

To review, by the beginning of 2009, Aaron Fisher had made rather vague allegations that Jerry Sandusky had molested him after his mother got the idea that the molestation must have happened and alerted the school principal. Fisher's disclosures came in the form of answering "yes" or "no" to leading questions. He had supposedly told Gillum that he and Sandusky had engaged in oral sex, but then he denied it to the police. Fisher was emotionally overwrought and was indeed the "screwed-up kid" that Sandusky perceived him to be.

When Trooper Cavanaugh submitted a report to the Clinton County District Attorney Michael Salisbury in late January 2009, he noted that most of the allegations took place in Centre County, so (with probable relief) Salisbury sent it over to Centre County District Attorney Michael Madeira. But Madeira was married to the sister of one of Sandusky's adopted children, so he recused himself, asking the Pennsylvania Office of the Attorney General to take the case.*[61] There, it was assigned to Senior Deputy Attorney General

---

* Extensive legal analysis on the Penn Law Fumble website reveals that a 1990 Pennsylvania law, modified in 1994, specified that Children and Youth Services, part of the Department of Public Welfare, should investigate sex abuse allegations, not the Attorney General's Office. Ironically, the law, which created CYS, was intended to avoid the disastrous false allegations that resulted in the day care hysteria cases of the 1980s (McMartin, Little Rascals, Fells Acres, Wee Care).

Jonelle Eshbach, who had considerable experience with child sex abuse cases, particularly during her time as an assistant district attorney in York County.[62]

Under Eshbach's direction, on March 19, 2009, police officer Timothy Lear interviewed Aaron for another hour with Gillum by his side.[*63] "He was nodding his head yes or no as Lear asked him pointed questions about the nature of the sexual abuse," Gillum wrote. "We needed verbal answers for the record, and it was hard to keep asking him to state his answers out loud. Aaron gave one- or two-word answers about where he was touched and what happened to him, and when it got to the more graphic details of oral sex, Aaron was still reluctant to state any details. He just kept nodding to indicate that abuse—and particularly, that oral sex—had happened."[64] So apparently Fisher was now at least nodding affirmatively that oral sex *had* occurred. Still, Gillum was frustrated at "this extremely fragile fifteen-year-old boy whom I can barely get to talk to me about the details of the sexual abuse." He assumed that Fisher was reticent because "he's not only traumatized but also scared to death that Sandusky is going to kill him, even by going so far as to hire a hit man."[65]

This assumption by Gillum, which he transmitted to Fisher, is part of the process of the demonization of Jerry Sandusky, turning him into a Monster, and is quite similar to the paranoia that therapists purveyed to clients about mythic, satanic, ritual-abuse cults that were supposedly out to kill their clients.[66]

Nonetheless, something in Aaron Fisher still rebelled against the effort to incriminate his former mentor. Mike Gillum noted that Fisher was stunned when he realized that the stories he had told in therapy might harm Sandusky. When Officer Lear boasted to Fisher that he "would put the cuffs on anybody," Fisher's "eyes got real wide and he became very quiet." He answered Officer Lear mostly by nods. At last they prompted Fisher to give one- or two-word answers. "He looked down at the floor as if he was ashamed."[67] Of course, his shame could have derived from revealing oral sex acts, but it could also have derived from his uncertainty about whether he was telling the truth. Gillum reported that Fisher "asked me very detailed questions about if Sandusky went to prison, how long he would be there. He worried that something bad would happen to

---

* Timothy Lear, thirty-one, was suspended without pay in August 2009, after his ex-girlfriend accused him of breaking into her house, grabbing and bruising her, and accusing her of having an affair. Lear was replaced in the Sandusky investigation by police officer Scott Rossman.

Sandusky and said that all he wanted was to get away from him. He wasn't looking to punish him."[68]

The prosecutor, Jonelle Eshbach, meanwhile was pressuring Gillum to get Fisher to come up with details. "She hoped he would become more comfortable and discuss in greater depth the details that were relevant to the case. She made it very clear that the standard of evidence required by the Attorney General's office before they could even begin to prosecute the crimes inflicted on Aaron had to be far more comprehensive." Gillum reassured her that Fisher was likely to comply. "With most child victims of sexual abuse, their information comes in layers."[69] This is in fact usually true of *false* allegations more than real ones. A growing and malleable sex abuse narrative, influenced by therapy, is often a warning sign that false memories are being developed.[70]

The other thing that repressed memory therapy often does is to make subjects worse rather than better. "Once I started therapy with Mike and began to tell him everything," Fisher said, "the nightmares actually got a lot worse. . . . They were nightmares about what happened to me all those times Jerry was doing things to me and making me do things to him."[71] Instead, it is possible that these nightmares were fantasies induced by therapy and then the nightmares themselves were taken as "proof" that the abuse had taken place. This is exactly what many repressed memory therapists did with clients—warning them that they would have nightmares about abuse that would then prove that the abuse occurred, thus becoming a self-fulfilling prophecy.[72] "I went from nightmares about Jerry abusing me to nightmares about Jerry having people come after me and kill me and my family and take things from me. . . . They were so graphic in detail that even after I woke up I could recite everything that happened and everything that was said. . . . Those nightmares were my reality."[73]

Aaron Fisher was becoming a much more disturbed young man. The counseling process, in which he vividly imagined how Jerry Sandusky might have abused him, was blurring his already weak boundaries between reality and fantasy. Nightmares became more frequent and more vivid after therapy began. He became suicidal.[74] He was hospitalized three times for anxiety or "conversion disorder" under Gillum's care, which Gillum described as "deep psychic pain from deep in your unconscious."[75]

Mike Gillum thought that Fisher's fears of being killed by a hit man hired by Jerry Sandusky were appropriate, and he validated them. "In no way at all did I think he was paranoid," Gillum recalled. "I did not and would not discount or dismiss Aaron's fears; I knew he was entitled to have them."[76] Fisher was generally so fearful that he made a report to his high school in October 2010 that a man from Second Mile wearing a dark suit and worn pants had approached him between classes. Asked about this report during the trial he said he had been "startled and confused," and that throughout that entire school year "I did nothing but watch the entrances of the school to make sure somebody wasn't going to come into the school and talk to me and throw me into an anxiety attack."[77] An investigation indicated that no such mysterious man had approached him.[78] In the same month, Fisher drove into a tree, fracturing his skull. His mother wondered whether the evil Jerry Sandusky had somehow sabotaged the car.[79] Fisher later recounted how he unsuccessfully attempted suicide, slicing his forearms with a razor and trying to hang himself in his closet.[80]

Despite Fisher falling apart, the daily therapy began to pay off in other ways. "Eventually," said Gillum, "Aaron told me in no uncertain words that it was after that second summer at camp, when he was twelve, that the intensity of the sexual acts escalated to oral sex, which Aaron was forced to perform as well as receive."

Gillum was teaching Fisher that he had dissociated during his theoretical abuse, which was one of the reasons he hadn't remembered it. "With Sandusky's help," Gillum wrote, "Aaron managed to disassociate himself from the grim reality of abuse, as victims do."[81] Fisher parroted the same jargon about dissociation that Gillum had taught him: "I spaced. I took myself *out of my body* and away from him and out of that basement room."[82] This stereotypical language could have been taken verbatim from many classic repressed-memory accounts.

After Timothy Lear was suspended from the force for assaulting his ex-girlfriend, Trooper Scott Rossman became the new interrogator, asking Fisher things such as, "Did he ever try to put his dick in your butt? I mean his penis in your anus?"[83] Finally, in a meeting held in Gillum's therapy office on June 8, 2009, Rossman got Aaron Fisher to say that he and Sandusky had performed oral sex on one another.[84]

Rossman also began to search for other potential victims, with encouragement from Gillum, who was sure there must be others. "He wanted details about my school and when Jerry was there and what were the names of other kids and where did they live and what did they look like," Fisher said. "Later I found out that Trooper Rossman and some agents in the attorney general's office went out scouring neighborhoods, just like cops do in the movies. They worked a fifty-mile perimeter."[85]

Eventually, the police would also begin to question other Second Mile alums, particularly those named in Sandusky's 2000 book, *Touched*. Nevertheless, police investigator Joseph Leiter would later admit, not knowing he was being tape-recorded: "It took months to get this first kid [to say he was abused]. . . . It just took repetition and repetition and finally we got to the point where he would tell us what happened."[86]

Two grand juries investigated charges of child abuse against Jerry Sandusky, at which Aaron Fisher was the star witness. Grand juries are little-understood affairs. They resemble trials in that they have jurors (twenty-three of them in Pennsylvania, hence the name "grand jury," versus the twelve jurors in a normal trial) who listen to sworn testimony. But unlike regular trials, grand juries are held in secret, for the purpose of determining whether there is enough evidence to pursue a criminal indictment. In a grand jury, the prosecutor presents a case, but there is no defense lawyer present, and no cross-examination is allowed. Nor are transcripts ever made public. Grand juries meet for three or four days per month and can last up to two years. Each panel of jurors can hear evidence in several different cases. In Sandusky's case, the 30th Pennsylvania grand jury met to consider the allegations from June 2009 until early 2011. Then the 33rd Pennsylvania grand jury, with a different jury pool, took it up again in March 2011.[87]

At his first grand jury interrogation, which convened in June 2009, "Mike prepped me and told me what to expect," Fisher recalled. "Mike had permission to sit in the courtroom with me." But when asked about the alleged molestation, Fisher just started to cry. He blurted out "No!" when Jonelle Eshbach, the assistant attorney general, asked whether oral sex had occurred. He broke down weeping. Due to his disturbed emotional state, a recess was called so that Fisher could receive medication and a pep talk from Gillum. After the break, Fisher performed more satisfactorily, providing Eshbach with the anticipated answer of "yes," but continuing to weep.[88] Maybe he broke down because he was revealing the shameful truth about oral sex. But it is also certainly possible that Fisher was so emotional and conflicted that he initially denied that abuse had occurred because he actually knew, despite all the therapy, that abuse had *not* occurred.

After the first grand jury session, "Aaron continued to come in for therapy at least once a week . . . and we held several phone calls in between sessions," Gillum recalled. "I had an open arrangement with Aaron and Dawn to the effect that if either of them needed me for whatever reason, they could call at any time—day or night."[89]

The grand jury refused to indict Sandusky. "The first grand jury said that Aaron had trouble responding clearly and didn't elaborate as much as he could have or should have. . . . Jonelle would say something like, 'He then would touch you in a sexual way,' and Aaron would answer yes or no. In the second [session of the] grand jury, the jurors wanted Aaron to narrate the story in his own words. They wanted all the gory details."[90]

Gillum was frustrated, suggesting that he could testify instead of Aaron under the "Angel Act," also known as the "Tender Years Exception to the hearsay rule." In that case, "I could have testified as though I was the child if I deemed that the child was too fragile and the court concurred." Instead, "Jonelle and I gave him (Aaron) some more coaching and emphasized that he had to state exactly what happened. Jonelle explained that she didn't want anyone on the jury to say that she had been leading the witness."[91]

Of course, leading the witness is exactly what they were already doing with the "coaching" sessions, with the months of therapy, with the assumption and insistence that he had been abused, and with Eshbach's leading questions. By the time he testified again to the grand jury, reconvened on November 16, 2009, Aaron Fisher's testimony and memory had been irrevocably contaminated. "Once Aaron took the stand, Jonelle . . . pushed him a lot harder that second time. To Fisher's credit, he managed through tears to be more of his own advocate and narrator, until he literally collapsed."[92] He began to perspire, went pale, and sank to the floor. Then he vomited.

"The second grand jury (actually the same pool of jurors in the 30th Pennsylvania grand jury, meeting again) still did not feel that Aaron's testimony was strong enough to make a case for an arrest." Time dragged on. Fisher continued therapy and continued to get worse, becoming severely depressed and experiencing panic attacks and excruciating abdominal pain by August 2010. He also began to talk about suicide. "He was truly beginning to come apart," Gillum observed.[93]

All of this should be familiar to those who have studied the impact of repressed memory therapy. As one woman told Bass and Davis in *The Courage to Heal*, "Breaking through my own denial, and trying to fit the new reality into the shattered framework of the old, was enough to catapult me into total crisis. I felt my whole foundation had been stolen from me. If this could have happened and I could have forgotten it, then every assumption I had about life and my place in it was thrown up for question." Another revealed, "I just lost it completely. I wasn't eating. I wasn't sleeping. . . . I had terrible nightmares about my father. I was having all kinds of fantasies. . . . Physically, I was a mess. I had crabs. I hadn't bathed in a month. I was afraid of the shower."[94]

Similarly, in her book *Repressed Memories*, Renee Fredrickson told the story of her client, Carolyn. "Her anger and grief were enormous. For months she suffered emotionally, physically, and spiritually. She had crying jags, eating binges, suicidal feelings, and bouts of depression." Fredrickson unquestioningly assumed that all of these were symptoms of abuse. "I never felt like my problems were connected to my past," Carolyn told her. "To be honest, they still don't seem related." Another patient exclaimed during a session: "But I feel like I'm just making this up!" Fredrickson ignored her concern. "I urged her to continue, explaining that truth or fantasy is not of concern at the beginning of memory retrieval work."[95] Thus, it was common for many who underwent repressed memory therapy to fall apart in the same way that Aaron Fisher did. The repressed memory therapists always interpreted these symptoms as the result of the abuse, when in fact they were caused by the therapy itself.

AARON FISHER'S MONSTER

On April 11, 2011, a new grand jury met to hear Aaron Fisher's testimony.[96] This time, as Fisher recalled in his book, "the new grand jury allowed me to read my testimony, since I had given it twice before."[97] According to Mike Gillum, Fisher just read aloud from his previous testimony, even though it had been deemed to be too vague and uncertain, one-word answers in response to leading questions. Gillum denied that he helped Fisher write the testimony that he read aloud.[98]

At this point, "the nightmares were picking up speed again, but this time I was also sleep walking," Fisher wrote in *Silent No More*. He would yell, "Get away!" and "Leave me alone!" By this time, as he himself observed, "My monster was real."[99] Jerry Sandusky's transformation into a Monster was complete.

Near the end of August 2011, however, Aaron Fisher got cold feet. During a meeting with Gillum, the prosecutors, and the police, Fisher said, "I'm out. That's it. I'm not going to be your witness anymore." Gillum interpreted this as Fisher expressing frustration that Sandusky had not yet been arrested, which may have been the case, but it also could have been Fisher's frustration at having been pushed and pushed to create stories that he knew deep down were not true. Even Gillum seemed to recognize this on some level. "If not for my pushing him along, he (Aaron) might have backed out a long time before this, and to this day I still question myself about how much I pushed him," he wrote.[100]

But Gillum did convince Fisher to testify, and on November 5, 2011, Jerry Sandusky was arrested. "I never thought the arrest would happen," Fisher said, "and when it did, something didn't feel right about it."[101] The arrest came just before Fisher's eighteenth birthday. At this point, he had been under Gillum's influence for three years.

By this time, the police had succeeded in locating five other Second Mile boys who were willing to say that Sandusky had molested them, along with the anonymous "boy in the shower" of the McQueary incident (they did not yet know that this boy was Allan Myers, who came forward soon thereafter to defend Sandusky), and a hypothetical hearsay victim based on testimony of a Penn State janitor (who said another janitor, Jim Calhoun, who was now suffering from dementia, had witnessed the abuse). By the time of the trial, they had come up with two more alleged victims.

When Aaron Fisher testified during the 2012 trial, the inconsistencies of his allegations were exposed. He couldn't remember what he had said about the abuse and couldn't keep it straight. "I don't remember dates of when I told people anything. All I know is that it happened to me. I honest—I don't even want to be here."[102] That could be explained easily if he had recovered memories that were unconnected to reality. If a witness's testimony is not based on real events, naturally he doesn't have anything to connect it to. For example, Fisher offered four guesses about when oral sex allegedly occurred. *One:* It stopped a month before or after his birthday on November 9, 2007.[103] *Two:* It started in the summer of 2007 and continued until September of 2008.[104] *Three:* It started November of 2007 and continued until the summer of 2008.[105] *Four:* It only started during 2008, going into 2009 (impossible, since he made his allegation in the fall of 2008).[106]

Indeed, Fisher's testimony over the course of the investigation was erratic. In June of 2009, Fisher told Scott Rossman that he had performed oral sex on Sandusky many times, and that Sandusky had ejaculated, keeping his eyes closed. A week later he said it only happened once. Yet in November 2009 he said he had never performed oral sex on Sandusky.[107]

When reminded of his previous testimony, he complied by then saying it *did* happen. During the trial, when he was confronted with the fact that his testimony had changed frequently and asked why that was, Fisher told the jury that he had "white lied" to save himself embarrassment, because he was scared, because he was under stress and didn't know what to do.[108]

In his testimony, Fisher also said that after he began to stay overnight at the Sandusky household, "I acted out. I started wetting the bed. I got into fights with people."[109] But in fact, according to one of Fisher's childhood friends and the friend's father, Fisher had wet the bed repeatedly on sleepovers before he ever met Sandusky.[110]

But none of these issues—Fisher's bed-wetting, his confusion regarding dates or places, or his changing story about oral sex—provided sufficient reason to disbelieve his story. A reporter attending the trial described Fisher's testimony: "The sobs from the witness stand were loud and prolonged, the cracking voice of Victim No. 1 in the Jerry Sandusky child sexual molestation trial gasping for breath as he detailed repeated acts of oral sex with the former Penn State defensive coordinator." The testimony had a profound effect on the audience, including the jury. "The sighs and sniffs echoed around a rapt Centre County Courtroom as jurors looked on, a couple noticeably disturbed. A few grimaced at the retelling and shook their heads." The reporter's dramatic story continued:

> The witness then breathed heavily. He followed with a deep sniff of his nose, then hung his head and openly wept. "He . . ." More sobs. "He put . . ." There was another prolonged sigh. An attempt at a breath. A loud cry. "He put his mouth on my privates," the witness said through a broken voice, seemingly just trying to spit it out. "I spaced. I didn't know what to do with all the thoughts running through my head. I just blacked out. I didn't want it to happen. I was froze."[111]

In fact, in the trial transcript at that point, when Fisher talked about oral sex, he used telltale language to indicate that these were recovered memories. Gillum had probably explained that Fisher couldn't really recall the oral sex clearly because he "spaced," he "blacked out," he was "froze."*[112] Perhaps Gillum had explained that Fisher had dissociated, blanking it all from his memory. Fisher continued: "He blew on my stomach, and then it, it just happened. I don't—don't even know."[113] Indeed, it is possible that he truly *didn't* know.

Fisher said that he had stayed overnight in the Sandusky household about one hundred times between 2005 and 2008. His mother "kind of let me do my own thing." In fact, "in some ways she encouraged it."[114] He said that he had been repeatedly molested in the basement, yet he willingly continued to return for additional rounds of abuse for three years. The only explanation he gave for not confiding in his mother was that he was afraid she might not believe him and that he was embarrassed and scared. He frequently used the line, "I couldn't." During his alleged abuse, he couldn't move. He was "froze." He couldn't talk.[115] Understandably, the jury accepted this highly emotional testimony and found Jerry Sandusky guilty of all the charges concerning Aaron Fisher.

Therapist Mike Gillum did not testify.

---

* The idea of being "frozen" during sexual abuse took on a life of its own. "I don't think I've seen a (sexual abuse) complaint in the past year that didn't use the word *frozen* somewhere," a defense lawyer observed in 2017.

CHAPTER 5

Jonelle Eshbach's Mounting Frustration

B EFORE EXAMINING the stories of the other alleged victims, it is important to understand how the investigation proceeded and why it took so long to file charges and arrest Sandusky, three years after Aaron Fisher's initial allegations. Jonelle Eschbach, the senior deputy attorney general in the Pennsylvania Office of the Attorney General, was the key figure driving the case.

In the spring of 2009, Eshbach was becoming incredibly frustrated. On May 1, 2009, based only on Aaron Fisher's rather shaky testimony, Eshbach had written a request for a grand jury to look into the Sandusky case. "It is believed that other minor males have been similarly assaulted through this connection [with the Second Mile]," she wrote. "Witnesses with knowledge may be too embarrassed or intimidated to admit their knowledge of the violations because the actor is well-regarded and influential and is also known as the founder of a charity that raises funds for and serves disadvantaged children. Young men who are potentially involved are in fear of revealing what they know due to the suspect's power and influence."[1]

These assumptions are what drove the investigation. At the onset of the case, Trooper Joseph Cavanaugh had asked administrators at Fisher's high school for the names of other students whom Sandusky had mentored, and he interviewed those four boys. All denied that Sandusky had molested them. Yet Eshbach was convinced that Jerry Sandusky was a pedophile and *must* have been abusing many other boys, and that any denials were simply because they were "embarrassed or intimidated." She would push and push this case over the next two and a half years, along with State Trooper Scott Rossman and Anthony Sassano, a drug agent for the Office of the Attorney General, both of whom joined Eshbach as primary investigators in May 2009.[*2]

It was unusual for a Pennsylvania grand jury to be used as a tool during a criminal investigation. The grand jury system was designed to investigate public corruption or organized crime, not to fish for evidence of sexual abuse.[3]

When Rossman testified before the grand jury on June 16, 2009, he "expressed the belief that Sandusky had victimized others," but there was no evidence to back up that claim. Shortly afterward, Rossman interviewed Frankie Probst and Frankie Aveni, boys whom Sandusky had befriended and helped. Both denied that Sandusky had sexually abused them, but they told the officer that Sandusky would hug them or put his hand on their knees when driving, which Rossman interpreted as "grooming behavior."[**4] Later in 2009, Rossman interviewed Matt Sandusky, whose mother hated Sandusky for adopting her son. Matt vehemently denied that his adoptive father had ever touched him inappropriately.[5]

Agent Sassano didn't come up with much either. In September 2009, he emailed Eshbach and Rossman, suggesting that they get a search warrant for Sandusky's computer, find out how Sandusky might have arranged for Aaron Fisher to get tickets to Philadelphia Eagles games, look at Sandusky's employment records at Penn State, and see whether Centre County Children and Youth Services had any other complaints about Sandusky. Of all his suggestions, the only one that eventually bore fruit was the discovery of the 1998 complaint about the shower with Zach Konstas. Sandusky's computer held no child pornography or other incriminating evidence, and he had a spotless record at Penn State. "Scott dug up some info on another potential victim," Sassano wrote. "We will be pursuing this matter." But nothing came of it.[6]

In January 2010, Jonelle Eshbach wrote a memo to her boss. "Sandusky was routinely surrounded by young men [from the Second Mile program], although we have been unable to develop any

---

* Sassano was assigned to the Bureau of Narcotics Investigation and Drug Control at the Office of the Attorney General, which led some people to assume that Sandusky, who didn't drink, smoke, or take drugs, was also being investigated for illegal drug use. But Sassano had investigated sexual-assault cases during his twenty years of work for the Altoona Police Department and expressed interest in the Sandusky case. The investigation had nothing to do with narcotics.

** Frankie Probst later told a reporter that Sandusky was "a down-to-earth, really nice guy that would do anything for you. I guess he took a liking to me and the relationship grew to kind of like a fatherly figure." But he came to feel that Sandusky demanded too much of him in his teenage years, and he went on to claim abuse and receive a hefty settlement in 2017.

victims other than the one minor victim [Aaron Fisher] who has testified before the Grand Jury." She added that she was suspicious
that Sandusky had retired from coaching in 1999 "at a relatively
young age and rather abruptly. . . . We therefore are seeking any
records which might indicate that his reason for leaving the university's employ was other than by his own choice."[7] Internal emails
discussing Sandusky's planned retirement revealed that Paterno
had told Sandusky that he would never replace him as head coach,
and that Sandusky wanted to take advantage of an early retirement
window in order to spend more time on the Second Mile program.[8]
His retirement had nothing to do with the 1998 shower incident.
But Eshbach's attempt to "develop" more victims would continue.

By the time Eshbach wrote her first draft of a grand jury presentment in March 2010, she still only had Aaron Fisher as her sole
Sandusky victim. She included a curious assertion in the draft: "A.
F. testified that Sandusky performed oral sex on him more than 20
times in 2008 and 2009 . . . Termination of contact with Sandusky
occurred in spring of 2009."[9] Those facts could not be accurate,
since Fisher's first allegations occurred in the fall of 2008, and after that time Sandusky certainly did not see him, much less force
him into oral sex. Regardless, as we have seen, Fisher's grand jury
testimony had consisted primarily of unconvincing, one-sentence
responses to leading questions.

Eshbach sent an email to Tony Sassano and Scott Rossman on
March 15, 2010. "Guys," she wrote, "Here's the draft currently under
review. . . . I will let you know but suspect the Grand Jury will approve it in April. Then we will talk about coordinating the arrest."[10]
But by April 19, she still hadn't heard anything from her superiors
at the Office of the Attorney General. "I keep asking . . . no word,"
she emailed Sassano. She still had no answer by May 28, 2010,
when she wrote to Sassano: "Despite asking, begging, pleading, I
have heard nothing." She made a few minor edits and resubmitted
the draft presentment. "I know I sound like a broken record," she
wrote to her boss, Richard Sheetz, on June 14, 2010. "On Friday,
you mentioned me jumping in front of a bullet. Is this approved for
submission to the Grand Jury this week or not?"

A month later, Eshbach wrote again to Sheetz and two other
higher-ups: "The grand jury asked me again, as they have for the
last 4 months, why we don't have that particular presentment for
them. They are very anxious to approve it. Likewise, I continue
to get calls and mail from the victim's mother and therapist. Can
someone please tell me what the hold up is?" On August 12, 2010,

Eshbach forwarded an email from Dawn Daniels, Fisher's mother, asking, "Why is this not been dealt with already? This is causing my family a lot of stress and anxiety." Eshbach wrote a cover note: "This is my fourth message from the victim's mother on Sandusky. Does anyone want to answer my questions about why we are stalled since winter?"

Finally, in a response on that same day, Frank Fina, who headed the Criminal Prosecutions section of the Office of the Attorney General, answered her. "We are still working on the case," he wrote, "looking for better corroboration of our single victim. We need to do everything possible to find other victims." Eshbach duly notified Sassano, "My bosses have directed that we try harder to find any other corroboration for A. F. At this point, they are unwilling to allow the presentment to go to Grand Jury as it stands right now."[11]

Thus, according to a 2014 review of the Sandusky case conducted by Geoffrey Moulton for the Pennsylvania Office of the Attorney General, the case was stalled by the time Tom Corbett, the presiding attorney general, was elected as governor. "As of November 2, 2010, the date of the Pennsylvania gubernatorial election, little progress had been made in finding additional victims," wrote Moulton. "The only identified victim, A. F., was in bad shape both physically and emotionally." The following day, Jonelle Eschbach wrote yet another plea to her superiors. "I am worried about this boy. Can we *please* meet Thursday about this? It's 'critical timing' for this case and this kid." She recalled that in terms of finding new victims, the case was "dead in the water," and as Moulton put it, she feared that "the case might be slipping away."[12]

Eshbach sent her email at 10:51 a.m. on November 3, 2010. Twelve hours later, at 10:35 p.m., someone calling themselves "A Concerned Citizen" sent an anonymous tip to Centre County District Attorney Stacy Miller, who passed it on to State Police Trooper Scott Rossman. "I am contacting you regarding the Jerry Sandusky investigation," read the email. "If you have not yet done so, you need to contact and interview Penn State football Assistant Coach Mike McQueary. He may have witnessed something involving Jerry Sandusky and a child."[13]

The tip came from a Penn State football fan named Christopher Houser, who had gotten into an email dialogue with Mike McQueary's older brother, who had mentioned something about the McQueary shower incident. On November 23, 2010, Scott Rossman interviewed Mike McQueary, who told him about the shower incident with the slapping sounds that he had interpreted as sexual.

In retrospect, when Rossman told him about the new allegations, McQueary was even more certain that it must have been Jerry Sandusky sodomizing a child, and he now revised his memory to assert that he had actually seen Sandusky behind the boy against a shower wall, although the story he told of what he actually saw would morph over time. He misplaced the event by a year, saying that it had occurred in March 2002 rather than December 2000.[14] McQueary testified shortly thereafter to the Sandusky grand jury.

RAMPING UP THE INVESTIGATION

As Moulton observed, "Finding McQueary was enormously important to the investigation." The McQueary story galvanized the police and the Attorney General's office. "From January 2011 through the filing of charges on November 4, 2011, the investigation proceeded rapidly and aggressively, with investigators and prosecutors conducting hundreds of interviews, issuing over 100 subpoenas."[15]

State Trooper Joseph Leiter joined the investigation to help Scott Rossman. On January 3, 2011, Rossman and Leiter went to the Penn State and State College police departments, looking for any reports on Sandusky, and they thought they hit pay dirt with the 1998 report of the previous shower incident with Zach Konstas. True, that investigation had uncovered no sexual abuse, and no charges were ever filed, but there Sandusky had been, hugging a boy while naked in the shower. To Rossman and Leiter, this was clearly "grooming" activity.

The policemen then wasted a good deal of time tracking down gossip on the Internet suggesting that Sandusky's retirement from the Second Mile was linked to child sexual abuse, but none of those who posted the rumors had any first-hand information.[16]

Around this time, reporter Sara Ganim, who had gotten wind of the Sandusky grand jury proceedings (probably through a leak from someone in the Attorney General's office), contacted Debra McCord, Zachary Konstas's mother. Ganim gave McCord the name and number of police investigator Joseph Leiter, who was looking for additional victims. Ganim told McCord to call the investigator if she wanted the case to go forward against Sandusky, because otherwise the case might be dropped.[17] McCord identified some of the other Second Mile boys with Sandusky in a photograph that had appeared in *Touched*, Sandusky's 2000 autobiography. The photo showed a smiling Jerry Sandusky with eight apparently relaxed, happy young boys in his kitchen after attending a Penn State home

Jerry Sandusky around 1999 with Second Mile kids: From left: Dustin Struble, Jason Smeal, Brett Houtz, Michal Kajak, Frankie Probst, one unidentified, Brendon Kempton, and Zachary Konstas.

football game (a ninth boy's head is just visible behind Sandusky). Sandusky had his arms draped around two boys' shoulders.[18]

Debra McCord identified Dustin Stuble, Michal Kajak, and Brett Houtz, all friends of her son, and all of whom would eventually testify that Sandusky had molested them.

A new grand jury, the 33rd in Pennsylvania, with a new panel of jurors, was convened on March 10, 2011, when Sassano and Rossman gave the jurors a synopsis of their version of the case thus far.[19] Jonelle Eshbach was now more confident that she would be able to revise her long-delayed presentment, adding McQueary, Konstas, and perhaps others. Eshbach had an ally in incoming attorney general, Linda Kelly, who had been appointed by newly elected Governor Tom Corbett to replace him. Kelly was officially confirmed in May.

Reporter Sara Ganim's first stories on Sandusky appeared on March 31, 2011, making the sex abuse allegations against Sandusky public for the first time, only three weeks after the new grand jury convened, and she would fan the flames in the media in the months to come.[20]

"Jerry Sandusky, a former assistant coach with Penn State football, has been the subject of Internet rumors for months," wrote Ganim in her first article. "Now, sources close to the case confirm that a grand jury is hearing testimony connected to a 15-year-old's allegations that he was inappropriately touched several times over a four-year period by Sandusky." Ganim also mentioned the

1998 shower incident with Zachary Konstas, writing that "the boy claimed Sandusky washed his body during the shower, sources said," though Konstas had made no such claim in 1998.[21]

The afternoon that Ganim's article appeared, long-time Penn State janitor Ronald Petrosky called the Pennsylvania State Police to say that another janitor named Jim (later identified as Jim Calhoun) had allegedly told him that he'd seen Sandusky doing inappropriate things with a boy in the shower at the Lasch building in the late 1990s (the date was later changed to 2000), which would turn into the search for yet another victim, who was never located. But that didn't stop the prosecution from including this "phantom" victim in the trial.

By May, four new investigators had joined the Sandusky team, which was now known as a "task force" and given its own office space. Agents Michael Cranga and Timothy Shaffer were added from the Office of the Attorney General, and brothers Mark and Robert Yakicic, both troopers for the Pennsylvania State Police. Tony Sassano was now working full time on the investigation and took a leadership role. That month, the investigators conducted over sixty interviews, searching for new victims.

On June 3, 2011, Sassano sent a memo urging that Sandusky should be arrested soon. "We will have four victims who will testify," he said, listing Aaron Fisher, Dustin Struble, Zachary Konstas, and Brett Houtz. He also listed "three incidents witnessed by PSU staff," including the Mike McQueary story, the Jim Calhoun janitor story, and another janitor, Brian Huffman, who was supposed to have witnessed another shower incident, though Huffman's saga must not have been very convincing, because he was never called as a trial witness.

In the same memo, Sassano complained that Michal Kajak "has not been cooperative, refusing to return calls and respond to emails. After him, we have no substantial information to follow up on for other potential victims, other than the hundreds of names listed as being the 2nd Mile." He added: "We have recently been interviewing kids who don't believe the allegations as published and believe Sandusky is a great role model for them and others to emulate." The fact that many of the boys Sandusky mentored thought he was a great guy and denied that he had abused them apparently had little impact on Sassano or the other investigators. He concluded his memo: "I believe our case against Sandusky is strong at this time and ready to proceed to charging. . . . I anticipate that after arresting Sandusky, other victims will come forward."[22]

The police never revealed how many of the Second Milers refused to accuse Sandusky, who had been a mentor and father figure for many of them. As the Grand Jury Presentment stated: "Through the Second Mile, Sandusky had access to hundreds of boys."[23]

One of the young men Sassano complained about, who thought Sandusky was a "great role model," was Peter Mali, who spoke with Joseph Leiter in May 2011, telling the police investigator that "Sandusky did the things he did out of a true concern and care for kids, and that Sandusky never made him feel uncomfortable." Mali said that Sandusky "did things out of innocence and that his motive always seemed to be that of concern for the well-being of kids." He recognized that Sandusky was ill-advised to shower with kids, but that "nothing happened between them and that Sandusky never forced him to do anything. Mali is grateful for the time Sandusky spent with him and provided him guidance and put him in the right direction."

Leiter was disappointed but undaunted. "I ended the conversation by availing Trooper Rossman and I to him should he recall anything and need to report it to us," Leiter wrote in concluding his report.[24] In other words, Leiter hoped that Mali might recover some abuse memories. Otherwise, he was not interested in hearing what he had to say.*[25]

On June 7, 2011, Sassano and Rossman finally got Michal Kajak to talk to them. He recounted the usual Sandusky behavior—hand on the knee in the car, playing games, working out. They took only one shower together. But then he said (according to the police report) that Sandusky had grabbed his hand and placed it on Sandusky's erect penis. Now they had a fifth victim.[26]

A June search of Sandusky's home failed to find any child pornography, only hundreds of photos of various Second Mile boys, including the alleged victims, and typed lists of Second Mile participants. Some of the names had handwritten asterisks by them, including Aaron Fisher and Sebastian Paden, who would later be added to the victim list. During the trial, the prosecution would make much of the "asterisk kids," but Sandusky asserted that he was simply marking the names of Second Mile kids who had expressed an interest in getting tickets to Penn State football games.[27]

---

* According to a December 2011 police report, Joseph Leiter finally got Mali to say that "Sandusky would often stand behind him and press his erect penis against Mali's back." Leiter prompted him further, asking if Sandusky ever blew on his body. "Mali sat straight up, his eyes widened, and said there was something familiar with that." But Leiter decided not to have him testify before the grand jury because he needed additional "time to resolve some of these issues" of his recovered memories.

On July 21, 2011, Jonelle Eshbach told the grand jury, "You aren't going to get a presentment at this time. . . . We're tying up every end and things are still coming in." Scott Rossman explained to the grand jurors that they had compiled a list of around 250 Second Mile alums. "What we figured was there was a general area that Mr. Sandusky is probably willing to travel. . . . So we did a circumference of roughly an hour distance from his home in State College and we came up with areas like Mill Hall, Clinton County, Altoona, Snow Shoe, Moshannon, Jersey Shore, and Renovo." In July, the Sandusky task force interviewed over one hundred young men who had gone through the Second Mile and attempted unsuccessfully to interview many others. One of the interviewees was Jason Simcisko, who denied that Sandusky had sexually abused him. Obviously, none of the other interviewed Second Mile alums alleged abuse either. Their interviews were ignored and never made part of the trial record.[28]

The interviews continued into August without eliciting any new allegations, but on August 18, 2011, Tony Sassano re-interviewed Jason Simcisko, "based upon information provided to Agent Sassano by another Second Mile participant," according to the Moulton report. It appears possible, then, that some kind of communication and influence between potential "victims" was taking place. This time, Simcisko said that Sandusky had hugged him in the shower and that he had felt his penis rub against him. Now they had their sixth alleged victim, plus the McQueary and Calhoun stories.

Throughout September and October 2011, the task force members interviewed many more former Second Mile participants and their family members. None of them would say that Sandusky had molested them, though several described what the investigators called "grooming" behavior, such as hands on knees, hugs, or tickling.[29]

Meanwhile, in early September 2011, Jonelle Eshbach began to revise and expand her first draft of a grand jury presentment, which had featured only Aaron Fisher. Now she emphasized the McQueary and janitor stories, while adding the five other alleged victims. Eshbach also briefed Attorney General Linda Kelly in detail about her version of the case. By early November, Eshbach was finally ready to have her presentment endorsed by the grand jury and to arrest Jerry Sandusky.[30]

CHAPTER 6

Four More Alleged Victims

N OW LET us look carefully at the shifting testimony of the alleged victims. Although their names became public during the trial, and they appear in the trial transcript, they are usually called only "Victim Number 1" and so forth in the media. This tends to depersonalize them, turning them into stereotyped cardboard cutouts of assumed "victims." Not only that, the numbering doesn't match the way they came forward chronologically as the case against Sandusky developed. Therefore, where possible, real names are used throughout this book, presented in a more logical order. We've already covered Allan Myers ("Victim Number 2"), Zachary Konstas ("Victim Number 6"), and Aaron Fisher ("Victim Number 1"). Let us now turn to the rest of the alleged victims who testified at the trial.

DUSTIN STRUBLE, VICTIM NUMBER 7

Dustin Struble (eventually to be labeled "Victim Number 7"), born on October 10, 1984, was two years older than Zachary Konstas. The two had been friends since their Second Mile days. The police first tried to contact Struble in January of 2011, but he avoided them initially because he had heard about the allegations against Sandusky and was beginning to worry that perhaps he really *had* been abused. He began to rethink things like Sandusky putting his hand on his knee in the car. Maybe there had been more to it. When he finally drove to the police station, he said that "it was almost like a tidal wave hitting me full force, and that's when for me everything sort of started unraveling."[1]

State Trooper Joseph Leiter interviewed Struble for the first time on February 3, 2011. The interview was not tape-recorded, but according to Leiter's notes, Struble said the Second Mile was "a great program and helped him tremendously." Yet he did tell Leiter that he had been thinking about the way Sandusky used to put his hand on his knee while driving, and now he thought he remembered Sandusky moving his hand slowly up towards his crotch sometimes. And other times, he thought Sandusky may have been trying to slide his hand down his back under his underwear waistband. When he spent the night at the Sandusky home, he remembered now that sometimes Sandusky would "cuddle" next to him on his bed briefly, though they were both fully clothed. Yes, he had taken showers with Sandusky, but nothing sexual had taken place there. He'd given him bear hugs at times, but not in the shower. They had wrestled around, but Sandusky had never touched him inappropriately.*

Leiter showed Struble the photos in Sandusky's book, *Touched*, and was excited when he identified the boys in the photos so that the police could then interview them, including Brett Houtz, Michal Kajak, Jason Simcisko, Zachary Konstas, Frankie Probst, and Brendon Kempton. All but the last two would end up being alleged victims at the trial.

At the end of the interview, Struble told Leiter that Sandusky was an "overly friendly person" who "makes me feel weird," but "if I can go with Jerry I'll put up with it." Leiter was excited that Struble was open to the idea that Sandusky might have abused him, with hints that he had tried to put his hands on his crotch or down the back of his pants, but that wasn't enough. In ending the interview he "advised Struble that as he recalls events to please contact me and we can set up another interview. Also, if he begins having difficulties with his memories to contact me so that assistance can be found."[2]

After a second interview with police, Struble told them that he was entering psychotherapy on February 22, 2011. Zach Konstas would subsequently ask about Struble's counseling experience during phone calls. He wanted to know if he had "remembered anything more," indicating that Struble was in the process of recovering memories during therapy.[3] From the context, it is likely that Konstas was also trying to "remember" more during therapy sessions of his own.

Dustin Struble grew up with both parents and two sisters in Milesburg, Pennsylvania. He was referred to the Second Mile program by a guidance counselor in 1995 and attended Second Mile camps for three consecutive summers, beginning that year. He said that he loved the experience, and he got to know Jerry Sandusky, occasionally spending the night at the Sandusky home.

---

* Sandusky recalls hugging Struble and tucking him into bed, but not showering with him.

In 2004, Struble wrote in his own handwriting on an application for a scholarship from Second Mile, "Jerry Sandusky, he has helped me understand so much about myself. He is such a kind and caring gentleman, and I will never forget him." Struble attended Penn State football games and tailgating parties every year for fourteen years with the Sanduskys, until he was twenty-five.

On April 11, 2011, Struble testified at the Sandusky grand jury proceeding. He said nothing about bear hugs, hair washing, or being dried off in the shower. He said that Sandusky had put his hand on his waistband, but "I can say he never went the whole way down and grabbed anything."[4]* He denied that Sandusky had kissed him and said that Sandusky had never touched his privates or fondled him at all over his clothes. Indeed, Struble said that Sandusky had never had any physical contact with him at all in the shower. When he did shower with Sandusky, also present were "other assistant coaches or players or there was a couple random people that were in there from time to time . . . they would just be passing through and say hi . . ."

After his grand jury testimony, Struble signed a contingency agreement with State College, PA, attorney Andrew Shubin, meaning that the lawyer would only be paid if Struble received compensation. Lawyers in such cases typically receive from thirty-three to forty percent of the total payment.[5] Before the June 2012 trial, Struble met with Shubin from ten to fifteen times. During his trial testimony, he claimed not to know the contents of the contingency agreement he had signed.

As late as January 2012, Struble apparently was still ambivalent about his feelings for Sandusky. That month, when he ran into Todd Reed, a Sandusky *protégé* and supporter, he told Reed that he and his friend Zach Konstas were both "very shocked" by the allegations and that "Zach was crying on the phone [with Dustin Struble] because he was upset about Jerry Sandusky and this situation. . . . Zach was upset because his mom was pushing Zach to accuse Jerry."[6]

By the time of the trial, Struble had changed his story, asserting that Sandusky gave him bear hugs, washed his hair in the shower, and then dried him off. He said that he had only disclosed these details to his attorneys and prosecutor Joe McGettigan a few months before the trial. Now he testified that Sandusky put his hand down

---

* Although the transcript of the grand jury testimony is not available to the public, defense attorney Joe Amendola had access to it, and these quotations from it emerged during his cross-examination of Dustin Struble during the trial.

his pants and touched his penis in the car, that Sandusky had grabbed him in the shower and pushed the front of his body up against the back of Dustin's body, that Sandusky had touched his nipples and blown on his stomach. Now he said that he never saw anybody else in the shower area, implying that he and Sandusky were alone there.

Defense attorney Joe Amendola challenged Struble, asking why he had changed his testimony so radically since the previous year.

> *Amendola*: "But today now you recall that he put his hand down pants, Mr. Sandusky [did], and grabbed your penis?"
>
> *Struble*: "Yes. That doorway that I had closed has since been re-opening more. More things have been coming back and things have changed since that grand jury testimony. Through counseling and different things, I can remember a lot more detail that I had pushed aside than I did at that point."[7]

Struble went on to explain more about how his repressed memories had returned in therapy. "Through counseling and through talking about different events, through talking about things in my past, different things triggered different memories and [I] have had more things come back, and it's changed a lot about what I can remember today and what I could remember before, because I had everything negative blocked out. Now with the grand jury testimony was when I was just starting to open up that door, so to speak."[8]

Further defending his changed testimony, Struble explained: "No, that testimony is what I had recalled at that time. Through—again, through counseling, through talking about things, I have remembered a great deal more things that I blocked out. And at that time, that was, yes, that's what I thought but at this time that has changed."[9]

During his testimony, Struble also revealed that he and Zachary Konstas had talked about how the repressed memory therapy was going. "Zach would ask me sort of what happened to me almost—I feel so that he could confide in me. But he had asked me if I remembered anything more, if counseling was helping, just all kinds of random things."[10]

When Prosecutor McGettigan asked Struble why he hadn't disclosed Sandusky's abuse to the police during his first or second interrogation, Struble explained: "I had sort of blocked out that part of my life. Obviously, going to footballs games and those kind of things, I had chose sort of to keep out in the open, so to speak. And then the more negative things, I had sort of pushed into the back of my mind, sort of like closing a door, closing—putting stuff in the attic and closing the door to it. That's what I feel like I did."[11]

Dustin Struble was the only alleged Sandusky victim who agreed to speak to me on the record. In October 2014, I spoke with him at length in his home in State College, Pennsylvania, with follow-up by email and phone, and he verified that he had recovered memories of abuse and that he thought the door to his abuse memories was still only part way open. He remained in therapy with Cindy MacNab at The Highlands in State College, who had apparently been suggested by his lawyer, Andrew Shubin.

"Actually both of my therapists have suggested that I have repressed memories, and that's why we have been working on looking back on my life for triggers. My therapist has suggested that I may still have more repressed memories that have yet to be revealed, and this could be a big cause of the depression that I still carry today. We are still currently working on that."[12]

I tried to clarify how his memories came back, asking whether that happened during therapy sessions and whether his therapist used any form of trance work. No, he said, no hypnosis, but MacNab would prod him for more details, asking, "Well, do you remember this? What happened here? Did you sleep up here or down there?" In response, Struble came up with "a lot of like detailed memories and even some vague memories came back during either therapy sessions or I guess you could say 'trigger.'"

The therapist must have explained how repressed memories might come back in response to "triggers," and that Struble should pay close attention to anything that might bring back sex abuse memories outside of therapy. Struble told me about two such "triggers" in particular that helped him visualize abuse memories. In a store, he saw some mesh shorts on sale that set off alarm bells, because Sandusky always brought mesh shorts for him to wear when they were working out. Another time, he saw a man with abundant grey chest hair, like Sandusky's. Struble told me that he used to shave his chest hair when he was in high school, and now he concluded that this must have been because he had repressed memories of abuse by Sandusky.

None of this surprised me. In my research on repressed memory therapy, I had found many people in repressed memory therapy who became convinced that they *must* have been sexually abused and forgotten all about, and they became obsessed with recalling it. The role of *expectation* is central to understanding how people came to visualize mythical abuse, whether it be through hypnosis, dream analysis, group pressure, induced panic attacks, so-called "body memories," or alleged "triggers" such as the mesh shorts. It became a self-fulfilling prophecy. If they came to expect that something would trigger them, it was almost inevitable that something would.

Plus, if people didn't recall particular events or details, therapists would tell them that *that* was further proof that they had repressed the memories, and that there were still more to come. "When I try to think back," Struble told me, "there is like a fog there almost, like a black curtain." Thus, ordinary forgetfulness becomes sinister. And Struble's former drug use became evidence that he used drugs as "coping mechanisms."

Struble also explained that, after the trial, he had been in a fifteen-week group with other alleged Sandusky victims, and that this had reinforced his abuse memories and called forth more of them. "As far as being able to go back and confront my memories from the past, going back in detail, that group therapy session has had the biggest impact, just seeing the different stages that people were at and hearing people echo the stuff that I couldn't think to say." This group contagion would become intense. "Once a couple of people are engaged, then it kind of picks up the rest of the group."

Summarizing his experience, Struble wrote to me that "the memories come back instantly but fragmented, almost like a light bulb going off in your mind but with a sick feeling accompanying it. Most of these triggers occur at random places/times and are utterly unexpected. For me it feels like a giant puzzle that I seemingly stumble into key pieces. However, I feel like there are a few more missing pieces that are needed to solve this particular puzzle. When these events happen, I do discuss them with my therapist most of the time."[13]

I had heard this analogy to putting puzzle pieces together from many others who sought their repressed abuse memories, as I wrote in *Memory Warp*. In the repressed memory bible, *The Courage to Heal*, the authors explained that the process of reassembling the disparate memory fragments could be intellectually stimulating, "a lot like putting together a jigsaw puzzle or being a detective." They quoted a woman who had come to believe she was abused: "Part of me felt like I was on the trail of a murder mystery, and I was going to solve it. I really enjoyed following all the clues."[14]

I have to say that I liked Dustin Struble, who had just turned thirty, had bought a new house and car with the compensation money he had received from Penn State, and was planning to get married the following year. Bored at home, he went back to working part time as a cook at the Eat'n Park restaurant. He considered himself an introvert and still struggled with depression. He used to smoke a lot of marijuana but stopped after he was arrested for selling it, and then he lost most of his friends when the police coerced him into taking part in a sting operation. "I take legal drugs now," he said. "I was on six but now just four—Celexa is an anti-depressant, Xanax for anxiety, Adderall for ADHD, and Ambien to sleep at night."[15]

It was very clear that Struble, a personable but troubled young man, now truly believed that Sandusky had abused him, based on his recovered memories. I asked what he would have told me about Jerry Sandusky if I had asked him in 2010, before he heard about the allegations, and before he spoke to the police. "I would have said I went to games with him and that we were friends. At that point I was completely shut off to the negative aspects of it. I had completely isolated that, you know, really, I wasn't really aware of it."[16]

MICHAL KAJAK, VICTIM NUMBER 5

Michal Kajak, who also appeared in the now-infamous photo, was born on August 8, 1988, and grew up in State College, Pennsylvania, with his Polish immigrant parents and an older brother. He grew up bilingual, since the family spoke Polish at home. Kajak attended Second Mile summer camp in 1999, 2000, and 2001, and continued to attend Penn State football games and tailgate parties with Jerry Sandusky. He never stayed overnight at the Sandusky home.

When the police first interviewed Kajak on June 7, 2011, he said that Sandusky sometimes put his hand on his knee while they were driving, but so did his uncle.*[17] He said that he had showered only once in the morning with Sandusky during football season in 1998, though this is impossible, since he didn't meet Sandusky until the following year, when he first attended the Second Mile camp. Sandusky doesn't recall ever showering with Kajak. Then, according to Trooper Scott Rossman's police report (the interview was not tape recorded):

> [Kajak said he] was really uncomfortable because he did not shower with other people before. Kajak related he remembered turning around and seeing Sandusky naked. He remembered that Sandusky's penis was really big. Kajak related he was embarrassed so he turned away from Sandusky and looked at the wall. At this

---

* Jerry Sandusky's father did the same thing to him and other children. "I squeezed what I called their 'weak spot' (just above the kneecap)," Sandusky wrote. "It was my way of showing enthusiasm for having the opportunity to see them."

point I observed that Kajak was really uncomfortable and he began to cry. I asked Kajak if something happened in the shower that probably should not have happened and he said yes. Kajak asked me if he was molested and I related I did not know. Kajak related that there was not any penetration so he did not think he was molested.[18]

Then, according to the police report, "Kajak was still crying and was extremely uncomfortable," Rossman wrote. "He related he did not want to remember this stuff. I told Kajak that he needed to tell the whole truth about everything that happened. Kajak continued to cry and said he did not want to remember." Kajak finally said that Sandusky had taken his hand and placed it on Sandusky's erection for a few seconds during this single shower they took together. "Kajak related he did not really know what an erection was back then, however, he knows now and it was definitely an erection."[19]

In a subsequent speaker-phone interview on November 9, 2011, the police pressed him harder, wanting to know if he had been sodomized. This interview took place a few days after the explosive Grand Jury Presentment was made public, and Kajak said that he "cannot escape this (the Sandusky scandal) as he sees it everywhere he goes and hears people talking about it." In this high-pressure, emotional atmosphere, Kajak now remembered a second shower, during which Sandusky grabbed his penis and wiggled it from side to side. Kajak said he didn't recall sodomy, but he remembered how he used to touch his own butt and wondered why he did that. The implication was that perhaps he had repressed the conscious memory but had a "body memory" that caused him to fondle his own posterior. But we do not know whether Kajak was in therapy.

During this interview, the three officers, James Ellis, Joseph Leiter, and Tony Sassano, also wanted to know if Kajak might be Phantom Victim 8, supposedly seen by a janitor who now has dementia (see Chapter 9). Kajak didn't know if he was that unknown boy, but he said he never held hands with Sandusky, which the Phantom Victim was supposed to have done. This is another indication that the police were feeding potential victims information from other allegations, thus providing cross-contamination of memories and evidence. "He wants to say no about oral sex," the notes said, though he *did* remember Sandusky being in front of him and low in the shower. But he couldn't bring himself to say he gave Sandusky oral sex. "It doesn't seem possible," he said, which must have disappointed the officers, for whom oral sex appears to have been a kind of holy grail.[20] "Kajak promised to contact us again if he remembers anything additional," Leiter concluded hopefully in his report.[21]

At the trial, Kajak testified that he had worked out and showered with Sandusky only once, but now the date for this shower was moved to 2001, three years later than the original estimate, as well as being moved to a new location, the Lasch Football Building (built in 1998), perhaps in an effort to make Penn State liable for damages.*

On the stand, Kajak related an updated story. In the sauna, he said, Sandusky had unwrapped his towel and sat on it. "I noticed that his penis was enlarged, but I didn't understand the significance of it back then." Since he was now claiming he had been thirteen years old at the time, it is hard to imagine that he would not have known the significance of an erection.

Then, in the shower, Sandusky had allegedly lathered soap on Kajak's shoulders, forcing him against the shower wall so that he felt Sandusky's body and erect penis on his back. Then Sandusky was supposed to have taken Kajak's hand and forced him to touch his penis. Kajak said he then ran off and left the shower before Sandusky could do anything else.[22] When asked by the prosecuting attorney about disclosure, he said that he never said anything about the shower to anyone until his first meeting with the police in June 2011, and then later to his girlfriend.

There was a good deal of confusion as to when this alleged incident was supposed to have occurred. On June 17, 2011, at the grand jury proceedings, Kajak testified that Sandusky had abused him during the 1998 football season. At trial the following year, he shifted the date by three years, testifying that it had happened after his birthday, August 8, 2001, but before September 11, 2001. In another apparent glitch during his testimony, Kajak said it had occurred in 2002, perhaps because the McQueary incident date was at first erroneously set in March 2002.[23]

Joe Amendola, the defense attorney, went to a great deal of trouble getting Michal Kajak to state repeatedly and emphatically that he was very confident of the new date, apparently leading up to a presentation of proof that Jerry Sandusky had stopped bringing

---

* Two prominent Penn State administrators, Tim Curley and Gary Schultz, had already been charged with conspiring to cover up Sandusky's alleged abuse in the Lasch building shower on February 9, 2001 (the McQueary incident), so any Sandusky "victims" who claimed abuse after that date might be compensated generously, despite the fact that Sandusky was banned from bringing Second Mile kids to exercise on the Penn State campus after the McQueary complaint.

youth to the Lasch building and its shower facilities after February 2001.[24] For inexplicable reasons, Amendola stopped his cross-examination before presenting this information, so the jury heard nothing to raise doubts about Kajak's redesigned, time-shifted story.*

Kajak is the only alleged victim to have made allegations during his first contact with the police. We have no way of knowing whether Michal Kajak was in repressed memory therapy. (I tried to interview Kajak, but he would not speak to me.) By the time he spoke to the police in the summer of 2011, however, the abuse allegations against Sandusky had been publicized by reporter Sara Ganim, who had also contacted Zachary Konstas's mother, who had, in turn, suggested that the police interview Kajak as a potential victim. We also know that Zach's sister had talked to Kajak about the allegations.[25]

It is thus possible that he spoke with his friend Dustin Struble, who was "remembering" his own abuse and might have helped him with his own shower story. Kajak's allegations do not fit the *modus operandi* that the police otherwise thought Sandusky used. He was supposed to have "groomed" boys carefully before attempting more overt sexual abuse. The idea that he would have acted this way during the very first shower must have seemed odd, even to the police.

JASON SIMCISKO, VICTIM NUMBER 3

Another Second Miler alleged victim was Jason Simcisko, born on January 1, 1987. He grew up in Moshannon, Pennsylvania, a small town about thirty miles north of State College, with his single mother and a much younger brother. Jason fought with his mother and was estranged from his father and got into a great deal of trouble at school. He was referred to the Second Mile from the Big Brother program. In 2002, at the age of fifteen, he lost contact with Sandusky after he was placed in two group homes and then foster care. When he came of age, he joined the Army and served in Iraq. At the time of the trial he was unemployed aside from serving in the Army Reserves.

On July 19, 2011, Simcisko was questioned by police brothers Mark and Robert Yakicic, as part of the increasingly urgent search for more Sandusky victims. He told them that nothing inappropriate had ever happened between him and Jerry Sandusky. When the policemen asked if Sandusky had helped him rinse off in the

---

* In March 2017, at the trial of former Penn State president Graham Spanier, Kajak changed the date of his alleged abuse yet again, to the summer of 2002, asserting that he remembered that it was *after* 9/11.

shower, perhaps lifting him up to the showerhead, Simcisko replied, according to the police report: "There might have been something like that. I don't exactly remember, but it sounds familiar."

He went on to say, "I lost touch with him (Sandusky) around the time I went into 10th grade. I was in trouble a lot then; in and out of foster homes and stuff. He made me feel special, giving me stuff and spending time with me. I just always took it that he was trying to make sure I kept out of trouble. I don't believe any of this stuff is true and hope that he's found not guilty." The Yakicic brothers left disappointed but noted that Simcisko "agreed to call if he recalled anything further."[26]

Then, like Dustin Struble, Simcisko became a client of lawyer Andrew Shubin, and by the time he spoke again to Penn State trooper Scott Rossman on August 18, 2011, he had changed his mind. Now he said that he had been at the Sandusky household some twenty times, and Jerry Sandusky had rubbed his shoulders, washed his hair, and given him bear hugs in the shower. On one occasion Simcisko thought he felt an erection when Sandusky hugged him from behind. He also said that Sandusky had touched his penis "several other times." At bedtime during sleepovers, he said that Sandusky would rub his shoulders and tickle him, and that he had touched his genitals through the athletic shorts he wore to bed.[27]

By the time he testified at the trial on June 22, 2012, Jason Simcisko had remembered even more abuse. Now he said that he had spent *fifty* overnights at the Sandusky household, where he was tickled, kissed on the shoulder, rubbed on the stomach, and had his penis touched practically every night he was there. He said that Sandusky had washed his buttocks. He asserted that he had first disclosed this additional information to his attorneys and Joe McGettigan, but no one else.

When asked to explain the discrepancies in his testimony, Simcisko said, "Yes, but then I thought about it more. Like, everything—everything that's coming out now is because I thought about it more. I tried to block this out of my brain for years."[28] Although Simcisko did not use the term "repressed memory," he was apparently referring to this discredited phenomenon.

When asked, Simcisko couldn't recall when he first saw his attorney. "It was before or it was after the grand jury," he said, "and it was after the [canceled] preliminary hearing."[29] He said that he had met with his lawyer six times and discussed (i.e., prepared, shaped, and rehearsed) what he was to say in court. He couldn't recall the content of the agreement he signed.

When prosecuting attorney Joe McGettigan questioned Simcisko, it became poignantly apparent that Jerry Sandusky had treated him with kindness and compassion, in sharp contrast to his own family:

> *McGettigan*: Did you have fun [with Sandusky]?
> *Simcisko:* Yes.
> *McGettigan:* Did you like spending time with him?
> *Simcisko:* Yes.
> *McGettigan:* And most of the time did he treat you nice?
> *Simcisko:* Yes.
> *McGettigan:* In fact, did he treat you nice all the time?
> *Simcisko:* Yes.
> *McGettigan:* Did you like him?
> *Simcisko:* I loved him.
> *McGettigan:* Did he ever tell you how he felt about you?
> *Simcisko:* Yes.
> *McGettigan:* What did he say?
> *Simcisko:* That I was like extended family, unconditionally loved.
> *McGettigan:* And how did that make you feel?
> *Simcisko* : Like a family, like—like I was part of a family.
> *McGettigan*: And did you feel like part of your own family with your mother and your brother at that time?
> *Simcisko*: Not really.[30]

It became clear during his testimony that Jason Simcisko did indeed feel bitterness and anger towards Jerry Sandusky, but it had nothing to do with any alleged sexual abuse. It was because he thought that Sandusky had not cared enough to keep track of him once he entered the foster care system.

> *McGettigan:* Did there come a time . . . when you weren't living with your mother and your brother?
> *Simcisko*: Yeah. The reason why I broke it off with Jerry is because I had to go away. I got sent away to a group home, to two different group homes and then in foster care, where I eventually graduated out of. I had no further contact after that point.
> *McGettigan:* Well, you didn't really break if off with the defendant, did you?
> *Simcisko*: No, not really, but—
> *McGettigan:* When you went to foster care, were you mad at your mother?

Simcisko: No—well, a little bit, yeah, because she had sent me there. I mean—

McGettigan: Was there anybody else you were mad at?

Simcisko: Jerry.

McGettigan: Why?

Simcisko: He never contacted me, never—my mom never even heard from him to find out where I was.

McGettigan: And how long were you in the group home and then in foster care?

Simcisko: I'd say about three years.[31]

After Simcisko described the enhanced criminal version of the bedtime ritual to the jury, McGettigan asked, "Were you even mad then? Were you mad at him then?" He answered that he had not been angry.

McGettigan: Are you mad at him how?

Simcisko: Yes, I'm infuriated right now.

McGettigan: Are you just mad or is there something else?

Simcisko: I'm mad. I'm enraged. I'm hurt.

McGettigan: Why are you hurt?

Simcisko: Because he could just forget about me like I was nothing after I got sent away and that was it, no more Jerry.

McGettigan: Did you still care about him when you were in your group home?

Simcisko: Yes. I would pray he would call me and maybe find a way to get me out of there, adopt me or something. That never happened."[32]

Jason Simcisko may or may not have needed repressed memory therapy to nourish his abuse allegations, after he at first denied to the police that Sandusky had abused him. But it is abundantly clear that the twenty-four-year-old who testified at the trial had truly felt part of the Sandusky family, and that he had felt abandoned and betrayed when Sandusky did not save him from foster care. He knew that Sandusky had adopted Matt, who was much more difficult and troubled than he was. Why not him? Why not Jason?

Simcisko didn't know that Sandusky had, in fact, called his mother to ask how he was and whether he could see him. She told him that he was in a psychiatric hospital, which would not allow non-family visitors.[33]

CHAPTER 7

The Star Victim

B RETT HOUTZ, known as "Victim Number 4," was another one of the Second Mile kids in the photograph in Sandusky's book, and he would prove to be one of the most effective witnesses during the trial. He lived five doors down from Jason Simcisko at Spring Brae Apartments from 2007 until 2011, so they may have discussed what they would say about Jerry Sandusky as they both geared up with lawyers in 2011, though Houtz said that they were not friends and that he had in fact been unkind to the younger Simcisko when they were children. "I wasn't the nicest kid when I was little. I was kind of a bully."[1]

Houtz, born on September 9, 1983, grew up in Snow Shoe, Pennsylvania, spending most of his childhood next door at his grandmother's house. He didn't get along with his stepfather, nor did he care for his grandfather. He rarely saw his biological father.[2] In school, he got into trouble frequently, which is why he ended up attending the Second Mile summer camp in 1996 and 1997.

Sandusky recalled that the first time he met Brett Houtz in 1997 as a fourteen-year-old Second Miler, the boy showed him a card trick. *This is a bright kid*, he thought to himself. Indeed, Houtz was classified as "gifted," but he didn't perform well in school. Sandusky took on Houtz as a challenge. "How could we get this young man as interested in school as he was in magic?" Sandusky wondered. So he invited him to picnics and football games, encouraged him to play sports, and finagled sporting equipment for him. He asked Penn State football players such as LaVar Arrington to visit him at school to encourage him with academics. "I tried to set up a pilot program of studying and exercising in order to motivate him."[3]

But when Houtz turned sixteen in 1999, he pulled away from Sandusky's influence and became confrontational and disrespectful, according to Sandusky. He began to use drugs, stole a car, became sexually involved with a girl, did poorly in school, quit his sports.*[4] "It hurt me and others to see him throw everything away," Sandusky recalled.[5] Worried about Houtz, Jerry Sandusky wrote up a contract on January 10, 1999, which both Sandusky and Houtz signed, whereby Houtz would be awarded $1,000 towards college tuition if he met high school expectations. "This program is unique and designed to help support a special person," the contract began, "one who is committed to become a productive citizen. Somebody who is a team player, cares, cooperates with others and appreciates the efforts of all the people who make this possible. The expectations are high and the reward is significant. It is designed for a long-term commitment."[6]

During the trial, Houtz said that it was "an incentive for me to start doing more . . . getting better in school." He didn't take the contract seriously. "So I'm just signing it to shut him up," he said. As Houtz recalled dismissively, he got only "little things. Not a whole lot of money. Mostly because I didn't really cooperate with it."[7] Sandusky's sanctimonious advice drove Houtz crazy. "He would tell me every day, well, you need to do this or you can do this."[8] In his testimony, Houtz described how he pulled away from Sandusky. "I started to get older. You know, I had gotten a girlfriend . . . so I tried to distance myself. . . . I would say, 'Okay, yeah, we can do whatever.' Then when he would come to meet me, I would just make sure I wouldn't be there."[9]

Sandusky wrote several long, heart-felt letters to Houtz around this time, discovered among Sandusky's papers through search warrants, though he apparently never sent some of them. In "The B-J Story," Sandusky wrote: "Brett is a young man that came into Jer's life. It was a difficult time for Jer because he had [just] lost his dad. Jer and his dad shared so much, did so many things together. Brett came along and he and Jer seemed to enjoy the same experiences. Both seemed to be in need. They loved playing games, competing, singing, laughing, sharing experiences, just being themselves."[10]

Another letter, signed "Jer and Tim," was written in Sandusky's handwriting. "I write because you mean so much to us. I write because I am concerned about all of us. I write because I have seen

---

* During the trial, Houtz talked about getting "out of rehab," but then denied that he ever got in trouble for drugs. Perhaps he had voluntarily entered drug rehab without being forced to do so, though he went into the program directly from a juvenile detention center.

the hurt on Tim's face when you don't show for him, even though you have given your word [refers to Tim Janocko, a high school football coach and friend of Sandusky's]. I write because of the churning in my own stomach when you don't care. I write because I still hope that there will be meaning to the time we have known each other." Later in the letter, Sandusky wrote: "We seem to be a convenience. When it's inconvenient or a better deal comes along, you leave a trail of broken promises. . . . You don't understand or choose not to worry about loyalty, commitment, or caring. The motivation is to get what you want regardless of others."[11]

Another letter, written in 1999, began: "I hope that writing some of my thoughts will not annoy you as much as I do personally. We have known each other for almost two years, gone through many highs and lows. There was tremendous encouragement as we went through last summer and into fall. You seemed like you had bought into everything and were doing well. . . . It's your song, your choices, your life. I like to fill a small part of it and I will be there if you want. I have believed and stuck up for you. I care, Jer."[12]

In that same letter, Sandusky included inspirational quotes from the likes of John F. Kennedy and Theodore Roosevelt, though the jury did not hear them. "Life was not designed as a prison in which man awaits his execution," Kennedy's quote began. "It is not necessary to stay with what you have. You have the capacity for great achievements, great loyalty, and great love. And I would say to you, if you have this dream to make things better, don't sell out short. Don't back away. If you have a song to sing, sing it." Teddy Roosevelt contributed: "The credit belongs to the man who is actually in the arena—whose face is marred by dust, sweat, and blood; who knows the great enthusiasms, the great devotion, and spends himself in a worthy cause."[13] These uplifting if somewhat hackneyed quotes were vintage Sandusky fare.

"You must keep trying, keep pushing," Sandusky wrote in another message to Houtz. "You may even get discouraged. Soccer or school will not always be perfect, but you <u>must keep trying to go forward</u>. Success and happiness will be a journey!"[14]

As Houtz pulled away from attempts to get him to buy into the program that was supposed to help him, a frustrated Sandusky sought to remind him of the good times they had shared: "Try not to ever forget all of those who care. Try to remember canoes, squirt guns, water balloons, fighting outside miniature golf, Polish soccer, basketball, racquetball, football, swimming, studying, lifting, working, golfing, volleyball, kick ball, soccer (Communist Tim), laughing, hurting, arguing, crying, caring, and so much more <u>fun</u>."[15] This was certainly an ironic message if part of that "fun" had been sexual abuse.

In his testimony, Houtz dismissed such messages from Sandusky as "almost, like, creepy love letters," and that is certainly the way the prosecution presented them.[16] In the context of the horrendous abuse allegations, that's how they appeared to the jury as well. But it is also possible that Sandusky was being entirely transparent, that he really was concerned that Houtz's future was at stake and that his intervention and caring might make a difference. As Sandusky later wrote, "Brett's focus was on being cool, smoking, getting a high out of sex and drugs. It tore me apart to watch this happen. What could I say or do? The letters were my attempt to make a difference, to help him realize how many people had cared about him and supported him."[17]

The prosecution did not submit this passage from a Sandusky letter to Brett Houtz as evidence during the trial:

> You care a little when you can impress your peers, that you hang out with players, or when you are given something. You care a little when you can impress some young lady. There's no real feelings. Your word means nothing. You have no loyalty. You have no appreciation. You have no work ethic. . . . There is no substance to your agreements. You live moment to moment. You are faltering in school. You listen to nobody but yourself. You don't want anybody in your life to try to help you. You discard them.[18]

"Didn't he spend time with you studying?" Sandusky's defense attorney, Joe Amendola, asked Houtz. "If you want to call it studying, I guess . . . him sitting there basically demanding things while I'm riding a bicycle." Houtz reluctantly admitted that Sandusky "told you time and again he wanted you to succeed."[19] Houtz also admitted that Sandusky "made comments like, you know, you're going to go to college some day," but he never took them seriously, "because I never, ever knew what to really do with my life, even when I graduated."[20]

Houtz managed to make it through his high school years, and Sandusky attended his high school graduation. Houtz later accepted free football tickets and participated in a Second Mile golf tournament with Sandusky in 2002, when Houtz was eighteen.

The young man ended up in a detention center, where Sandusky visited him. When he got out, Houtz entered a drug rehab program. Sandusky helped him get a job, which he quit. "Then I lost contact,"

Sandusky wrote. "Later, I learned that he had struggled. At one point he lived in the woods."[21]

Brett Houtz also had a reputation as a liar, though he said, "I wouldn't say I lied a lot. Like any other normal kid."[22] Megan Rash, the sister of Houtz's longtime friend Ryan Dixon, knew him for eighteen years and testified at the trial that he was dishonest and embellished stories.[23] In another interview, she called Houtz a "pathological liar" and said he was "always telling stories that were not true, always trying to be bigger and better than anyone else."[24] (Her brother Ryan Dixon died in a motorcycle accident in 2008.) During his own testimony, Houtz said that his mother disregarded his statement that Jerry was gay by saying it was just another one of his lies.[25]

Unlike many of those who turned on Sandusky in the year before the trial, Houtz did not maintain a close relationship with him as a young adult, but in 2010, when he was twenty-six years old, Houtz came back to visit the Sandusky family, bringing his girlfriend and their three-year-old son. Long-time family friend Elaine Steinbacher happened to be there during the visit and recalled that Houtz acted as if he were part of the family and that a big fuss was made over his son. Jerry Sandusky played with the little boy.[26]

A friend reported that when Brett Houtz first heard the news about the Sandusky grand jury investigation, Houtz was upset, not because he was a victim, but because he liked Jerry Sandusky.[27] But after reading Sara Ganim's March 31, 2011, article about the Sandusky allegations, Brett Houtz's biological father, Chris Swisher, called him late at night, waking him up. "Hey, did you see what's going on with your buddy?" Houtz wasn't close to his father. "My Dad wasn't the greatest person," he recalled. "He's usually just looking out for himself." During the phone conversation, his father said, "Well, maybe you should get a lawyer," obviously thinking of the possible financial gain. Houtz said that he "wanted nothing to do with that," but his father did some research and found sex abuse attorney Benjamin Andreozzi in Harrisburg, Pennsylvania.[28][*][29]

Andreozzi had carved out a niche for himself as a lawyer specializing in sex assault cases, taking them on a contingency fee basis. The day after Swisher called him, apparently without having

---

* Chris Swisher died of a heroin overdose the following year. He was an excellent car salesman, according to his colleague David McNitt: "He just knew how to bullshit people, knew all the angles. He was a kind of con artist." Swisher told McNitt, "My kid Brett is one of the victims. We're gonna get lots of money."

spoken to Brett Houtz, Andreozzi called the Pennsylvania Office of the Attorney General to say that he represented an adult male who had been sexually assaulted by Sandusky when he was a juvenile. But he refused to divulge Houtz's name, perhaps to assure that he would be involved with the case, should it prove to be remunerative.[30]

Andreozzi met with Brett Houtz four days later, on April 5, 2011, but despite the lawyer's earlier assertion that he represented a Sandusky abuse victim, Houtz wasn't cooperative. "The lawyer came to me," Houtz said. "I didn't even tell the lawyer anything to begin with the first time I talked to him."[31] Andreozzi was intrigued by what might become a high-profile case involving Penn State, but there didn't appear to be any way to blame the university, with its deep pockets. Sandusky himself was not a wealthy man, and his assets were jointly owned with his wife Dottie, so there was no way to get a lien on his house or pension. Still, Andreozzi agreed to represent Houtz for a small fee, just in case something more lucrative developed down the line.[32]

Two days later, when Corporal Joseph Leiter knocked on his door as part of their efforts to find possible Sandusky victims, Houtz told the policeman that he already had an attorney and that he wanted to talk to him before he would speak to the police.[33] "I didn't even tell the cops anything the first time I talked to them," he said during the trial.[34] Then he spoke again to Andreozzi, and this time he apparently decided to be more cooperative, telling his lawyer that Sandusky had indeed molested him.

A REVEALING INTERVIEW

Consequently, at the April 21, 2011, interview with Joseph Leiter and Scott Rossman, at the Rockview police barracks in Bellefonte, PA, attorney Benjamin Andreozzi was present. The two policemen told him that Sandusky had abused other Second Mile kids and encouraged him to tell them that he, too, was a victim. At first, Houtz was slow to comply, but during this long, tape-recorded interview, he eventually came through with a vivid, shocking account of abuse.

After fifty minutes of preliminary talk about harmless games, wrestling around, and showers, Houtz finally told some lurid stories that thrilled Rossman and Leiter. As they wrestled in the shower, Houtz claimed that Sandusky would pull him to the floor into a "sixty-nine" position, "his genitals in my face, and his face down by mine, basically." Sandusky would allegedly lick and kiss the inside of Houtz's legs. "How about your testicles?" Rossman asked. "Like did he mess with your testicles at all, kissing them, licking them?" Houtz, perhaps improvising, answered, "Kind of, kind of. It wouldn't be all out, you know what I mean." Rossman, frustrated: "But they would get touched?" Houtz: "Oh, obviously, yeah, I mean, his head's there, it's happening. And if it wasn't that way, it would be the other way to where he's pinning me down and he's arousing himself on my face, basically."

Rossman asked, "When he was aroused, did he have you do some things to him?" Houtz's response was disappointing and difficult to fathom: "He would want a hug then, usually, it depends." And so it went, with the policeman eager for more, and Houtz eventually providing new details. He said that Sandusky would "arouse himself" during their soap battles. "Right in front of you?" asked Rossman. No, Houtz said, "he wouldn't be real blatant about it," but he never explained exactly what he meant.

Houtz also told Rossman and Leiter that when Jerry and Dottie Sandusky had taken him to the Alamo Bowl in San Antonio, Texas, Houtz slept on a cot in the same room where the couple slept. One day after exercise, as Houtz was about to shower in the hotel room bathroom, Sandusky allegedly wanted to hug him and "start feeling me up." When Houtz objected, Sandusky supposedly said, "Well, you don't want to go back to Snow Shoe, do you?" Houtz lived in Snow Shoe, PA, though how Sandusky would have sent him back there wasn't clear. Then Dottie opened the door to the hotel room and the incident was interrupted.

At this point, a little over an hour into the interview, Houtz asked for a cigarette break. While he was smoking outside, Leiter and Andreozzi, the lawyer, discussed what they had heard. They thought that the tape recorder had been turned off, but it had not been, so we know what was said. Ben Andreozzi was pleased: "I thought Scott got further than I did with him," adding, "I wonder if there wasn't oral sex." Joe Leiter assured him, "Well, there is, I think we'll get to that. I'm hoping we can get his confidence, and we have all these other kids. The thing we found with Jerry is the first time they shower, it's just to get the feel. The second time, it's to move a little closer."

Andreozzi said, "I've got to get him. . . . I've only had a chance to talk to him, really one time, when I interviewed him, and it seems like we're getting a little bit more, and I was in a hurry, I only had an hour. Now we have more time." Leiter assured him that it would just take time and effort. "That's the way it was with the first one," he said, referring to Aaron Fisher. "It took months to get the first kid, after it was brought to our attention. First it was, yeah, he would rub my shoulders, then it just took repetition and repetition, and finally we got to the point where he would tell us what happened." Leiter was absolutely sure that Sandusky must have sodomized Brett Houtz, since he had mentored him for three years. "I know there's been a rape committed somewhere along the line."[35]

The conversation then turned to strategies to get Houtz to reveal more. Andreozzi asked, "Can we at some point in time say to him (Brett Houtz), 'Listen, we have interviewed other kids, and other kids have told us that there was intercourse and that they have admitted this, you know. Is there anything else that you want to tell us?'"[36]

Leiter saw no problem with that approach. "Yep, we do that with all the other kids. Say, 'Listen, this is what we found so far. You fit the pattern of all the other ones. This is the way he operates and the other kids we dealt with have told us that this has happened after this happened. Did that happen to you?'"[37]

Leiter made it clear that he was sure that Sandusky had abused the Second Mile alums he was interviewing, even when they refused to admit it. "We had a kid in here the other day who thinks the world of him (Sandusky). . . . We never got that far with him. I think we're going to talk with him again, because he left here—in fact I said to him, 'You know, we're done with you now, you're shot, your mind is absolutely a sponge.' I mean, this is a horrible thing to do, sit these kids down—I keep calling them kids—sit these people down and then they realize, oh man, I didn't realize that's what he was doing this whole time." In other words, part of the policeman's perceived task was to reframe the way potential victims viewed Sandusky's actual behavior with them, to get them to view it as "grooming" or abuse. If Sandusky was innocent, it was indeed a "horrible thing to do," but Leiter didn't even consider that possibility.

Then when Brett Houtz came back into the room, Leiter gave him a pep talk, as he clearly had done with other alleged victims, urging him to get with the program: "Before we start again, I just want to let you know you are not the first victim we have spoken to. We have interviewed probably, I'm going to say, nine—again I call them kids, I apologize—nine adults we have interviewed, and you are doing very well. It is amazing. If this was a book, you would have been repeating word for word pretty much what a lot of people have already told us. It is very similar." Actually, by that time, only Aaron Fisher, Dustin Struble, and Zachary Konstas were "victims" who would testify, and only Fisher claimed severe, prolonged abuse, after therapy with Mike Gillum. Leiter must have been including the McQueary and janitor stories, but that still only came to five alleged victims.

Having assured Houtz that they had interviewed other alleged victims, and that his story was very similar to theirs, Leiter explained that the abuse would follow an inevitable progression. "Often this progression, especially if it went on for an extended period of time, leads to more than just the touching and the feeling, that there has been actual oral sex that has taken place by both parties, and we have unfortunately found that there has been what we would classify as a rape has occurred." Leiter was stretching the truth considerably. At that point, only Aaron Fisher was claiming oral sex. Zach Konstas never said that Sandusky abused him, and Dustin Struble had thus far only come up with one shower incident in which he had allegedly touched Sandusky's penis.

As more alleged victims were subsequently uncovered, some of their shower stories were indeed similar, which could be, of course, because Sandusky repeatedly molested boys in showers or in his basement. On the other hand, it is possible that police, lawyers, and counselors were all feeding similar stories to the young Second Mile alums. This kind of "co-witness" contamination occurred in the classic daycare sex abuse hysteria cases in similar fashion, where the interviewers inadvertently cued children to say what they wanted to hear.

Leiter and Rossman, who had no training in sex abuse investigations, undoubtedly were unaware that they were doing anything wrong or that they were cuing witnesses as to what to say. In their minds, they were simply encouraging these young men to tell the truth. Yet, in a classic case of "confirmation bias," they had already predetermined in their own minds what that truth was. And in this case, Leiter was intent on getting Houtz to say that Sandusky had forced him into oral sex, which Houtz had not yet said.

Leiter went on: "As Trooper Rossman said, I don't want you to feel ashamed because you are a victim in this whole thing. What happened happened. He took advantage of you but when I—when we first started we talked, we needed to get details of what took place so these types of things happened. We need you to tell us this is what happened. . . . We need you to tell us as graphically as you can what took place as we get through this whole procedure. I just want you to understand that you are not alone in this. By no means are you alone in this."[38]

After that pep talk, which he thought was not being taped, Scott Rossman said, "Okay, we're going to restart the recording. It's now 12:37 on 4/21/2011 and again we're going to continue to record it."[39] During the rest of the interview, Houtz did indeed get more graphic, asserting that Sandusky would get him facedown in the shower, then hump between his buttocks until he ejaculated, or that he would push his erect penis against Houtz's face until he orgasmed. He said that these same activities took place in the new Lasch building's sauna rather than the shower, because the shower had no curtain or privacy.

But Houtz denied that there had been any penetration, by penis or finger, which clearly frustrated the police investigators. At the end of the interview, Rossman said, "Well, listen, what usually happens is when you start to think about things, especially things that you try not to think about, you know, it may be 3 o'clock in the morning, tonight, and you go, *Oh, my gosh, I remember this or I remember that* or whatever." In that case, Houtz should call them. "Sometimes things come up and you remember more things in detail, even though you may try not to think about it. . . . If there's things you think about and there's other things that you remember. . . ."

Houtz assured him, "I know what you're saying." Then they turned off the tape recorder but obviously discussed what else Houtz might reveal, because they turned the tape back on eight minutes later, so that Houtz could say, "Basically, I really don't want to talk any more today, but there are some things that were a little more significant that I just don't feel comfortable talking about at this moment, basically, that in the future, we can talk about." And with that tantalizing tidbit, the tape ended.[40] Eventually, by the time of the trial, Brett Houtz fulfilled their expectations, asserting that he and Sandusky had oral sex.

During his own trial testimony, Trooper Rossman admitted that he suggested similar things to other alleged victims, and that he saw nothing the matter with it, that it was an appropriate technique.[41]

When asked if he had ever turned the tape off during any other interviews with alleged victims, Leiter said he couldn't remember. In fact, none of the other interviews appear to have been recorded at all.[42] He may well have employed this technique regularly, however, explaining the types of allegations he hoped to hear and emphasizing how others had said the same kind of thing. He would imply that if they didn't say Sandusky had molested them, they would be disappointing him, and he would think they were hiding something, that they were lying or had repressed the memory. After admitting that he and Rossman had discussed their testimony on June 19, 2012, before their appearance in court, Leiter was confronted with the fact that Rossman had testified that they *hadn't* discussed it and was asked to explain it.[43] Of course, he couldn't. Rossman had apparently perjured himself, but neither the judge nor anyone else seemed unduly concerned.

During this testimony, Rossman admitted that during the initial interviews, many victims said that little or nothing had happened, but that they later added more serious allegations.

> *Amendola*: Did you ever in the course of interviewing these accusers who later led to charges; did, in your initial interview, any of them say to you that nothing happened or something minimal happened and then later add things to it?
>
> *Rossman*: Yes.
>
> *Amendola*: During the course of that transition from nothing happened or maybe some things happened minimally but then they became more serious, did you ever suggest to them that you think more serious things occurred but that they're just not telling you and there are other people out there who are saying the same things, that more serious things occurred?
>
> *Rossman*: Did I ever think that more occurred than what they told me? Absolutely.
>
> *Amendola*: Did you ever convey that to them when they weren't telling you what you might have thought occurred more seriously?
>
> *Rossman:* Yes.[44]

He said he thought that more had occurred than what they were telling him, so he pressed them repeatedly for more graphic material. He said he didn't think he was tainting the investigation by doing so.[45]

Judge Cleland dismissed concerns about the way Rossman and Leiter questioned Brett Houtz or other "victims" and whether their interview methodology was likely to lead to false allegations. "The issue is not whether or not the witness's testimony was corrupted by any questions," Cleland advised the jurors. "The purpose of the evidence is to show that the troopers didn't tell the truth, not that Houtz didn't tell the truth."[46] Of course, that makes absolutely no sense, nor is it legally correct. The evidence indicated bias, prejudice, and influence on the witness.

This revelation of the way Rossman and Leiter operated is crucial to understanding how the number of alleged victims mushroomed.

Police who are convinced that there are multiple victims, and who assume that abuse must have occurred, can let suspected new victims know what they expect to hear. They are often unaware that they are contaminating their interviews by such suggestive methods. They believe that they are simply encouraging victims to reveal the terrible things that someone *must* have done to them. The message is clear: *Others have told us that Sandusky abused them. We will be very gratified if you tell us something similar.*

DEVASTATING TESTIMONY

As with others, Brett Houtz's testimony morphed between his 2011 grand jury testimony and what he told jurors during the trial the following year. What he told the grand jury was bad enough. Rossman and Leiter had sought graphic testimony about oral sex, and they got it by the time Houtz testified. Houtz said that he remembered being touched inappropriately in a swimming pool and that the first molestation took place at Toftrees, a golf resort used by the Penn State football team. He described soap fights in showers that turned into wrestling, which would then become 69 positions in which Sandusky would insert his penis into Houtz's mouth, sometimes ejaculating. He said that Sandusky had attempted anal intercourse but that he had resisted and prevented that from happening. At the Alamo Bowl, Sandusky had threatened to send him home because he wouldn't cooperate with attempted oral sex in a hotel bathroom.*

Then, after the move to the Lasch Football building, a ritzy new Penn State sports complex completed late in 1998, when Houtz was fifteen, Houtz said in his grand jury testimony that all sex that did not occur in hotel rooms occurred in the sauna, because it was more private. Houtz said that Sandusky bought him cigarettes regularly, and that at one point Sandusky gave him $50, drove him to a drug dealer where he scored marijuana, and allowed him to smoke it in Sandusky's car—an allegation that, for anyone who knew the teetotaling Sandusky, was highly unlikely.[47]

It isn't clear how much Houtz's memory may have been enhanced by therapy or suggestive questions from the police or lawyers by the time he testified before the grand jury. He did sign an agreement with Andreozzi, which stipulated that he should enter

---

* Jerry Sandusky found this Alamo Bowl allegation preposterous. "Send him home for not having sex with me—that makes sense! What would I have told his parents? Wouldn't it be more likely I was upset with him because he was refusing to go to a luncheon when we had paid $50 for a ticket?"

counseling as part of their deal.[48] Part of Houtz's motivation may have been financial, since he was shortly thereafter evicted from his apartment because he didn't pay his rent.[49] Andreozzi saw Houtz at least five times, including his testimony during the grand jury proceedings and at police interviews. Houtz also spoke on the phone with his lawyer multiple times. During his trial testimony, Brett Houtz said that he met with the police and agents from the Office of the Attorney General at least ten times.[50]

Because of his graphic testimony, by far the most shocking firsthand account that prosecuting attorney Joe McGettigan had, Houtz was chosen as the lead-off witness for the trial on day one, June 11, 2012. By this time, Houtz had switched therapists and was in the hands of a master—Mike Gillum, who had worked with Aaron Fisher for three years to help unearth his memories.*[51]

On May 29, 2012, Gillum revealed in an affidavit: "I am currently in the early stages of treating a young man known as Victim #4 in the Grand Jury Report related to criminal charges against Jerry Sandusky." Gillum was asking the court to allow Houtz to testify without using his name, because "it is my opinion that the identification of Victim #4 in open court at the scheduled trial will obstruct his recovery process and create further emotional damage." Houtz's "recovery process" may have involved recovering more abuse memories. Gillum's request was denied, despite his assurance that using Houtz's name in court would traumatize him "and lead to further feelings of shame and humiliation" and would give him PTSD symptoms.[52]

During the trial testimony in June 2012, McGettigan asked Houtz to describe how in July 1997 he was invited to go to football games and taken to tailgate parties with other Second Mile kids. Interspersed with these bland and believable details were the general questions about showering crimes, with no specified dates. Houtz said that the abuse occurred in the coaches' shower area, that he could not fight back, that nothing was said about it afterwards, and that he didn't protest or tell anybody about it.[53] He didn't say anything about the abuse to his friends or his probation officer.[54] And no, Sandusky had never asked him to keep it quiet. Houtz explained: "It was basically, like, whatever happened there never really happened."[55]

---

* Mike Gillum was associated with an organization called Let Go Let Peace Come In, whose website was full of repressed memory references. Attorney Andreozzi was working with "Let Go," which was offering free counseling to alleged Sandusky victims, as of November 2011.

Houtz said that many coaches came into the locker room and shower area, and that he interacted with them and talked to them, but that he and Sandusky were never caught in the act because Sandusky would be alerted by the loud clicking of the four-button lock in the old coaches' locker room, which he could hear in spite of the shower noise.[56] Houtz said that Sandusky inserted his penis into his open mouth two or three times a week for years, with ejaculation sometimes occurring. He said it occurred "40 times at least." When asked by the prosecution if he'd ever thought of just saying he didn't want to continue, he said, "The thought always crossed my mind."[57]

During the trial, Houtz changed his grand jury story that the sex happened only in the sauna in the Lasch building. Now he said that the sex happened in the shower, too, apparently realizing that he needed to be consistent with the soaping, wrestling, and positioning tales. When questioned about how the attempt at anal intercourse arose, Houtz said they were chest to chest, estimating that he was so small that he only came up to Sandusky's waist "a little bit above the belly button."[58] That would have made Houtz about three and a half feet tall, the size of a six-year-old, when he was fourteen. McGettigan had trouble getting Houtz to create a credible story.

> *McGettigan:* Now at that time, about how high up on the defendant did you come? If I can use—
>
> *Houtz:* Lower. Much Lower. Probably about here is where I'd come up to him at.
>
> *McGettigan:* Let the record reflect indicating above the waist?
>
> *Houtz:* A little bit above the belly button, yes.
>
> *McGettigan:* Okay. And where were the defendant's hands on you if at all at the time this happened, if you were chest to chest? You weren't really chest to chest really, were you?
>
> *Houtz:* Yes.
>
> *McGettigan:* You were facing . . .
>
> *Houtz:* Well, yes. Right. Right. . . . That's the way we were turned. We weren't actually—
>
> *McGettigan:* Where were the defendant's hands on you?
>
> *Houtz:* Here, and then one managed to well, one managed to make its way down to my butt.
>
> *McGettigan:* Okay. And when you say managed to make its way down to your butt, what if anything did he do when his hand went down to your butt?
>
> *Houtz:* Slid his finger between my butt cheeks.[59]

Then Houtz said he turned the water off and left, before correcting himself by saying he didn't turn the water off but left without even rinsing off.

Later at the Lasch building, he said, when he was fifteen or sixteen, Sandusky soaped him up, then pushed him down flat on the tiles and attempted to slide his erect penis between his butt cheeks.

> *McGettigan:* And what did you do?
> *Houtz:* Got up and left.
> *McGettigan:* Well, the defendant was on top of you, how did you—
> *Houtz:* Yeah, no. I pushed. I pushed with all my might. Squiggled. Slided underneath him. Got out of there. I'm covered in soap too, you got to remember.[60]

During the grand jury, Houtz had said he was abused at the Toftrees resort, but there was no mention of Toftrees at the trial. McGettigan wrapped up by having Houtz agree that Sandusky put his penis in his mouth over forty times and that he had attempted sodomy. Houtz asserted that there was no reason for him to say these things other than that they were true.

Under cross-examination, Houtz claimed that Sandusky had taken him to the Penn State campus at the end of the summer of 1997, and that they had played basketball alone, from 6:00 p.m. to 9:00 p.m., from the end of the summer until year's end. Even though it was the busy pre-season and then football season, there were supposedly no other coaches or players around. Houtz then told defense attorney Joe Amendola that they had been "grappling around, like play boxing," which sounds like the kind of thing Sandusky really did. But of course he went beyond that.

Amendola asked him if Sandusky touched his privates during their first shower together. "That first time, yes," Houtz said, "but you got to understand that he never was really right for it with touching me. It was more like he wanted to be touched." So in the same breath, Houtz said that Sandusky did touch him, but then no, maybe he didn't.

This seems an odd assertion, given the number of times he alleged that Sandusky forced oral sex on him. He described being wrestled to the floor and having Sandusky sneakily try to slip his penis into his mouth. It seems implausible, given the fact that Houtz had working jaw muscles and teeth that would have made such an unwanted penile entry unlikely.

"I mean," Houtz said, "it would happen on quite a few—almost every time after that, that same sort of thing would happen. It would get, you know, more to where he's actually sticking his penis in my mouth, you know. There's even a few occasions where he ejaculates."[61]

When asked why he put up with all this abuse over the three years from 1997 to 2000, Houtz explained that he was picked on at school, and he wanted to be one of the cool kids, so he put up with sexual abuse in order to be seen as buddies with Sandusky.

Then he revealed that he may not in fact have *remembered* the abuse after it took place. "I don't even really want to admit that it's happening, you know," he explained, using the present tense to refer to the time of his abuse. "I have spent, you know, so many years burying this in the back of my mind forever." Since we know that Brett Houtz was in psychotherapy with Mike Gillum, this may be a reference to repressed memories.

But then he went on to say that he had "thought I was the only person. I had come to terms with that and just wanted everything to go away. But then I find out that this has happened over and over and over and over again forever, and I feel if I just would have said something back then, they wouldn't have had this happen to them. So I feel responsible for what happened to other victims."[62] It was thus unclear whether Houtz meant that he had repressed the memories and only recovered them recently, or whether he had always remembered it and "just wanted everything to go away."

Houtz's testimony would have been more credible, however, if he had said from the beginning that he was abused. Even after his lawyer found him, and the police initially contacted him, he did not disclose that any abuse had occurred. Then, like many other alleged victims, his story grew worse over time, with changing details. Of course, some abuse victims may be hesitant at first to reveal what happened to them, but the idea that they would initially deny any abuse, and then incrementally reveal it, is not proven by extensive research in confirmed cases. Therapists such as Mike Gillum believe that they must peel back a mental onion in layers. Many (though not all) real abuse victims simply tell the story of what happened to them, once they decide to do so. They do not elaborate and change their stories over time.

Also, since Sandusky was incredibly busy during football season, it was literally impossible that he could have been spending all this time with Brett Houtz during the summer and fall, as he asserted. Sandusky found time for dinner with his family almost every night, before going back to practice, according to his wife and children.[63]

During cross-examination, Houtz scaled back his estimate of several hundred oral rapes to fifty events total, including groping, kissing of thighs, and "any of that." In the late afternoon, he and Sandusky had supposedly played basketball or racquetball *hundreds* of times, twice a week during the summer of 1997 through the end of the year. "This was totally impossible," Sandusky later observed. "I was coaching. I can just see myself saying, 'Joe, I'll miss practice and meetings so I can play racquetball with this kid.' It took 30 minutes just to go to Brett's house to pick him up. It's ludicrous."[64]

Houtz insisted that no coaches or players were there because they were all done and gone by then. Besides, nothing inappropriate could be observed because there was a blue curtain extending all the way to the floor in the old sports building. Yet when questioned about the new Lasch facility, Houtz admitted that the shower area was open to all, there were no key codes, and anybody could walk in. Still, he said that he was abused fifty additional times in the Lasch shower area, when he would have been fifteen or sixteen years old. Houtz said that no one else used the new locker room.[65]

There is no question that Brett Houtz's testimony was powerful and believable to the jury, and that Joe McGettigan was wise to choose him as an opening witness. Defense attorney Joe Amendola was clueless about repressed memory therapy. During the trial, he never raised the possibility that vital testimony could have been enhanced or created through such counseling.

But Houtz also may have been tempted by the financial benefits of making allegations against Sandusky, as well as the sympathy and attention he garnered.

"Brett is a shrewd, manipulative person," Sandusky later asserted. "He played with people's minds, especially those who cared about him. Brett was all that mattered to Brett."[66]

— CHAPTER 8 —

Two New Hotline Victims

SABASTIAN PADEN, VICTIM NUMBER 9

T HE NEXT two alleged victims came forward after the media firestorm that followed the Grand Jury Presentment's release and Jerry Sandusky's arrest.

Sabastian Paden, born in 1993, seemed to be a Second Mile boy who was making it. His relationship with Jerry Sandusky began in 2004 when he was eleven, during his second summer in the Second Mile. He appeared to enjoy the times he was invited as a teenager to join the Sandusky family fun in their home, playing games in the basement. In the fall of 2011, he was eighteen, a little older than most in his high school class.

Paden's changed attitude towards Sandusky occurred incredibly quickly. Sometime in October 2011, the high school senior was seated in Beaver Stadium beside Sandusky, enjoying a Penn State football game with a friend.[1] Less than a month later, Paden rocked the grand jury with accounts of his former life as a virtual captive in the Sandusky basement.

The day Sandusky was arrested on November 5, 2011, with the Grand Jury Presentment leaked the day before, Paden's mother, Angella Quidetto, watched the television and reacted to Pennsylvania Attorney General Linda Kelly's plea for more victims to come forward. She called the high school and asked someone to call the hotline for her. The police quickly arrived. Sabastian Paden apparently knew nothing about her call until the police were knocking at the door.

Angella Quidetto had raised her son the best way she knew how. She had a boyfriend who did not live with her all the time. She worked at a sports bar and another establishment whose nature was not revealed during the trial. Sabastian's natural father at this point was keeping in touch with his son. Quidetto and Paden, apparently an only child (no other children were mentioned at the trial), lived in a trailer in McClure, Pennsylvania, about forty miles east of State College. At one point, Paden had to be placed in foster care, though the reasons for his removal from the home were not revealed during the trial. Paden was placed in therapy throughout grade school and through part of middle school.[2]

Unlike Ryan Rittmeyer, the other accuser who answered Linda Kelly's televised call for more victims, Sabastian Paden actually did spend significant time with the Sandusky family. According to Dottie Sandusky, he came to their home for twenty to possibly thirty visits over his entire association of six years (from 2004 to 2011) with them, with the overnights included.[3] This would have Paden visiting them about every other month. He enjoyed his time in their basement, because that's where the pool table, air hockey table, and other entertainments were, and he had his own guest bedroom and bath. His mother, for her part, didn't seem to mind having somewhere for him to go.

Paden was beginning his senior year in high school when his mother called his school to have someone call the hotline for her. When the police showed up unexpectedly at his door in early November, he told them that Sandusky had never abused him.[4] Around the same time, unaware of the police visit, Jerry Sandusky called Paden to ask if he would testify for him. "Sab reiterated that nothing ever happened but said he needed to speak with his Mom, and he asked me to call back," Sandusky recalled. By the time he called again a few days later, Paden had become an alleged victim, and the police tape-recorded the call, hoping to get Sandusky to say something incriminating, but he did not.[5]

Less than five days after Sandusky's arrest, Paden testified at another session of the Sandusky grand jury on November 9, 2011. There he told a truly horrifying story. The grand jury panel heard how Jerry Sandusky would pick up Paden at school and take him to the Sandusky home, where he was locked in the basement (although the lock on the door was from the basement side, so this aspect of his story was impossible). He was forced to eat all of his meals there, which were brought to him by Jerry Sandusky. Paden said that he barely had any contact with Dottie Sandusky, and that she never came down to the basement. Paden said that he was forced to perform oral sex on numerous occasions, and that Sandusky attempted anal intercourse over sixteen times, with actual penetration at times. Paden said that he screamed loudly for help during these attacks, knowing that Dottie was upstairs, but that no one came to help.

It is unlikely that repressed memory therapy was involved in encouraging Sabastian Paden's memories, at least at the outset, since his grotesque allegations arose within just a few days of his mother's phone call. It is instead likely that he was either telling the truth or that he was consciously lying, at the urging of his mother and in search of remuneration and sympathetic attention.

Seven months later, during the trial, the narrative had evolved somewhat. It continued to change, even during the short time Paden was testifying. He apparently had a hard time remembering how the story was supposed to go.

When the prosecution questioned him, Paden said that in 2005, 2006, and 2007 he spent almost every weekend from Friday afternoon to Saturday in the Sandusky home (the same time frame in which Sandusky was supposed to be molesting Aaron Fisher most weekends). He estimated that he had been there from 100 to 150 times. He said Jerry Sandusky kissed him during each visit and forced him to perform oral sex quite a few times. Paden said that he slept alone in the basement and that Sandusky "put his penis in my butt" at the age of maybe thirteen, or perhaps it was fourteen, or come to think of it, fifteen. When asked to describe the anal assault, he said, "He came in. I sucked his penis, and then he got real aggressive and just forced me into it and I just went with it. There was no fighting against it."[6]

As Jerry Sandusky later pointed out, "Aaron Fisher and Sabastian Paden gave the same time frames for their outlandish number of overnights at our home. However, they only saw each other once." They alleged that during all these times, they slept in the same bedroom, in the same bed.[7]

Paden's story changed again when answering the defense attorney's questions. Now he said he spent every weekend from Friday to Sunday, not Saturday, and the weekly visits continued through 2009, not just 2007.[8] Again, he said he was alone, that there were no other kids there—not any of the Sandusky children or any other Second Mile children. Sandusky allegedly made Paden touch his penis, after which he made Paden perform oral sex. "He made me give him a . . . oh, how do you . . . suck his penis, is how you put it."[9] When asked exactly how that happened, Paden described it as Sandusky coming in, lying on top of him and then he "kind of forced it in."[10] He denied that he wanted this to happen and pointed out that he was overpowered. "What was I going to do? I mean, look at him. He's a big guy. He was bigger than me at the time, way bigger than me."[11]

Then Paden made a new and startling claim of going without food during his entire stay in the basement each weekend. He was now telling the jury that he had been starved during his captivity in the basement. Instead of sticking to the original story he had told to the grand jury, including having his meals delivered by Sandusky, he created a completely new version of his basement captivity. He claimed "he never really ate anything at the Sandusky house."[12] When given a chance to modify that assertion to make it more credible, he continued to insist that he never ate anything at the house. Then, perhaps realizing that he must have eaten somehow, he went on to say that he was taken out to eat on occasion.

Paden also changed his first account of being forced to stay in the basement against his will and later said he liked it there because that's where the games were. "I would go down there and play games and stuff because down in the basement he has, like, a pool table, an air hockey table, one of them shuffleboards and a TV, a couch, a dartboard, a bathroom, and then a bedroom, and there's games and stuff down there."[13] Apparently he got carried away with these pleasant, real memories, testifying that he "would go down there," forgetting that he had claimed before that "he was always down there,"[14] because he had supposedly been forbidden ever to come up out of the basement.

Paden's testimony was replete with contradictions. He told the prosecutor that the last time he stayed at the Sandusky house was when he was fifteen. He told the defense his last visit was at the age of sixteen.[15] Although he first testified that he spent at least every Friday night and Saturday, and possibly Sunday, too, in the basement for about four years in isolation (other than Sandusky's assaults), which would have amounted to two hundred days, he changed that story in answer to questions by the defense attorney. Now he did remember other kids being present, but he could not recall their names. "That's been a long time." That long time would have been a few years back. He went on to tell about going to a fund-raising golf tournament with other Second Mile kids. So his first story was that he was always alone in the basement.[16] He later said that he was around other kids.

Paden's mother, Angella Quidetto, testified for the prosecution three days after her son's testimony. She said he never told her anything and that she didn't ask. Indeed, he still hadn't told her any details. Her estimation of the time he had spent at the San-duskys was significantly less than her son's. Sabastian was not there continually every weekend of the year, she said. His visits ran from spring to Christmas at the rate of a few times each month—still more than Dottie Sandusky estimated.[17]

Quidetto was aware that her son had said that he had bled from the alleged anal rapes and now she explained why she never no-ticed anything suspicious. The defense had asked Paden during the previous week about any problems with rectal bleeding, and how he managed to prevent his mother from catching on. He was vague and just said he had his "own way" of handling it.[18] Sabastian's mother now devised an alibi for that. She said that his underwear went missing.

The prosecution introduced this opportunity when she was asked about gifts from Sandusky. She broke down and wept as she said, "I wish he (Jerry Sandusky) would have just gave him some underwear to replace the underwear that I could never find in my laundry." Under cross-examination, she said she always wondered why "there was never any underwear, never socks."[19] (It was un-clear how the socks were involved in the sexual assaults.) Did she ever ask Sabastian about the missing underwear? Yes, but he told her that he had accidents in them and threw them out.

She also bolstered the believability that he had been sodom-ized by testifying to his constant complaints of stomachaches and bathroom problems. She told defense attorney Amendola that she took him to the doctor, but that a complete physical was not done.[20] Remarkably, Amendola apparently did not request Paden's medical records, and this testimony was allowed to stand as "evidence" for the supposed abuse.

Angella Quidetto was oddly ignorant about the terrible crimes that supposedly had occurred to her teenaged son, even though he had been talking about them the previous year to the grand jury and now during the trial. She said she never asked him any ques-tions about his abuse. Sitting on the witness stand, she told the jury that she didn't know what specifically happened to her son. But "I can just imagine what happened to him."[21]

What could she say about the activities that her son was in-volved in with Jerry Sandusky? Quidetto told of Sandusky tak-ing him to church, playing racquetball, swimming, going to see Sandusky's mother in a nursing home, and playing games in the Sandusky recreation room in the basement. What kinds of gifts did Sandusky give to Sabastian? Nike apparel, sneakers, athletic clothes, and a racquetball set.[22] All of these gifts were now seen as diabolical bribes to secure his silence.

Sandusky had originally thought that Sabastian Paden was going to help him with his defense efforts. He was on friendly terms with both Paden and his mother right up to the time of his arrest. In addition to Paden himself, Sandusky had taken both his mother and biological father to football games in 2009, 2010, and 2011. Paden's father had visited Sandusky's home with him.[23] The defense tried to use these facts in Sandusky's favor. Amendola asked Quidetto whether she knew that Sandusky had asked her son for help with his defense.

Yes, she said that she was aware that Sandusky had asked Sabastian to help him, and she knew Sabastian was asked to "make an affidavit or some kind of statement on what kind of character person he was." However, she thought it was perfectly awful that her son's mentor would now need or ask for help "after all these accusations were going on." She considered it very inappropriate for Sandusky to ask her son to get involved by telling the truth to the police. "Why would he call my kid after he was being accused of things like this?" she lamented to the courtroom.[24] Why indeed, given the horrific abuse her son would testify to? It is difficult to conceive that Sandusky would have asked Paden to be a character witness for him if he had been sodomizing him in his basement prison for all those years.

Sabastian Paden's civil attorney, Stephen E. Raynes, did not succeed in getting the settlement that they wanted from Penn State University through the attorneys that were handling those payments. Evidently, Kenneth Feinberg, who was in charge of making settlements to the families of the 9/11 terrorist attacks and who was now appointed to dispense a total of $60 million of Penn State's money, was not generous enough to suit Raynes. Paden was one of two holdouts (Zachary Konstas being the other) negotiating for more money. In order to strengthen his civil claim, Paden's attorney had to provide a direct link to the university to explain why Penn State was to blame for Sabastian's alleged abuse. Thanks to the fact that Joe Paterno was not alive to dispute any allegations, Raynes and Paden were free to produce their own account of Paterno's personal interaction with Sabastian Paden.

The lawsuit claimed that Sandusky's former boss, Coach Joe Paterno, invited the boy and Sandusky to have lunch with him at Beaver Stadium and tour the stadium, despite the late coach "being alerted years earlier to Sandusky's sexual assault of young boys. . . . Each time Sandusky and Sabastian Paden encountered Paterno, Paterno greeted Sandusky, endorsing Sandusky's favored status with Penn State."[25]

Jerry Sandusky denies that he and Paden ever saw Paterno. "The only time I was ever ate lunch with Joe Paterno was with a recruit, while coaching. He (Sabastian Paden) didn't play football, and I wasn't coaching in those years."[26] Joe Paterno and Jerry Sandusky had never spent much time with each other off the football field and were not close socially.

Raynes made the following statement as part of the lawsuit: "It was the inviolable culture of financial and sporting success of Penn State football that made possible the horrific sexual abuse that forms the basis of this lawsuit." In other words, Raynes was arguing that a successful football program leads directly to sexual abuse, and therefore the institution must pay. Since that is obviously absurd, and they needed some kind of direct tie-in, Raynes and Paden came up with the luncheon date with the legendary Joe Paterno.

Even though Sabastian Paden was probably not in repressed memory therapy before he gave his original testimony to the second grand jury in November 2011, what his attorney was now blaming on Sandusky sounds all too familiar. "Victim 9's lawyers said he has suffered depression, post-traumatic stress disorder, flashbacks of abuse at Sandusky's hands, sleep disturbance and other problems." It is consequently likely that Paden had been seeing a therapist who assumed the reality of his abuse narrative.[27]

The predicament in which Paden found himself, when the police unexpectedly came knocking, is anybody's guess, along with what his mother may have told him to say. He was still living in her home with a year to go to finish high school. At one point in his life, he had been taken out of that same home and put in foster care. All we know is that his story was inconsistent and difficult to believe. Despite allegedly being held a virtual prisoner in the Sandusky home and repeatedly forced into oral sex and sodomy, Paden had continued to return over and over again, for years, and had never said a word about the abuse to anyone. He remained friends with the Sandusky family until the month before Jerry Sandusky's arrest.

Especially suspicious is the fact that Paden refused to disclose anything to the police when they first came to the trailer to speak to him, but then he changed his mind and told the grand jury about being a sex slave in the basement with no freedom of movement.

RYAN RITTMEYER, VICTIM NUMBER 10

Ryan Rittmeyer was born on February 27, 1988. At age ten, in 1998, he lived in Moshannon, Pennsylvania, with his mother, stepfather, and stepbrother. He had last seen his biological father at the age of four. Rittmeyer attended the Second Mile summer camp for three consecutive years, starting in 1997. In 1998, his roommate was Jason Simcisko. That same year, he was placed in foster care with Cheryl Sharer in Milesburg, PA, and attended his second Second Mile summer camp. After being in the foster home for eleven months, he lived with his grandparents in Maryland and later lived again with his mother and stepfather.

Rittmeyer was incarcerated twice—for burglary in 2004, at age seventeen, and in September 2007, when he was twenty, for burglary and assault. He and a teenager assaulted an elderly man on the street, punching him in the face and leaving him with permanent injuries. They robbed him of his backpack, which held a camera and three books, but no money. Rittmeyer was sentenced to twenty-one months in prison and was released in 2009. At the time of the trial, he was married, with a pregnant wife. It is unclear whether or not he had been able to find a job, which is difficult for an ex-con.

Following the Sandusky arrest on November 5, 2011, Pennsylvania Attorney General Linda Kelly publicized a hotline number, which Rittmeyer called. He subsequently found a lawyer (or vice versa), Andrew Shubin, whom some might call the Gerald Sandusky ambulance chaser, since he specialized in representing former Second Mile kids. He eventually represented nine of them.

At his first police interview with Officer Michael Cranga on November 29, 2011, Ryan Rittmeyer said that he knew Jason Simcisko. He also said that Jerry Sandusky had groped him in a swimming pool. Then, while driving a silver convertible, Sandusky had allegedly opened his pants to expose his penis and told Rittmeyer to put it in his mouth. When he refused, Sandusky became angry and told him that if he didn't do it, Rittmeyer would never see his family again. Rittmeyer said that he still wouldn't do it, and when he got home, he told his mother he didn't want to go to Second Mile programs any more.* "His life went downhill" subsequently,

---

* In fact, on an application for the 2000 Second Mile camp, Rittmeyer and his counselor requested that he be accepted, stating that he had enjoyed the camps.

Cranga wrote in his report, which Rittmeyer apparently blamed on this traumatic event.[28]

During his grand jury testimony on December 5, 2011, Rittmeyer changed and amplified his story somewhat, saying that after he refused the demand for oral sex in the car, Sandusky got quiet and then talked about something else. It was the *second* time he demanded oral sex that Sandusky got mad and threatened him, but then he took it back. Now Rittmeyer was saying that something sexual occurred almost every time he saw Sandusky throughout 1997, 1998, and part of 1999, once or twice a month. Finally, Rittmeyer said that he eventually complied and gave Sandusky oral sex, and vice versa.

During the trial, he reverted to saying that in the car, after the refused oral sex incident, Sandusky got angry and threatened him but then apologized and told Rittmeyer that he loved him. When confronted with his dissimilar stories, he attempted to resolve them by saying Sandusky had been quiet but had a displeased look on his face. This abuse allegedly took place from the fall of 1998 to early 1999.

Rittmeyer also added new stories during his June 22, 2012, trial testimony. He described being invited to a football game. At some point in time, although he couldn't remember days or times or connected events, he was taken to the Sandusky basement, and after wrestling around, Sandusky abruptly and silently pulled his shorts down and began to perform oral sex on him. His reaction to that was to freak out, get nervous and scared. It lasted only a couple of minutes, after which Sandusky went upstairs. On cross-examination, he said he didn't know if Dottie was home but that he didn't see her.

Rittmeyer said that he went to Sandusky's house five times, presumably despite this disturbing assault and threat. He also added that Sandusky had reached up inside his shorts as he was sitting on Sandusky's shoulders in the pool and grabbed his genitals.* He testified that after a trip to Nittany Mall he was taken to the house and had oral sex performed on him, and he did the same to Sandusky in return. After that, he was taken home to his foster parent, Cheryl Sharer. He did not tell her about the abuse in the pool or anywhere else. He never told anybody, he said, because he was scared, ashamed, and embarrassed.

---

* Sandusky points out that pool rules prevented him from having children sit on his shoulders.

Upon questioning by defense lawyer Joe Amendola about the attack-in-the-basement story, trying to pin down a time, Rittmeyer said that the first time he went to the Sandusky residence was in 1997 before a football game, and that there were other children there and Sandusky's wife. He then contradicted himself, saying that the first time he went to the house *nobody* else was there, not even Dottie Sandusky.[29] He said he did not tell Jason Simcisko, his Second Mile roommate, that Sandusky grabbed his genitals in the pool during camp in the summer of 1998.

When asked to provide information about the alleged times Sandusky picked him up and took him to his home to assault him, Rittmeyer was vague and said he couldn't recall days.[30] He did say, however, that these visits usually occurred late in the afternoon to evening time, when nobody else was in the home, and that he was always taken home at night. This is an unlikely scenario, since Jerry Sandusky was otherwise occupied as a defensive linebacker coach at Penn State during the fall when Rittmeyer alleged he was abused.[31] That same logistic problem would plague other alleged victims' testimony as well. Sandusky somehow managed to run around in a near-constant priapic state, sexually assaulting boys, even as he worked as an extremely busy college football coach, only appearing at his home for dinner.[32]

Under cross-examination, Rittmeyer expanded the time frame for the alleged abuse, saying that it occurred in 1999 as well as 1998. Confronted with a statement on an application to attend the 2000 Second Mile Camp, indicating that he enjoyed the camps, he said that was an inaccurate statement.

Jerry Sandusky never owned any kind of convertible, nor was it likely that he borrowed or rented one, which would have been quite out of character for him. The Ryan Rittmeyer testimony, filled with inconsistencies as well as a mythical silver convertible, appears even more questionable because the Sanduskys said that they couldn't even remember him, whereas they readily admitted knowing the other Second Mile accusers. He may have been one of the Second Mile kids who came to their home, but Dottie Sandusky didn't know his name, and Jerry Sandusky said that if he met him on the street, he would not recognize him.[33]

CHAPTER 9

The Phantom Victim: Number 8

E'VE NOW covered all of the alleged victims who testified at the trial, but in addition there is "Victim Number 8," who never testified because he may never have existed, which is why I am calling him the Phantom Victim. He was the creation of Penn State janitor Ronald "Buck" Petrosky, who told the secondhand story of what another temporary janitor, Jim Calhoun, had allegedly told *him*. In other words, this is classic hearsay testimony—indeed, it is *double* hearsay, since it is two steps removed from an actual victim testifying to something that allegedly occurred. And the reason the temporary janitor didn't testify is that he was apparently suffering from Alzheimer's disease at the time of the trial and had been institutionalized.

Petrosky, a long-time janitor at Penn State, testified that he called the police at the end of March 2011, after reading a newspaper article in the *Centre Daily Times* about Mike McQueary supposedly having witnessed Sandusky committing sodomy with a ten-year-old in the showers at the Lasch building.* Petrosky said that the story sounded a lot like something he remembered from eleven years ago. He told the police that the incident occurred during a time that the Penn State football team was out of town on an away game, playing Ohio, during the fall of 2000.[1]**[2]

---

* Petrosky's supposed motivation for calling the police is impossible, because the first reporter to write about the Sandusky case was Sara Ganim in the *Patriot-News* on March 31, 2011, and she did not write about the McQueary story. In fact, Petrosky called the police after he read Ganim's article that day.
** The Commonwealth's "Bill of Particulars" stated that the crime concerning Phantom Victim 8 took place from November 20-27. Petrosky said that it occurred during an away game with Ohio State. The football season ended on November 18, 2000. The Ohio game took place on September 23, 2000. The last away game was played on

During the trial, on the witness stand on June 13, 2012, Petrosky described how an older janitor named Jim Calhoun became very upset during one night's late shift, which went from 7:00 p.m. to 3:00 a.m. in the morning. He recalled hearing Calhoun, a temporary employee, cleaning the toilets in the staff locker room in the Lasch building as Petrosky was entering the shower area in order to clean it. Petrosky hooked his hose up under the sink. Then, as he started to enter the shower, he saw the lower half of two people's legs in the shower area. One set of those legs was hairy, and the other set skinny. This was rather odd testimony, since the shower area was a wide-open space with five showerheads and no curtains, so he would have seen two whole naked bodies, not just legs. Not wanting to interrupt, he said, he dropped his hose and backed out. Then he went back in the hall and mixed up his chemicals.

Petrosky said that he waited there in the hall for them to finish and leave, so that he could get on with his work. He estimated that he was about two feet away from the locker room exit. Then Jerry Sandusky and a small boy walked out. He noticed that their hair was wet and that they were carrying gym bags. Petrosky recalled saying, "Good evening, Coach," explaining that he must have said that, because, "If I ever see him, I call him Coach."[3] Then he stood there watching them as Sandusky and the boy walked out the door and down the long hallway towards the double doors where the stairs went up. About three-quarters of the way down the hall, he said he saw Sandusky take the boy's hand in his. They walked through the doors, and then "of course, I never, I didn't see them again."[4]

Petrosky said that he then finished mixing his chemicals and was going back into the locker room, when he met Jim Calhoun, who was white and shaking. He spent about five minutes trying to calm the older man down. "I could see he was upset. His face was white. His hands was trembling. I thought it was a medical condition. I said, 'Jim, what's wrong?' And this is how he said it to me. He said 'Buck, I just witnessed something in there I'll never forget the rest of my life.' I said, 'What are you talking about, Jim?' He said, 'That man that just left, he had this – the boy up against the shower wall licking on his privates.' I said, 'Are you sure that [was the] man that just left?' He said, 'I'm sure.' I said, 'You know who that is?' I said, 'That's Jerry Sandusky.' He didn't know who he was but he knows what he seen that night."[5]

_____

November 11. So what Petrosky testified to did not fall into the necessary time frame. During an appeal on January 30, 2013, the judge refused to consider the issue because the defense had not raised it properly at trial.

Petrosky said that he then called his fellow janitors to a nearby meeting room, where Calhoun "told the other guys the same story." Calhoun was so upset that "we thought he was going to have a heart attack. We kept people with him all night throughout the night and made sure, you know, he was all right."[6]

"And was that all?" asked prosecuting attorney Joe McGettigan. No. Later that night, Petrosky was looking out the windows from the second-floor office area and saw a car cruising in the parking lot. "And I seen Jerry Sandusky drive real slow by. That's when I—yeah, it was about 10:00, 10:30, 11:30 pm—." And was that all? No, not all. He saw him again around 2:30 a.m. "I was taking the garbage out. I seen him one more time drive real slow. He never got out of the car or nothing. . . . He didn't have the boy with him then."[7]

McGettigan asked Petrosky, "Did you ever go and tell anyone what Mr. Calhoun said he saw?" Speaking for Jim Calhoun, he replied, "No, he never did."[8] Petrosky could not actually have known this, since theoretically he was not in contact with Calhoun after this event. And did anyone else tell anyone? No, not that Petrosky could recall. And even though Petrosky saw Sandusky in the building many times afterwards, he never said anything to him either.

On May 18, 2011, a year before the criminal trial, Ronald Petrosky told a somewhat different story to the grand jury. First, the location within the Lasch building was different. In this earlier version, the abuse had allegedly occurred in the assistant coaches' locker room, not the staff locker room. Of greater import, in his grand jury testimony Petrosky said he waited ten minutes before going back to clean the shower stall, which he did *before* Jim Calhoun allegedly told him what he'd seen: "I went back in, and I finished cleaning the shower. And I came back out. I unhooked my hose and [was] winding the hose up, and then Jim came up, and I could tell he was upset."[9] Petrosky said that when he cleaned a shower, he sprayed chemicals on the wall and then waited ten to fifteen minutes before spraying it off.[10]

That would mean that about a half hour must have elapsed between the time Sandusky and the boy were showering together and the time Calhoun spoke to Petrosky. The former coach and child would have left the shower, dried off, gotten dressed, and walked down the long hallway. Then Petrosky cleaned the shower and was putting away his hose. You might think that the timing wouldn't make that much difference—who cares *when* the distraught janitor revealed what he had seen? But *legally*, it made a big difference.

Before Petrosky told the jury what he heard from Calhoun over a decade beforehand, the defense attorneys tried to get Judge Cleland to bar the hearsay evidence from the courtroom. These arguments, held out of hearing of the jury, are enlightening. The prosecutors, Joe McGettigan and Frank Fina, told the judge that they had two witnesses who would testify to Jim Calhoun's outbursts in 2000. The second man, fellow janitor Jay Witherite, would be heard after Petrosky testified.[11]

The prosecutors realized that they had a big problem with Petrosky's story. In order to be admissible in court, hearsay evidence qualifies only if it was an "excited utterance" that occurred immediately after the event that prompted the outcry. What Calhoun supposedly said to Petrosky, as described to the grand jury, did not meet that legal definition. It was excited, but it wasn't immediate. Another problem was that they had no other evidence in any form to make the hearsay evidence admissible. Hearsay evidence was not legally supposed to stand by itself. The fact of an "excited" utterance does not prove there had been an "exciting" event. There was no known victim. There was no direct witness.

Therefore, perhaps in order to get around this obstacle, one key element in the story was changed for the trial. McGettigan told the judge that he wanted him to know upfront that there were changes in Petrosky's testimony, but that they were insignificant. "I can only say as an officer of the court that I spoke with him (Petrosky). I don't think there's anything dramatically different, but, you know, the written statements, grand jury testimony—they (defense attorneys) have what—I have spoken with him, and my understanding. . . ." Perhaps the court reporter didn't get precisely what McGettigan said here, which is confusing and unclear, but it was apparently satisfactory to the judge, who responded: "I don't think you could fake representation. If that person takes the stand, that's what they're going to say."[12]

The sequence of events was changed from cleaning first (before hearing Calhoun's story) to cleaning after. This would shorten up the time so the utterance might fall into the "spontaneous" range. The prosecutors hoped that this change in Petrosky's testimony would allow the testimony to be heard, even though it was obviously different from what was first said.

Prosecutor Frank Fina told the judge that in Pennsylvania, circumstantial evidence was enough to convict with a sole eyewitness. Indeed, an excited utterance could be the only linchpin between that defendant and the crime. "So [it is] certainly novel, judge, but

I would assert we have gotten the ball over the finish line here. Maybe by a hair."[13]

Judge Cleland was intrigued. He asked Fina if other alleged crimes in this case might also be considered evidence. Fina said they could. Cleland asked again, "Can the jury consider that other crimes have been committed in the shower room and therefore the pattern would sustain a guilty verdict on #8?" Fina gave him permission to do so, saying, "Yes, your honor, on the theory of course of conduct evidence, yes."[14]

Defense attorney Karl Rominger complained that it was problematical when a prosecutor was allowed to pile on charges, flimsy or not, and then use those charges to prove other charges. He said that allowing such hearsay would mean that they could never confront the witness. "If you allow the excited utterance in as substantive evidence, we never get to cross-examine an unavailable witness." Rominger argued that the recent rulings trended to support "more confrontation rather than less." The judge snapped, "You're talking to the wrong court about trends."[15]

Cleland ruled in favor of the prosecution, as he would in many other instances during the Sandusky trial. Petrosky could give his hearsay testimony. When he was finally allowed to take his place on the stand, Petrosky told the jury what the prosecution needed him to tell them. But Jay Witherite was never called to the stand, nor were any of the other janitors who were supposed to have stayed all night with Jim Calhoun to make sure he was all right.

All versions of the story had the janitors deciding as a group to keep mum about it, leaving it to Jim Calhoun, who was the eyewitness, to report what he had seen, if he had indeed seen something disturbing. The jury was told that Ronald Petrosky never told anyone about this incident until eleven years later, and neither had anyone else. Making the charges stick would rest solely on the credibility of Ronald Petrosky.

It is odd that the prosecution did not call Witherite to testify, since they apparently had him ready to do so, and he allegedly had corroborated Petrosky's testimony during the second grand jury proceedings.[16] Perhaps he would *not* have corroborated his evidence, and the defense did not depose him or call him to the stand either. We simply don't know. My attempts to find Witherite to talk to him failed.

Ronald Petrosky's grand jury testimony, as written up in the Grand Jury Presentment that was leaked on November 4, 2011, was quoted extensively by the media in the run-up to the trial.

"Jim said he had fought in the Korean War, seen people with their guts blowed out, arms dismembered—[but] 'I just witnessed something in there I'll never forget,'" according to the Presentment.[17] The clear implication was that what Calhoun had allegedly seen in the shower was worse than war atrocities.

Petrosky's narrative was detailed and vivid. He forgot himself and spoke for his protagonist, Jim Calhoun, seeming to know what he thought and did. Although he wrongly situated the event around an Ohio game, and recalled other details incorrectly, he had no trouble recalling word for word the horrifying details Jim Calhoun had told him over a decade ago. Yet this was about an event he didn't think serious enough to report to the police at the time.

Ronald Petrosky's story should never have been put before a jury. It wasn't even real hearsay. It was a reconstructed memory, swayed by current attitudes. Petrosky certainly would have heard about the McQueary story from his police interviewers, and with encouragement, he pieced together a likely scenario and rehearsed it in his mind until it became as real as a mental movie to him.

The afternoon Petrosky testified, the din in the courtroom made by noisy fans made listening difficult, both for Petrosky, who was hard of hearing, and the entire courtroom.[18] It was near the end of a long day. Otherwise, Amendola might have done a better job pointing out the inconsistencies in the narrative and why they mattered. And he might have asked why no other janitors who were there the night of the alleged abuse were called to testify. Instead, he said, "That's all I have."[19]

Ronald Petrosky's usefulness as a propaganda tool was proven many months before the trial. Sports commentator Bob Costas interviewed Jerry Sandusky on November 14, 2011, only nine days after the Grand Jury Presentment had been made public, an interview for which Sandusky was disastrously ill-prepared. During the interview, Costas inadvertently misrepresented the Petrosky evidence as follows:

> Costas: A janitor said that he saw you performing oral sex on a boy in the showers in the Penn State locker facility. Did that happen?
> Sandusky: No.
> Costas: How could somebody think they saw you do something as extreme and shocking as that, when it hadn't occurred, and what would possibly be their motivation to fabricate it?
> Sandusky: You would have to ask them.

Costas had misconstrued Petrosky's testimony. Petrosky had not claimed to have witnessed any abuse. He was repeating hearsay evidence from someone else now suffering from dementia. And Sandusky didn't know enough to correct Costas. This interview helped to enshrine the popular but false belief that a janitor with no motive to lie had been an eyewitness to Sandusky sexually abusing a child in a shower.

This set of charges lacked not only any physical evidence or any direct eye-witness testimony—it lacked a victim. It featured one changing story, from one man, who didn't report it for years. Yet it stuck. The Petrosky story was more than satisfactory to the jury, which found Jerry Sandusky guilty of all the charges. They could picture it happening. It was a vivid tale of horror, something like the shower scene in Alfred Hitchcock's *Psycho,* transferred to the Lasch building. And most reassuring of all, there was no reason for Petrosky to lie (other than, perhaps, the desire for attention, sympathy, drama, and a genuine desire to "do good" that may have transformed his memory dramatically in hindsight.) Therefore, there was no reason to doubt.

It turns out that Trooper Robert Yakicic had tape-recorded an interview with Jim Calhoun on May 15, 2011, before he was deemed to be too demented to testify.[20] The interview took place at a nursing home, where Calhoun's daughter Trudy led the initial interview caught on tape. At first, Calhoun appeared to be halting and confused, perhaps in the early stages of Alzheimer's. Yes, he remembered working for "JoePa," Paterno, but he couldn't recall the other coaches' names. "We had so many coaches up there." Yet when Trudy mentioned Sandusky's name, he brightened and verified that he was "a pretty good guy."

When Trudy asked him whether her father had seen "anything bad happen up there with, maybe, somebody younger and an older man," Calhoun said, "There was bad things that happened to those kids up there for years. It's been going on for years, Trudy . . . I seen things happen to young kids, sexual. . . . I saw things that sexually happened to them. It should have never happened to *any* kid." Trudy tried to get details but concluded that her father might be too embarrassed to tell her, so she let police investigator Bob Yakicic take over. Calhoun told him, "I saw him (a boy) get sucked. . . . It was terrible to see it. It was something in my life I never wanted to ever see again. . . . I was shaking like a leaf."

When asked how old the boy was, Calhoun said that he was "more than just a kid . . . way over 10 [years old]," but that the perpetrator was "much older." Calhoun couldn't remember this older man's name, but "I know that if I saw the man again, I could recognize who it was." Finally, Yakicic asked, "Mr. Calhoun, do you remember Coach Sandusky?" Yes, he did. "Do you remember if that was Coach Sandusky you saw?" Calhoun immediately answered, "No, I don't believe it was." Surprised, Yakicic said, "You don't?" Calhoun went on, more emphatically. "I don't believe it was. I don't think Sandusky was the person. It wasn't him. There's no way. Sandusky never did anything at all that I can see."

The former janitor went on to explain that he had only recently gotten his job at Penn State when he saw the incident in the shower, so he didn't report anything. "I was a new man, and I could have lost my job."[21]

It seems that Jim Calhoun probably did witness oral sex in the Penn State locker room, which deeply disturbed him. During this taped interview, his voice broke, and he began to cry as he talked about it. But it clearly wasn't Jerry Sandusky whom he saw, and the person being fellated wasn't a young boy but an older teenager or young adult. That night Calhoun probably *did* tell Ron Petrosky what he saw, but not that it had been Sandusky. Ten years later, when the Sandusky scandal broke, Petrosky recalled the story and erroneously concluded that it must have been Sandusky whom Calhoun had seen, and his memory changed to incorporate the now-infamous coach, and he added other fictional details such as Sandusky cruising the parking lot at 2:30 a.m. in his car.

Amendola later claimed, under oath, that he knew about this taped interview with Jim Calhoun. "We had a transcript of it, and I believe we even played it." Incredulous, his cross-examiner asked, "You're certain you did review this transcript and the tape before the trial? You're certain of that, I take it?" Amendola backed off. "Pretty sure. . . . Can I say today that I definitely got that before trial and reviewed it? I can't tell you that today."

It would, in fact, have been beyond comprehension if Amendola had known that janitor Jim Calhoun, over a year before he was declared incompetent to testify, had clearly stated on tape that Jerry Sandusky was *not* the man he saw abusing a child in the shower, and that the lawyer had failed to introduce the tape into evidence. It is more probable that he never listened to this taped interview.[22]

CHAPTER 10

Matt's Flip

THAT ACCOUNTS for the ten alleged victims presented during the Sandusky trial, but one more accuser made a big difference during the trial and resulted in Jerry Sandusky deciding not to testify. Matt Sandusky, the last of the six children to be adopted, had stood by Jerry Sandusky during the investigation. In 2009, he had told the police that his adoptive father "did not ever touch him in an inappropriate way." They had a few disagreements over the years, but "it was not about anything sexual." In 2011 he had testified in front of the grand jury that his adoptive father had never abused him. "They tried to get me to say stuff, they tried to break me, but they couldn't do it," he bragged to his siblings afterwards.[1]*

Yet in the middle of the June 2012 trial, he "flipped," as the rest of the family put it, going to the police to say that he, too, was a Sandusky victim. As a result, he would later collect millions of dollars in compensation from Penn State, star in the documentary *Happy Valley,* and appear on Oprah Winfrey's television show, where he told Oprah how he had only recently unearthed memories of abuse through therapy. Until then, he said, "I didn't have these memories of the sexual abuse."[2]

Before we examine Matt's flip in detail, it is important to understand how he came to be a part of the Sandusky family. Matthew James Heichel was born on December 26, 1978. His mother Debra was eighteen years old, married only recently to his father, Matthew Martin Heichel. They had two more children, Ron, born a little over a year later, and Stephanie, a few years after that. The couple

---

* I was able to speak to Matt Sandusky, a soft-spoken young man, in a State College café in October 2014, but he insisted that our conversation remain off the record, so the following account is based on public documents and other interviews.

divorced when Matt was six. When Jerry Sandusky got involved with Matt through the Second Mile program, the family was living in a trailer in Howard, Pennsylvania, in impoverished circumstances.

Jerry Sandusky wrote in some detail about Matt Heichel in his 2000 autobiography, *Touched*:

> Matt was around seven or eight years old when he first became involved in the Second Mile. He would visit our house occasionally, but he was never one to get very attached to anyone. He would stand off in the corner somewhere and watch as I would be wrestling with the other kids. He became an instant challenge for me. I didn't want to see him go through life by himself at such a young age. I didn't want to lose him to whatever other fates might have awaited him, so I kept trying and trying to pull him in.[4]

As Matt spent more time with the Sandusky family, he became particularly close to Sandusky's wife, Dottie, and daughter, Kara. "But he was still very shy and quiet," Sandusky wrote in *Touched*. "He lived with his biological mother, brother and sister. His mom (Debra) was a person who tried very hard, but she kind of went from one crisis to another and never really gained control of all the circumstances she was faced with. As a result, Matt seemed to be neglected in many ways." Sandusky had the impression that he was "put down a lot and told that he really wasn't any good." Sometimes when Sandusky drove him the twenty miles back to his trailer in Howard, Pennsylvania, no one was home. At one point, Matt told Dottie and Kara that his mother was being abused by her boyfriend and that he, Matt, just wanted to get out of that situation.[5]

When Matt was in eighth grade, he was constantly in trouble at school for disciplinary problems. "I convinced his mother to start a program where he could study and work out and spend time with us," Sandusky recalled, "and in turn, he would be rewarded with money that would go into a fund for his college education." Sandusky did this kind of thing with other Second Mile kids, such as Brett Houtz, and he had Matt sign a contract, hoping it would help him to change his behavior and life. Things seemed to be going well, and Matt enjoyed going to the Citrus Bowl in Orlando, Florida, with the family.

But then things went downhill. "Matt started missing his responsibilities with me, and I had to try and track him down." In addition, his mother "became very jealous" and resentful of the Sanduskys. Jerry Sandusky gave Matt a lecture. "I told him he had to stop lying to people and accusing others for the problems that he had to deal with. I told him he had to have the strength and courage to fight out of the lifestyle that was making him so despondent."

Then Matt's mother and her boyfriend called a halt to the Sandusky program and refused to let Matt visit their home any more. Debra apparently felt that she was being unfairly judged and resented the help that was being forced on her. She later expressed the sentiment that her son was being stolen from her. Once Matt began to be somewhat less of a problem for her, she decided to end his association with the Sanduskys. Matt expressed his unhappiness about it to Jerry Sandusky.

"Time went on and I couldn't see him very much," Sandusky recalled. "I went through all kind of channels, such as children and youth organizations to probation systems, trying to devise a way for Matt to be relieved of those difficult circumstances he was embedded in." But nothing came of his efforts. Then Sandusky learned in December 1994 that Matt had gotten himself into serious trouble with the law with possible arson charges. Matt and his cousin had set fire to a barn while they were cutting school.[6]

At the time, Jerry Sandusky was in California as the defensive coach for the Penn State Nittany Lions before a victory in the Rose Bowl. He made a few phone calls to explore the possibility that Matt could live with his family, and he asked Tim Janocko, a close friend and high school football coach, to visit Matt at the juvenile detention center to ask if he wanted to do that. Considering that the only other option was remaining locked up, Matt said he would. The Sanduskys were told that Matt and his cousin claimed that they had just been smoking cigarettes, and the fire started when they attempted to hide them in the hay. While authorities were still looking into the cause of the fire, plans were finalized to transfer Matt to the somewhat more controlled, and hopefully safer, environment of the Sandusky home.[7]

A Children and Youth Services report from December 1994 recommended the placement:

> Overall, Jerry and Dottie are intent on making a difference in Matt's life. They have had three foster children already, one of whom they adopted, in addition to four others [whom they had adopted]. They understand the philosophical nature and goals of foster parenting, and I believe they have realistic expectations in regard to Matt's placement. They can offer him a stable, loving home environment which will give him maximum opportunity for growth.[8]

But as a foster child, Matt did not respond to the touted advantages of a middle-class environment by following the rules or cooperating with Dottie and Jerry Sandusky. He ran away for a day that winter. He exposed himself repeatedly to Kara Sandusky, who was five years older, and who just tried to avoid him.[9] And then in August 1995 an unexpected guest came to join the family.

A MODERN ROMEO AND JULIET

The Sanduskys learned from friends that seventeen-year-old Anne (not her real name) had moved in with her sister in another state when she became pregnant the year before, but now she wanted to enroll in college and needed to find a way. Jerry and Dottie agreed to have her move into their home with her infant son, so that she could attend Penn State. At the time, Kara and Jon were the remaining children at home. "This family was unlike any I'd ever witnessed," Anne recalled. "Church every Sunday, nightly family meals at the table, game nights. I now know that this *should* be the norm, but I wasn't familiar with all this togetherness and structure." She felt like an outsider and quickly bonded with sixteen-year-old Matt, the other "outsider" in the house.

With Dottie's help, the teenaged mother got a job and enrolled at Penn State in the fall. Anne and Matt began a secret sexual relationship that continued for months but was eventually disrupted when the Sanduskys discovered what was going on early in 1996. Jerry and Dottie Sandusky sternly confronted the pair, demanding that they stop their affair immediately.

In response, the two teenagers vowed to end their lives together as a modern Romeo and Juliet, taking the family car one night and overdosing on aspirin. Anne woke up in the hospital and was transferred to a psychiatric unit for a few weeks before she was sent to a group home in her home state. With the benefit of nineteen years' hindsight, she summed up the event as "us being ignorant kids and wanting to die because life stunk and we weren't getting our way."[10]

Sixteen years later, when Matt claimed that Jerry Sandusky had abused him, he strongly implied to the police that he had attempted suicide because of the alleged abuse. During his 2014 interview with Oprah Winfrey, he allowed this impression to be broadcast on national television. "So you move in [to the Sandusky home] at 16, and you think this is going to save you from going to a detention home or a military camp or wherever because he's convinced you that this is your saving grace in that moment. By the time you're

17, you had tried to commit suicide. Did the abuse subside after the suicide attempt?" Yes, Matt answered.[11]

Looking back on their time together, Anne said that Matt had talked about Jerry Sandusky putting his hand on his leg in the car, but they just joked about it. "Matt never mentioned actual sexual abuse to me," she wrote. "That strikes me as odd, and when listening to Matt's audio [interview with the police] about the abuse that took place and him mentioning that he wanted nothing more than to die at that time, hence the suicide attempt . . . If he wanted to die because he was abused, I never had a clue about that."[12]

After Matt and Anne's dramatic but failed suicide effort, "everything hit bottom," as Jerry Sandusky recalled.[13] The attempted suicide forced the authorities to reconsider Matt's placement with the Sanduskys. Terry Trude, the probation officer associated with Children and Youth Services who worked at the high school, raised objections to the arrangement. Although his opinions have been taken in hindsight as an indication that the Sandusky family was to blame for the many self-destructive acts of Matt Heichel, it is unlikely that Trude drew that conclusion in 1995. The probation officer was simply less idealistic and more practical than Jerry Sandusky on the topic of delinquent behavior and its causes and cures.[4]

But Dr. Fox, the psychiatrist assigned to Matt's case, recommended that he be returned to the Sanduskys' care because that was what Matt said he wanted, and the judge agreed. Matt Heichel was returned to the custody of Jerry and Dottie Sandusky. He was diagnosed as bipolar and was put on Prozac.[15] But Matt, then seventeen, continued to rebel. He stole money from the family and generally proved to be unmanageable.[16] "Things still continued on a downward trend until the whole situation looked very bleak," Sandusky recalled. "I started to withdraw from Matt because I just couldn't deal with the hurt any more. I felt we had done everything we could for Matt, and the end of our relationship was approaching. I told him there was nothing left and that we had played our last card."[17]

A TEMPORARY TURN FOR THE BETTER

At this point, Matt appeared to turn himself around. He brought Jerry Sandusky one of the corny inspirational articles his foster father had given him, called "Keep Climbing," with the message never to give up. "I love you," Matt told Sandusky. "From that point on, it seemed Matt had changed," Sandusky wrote in *Touched*. "He got tutored for his college boards and began to do very well in school." When he was eighteen, Matt asked to be officially adopted, since he would be eligible for a 75% Penn State tuition discount as Sandusky's son. And so in 1997, he became Matt Sandusky.[18]

Two years later, twenty-year-old Matt told a reporter for *Sports Illustrated* how much it meant to him to become a foster child and then a Sandusky:

> My life changed when I came to live here (in the Sandusky household). There were rules, there was discipline, there was caring. Dad put me on a workout program. He gave me someone to talk to, a father figure I never had. I have no idea where I'd be without him and Mom. I don't even want to think about it. And they've helped so many kids besides me.[19]

In his memoir, Jerry Sandusky concluded the story up through mid-year 2000: "Matt is still a student at Penn State, and we all, at times, still experience some highs and lows. There will always be battles." But he hoped they would fight them together. "He had the strength and the courage to stay loyal to us when we weren't sure what would happen. He could have hurt us."[20] In retrospect, those words became eerily prophetic.

The years after the publication of *Touched* (2000) were not a smooth glide to success for Matt Sandusky. In spite of his new name and status as a Sandusky, Matt continued to maintain a close relationship with his troubled younger brother Ronald. They were caught trying to steal computers from Penn State. Ron opened a charge account fraudulently in the Sanduskys' name. Matt used his parents' credit card without permission many times. In spite of his worrisome influence over Matt, Ron was not excluded from the Sandusky home. Matt dropped out of Penn State.[21]

Matt married Jill Jones in 2003 and started a family with her. They had financial problems and were sued several times over rent issues. Three children later, the marriage foundered, with Jones filing for divorce on May 26, 2010. She alleged that Matt harassed her during the separation.[22]

Before his marriage ended, Matt must surely have been under a strain. On August 23, 2009, his brother Ron Heichel ambushed his lover's husband in his own garage, blasting him once in the chest with a shotgun, and once again in the back after he fell. It took the police just four days to discover incriminating text messages on the

Matt Sandusky with children and Jerry Sandusky from Sandusky family 2010 Christmas booklet.

cell phones of the two killers. The murder was so poorly executed that it was featured on the *Stupid Criminals* TV show.[23] Ronald Heichel was sentenced to life for the murder, with the Pennsylvania Superior Court affirming his sentence on March 30, 2012, shortly before the Sandusky trial commenced.[24]

Jerry Sandusky says that he and his wife bailed out Matt many times. "Always feeling sorry for him, we have given him money. He would come with all kind of needs (rent, car payment, school debt, and others). He was always looking for a loan that seldom was repaid. When his car didn't work, he asked to borrow mine for a week. As would be expected, the week turned into two months. He returned it on the day he turned on me." From his vantage point in prison, Sandusky wrote: "It's ironic that we saved him from being institutionalized twice."[25]

Following his divorce in 2010, Matt returned to live with Jerry and Dottie Sandusky for about a year.

"Why would he move in with us in his thirties if I had abused him?" Sandusky later inquired. When Matt began to date Kim, who would become his second wife, he moved into her townhouse. She was doing well, with a good job and a nice car. At first, Matt didn't tell Kim about his brother's murder conviction. During this time, Matt was also being chased for back child support payments. Nonetheless, Matt's pursuit of Kim was successful. Over her father's

objections, they were married in December 2011, a few days after Jerry Sandusky was charged for two more alleged victims and
was placed under house arrest.[26] From that time until his "flip" in
mid-trial, Matt continued to support his adoptive father's claims of
innocence.

Matt's mother, now called Debra Long, had been subpoenaed
by the grand jury and eagerly repeated her past resentments and
suspicions. Matt was so angry about the bullying he experienced
at the hands of the Attorney General's office that he wanted to take
legal action against them. He carried boxes of documents for the
Sandusky attorneys.[27] His loyalty appeared unquestionable. What
could have caused such a drastic change of heart?

Right before the trial, Matt's extremely pregnant bride, Kim,
threw him out of her apartment, and he spent some unhappy nights
back at the Sandusky home. Then, mere days before the trial began, Matt was arrested for not paying the child support he owed
to ex-wife Jill and his three older children, and he spent the night
in jail before Jerry and Dottie Sandusky bailed him out.[28] Clearly,
Matt was not in a secure place either financially or emotionally. In
retrospect, Jerry Sandusky thinks that Matt had already begun
to act strangely towards him and that perhaps he was already in
therapy that encouraged him to reframe his past. "My guess is that
Matt was going to a therapist over a month before the trial. He mentioned liking the person. My further speculation would be that's
because he was being told what he wanted to hear."[29]

MATT'S RECOVERED MEMORIES

On Monday, June 11, 2012, the first day of the Sandusky trial, the
prosecution called Brett Houtz, five years younger than Matt, who
told compelling stories of Sandusky's soapy assaults in the Penn
State shower. Matt sat in the courtroom and heard Houtz mention a
time when Houtz, Jerry Sandusky, and Matt had played racquetball
together, then showered. Matt got to the shower first, then Sandusky and Houtz came in. According to Houtz, after a few minutes,
Jerry Sandusky started "pumping his hand full of soap and threw
it," at which point Matt turned off his shower and left. He said that
Matt's face looked "nervous."[30]

That evening, at the Sandusky home, Matt scoffed at Houtz's
testimony, saying, "This is ridiculous! Anyone can make accusations without evidence and get paid. I could, you could, anyone
could . . . but I actually have morals!"[31]

Yet Houtz's testimony apparently planted a powerful seed in Matt's brain. He, too, had slap-boxed in the shower with his adoptive father. Sandusky had put his hand on Matt's leg in the car, too, which Houtz said "freaked me out like extremely bad."[32] Sandusky had written contracts promising to pay for part of his college tuition, too, if he behaved himself in high school. He, too, had gone to bowl games with Sandusky, including the Outback Bowl and Alamo Bowl, along with Houtz.[*][33] Could something have happened to him, too? Could he somehow have forgotten it or actively repressed the memory?

Two days later, on Wednesday afternoon, June 13, Matt asked his mother, Dottie Sandusky, to watch his five-year-old son Andy (not his real name) for a couple of hours while he went to paint a porch.[**] But he was well dressed when he left and returned, so she doubted that he had been painting anything. In retrospect, it seems likely that Matt used his mother as a babysitter while he went to a therapy session.

That same day, probably after his therapy session, Matt texted his older sister Kara on her cell phone, asking to see her. Kara, who was married with two children and lived in New England, had flown back to Pennsylvania to attend the trial and to support her parents. "I did not want to go over to Matt and Kim's house, because of my experience with him—he had exposed himself to me, more than once. I said, 'Is your wife going to be there?' I didn't want to be alone with him. I didn't have a car, either." Matt reassured her. So Matt, Kim, and Andy came to pick Kara up around 7:00 p.m. While she and Matt talked, Kim and Andy went outside, where Andy rode his bike.

Matt started telling Kara how he had listened to Brett Houtz's testimony, "and all these things were coming back to me. I showered with Dad, too, but nothing sexual happened. And I don't think Dad did anything to Andy."[***] Then Matt apologized for exposing himself to Kara and for other things he had done. "But then he started blaming some of his past mistakes on Dad," Kara recalled. "Like he blamed his suicide attempt on Dad for overcontrolling him, and maybe he was alluding to what he thought was abuse. I don't remember all the things he brought up," Kara said. "Remember

---

[*] Matt was the team manager during the Alamo Bowl.
[**] Matt and Kim had joint custody of Andy, who had arrived on Tuesday night for a few days.
[***] After the allegations became public, Matt Sandusky's ex-wife Jill had suggested that Jerry Sandusky might be molesting his grandson Andy.

that this was in the middle of the trial, and I was under a huge emotional strain." She does remember that Matt said, "I am not doing this for money, and I'm not going to the police."

Matt told her that he had smelled something really strange in their parents' basement. "Then he starts telling me he has been hearing these weird voices calling his name," Kara said, and he told her that Tarot cards were revealing things to him. "OK, I think it's time for me to go now," she said, thinking that her adoptive brother was becoming unhinged.[34]

Clearly, Matt was extremely disturbed. It is possible that by the time he spoke to Kara, he had already gone to see Andrew Shubin, the sex abuse lawyer who came to represent him, and that Shubin had listened sympathetically to Matt's confusion and suggested that a particular psychotherapist might help him to remember more about what Jerry Sandusky might have done to him, explaining that he, like other alleged victims, might have repressed the abuse memories. And Matt may have already had therapy sessions before the trial as well as on Tuesday and Wednesday. He would later say that Houtz's testimony had "opened a door inside my head and deciphered what had happened to me," but it also probably required repressed memory therapy to help him come to believe that he was abused.[35]

On Thursday, perhaps following another therapy session, Matt went to the police. He told them that Jerry Sandusky had abused him, too, though his allegations were apparently rather vague, so the police scheduled a longer session with Matt on Friday morning, which was tape-recorded.[36] The full interview of the Friday session has not been made available, but someone leaked the tape to NBC News, which later ran excerpts of that second meeting with the police on Friday, June 15.

Matt said that when putting him to bed at night, Jerry Sandusky would blow on his stomach, then move his hand down his body and rub against his genitals, and that sometimes Matt would ball up into a fetal position to avoid contact. "It just became very uncomfortable, you know, just with everything that was going on," Matt said. The police detective asked what he meant. "With like the showering, with the hugging, with the rubbing, with the just talking to me. The way he spoke. And just, the whole interaction with him alone."

It is likely that Matt had indeed begun seeing a therapist to help him unearth memories. Jerry Sandusky said that Matt had told him he was seeing a therapist some time before the trial, and that he had encouraged him. "Dottie and I had been trying to get him to go to therapy forever." Then he observed that "Matt began to act weird a couple of weeks before the trial." He seemed more hesitant than the other children about plans to have him testify and had asked, "Why am I being singled out?" In retrospect, Sandusky thinks that Matt had been considering a flip to accuse him for some time. "I think I made a mistake when I told him that Allan Myers had flipped. His wheels started turning, I swear."[37]

Matt told the police that he was working with a therapist and that "memories of his abuse are just now coming back," according to the NBC announcer. When the police asked whether Sandusky had sodomized him or forced him into oral sex, Matt answered: "As of this time, I don't recall that."[38]

When and how did Matt Sandusky begin searching for abuse memories with a repressed memory therapist? It could be that he had begun the process during his therapy in the month before the trial began. Alternatively, his new lawyer, Andrew Shubin, may have suggested a new therapist, who specialized in repressed memories, for him to see. Shubin told reporter Sara Ganim: "The folks we are talking to are largely folks in their 20's, who in a lot of cases have never told their story before." Aided by "a team of psychologists and social workers, the attorneys plan to aid the alleged victims by providing mental help and possible legal recourse," Ganim wrote.[39]

Matt's confused state, in which he was hearing voices, might have made him even more susceptible to suggestion and unclear about what was real and what was not. It is likely that he took things he had always remembered, such as Jerry Sandusky tickling him, blowing raspberries on his stomach, and taking showers with him after workouts, and began to add imagined details such as his genitals being rubbed.

Anne, whose affair with Matt when they were teenagers precipitated their suicide pact, had now been happily married for many years. She had not had any recent contact with Matt, but she followed the case in the media and concluded that Jerry Sandusky probably did not abuse Matt or any other boys. "An innocent man should not be in prison," she wrote. Though they were intimate with one another and lived in the Sandusky household, Matt never told her anything about being sexually abused. "Aside from that," she wrote, "I just can't understand a person being abused for so many years and then choosing to be adopted at the age of eighteen. He'd be free to move out—why would he stay? That makes no sense to me."[40]

In 2014, Matt Sandusky spoke to Oprah Winfrey about his alleged abuse. By this time, he *had* remembered oral sex. "For him to have done those things to me," he said, "for him to have performed oral sex on me, forced me to do the same to him, for him to kiss me on the mouth—" Winfrey interrupted him to ask, "So here's the tough question. Did he ever try to anally penetrate you?" To which Matt Sandusky answered, "Yes. I mean, he did digitally with his fingers, and he did try, but I was never anally penetrated."

Matt made it clear to Winfrey that he had not recalled sexual abuse until he was in repressed memory therapy, but this apparently did not make her skeptical in the least. "So based upon what you're telling me," Winfrey said to him, "you actually repressed a lot of it." And Matt replied, "Uh-huh, absolutely. The physical part is the part that, you know, you can erase."

When she asked him about first coming forward to talk to the police during the trial, he said, "It was a confusing time." It wasn't as if he heard Brett Houtz and all his own abuse memories came rushing back. "My child self had protected my adult self," he explained. "My child self was holding onto what had happened to me—and taken that from me—so I, I didn't have the memory of—I didn't have these memories of the sexual abuse—or with him doing all of the things that he did."

As he listened to Houtz and other alleged victims, he felt somehow that "they were telling my story," but he apparently didn't remember abuse right away. "They were telling—you know, all of these things start coming back to you, yes, [and] it starts to become very confusing for me and you try and figure out what is real and what you're making up."[41]

It is very likely that a therapist taught Matt Sandusky that his "child self" had hidden his abuse memories from his "adult self"—a version of "inner child" therapy, an antecedent to a belief in multiple personalities, as I documented repeatedly in *Memory Warp*.[42] Such therapists often dismiss their clients' uncertainty, telling them that doubts about their recovered memories are common. They might not seem real, they may be confusing. It might seem to the clients that they are making them up. But not to worry, they are real.

The idea that he might have been abused and had repressed the memories must have become appealing to Matt Sandusky by the time of the trial. Here were all these other Second Mile alums getting attention and sympathy, and they would also probably get a substantial amount of money. Matt had wanted to become a Sandusky when that name was a magic ticket to cheap tuition and respectful attitudes. Now that the name had become a huge liability, a stigma, he found a way out of it. He would later change his last name to Davidson, only to reclaim "Sandusky" when it became clear that it would be useful again. With his wife, Kim, he started the Peaceful Hearts Foundation, with a website explaining, "We believe every child and survivor of childhood sexual abuse should feel safe, supported."[43] Who could possibly disagree with such goals?

And now everyone praised Matt Sandusky for how brave he was to come forward and reveal his abuse. No one mentioned that if he was telling the truth now, then he had perjured himself under oath during his grand jury testimony. But of course he hadn't really perjured himself consciously, because he *hadn't remembered the abuse* when he had spoken before the grand jury. That makes Oprah Winfrey's praise for Matt ring rather ironic: "It takes a lot of courage to step up and to speak your own truth."[44]

MATT'S BOOK

In 2016, Matt Sandusky wrote *Undaunted: Breaking My Silence to Overcome the Trauma of Child Sexual Abuse*, in which he offered a much-revised version of his life story. For instance, he presented his suicide attempt as the result of his alleged abuse. People "would say it was two dumb kids with a Romeo and Juliet complex. It would never have been thought that I took my life because a man that the entire world worshiped, it seemed, was sexually abusing me."

Unlike in his 2012 police interview or 2014 conversation with Oprah Winfrey, in his book Matt Sandusky avoided using the term "repressed memories"—he now preferred the term "dissociation"—but there were numerous hints that he had not actually recalled the abuse until the trial. He printed a conversation with his "inner child" in which he had recovered a memory from when he was two years old (an impossibility because of infantile amnesia) of his biological father "holding the red-hot flame of a cigarette lighter to his tiny, fragile toes." He recalled this because this is "what I do now for my inner child. I tell him it is safe to disclose, to admit what happened, to me." He had to "access the traumatized child self" in order to heal. "I had kept my child self locked up in the prison of my pain and my silence, where he couldn't grow up."

About his alleged abuse by Jerry Sandusky, Matt wrote that his "mental escape mechanisms" allowed him to take his mind away. "This mental dissociation is common in rape victims. . . . They flee the only way they can—with their minds and hearts." When he unearthed his memories, "I felt like my mind had been a swollen wound full of infection and pus, and I had lanced it and all the poisonous junk had flowed out." He had finally chosen to disclose "something so deep, so personal, so buried." These were "things I had kept hidden deep within me [in] the deepest locked doors of my heart." The shame of the abuse led you to "put it away in a compartment of your brain, and lock the key to that dark place forever, [which is] the way a victim dissociates and denies." After he began to unbury the memories, "my mind was still in a fog."

Yet in *Undaunted*, Matt Sandusky was careful to deny that he had repressed memories, for which I may be partly to blame. When I met him in October 2014, I told him I was particularly interested in the issue of repressed memories and wanted him to talk about how he had come to recall the abuse. He insisted on keeping our interview off the record, so I cannot quote from it. Two years later, in this book, he pointedly wrote that he did *not* have "recovered memory" therapy and that he had never really forgotten that Jerry Sandusky had molested him. "I [just] did my very best to try to put it out of my mind."

Given everything else he had already said about repressed memories, however, and what he wrote even in this book, that claim of "always-really-remembered" seems unlikely. In *Undaunted*, he wrote about the process of "incremental disclosure" that occurred gradually through his therapy. "The more I tried to block it out, the more visuals I would see. I had denied it for so long that now that I was owning up to it, the memories flooded over me. I had spent most of my life blocking out or dissociating from the victimization." By the time he wrote his book, he had been in therapy with a "specialized trauma therapist" for several years.[45]

THE RUSH TO JUDGMENT

— CHAPTER 11 —

A Moral Panic and Its Aftermath

NOW THAT we have looked in detail at the ten alleged victims introduced at the Sandusky trial, plus Matt Sandusky's mid-trial flip, we have seen how weak the evidence for Sandusky's guilt was, despite the multiple accusers.

To put the case into better context, it is important to go back and look at the way the legal system and media created what sociologists call a "moral panic" in the run up to the trial, during the courtroom drama, and in its aftermath, in which more putative victims came forward. They may have been true sex abuse victims, of course, or they may have been motivated by the money that Penn State announced it would be paying, or both.

The term "moral panic" goes back a long way, to 1830. In his 1972 book, *Folk Devils and Moral Panics*, Stanley Cohen stated that a moral panic occurs when a "condition, episode, person or group of persons emerges to become defined as a threat to societal values and interests."[1] The perceived threat is demonized and becomes a source of true panic, often without foundation. Examples include the great witch hunts of the fifteenth through seventeenth centuries, anti-Semitic pogroms, fear of child abductions, Satanic ritual abuse cults, and, at least since the 1980s, predatory pedophiles.

Some of these objects of societal fear, such as the Satanic ritual abuse cult scare, were complete myths. Others, such as pedophiles, are all too real. Sexual abuse of children is abhorrent, but it has become the crime for which people are routinely judged to be guilty until proven innocent, and the definition of sex abuse can range from a hug or a hand on the knee to rape.

As historian Philip Jenkins wrote in his 1998 book, *Moral Panic: Changing Concepts of the Child Molester in Modern America:*

Images of the sex offender have changed dramatically and cyclically over time. Originating in the Progressive Era, the imagery of the malignant sex fiend reached new heights in the decade after World War II, only to be succeeded by a liberal model over the next quarter century. More recently, the pendulum has swung back to the predator model; sex offenders are now viewed as being little removed from the worst multiple killers and torturers.[2]

When a high-profile person is accused, it becomes all the more likely to turn into a rush to judgment, as occurred in the case of Jerry Sandusky. Why should that be the case? Partly, it is because of the widespread idea that the high-and-mighty take advantage of their positions to abuse children. While that may sometimes be the case, it has become almost a stereotype that the respected pillar of the community is guilty if accused of abuse. The same is true for caretakers such as teachers, daycare providers, or others who work with children—there is a widespread assumption that these people must have chosen their profession in order to have access to innocent, young children whom they could abuse. Sandusky fit the bill in both categories—a pillar of the community, idolized as part of the Penn State football phenomenon, who created the Second Mile, a program for troubled children, and who served as a personal mentor and supporter for many of those children.

As a moral panic builds, it applies enormous pressure on everyone in a society to conform to its belief system, or they, too, might be considered part of the problem. If they appear to be apologists for a pedophile, for instance, they might be accused of being pedophiles themselves. The level of anger or ostracism leveled at anyone who questions the conventional wisdom can be astonishing. In 1692, that proved true of anyone who questioned the guilt of those accused of witchcraft in Salem, for instance—and consequently, there were few such skeptics who dared to go public with their doubts. In similar fashion, the moral panic that built over the Sandusky case made it virtually impossible for anyone to express doubts about the case.

Indeed, even Philip Jenkins, the author of *Moral Panic*, expressed his firm opinion that Sandusky was a multiple molester, well beyond the crimes for which he was convicted. Jenkins, a professor at Penn State, wrote that pedophiles are "truly compulsive and they claim vastly more victims during their criminal careers, possibly two or three hundred." So what about Sandusky? "Where are the rest of the victims? Unless Sandusky departed radically from the usual pedophile pattern, then he would have been molesting at least from the age of twenty, say, in 1964." Yet at the time he wrote, the public allegations only went back to the 1990s. "Nobody becomes a pedophile overnight at age fifty," Jenkins observed.

One might think that Jenkins was intending to cast doubt on Sandusky's guilt, but instead he was hypothesizing that there were dozens more unknown victims.* He noted that Sandusky had started the Second Mile program in 1977, the year before the notorious North American Man-Boy Love Association (NAMBLA) was formed to promote the idea that male pedophilic abuse of boys was a legitimate expression of love. "In these very years, pedophiles genuinely were more likely to act out on their desires," Jenkins concluded.[3]

When a professed skeptic such as Philip Jenkins made such assumptions, it was hardly surprising that the new Pennsylvania attorney general would as well. To replace him as attorney general, Tom Corbett appointed his friend Linda Kelly, after making his successful run for the governor's office. Kelly officially took office in May 2011. When she inherited the job, Kelly also had an ally in another Corbett appointee, Frank Noonan, the new commissioner of the Pennsylvania State Police, fresh from his duties as the former chief of investigation under Corbett as attorney general.

When Kelly and Noonan took over, the case concerning Jerry Sandusky had been limping along for more than two years, with prosecutor Jonelle Eshbach continuing to pursue it, while becoming more and more frustrated. A teenager, Aaron Fisher, and his therapist, Mike Gillum, were alleging child sex abuse, based on memories Gillum was helping Fisher to identify in therapy, but the 30th Pennsylvania grand jury had found the testimony insufficient and refused to indict Sandusky. Jonelle Eshbach, Tony Sassano, and Scott Rossman had been unable to locate any more victims in spite of extensive searching.

THE INVESTIGATION CATCHES FIRE

But Mike McQueary's shower story changed everything when he told it to the police in December 2010. The McQueary allegations lit

---

* Some alleged Sandusky victims did come forward claiming abuse from earlier years, but the statute of limitations prevented their cases from being heard. It is difficult to conceive, however, that Sandusky had been serially molesting boys for all those years without any of them telling anyone. It is also possible that such allegations were false, influenced by the search for repressed memories and/or financial gain. Some of these cases will be covered in the pages to come.

a fire under the investigation, just as Linda Kelly was about to take charge. Kelly later complained of the "uncooperative atmosphere" from some officials, but that didn't stop her.[4] Apparently a true believer in repressed memories herself, given her later statements, she approved of a full-scale operation to uncover other victims, whom she and Eshbach imagined had to be out there. Perhaps these victims had forgotten their abuse, too.

The police interviewers encouraged young men to disclose abuse, even if they initially denied it. They would ask Second Mile alums to call them if they remembered anything abusive, anything at all. And until the would-be victims were in therapy and able to unearth memories, perhaps they would not even know to come forward.

As a long-time personal friend of now-Governor Tom Corbett, Linda Kelly was given additional funds to hire a small army of twelve agents and investigators (eight from the state police, four from the attorney general's office), whose only job was to find new Sandusky victims.[5] Mike Gillum listed the Office of the Attorney General as a customer, although Aaron Fisher was his client through Children and Youth Services in Clinton County.[6] Gillum would counsel Brett Houtz, in addition to Fisher, as well as three other alleged Sandusky victims.[7]

When Sara Ganim published her initial bombshell articles on March 31, 2011, leaking news of Sandusky's grand jury investigation, it stunned residents of State College, most of whom naturally assumed something really criminal was going on, or why would there be an investigation? Ganim also helped the prosecution when she contacted Debra McCord, the mother who had called in an unfounded report to the police in 1998 about her son Zach Konstas's shower with Sandusky. Somehow having obtained inside information (probably leaked from someone in the Pennsylvania Office of the Attorney General), Ganim told the mother to call Detective Joseph Leiter if she wanted the case against Sandusky to go forward.

Soon, many of her son's Second Mile friends were contacted by Pennsylvania State Police detectives. The two policemen who led the investigations were Joseph Leiter and Scott Rossman, who had in the meantime apparently been inculcated into the repressed memory dogma, if they were not already believers. The detectives encouraged potential victims to pursue abuse memory recovery, but they also used contaminating, suggestive interview techniques, as they revealed during their trial testimony and in the accidentally taped planning session about how to get Brett Houtz to reveal more severe abuse.

They would tell Second Mile alums that they *knew* that Jerry Sandusky was a pedophile, that many others were telling them that he had molested them in the shower, in his home's basement, or in hotel rooms, and that they, the young men, would be brave to reveal how Sandusky abused them. When the Second Milers said that Sandusky had done nothing inappropriate with them, Leiter and Rossman made it clear that they were disappointed and that they did not believe them. They implied that if the potential victims thought hard about it, they might unbury some sex abuse memories, especially if they went to therapy. It is possible that the detectives also let drop that not only would they be courageous to reveal their abuse by Sandusky, but that there might also be some substantial monetary reward down the line.

Attorney Benjamin Andreozzi suggested that the police say, "Listen, we have interviewed other kids, and other kids have told us that there was intercourse and that they have admitted it. You know, is there anything else that you want to tell us?"[8] Whereupon Joseph Leiter verified, "Yep, we do that with all the other kids. Say, 'Listen, this is what we found so far. You fit the pattern of all the other ones. This is the way he operates, and the other kids we dealt have told us that this has happened after this happened. Did that happen to you?'"[9]

Note that out of an estimated six hundred young men the police interviewed, only six eventually accused Sandusky before the accusations created a media firestorm, and only one, Michal Kajak, made a sexual allegation during his first encounter with police.[10] As we have seen, Kajak may have already been influenced by his friends, Dustin Struble and Zach Konstas, and Kajak's story then grew and shifted in both location and time.

Because only one interview was tape-recorded, and records of therapy sessions remain hidden, it is impossible to know exactly how the accusations were elicited. But police reports show that they routinely suggested to Second Mile graduates that they might recall abuse, even though the young men initially denied that Sandusky abused them. For instance, at the end of Joseph Leiter's police report after his initial interview with Dustin Struble, Leiter wrote: "I also advised Struble that as he recalls events to please contact me and we can set up another interview. Also, if he begins having difficulties with his memories to contact me so that assistance can be found."[11]

Finally, Jonelle Eshbach was ready for the new Sandusky grand jury, the 33rd Pennsylvania panel that first heard testimony about the Sandusky case on March 10, 2011.[12] Now Frank Fina, one of her superiors who had been unwilling to press the case when it had just one unconvincing teen accuser, took part in questioning witnesses, too. In his third time testifying before a grand jury, Aaron Fisher, "Victim Number 1," was well-prepared, allowed to read aloud his testimony, and this time there were a few more alleged victims.[13]

Jonelle Eshbach knew how to spin the former grand jury testimony in her own special way. She had begun to number the alleged victims, along the lines of Dr. Seuss's Thing One and Thing Two. She conspicuously left out the word "alleged," so that from then on, everyone would refer simply to victims, with the clear assumption that they *were* indeed sex abuse victims. Victim 2 (Allan Myers) was not called to testify, since he remained unidentified, and he would come forward to defend Sandusky after the grand jury proceedings. Nor was Mike McQueary called to testify. Eshbach relied on his testimony to the 30th grand jury in December 2010.

New Victims 3, 4, 5, and 7 (Jason Simcisko, Brett Houtz, Michal Kajak, and Dustin Struble) were lined up. Victim 6, Zachary Konstas, also testified in front of the new grand jury, and though he still didn't recall Sandusky molesting him in the shower in 1998, he now made the experience sound somewhat sinister. As the *coup de grace*, Eshbach added the janitor, Ronald Petrosky, who talked about hearsay Phantom Victim 8.[14]

With eight so-called victims, Jonelle Eshbach was ready to write up her summary of the testimony from the two grand juries, massaging it to appear quite damning, with eight victims saying that Sandusky had abused them, even though two of them remained unidentified. Her ace in the hole was the McQueary story. In the Grand Jury Presentment, posted briefly on Saturday, November 4, 2011, then officially the next day, Eshbach wrote that McQueary had witnessed Victim 2 "being subjected to anal intercourse by a naked Sandusky" in the Lasch building shower, even though that wasn't what McQueary had said.[15] "I feel my words are slightly twisted and not totally portrayed correctly in the presentment. I cannot say 1,000 percent sure that it was sodomy," McQueary wrote in an email to Eshback a few days later. "I did not see insertion." He also emphasized that "never ever have I seen JS [Jerry Sandusky] with a child at one of our practices."

Eshbach emailed back to tell him to keep his mouth shut. "I know that a lot of this stuff is incorrect and it is hard not to respond," she wrote. "But you can't." In later testimony, Eshbach explained: "My advice to Mr. McQueary not to make a statement was based on the strengthening of my—and saving of my case."[16]

Eshbach wrote that the grand jurors found McQueary's testimony "extremely credible," but one of the jurors, Stan Bolton, later told a reporter that he was quite skeptical of McQueary's claim that Sandusky had been sexually abusing the boy in the shower, because McQueary didn't actually witness penetration. "This planted a seed with me—either you saw it or you didn't," said Bolton. The prosecutors "kind of glossed over it and moved on to who [McQueary] told."

So did Jonelle Eshbach in the Grand Jury Presentment, in which she implicated Penn State Coach Joe Paterno, Athletic Director Tim Curley, Senior Vice-President for Finance and Business Gary Schultz, and University President Graham Spanier for failing to report the McQueary incident to the police. While the elderly Paterno now recalled that McQueary had thought "something of a sexual nature" was going on, Curley and Spanier said that they were under the impression that it was just Sandusky "horsing around" with the boy. Schultz thought that Sandusky may have inadvertently touched the boy's privates while wrestling but that it was "not that serious" and said that he "had no indication that a crime had occurred."[17]

In the Grand Jury Presentment, a twenty-three-page document, Eshbach wrote that Sandusky had performed oral sex on Victim 1 (Aaron Fisher) more than twenty times. There was no mention, of course, that he had recalled all of this abuse in long-term therapy with Mike Gillum. She also wrote that elementary school wrestling coach Joe Miller had walked in on Sandusky and Fisher at the high school one evening, where "Sandusky was lying under Victim 1 with his eyes closed." When Miller unexpectedly walked in, Sandusky allegedly "jumped up very quickly and explained that they had just been wrestling." Yet, in his subsequent testimony, Miller denied that Sandusky had leapt to his feet, and both Fisher and Sandusky said that they were indeed wrestling after Fisher fell off a climbing wall.[18]

Then Eshbach went through the other "victims," making the alleged abuse sound as sinister as possible, even when there wasn't much to tell. Victim 3 (Jason Simcisko), for instance, thought that he once felt an erection when Sandusky hugged him from behind and that he remembered that twice Sandusky had brushed his genitals through the athletic shorts he wore to bed. Like those of the other alleged victims, his memories would get enhanced and more abusive by the time of the trial.

Victim 7 (Dustin Struble), another newly found witness, didn't say much either. According to the Presentment, Struble was uncomfortable with Sandusky putting his hand on his knee in the car, but he said that Sandusky had never touched his genitals. "Victim 7 testified that he has a 'blurry memory' of some contact with Sandusky in the shower but is unable to recall it clearly."[19]

We have already covered each of the alleged victims, so it isn't necessary to go over those cases in detail here. Suffice it to say that the way the Presentment was worded was appalling in its cumulative impact and strongly indicated that Jerry Sandusky was indeed a serial molester of boys. Eshbach made it sound as if all of the testimony were recent and heard by the 33rd grand jury, but in fact neither McQueary nor Konstas had given new testimony, and two of the alleged victims were unidentified. Eshbach was a master at spinning the stories she did have, however, quoting the hearsay statement about temporary janitor Jim Calhoun, now institutionalized with Alzheimer's, that he had fought in the Korean War, "seen people with their guts blowed out," but that what he had allegedly seen in the shower was even worse.[20]

Even before the Grand Jury Presentment was officially made public on Saturday, November 5, Sara Ganim began to fan the media flames in the *Patriot-News*. On Friday, November 4, she published the breaking news that Jerry Sandusky had been indicted. It turned out someone had messed up and posted the Grand Jury Presentment too soon. Sandusky was in Ohio seeing family members, and the whole thing was supposed to come down the following Monday, November 7. But somehow the charges and Presentment got posted on the Pennsylvania state court docket system on November 4.

Ganim pounced. "Jerry Sandusky's public persona was almost perfect," she wrote, "a revered Penn State football defensive coordinator who helped lead the team to two national titles, then dedicated himself to bettering kids through his charity and in his personal life." But that was all over now. "On Friday, the state attorney general's office indicted Sandusky with 40 charges of sex crimes against boys—some dating to Sandusky's coaching days at Penn State."

Ganim continued: "The indictment follows an almost three year investigation by the attorney general that started in early 2009, when a Clinton County teen boy [Aaron Fisher] told authorities that

Sandusky had inappropriately touched him several times over a four-year period." She punctuated the article with an anonymous quote from Debra McCord, the mother of Zachary Konstas, who had been upset when she discovered that Sandusky had showered with him in 1998. "'I just got goosebumps, seriously,' said the mother of one victim after the filing Friday. 'I just lived with this for so long, and it killed me when people talked about him like he was a God, and I knew he was a monster.'"

Clearly, Ganim was already in close touch with Debra McCord and other mothers of purported Sandusky victims. In the same article, she also quoted Debra Long, the biological mother of Matt Sandusky, the troubled young man who went to live as a foster child with the Sandusky family in 1995 at the age of sixteen, then was adopted two years later. At this point, Matt had testified in defense of his adoptive father in front of the 30th grand jury. Long, his biological mother, had always been bitter that her son had chosen the Sandusky family over her, and now Ganim quoted her as having "raised concerns about the behavior of her son and Sandusky once her son went to live with the Sandusky family in 1995. 'We tried to stop it back then,' Long said." Ganim quoted another anonymous mother as saying, "I've been told different things and nothing ever came to pass. Personally I just thought he was going to get away with it again."

— CHAPTER 12 —

Media Blitz

T HIS ARTICLE on Friday, November 4, 2011, was the beginning of an avalanche of coverage by Sara Ganim that would bury Sandusky's chance of a fair hearing. Ganim would publish twenty-two articles on the juicy Sandusky scandal over the next week. Eventually, her Sandusky coverage would net her a Pulitzer Prize. She was the point journalist for what would become a national obsession with the evil Jerry Sandusky.

In one of her three articles that Friday, she wrote about the 1998 shower incident with Zachary Konstas and noted that Ray Gricar, then the Centre County district attorney, decided not to pursue any legal action, since the sex abuse concerns were unfounded. As we have seen, that decision was reasonable, since Konstas said that nothing sexual had occurred, despite repeated attempts to get him to reveal something. But Ganim made it look like Gricar had hidden the abuse. "Gricar disappeared in 2005 and was declared dead earlier this year," she concluded, thus introducing a bizarre conspiracy theory that somehow Gricar's disappearance, four years after he ruled on the shower incident, had something to do with Sandusky.[1]

The Sandusky charges were removed from the court system website that Friday, but the news had already leaked. Jerry Sandusky, having just learned that he had been charged, drove back from Ohio and turned himself in on Saturday morning, November 5, 2011. The police pressured him to confess to the multiple allegations, but he vehemently denied that he had ever molested anyone. He was released on $100,000 bail. The state then officially posted the bombshell Grand Jury Presentment. The *Patriot-News* immediately posted a copy on the newspaper website.

Ganim had lined up child abuse experts who made it sound as though Sandusky's love and care for children, along with his high profile, made him the perfect pedophile candidate. On Saturday, November 5, 2011, she published a story quoting clinical psychologist Stanton Samenow, who told her that "whereas someone with normal sex habits might think of sex two or three times a day, people who prey on children live moment to moment thinking about how they can get access." Typically, Samenow said, such "predatory behavior starts in late teens or early adulthood." If Sandusky had begun molesting children that far back—fifty years ago—he had done a remarkable job of hiding his activities.

Ganim also quoted Tammy Lerner, who said that she herself had been a victim of childhood sexual abuse and now worked with the Foundation to Abolish Child Sex Abuse. She said that pedophiles grew more dangerous the older they got. "It's more of a control and power issue and they just get better with age, and maybe trusted more by parents and have more access to children." Samenow compared many pedophiles to Pied Pipers. "For many of these people, they have very magnetic personalities and do very good things for kids . . . so most of the public sees that side. Of course they are very kind to kids, good to kids, kids look up to them. All of this is the reputation they established, which does make it easier to get away with things on the side."[2]

A great deal more of this kind of profiling expertise would roll over Sandusky in the months to come. Some of these generalizations may be true in some cases, and the theory of a "nice guy, pillar of the community" pedophile will be explored in a later chapter. Some pedophiles *are* charismatic and really do good things for children, though many others are socially inept or do nothing but harm. Not all people who choose to work with children—teachers, daycare workers, pediatricians, coaches, scout leaders, activists, or do-gooders—are pedophiles. Yet many people now regarded Sandusky's creation of the Second Mile organization as evidence that he must have been a pedophile.

To ram that point home, Ganim published another article the following day in the Sunday paper with the headline "Former Coach Jerry Sandusky Used Charity to Molest Kids," in which she quoted Sandusky's autobiography, *Touched*, published in 2000: "We've continually tried to reach out to thousands of young people and tried to do more for them," he wrote. "As much as we can. To make it even better, the reaching out has always been a lot of fun. Especially at the summer camps, where I've enjoyed wrestling and swimming with the kids. I even had to have knee surgery in the summer of 1991 because of my fooling around."[3] In retrospect, Sandusky's playful self-deprecation now looked ominous. *Reaching out* and *fooling around,* indeed.

In the same article, Ganim quoted Attorney General Linda Kelly, who contended that "the inaction of top officials at Penn State allowed Sandusky to abuse the most recent victim for several years. Athletic Director Tim Curley and Vice President for Business and Finance Gary Schultz were both charged with perjury and failure to report a crime related to charges filed against Sandusky. They could face as much as seven years in prison."

Ganim did not point out that the perjury charges made no sense, because they were based only on the revised testimony of Mike McQueary. Since more people testified that McQueary had *not* said in 2000 or 2001 that he had witnessed sexual abuse, if anyone were to be charged with perjury, it would logically be McQueary. Instead, Curley and Schultz were indicted, which meant—perhaps not so coincidentally—that they would not be able to testify in the forthcoming Jerry Sandusky trial.

Linda Kelly told Ganim: "Despite a powerful eyewitness statement about the sexual assault of a child, this incident was not reported to any law enforcement or child protective agency, as required by Pennsylvania law. Additionally, there is no indication that anyone from the university ever attempted to learn the identity of the child who was sexually assaulted on their campus or made any follow-up effort to obtain more information from the person who witnessed the attack firsthand." In this article, Ganim identified the "powerful eyewitness" as assistant Penn State coach Mike McQueary.

In a separate article that Sunday (there were five that day related to the Sandusky case), Ganim quoted beloved Coach Joe Paterno, eighty-four, who issued a written statement that McQueary had told him that Sandusky had done "something inappropriate" in the shower with a boy, but he had obviously assumed it was Sandusky's typical, well-known antics of "fooling around" with kids. Paterno then strongly implied that he thought Sandusky, with whom he had clashed repeatedly both personally and professionally, was guilty, though he was careful to qualify it somewhat: "The fact that someone we (he and his wife Sue) thought we knew might have harmed young people to this extent is deeply troubling. If this is true, we were all fooled, along with scores of professionals trained in such things, and we grieve for the victims and their families. They are in our prayers."[4]

In another article published that Sunday, Ganim wrote: "Whispers swirled on campus and in Harrisburg that the university's executive trustees were meeting Sunday night in Old Main to possibly consider President Graham Spanier's future."[5]

And in a fourth piece stuffing the Sunday paper, Ganim quoted from sports commentators around the country, all rushing to judgment, many referring ironically to "Happy Valley," a nickname for State College, nestled between Mount Nittany and Bald Eagle Mountain, presumably so contented because of its great football program.* "Happy Valley has become Creepy Valley," wrote the *Chicago Tribune*'s David Haugh. "Big Ten officials should demand the timely eradication of scandal from a once-proud program, Paterno's legacy be damned." In the sports world, the idea of a high-profile college football coach being a pedophile, or ignoring child rape, was horrific beyond description. Sports was all about being manly, courageous, and forthright, all attributes that Joe Paterno, known fondly as JoePa, had exemplified throughout his long and honorable career.

Washington Post columnist Mike Wise sarcastically called Paterno "Happy Valley's homespun saint" and asked him in print, "While you were regaling everyone with sappy tales about meeting your wife 50 years ago over ice cream at the local creamery in State College, Pa., did you have any idea what your longtime defensive coordinator was doing in the company of young boys?"

Mike Jensen of the *Philadelphia Inquirer* wrote, "The powers behind the powers can't just clean house. They'll need to build the house back up from the foundation." On Sportsjournalists.com, a writer posted: "The President [Graham Spanier], the AD [Curley], Paterno and Schultz need to be cleaning out their desks by midafternoon [today]." Greg Couch of Foxsports.com wrote that he was "sickened" by the Presentment and wondered "why no one did anything to help." He concluded, "We've got to stop treating football as a religion."[6]

In fact, that's just what Couch and the other sports commentators were doing. It was as if Penn State football were indeed a religion, and someone had desecrated the church. The only way to react properly was to perform an exorcism and get rid of the demonic elements that had allegedly infiltrated the sanctum. In

---

* Actually, State College was apparently nicknamed Happy Valley during the Depression, when the town survived better economically because of Penn State University, but few knew that—everyone assumed it was so named for Paterno's football team's success.

some measure, this accounts for the swift vehemence with which the sports community reacted, just one day after the Presentment was made public.

Only one person Ganim quoted expressed some caution against a rush to judgment. Lou Prato, the retired director of the Penn State All-Sports Museum, said, "People are innocent until proven guilty. I've read the 23 pages. I read the stuff, and if all that's true, my God, how did this happen? How did people allow this to happen? But we don't know if all of that's true, and people have to remember that."[7] But people did *not* remember that, and no one paid any attention to Prato's prattling.

Former Sandusky friends and supporters backed away.*[8] Gary Gray, a finance professor at Penn State, had played football for Sandusky and then served as his assistant coach while getting a graduate degree in 1975 and 1976, as Sandusky was planning to start the Second Mile program. When he read Sara Ganim's first article of March 31, 2011, revealing that a grand jury was investigating Sandusky, Gary Gray didn't believe that his old mentor could possibly have been a child molester, and he defended him in a letter to the editor:

> Jerry Sandusky has been a coach, mentor, racquetball partner and friend to me since I first met him in 1968. He is straightforward, honest and caring—a person that I have always admired. I have never known him to take an alcoholic drink, never heard him utter a cuss word (and he could have legitimately cursed at me on many occasions), or tell a lie. I remember well when The Second Mile was just his dream. He talked often about it and worked tirelessly to raise funds to start that charity (disclosure—I am a contributor) and he made it wildly successful. I do not believe the allegations against Jerry that were reported by the *Harrisburg Patriot-News* and on the front page of the *Centre Daily Times*. These newspapers are not reporting news—they are reporting vicious, hurtful rumors.[9]

Gray convened a group of other former Penn State football players who called themselves "The Lettermen," all Sandusky supporters. They planned to raise funds to help defray his legal expenses.

---

* Former Penn State offensive coordinator Fran Ganter was one of those who backed away, but in a January 2011 interview with police, Ganter said that "his four kids grew up around Sandusky and there was not ever a problem." Sandusky has told him that he would maintain his innocence "because he did not do anything wrong."

But when the bombshell Grand Jury Presentment was published, they all scuttled away. Sandusky had told them about Aaron Fisher and Zach Konstas—the only allegations the former coach knew about—but here were ten alleged victims, and a witness to sodomy. Gray read the twenty-three-page Presentment on his computer. "As I scrolled through it, my stomach churned and I wanted to vomit," he recalled. The Lettermen felt that Sandusky must have been lying to them. "The mood that day was one of a funeral without a corpse."

When Sandusky's lawyer, Joe Amendola, called Gray to discuss fundraising efforts, Gray cut him off. "Jerry is toxic. The world is now certain that he is a monster. Nobody is going to support him. The media already has found him guilty without the need for a trial. I pray that he is innocent, but even I have my doubts."[10]

LINDA KELLY, THE AVENGING ATTORNEY GENERAL

On Monday, November 7, 2011, Linda Kelly spoke to a room packed with TV cameras and reporters about the charges that her office had brought against three defendants—Sandusky, Curley, and Schultz. She began by saying she expected that all of the listeners had already read the Presentment and therefore could appreciate her outrage at "a serial sexual predator accused of using his position within the community to prey on numerous young boys for more than a decade."

But she focused primarily on Curley and Schultz. She made the case that the misdeeds of the administrators were primarily to blame for the alleged crimes of Sandusky. "And their inaction," she said, "likely allowed a child predator to continue to victimize children for many more years." She mentioned the Lasch building on the Penn State campus three times, Penn State eight times, and the showers and locker rooms three times each. It was clearly important to make Penn State directly liable.

She pontificated: "I'd like to emphasize that one of the basic principles of our legal system is that the witnesses are required to tell the truth when they're called before a grand jury. The truth, pure and simple, nothing more, nothing less. And that principle applies to everyone, from the ordinary man on the street as well as to those who occupy positions of power and influence, like the defendants in this case." But Jonelle Eshbach had not told the truth, pure and simple, in the Grand Jury Presentment, in which she had said that McQueary witnessed Sandusky raping a boy in the shower. That was a crucial misrepresentation that would influence everyone who heard about the allegations. McQueary's version was also refuted by testimony from four key witnesses—Paterno, Curley, Schultz, and Spanier—but Eshbach made sure that the 33rd grand jury appeared to find McQueary "extremely credible," even though the jurors on the 33rd panel never heard him in person, and she made equally sure that the three Penn State administrators were deemed noncredible.

At the end of her sermon about truth, ethics, the equal application of the law, and civic duty, Linda Kelly called for the unknown Victim 2 (the ten-year-old in the shower whom McQueary allegedly saw with Sandusky) to show himself. She said, "So today as we stand here, we encourage that person, who's now likely to be a young adult, to contact investigators."[11]

But that person, Allan Myers, had already been interviewed by the police and had strongly defended Sandusky. State Police officers Joseph Leiter and James Ellis had interviewed him two weeks before, on September 20, 2011. In the police report, Leiter wrote: "Myers said that he does not believe the allegations that have been raised and that the accuser, a kid from Lock Haven (Aaron Fisher), is only out to get some money. . . . Myers related at no time did Sandusky do anything that made him uncomfortable."[12] Until the Presentment came out, however, nobody knew what Jerry Sandusky was being charged with, not even the boy in the shower himself. When the inflammatory Presentment went public, Myers knew he must be "Victim 2."

On November 9, 2011, Myers went to the office of Sandusky's attorney, Joe Amendola, and gave a statement to his investigator, Curtis Everhart, an ex-FBI agent, saying that he had been the boy in the shower in the McQueary incident and that Sandusky had never sexually abused him. He said that the police were angry at him for not going along with the game plan and making allegations. (*See Chapter 1 for a full account.*)[13]

Myers had already published a letter in support of Sandusky six months previously, after Sara Ganim's first articles on March 31, 2011. His potentially exonerating testimony was very bad news for the prosecution, so they ignored it, continuing to promote the fiction that the identity of Victim 2 was unknown. Even when Myers subsequently found a lawyer and "flipped," apparently to make accusations, the prosecution didn't call him to testify.

After Linda Kelly's speech on that Monday, November 7, Frank Noonan, commissioner of the Pennsylvania State Police, took the mike. "This is not a case about football. It's not a case about universities, it's a case about children who've had their innocence stolen from them and a culture that did nothing to stop it, or prevent it from happening to others. These children are scarred for life." This notion that child sexual abuse invariably produces life-long harm, far worse than physical or emotional trauma, has been part of the child abuse advocates' dogma for many years. No one, of course, defends any form of child abuse, but emotional, stereotypical rhetoric about "stolen innocence" escalates emotional judgments and makes objective analysis difficult, especially in cases of actual innocence.[14]

In the case of Jerry Sandusky, there may have been no child sexual abuse in the first place, in which case any life-long scars of the alleged Sandusky victims would have resulted from the suggestive process that convinced these troubled young men that they had indeed been abused by their trusted mentor. Noonan concluded: "Child sexual abuse is a serious crime and I assure you, the Pennsylvania State Police will listen. If you or someone you know is a victim of sexual abuse, I leave you with three words: Nine - One - One." Linda Kelly had already given out a hotline number for additional putative victims to call.[15]

JOEPA FIRED, SAINT SANDUSKY ERASED

Events continued to pile on top of one another during the week. On Tuesday, November 8, the regularly scheduled weekly press conference with Joe Paterno was cancelled at the last minute by Board of Trustees member John Surma, the CEO of U.S. Steel, who had long sought Paterno's ouster.[16] On Wednesday, Paterno announced that he would retire at the end of the football season. He said he was "devastated" by the Sandusky case. "I have come to work every day for the last 61 years with one clear goal in mind: To serve the best interests of this university and the young men who have been entrusted to my care. I have the same goal today." That's why he was going to quit. "This is a tragedy," he said. "It is one of the great sorrows of my life. With the benefit of hindsight, I wish I had done more." He hoped to finish the season "with dignity and determination."[17]

But Joe Paterno was not allowed to retire with any dignity. That night, the Penn State Board of Trustees met to decide his fate. Just before they voted, Governor Tom Corbett told the Penn State board (of which he was an automatic member) via speakerphone,

"Remember that little boy in the shower."[18] After the board members agreed to do so (apparently without an official vote), they held a press conference to announce that they were firing Paterno, along with Graham Spanier.

Several thousand infuriated students rioted in downtown State College, throwing rocks and bottles and damaging a news truck and lampposts, while others went to Paterno's home to show their respect. "I love you guys," Paterno said. "It's going to be hard to get used to not being a coach."[19] The game that Saturday against Nebraska (which Penn State lost) was the first game Paterno didn't coach in sixty-one years. Ironically, he was in the hospital during the game, being diagnosed with lung cancer. He would die of it—and perhaps of a broken heart—two months later.[20]

On Thursday, Jerry Sandusky's portrait in a Penn State mural was painted over, replaced by a blue ribbon representing awareness of child sexual abuse. In 1999, when Sandusky retired, *Sports Illustrated* had dubbed him "Saint Sandusky, leader of linebackers, molder of men."[21] Now the iconic saint in the mural was painted over.

Sara Ganim found that the sister of one of the alleged victims was a junior at Penn State and quoted her: "I've just been really upset about it all because a lot of people aren't focusing on the victims in this, and instead they're focusing on other things, like football." She added, "If there was any pride left at PSU, it's gone now."[22]

By this time, even Sandusky's long-time friends and colleagues were in full retreat. On November 8, sports commentator Matt Millen, who had known Sandusky for thirty-five years, since he first played football for him in 1976, and who served on the Second Mile Board of Directors, spoke on ESPN about the unfolding scandal. He clearly had trouble wrapping his head around Sandusky being a pedophile. "Jerry Sandusky is your next door neighbor. He's the guy you've known your whole life. He's a helpful guy, he's a light-hearted guy, he's a smart guy, he's a willing-to-help person." How could Sandusky have done these things? "You've gotta be kidding me. I couldn't even imagine this."

But then Millen went on to observe: "Man's inhumanity to man is just mind-boggling . . . Where do we stop this stuff? . . . This is really an indictment of us as a society." Finally, he described the moral panic's onset quite eloquently. "There's a train coming down the tracks, whether you want to believe it or not, and it's headed right for you, so you better get ready for it."[23]

MCQUEARY'S QUANDARY

On Friday, Sara Ganim, who had publicly identified Mike McQueary as the "graduate assistant" in the Presentment who had supposedly witnessed Sandusky sodomizing a boy in the shower, wrote that McQueary was "getting blasted by the public for doing too little." He had received several death threats. The same day, newly appointed Penn State president Rodney Erickson announced that McQueary was being placed on administrative leave "after it became clear he could not continue coaching." Erickson pointedly continued: "Never again should anyone at Penn State feel scared to do the right thing."[24]

McQueary was hard to miss around town. He stood six feet five inches, topped by short bristles of bright, orange-red hair, which gave him the nickname Big Red. Now people were asking one another, "Why didn't Big Red stop it?" On Tuesday, McQueary had called an emotional meeting with his Penn State players. He looked pale and his hands were shaking. "I'm not sure what is going to happen to me," he said. He cried as he talked about the Sandusky shower incident. According to one of the players, "He said he had some regret that he didn't stop it." Then McQueary revealed that he himself had been molested as a child.[25]

Perhaps because he had been sexually abused, McQueary was particularly alert to possible abuse, and so he leapt to the conclusion that the slapping sounds he heard in the Lasch building locker room were sexual. It is clear from the testimony of Dr. Dranov and others that McQueary did not witness sodomy that night in December 2000. He *thought* something sexual was happening, but as he emphasized later, the entire episode lasted thirty to forty-five seconds, he heard the sounds for only a few seconds, and his glance in the mirror was even quicker. Ten years after the event, his memory had shifted and amplified, after the police told him that they had other Sandusky victims. Under that influence, his memory made the episode much more sexually graphic.

As we saw in Chapter 3, all memory is reconstructive and is subject to distortion. That is particularly true when many years have intervened, and when current attitudes influence recall of those distant events. It is worthwhile quoting here from psychologist Daniel Reisberg's 2014 book, *The Science of Perception and Memory: A Pragmatic Guide for the Justice System.* "Connections between a specific memory and other, more generic knowledge can allow the other knowledge to intrude into our recollection," Reisberg notes. "Thus, a witness might remember the robber's threatening violence merely because threats are part of the witness's cognitive 'schema' for how robberies typically unfold."

That appears to be what happened to McQueary, who had a "schema" of what child sexual abuse in a shower would look like. He had thought at the time that some kind of sexual activity must have occurred in the shower. The police were telling him that they had other witnesses claiming that Sandusky had molested them. Thinking back to that long-ago night, McQueary now visualized a scene that never occurred, but the more he rehearsed it in his memory, the more real it became to him.

"As your memory for an episode becomes more and more inter-woven with other thoughts you've had about that episode, it can become difficult to keep track of which elements are linked to the episode because they were, in truth, part of the episode itself and which are linked merely because they are associated with the epi-sode in your thoughts," Reisberg writes. That process "can produce intrusion errors—so that elements that were part of your think-ing get misremembered as being actually part of the original ex-perience." In conclusion, "it is remarkably easy to alter someone's memory, with the result that the past as the person remembers it differs from the past as it really was."[26]

On November 23, 2010, McQueary wrote out a statement for the police in which he said he had glanced in a mirror at a 45-de-gree angle over his right shoulder and saw the reflection of a boy facing a wall with Sandusky standing directly behind him.[*27] "I am certain that sexual acts/the young boy being sodomized was occur-ing (sic)," McQueary wrote. "I looked away. In a hurried/hastened state, I finished at my locker. I proceeded out of the locker room. While walking I looked directly into the shower and both the boy and Jerry Sandusky looked directly in my direction."[28]

But it is extremely unlikely that this ten-year-later account is accurate. Dranov was adamant that McQueary did not say that he saw anything sexual. When former Penn State football player Gary

---

* Mike McQueary, at that time a married man, apparently sent a "sexting" photo of his own penis to a female Penn State student in April 2010. He may have thought that was why the police wanted to talk to him, and why he didn't want to meet with them in his home. ESPN journalist Don Van Natta Jr. initially intended to include this information in a feature article about McQueary, but it was cut from the published piece. In 2017 McQueary, now divorced, texted another photo of his erect penis to a woman. Investigator John Ziegler obtained the text messages and photo and published them at framingpaterno.com.

Gray went to see Joe Paterno in December 2011, the month before he died, Gray told Paterno that he still had a hard time believing that Sandusky had molested those children. "You and me both," Paterno said. In a letter to the Penn State Board of Trustees after the trial, Gray recalled their conversation about McQueary telling Paterno about the shower incident. "Joe said that McQueary had told him that he had seen Jerry engaged in *horseplay* or *horsing around* with a young boy. McQueary *wasn't sure what was happening,* but he said that it made him feel *uncomfortable.* In recounting McQueary's conversation to me, Coach Paterno did not use any terms with sexual overtones."[29]

Similarly, in November 2011, when biographer Joe Posnanski asked Paterno about what McQueary told him back in 2001, Paterno told him, "I think he said he didn't really see anything. He said he might have seen something in a mirror. But he told me he wasn't sure he saw anything. He just said the whole thing made him uncomfortable."[30]

If McQueary had told Paterno, Curley, or other administrators that he had seen Sandusky in such a sexual position with the boy, it is inconceivable that they would not have turned the matter over to the police. This was not a "cover-up." Sandusky didn't even work for Penn State by the time of the incident, so what was there to cover up? Paterno and Sandusky had never really liked one another, and Paterno was famed for his integrity and honesty.[31] If he thought Sandusky was molesting a child in the shower, he would undoubtedly have called the police. It is clear that Paterno, Curley, Schultz, and Spanier took the incident for what it apparently was—McQueary hearing slapping sounds that he misinterpreted as being sexual.

McQueary gave five different versions of what he heard and saw, but all were reconstructed memories over a decade after the fact. They changed a bit over time, but none of them are reliable. McQueary had painted himself into a difficult corner. If he had really seen something so horrendous, why hadn't he rushed into the shower to stop it? Why hadn't he gone to the police? Why hadn't he followed up with Paterno or other Penn State administrators to make sure something was being done? Why had he continued to act friendly towards Sandusky, even taking part in golfing events with him?

When angry people began to ask these questions, that first week in November 2011, McQueary emailed a friend. "I did stop it not physically but made sure it was stopped when I left that locker room," he wrote. He now said that he *had* in essence contacted the police about the incident by alerting Joe Paterno, which led to Gary Schultz talking to him about it, and Schultz was the administrator the campus police reported to.[32] "No one can imagine my thoughts or wants to be in my shoes for those 30-45 seconds . . . trust me . . . I am getting hammered for handling this the right way . . . or what I thought at the time was right . . . I had to make tough, impacting quick decisions."

Subsequently, McQueary changed his story somewhat. He now recalled that he had loudly slammed his locker door, which made Sandusky stop the abuse, and that he had taken yet a third look in the shower to make sure they had remained apart.[33] At the trial, he said that he had "glanced" in the mirror for "one or two seconds," then lengthened his estimate to "three or four seconds, five seconds maybe." During that brief glance, he now said that he had time to see Sandusky standing behind a boy whose hands were against the shower wall, and that he saw "very slow, slow, subtle movement" of his midsection.[34]

But neither the newly created sodomy scene nor the slammed locker would save McQueary's career.

TWO MORE ALLEGED VICTIMS

When the Grand Jury Presentment came out, attorney Ben Andreozzi was amazed and excited. "My jaw just dropped, and I thought, *Oh, my gosh*," he recalled. "I knew right then there would be a good civil case against Penn State." He dropped the small fee he had planned to charge Brett Houtz in favor of a straight contingency fee agreement, somewhere between 25 percent and 40 percent of any cash settlement or award. Andreozzi would end up representing ten alleged Sandusky victims.[35]

On Friday, November 11, 2011, Sara Ganim wrote: "More than one tip has already come into the tipline that police have set up for potential victims."[36] One such tip came from Angella Quidetto, the mother of a Second Mile alum named Sabastian Paden. Only a month before, Paden, a high school senior, had attended a Penn State football game with his friend and mentor Jerry Sandusky. When the police came to talk to him, he had nothing to say. Yet when he testified before the reconstituted grand jury on November 9, 2011, only four days after Sandusky's arrest, he told the jurors how he was a virtual prisoner in the Sandusky basement, where he was forced into oral sex and sodomy, and where his screams for help were ignored.

Ryan Rittmeyer, another Second Mile alum, also called the hotline to claim that Sandusky had abused him, even though Jerry
and Dottie Sandusky couldn't even remember him. Rittmeyer would
later sign a contract with State College lawyer Andrew Shubin, who
came to specialize in Sandusky claimants. Rittmeyer claimed that
Sandusky had forced him to perform oral sex on him in a silver
convertible. Rittmeyer, too, testified before the grand jury.

It is possible that both Paden and Rittmeyer created stories in
order to cash in on the Sandusky abuse story, and that they each
tailored their stories to follow the pattern set in the Grand Jury
Presentment. Their narratives have already been covered in some
detail in Chapter 8. "But in the end," wrote Sara Ganim in her first
article about the hotline, "it's going to come down to credibility. Stories contradict each other. Grand jury testimony clashes."[37] Actually, in the end, incredible stories were readily accepted by the jury.
Logic and consistency didn't matter. The overwhelming number of
alleged victims did. At any rate, Jonelle Eshbach and Linda Kelly
gladly added Paden and Rittmeyer to their numbered list as Victim
9 and Victim 10, and both young men would testify at the trial.

It is noteworthy that the November 30, 2011, police report on
Ryan Rittmeyer listed him as "Victim #17" rather than his eventual designation as the tenth alleged victim. That means that seven
other young men must have come forward after the Grand Jury
Presentment was published on November 5, 2011, but that their
stories must have been so outrageously unbelievable that the Office
of the Attorney General refused to present them at trial.[38]*[39]

As prosecuting attorney Frank Fina observed four years after
the trial, about the alleged victims:

> Many of these young men had profound issues in their lives. Many
> of them had been severely damaged by abuse and by their lives.
> Some had mental health issues. And some had given dramatically
> inconsistent statements and conducted themselves in ways that
> made them, I believe, unusable as witnesses in this case.

Fina also admitted that there were, in fact, inconsistencies in
the stories of all of the alleged victims who *did* testify at the trial.[40]

---

* From a November 9, 2011, Pennsylvania State Police report, we know that one
person emailed, in reponse to the Presentment: "My ass is still sore after 10 years from
Jerry Sandusky playing with my virgin ass. He turned my asshole into a gaping pussy
hole. What are you going to do about it?"

LET GO LET MEMORIES COME IN

In the meantime, in the midst of the Sandusky media maelstrom, an organization called Let Go Let Peace Come In asked Mike Gillum to join its board. It was a perfect match, since the organization's website was loaded with endorsements of repressed memory therapy. "Let Go" was founded by Peter Pelullo, a self-proclaimed sex abuse survivor who wrote a book called *Betrayal and the Beast: One Man's Journey Through Child Sexual Abuse, Sexual Addiction, and Recovery* (2012), in which he wrote about being molested by two older boys when he was seven years old. He never forgot it, but it was only when he entered therapy in his fifties that he came to blame all his troubles, including his marital infidelities, on his childhood sexual abuse. "Post-traumatic stress disorder is the result of dissociation and unresolved anxiety," his therapist taught him. "While I grew physically and mentally over the years," Pelullo concluded, "the abuse left me so traumatized and frightened, all of my emotional development and growth had stopped in 1959."[41]

The book and website for "Let Go" featured "testimonials" from people like Maureen, in Bucks County, Pennsylvania, who wrote: "My sexual abuse was a suppressed memory. It wasn't until high school when I became sexually active that the memory of my attack resurfaced. My attacker was my uncle. I was around 4 or 5 years old. . . . Once the memory of my attack resurfaced, I have always felt betrayed, sad, scared, weak, angry all the time, DIRTY AND WORTHLESS." Unfortunately, this story is a stereotypical example of what happens when people develop illusory memories of abuse—for a time, at least, it tends to make them worse, not better.

The "Let Go" website bibliography featured books such as Judith Herman's *Trauma and Recovery*, which was among the most influential repressed memory books I critiqued in my books about repressed memory therapy.[42] The website also includes a list of supposed symptoms of sexual abuse, explaining, "Victims with a history of sexual abuse will often present secondary symptoms before the abuse is uncovered. It is important that these symptoms be recognized as a possible reaction to something greater than the symptomatic condition itself." These symptoms include a laundry list that could apply to most of us at one time or the other: *Trouble sleeping or excessive sleeping; Sexual acting out; Sexual problems or disinterest in sex; Discomfort with people that are the same gender as their abuser; A pervasive feeling of powerlessness; Depression;*

Drug/Alcohol addiction; Self-hatred; Repeated victimization such as rape or domestic violence; Unexplained physical or emotional numbness; Lack of trust; People pleasing/rescuing at an early age; Excessive need to control; Obsessive/compulsive behavior patterns; Low self-esteem/needy; Weak boundaries; Unhealthy choices in members of the opposite sex; Neurotic tendencies; Eating disorders; Chronic illness; Manic-depressive behavior (extreme emotions).

Several of the other listed symptoms are often the *results* of misguided repressed memory therapy that can then be taken as evidence for abuse: *Nightmares; Panic and/or anxiety attacks; A hunch or intuition that sexual abuse occurred; Self-mutilation, suicide attempts or strong suicidal wishes; Shame.* The list also includes *"Lack of memory of being a child or missing large blocks of their childhood."*[43] Of course, it's ridiculous to say that someone totally lacks childhood memories, but most of us cannot recall "large blocks" of our childhood. We tend to remember the best and worst things that happened to us, but not much of the rest. Repressed memory therapists frequently use this lack of complete childhood memory as "evidence" that abuse must have occurred.[44]

With Gillum on board, and in cooperation with self-identified "Sexual Assault Attorney Ben Andreozzi," Let Go Let Peace Come In began to offer free counseling to potential alleged Sandusky victims. "A few days before this book went to print," Pelullo wrote at the end of *Betrayal and the Beast,* "the foundation has subsidized 30 therapeutic trauma sessions for one of the young men associated with the Penn State childhood sexual abuse case involving Jerry Sandusky. The foundation is hopeful that these sessions will start this young man on his arduous journey to recovery and is prepared to help others from this tragedy as well."[45]

That young man was probably Brett Houtz. Mike Gillum revealed that he was counseling Houtz, Victim 4, an Andreozzi client, when he filed an affidavit trying to prevent Houtz's name from being revealed when he testified at the trial.[46]

Another therapist, Jennifer Storm, who had written books about being raped when she was twelve, served as a "victim advocate" for four alleged Sandusky victims, three of whom would testify at the trial. "A pedophile breaks your spirit and steals your soul," she said. "But with proper therapy and support, you learn to live with it."[47] Before the trial, Storm rushed a book into print called *Echoes of Penn State,* in which she assumed Sandusky's guilt. "The police, prosecutors, and medical professionals do everything they can to sensitively extract the appalling details from these children," she wrote. "We need to start removing the veil of denial from our lens and accept that monsters walk among us, and these monsters should be held accountable for their heinous actions."[48]

In an interview with me, Storm made her belief in repressed memories crystal clear. "I spend a lot of time with victims looking to unlock those memories that way and to prepare them for that experience when memory is brought to the front, when it is triggered. It's always there somewhere inside." She said that she did not treat the alleged Sandusky victims herself, but she referred them to other therapists. "Let me clarify that I was being a victim advocate, not doing traditional therapy. I was getting them through the system, throughout the trial, certainly helping to guide them to what to do next. Yes, I connected them with therapists."

She told me that in November or December 2011, when she hosted a Pennsylvania television show called *Smart Talk*, "We had an individual call in about the Sandusky case. He said on air that he had completely repressed what had happened to him, until it all came flooding back when he heard about the other victims."[49] She did not know whether he called the police or not.

In December 2011, the *Patriot-News* released a quick eBook, *Hear No Evil: How the Sandusky Sex Abuse Scandal Rocked Penn State, Toppled Joe Paterno, and Stunned a Nation*. The same month, "A Household Name" anonymously published *Why I Hate Jerry Sandusky*, while "An American Voice" penned *The Last Monster: Jerry (Disgusting) Sandusky*. In time for the Christmas season, "Uncle Herman" recorded "The Jerry Sandusky Christmas Song," with the warning that "most people will find this song highly offensive . . . very dirty . . . and inappropriate! But there will be a few of you who will find it absolutely hysterical."

On April 16, 2012, Sara Ganim was awarded a Pulitzer Prize for her coverage of the Sandusky case. The next day, William Morrow published *Game Over: Jerry Sandusky, Penn State, and the Culture of Silence*, by Bill Moushey and Robert Dvorchak, the culmination of the virtual conviction of Jerry Sandusky before he ever set foot in the courtroom. At the end of the book, they quoted Jennifer Storm, who praised the bravery of the alleged victims and said, "I keep seeing that little boy in the shower."[50]

— CHAPTER 13 —

The Accumulating Horror

S EVEN MONTHS and one week would pass from the date Jerry Sandusky was arrested to the day that the jury listened to the first alleged victim. In seven months, the story of a ten-year-old boy being raped in the open in a university shower by an old, gray-haired man had been repeated a thousand times and had become fodder for cartoonists and scriptwriters everywhere. It wasn't until May of 2012 that the defense lawyers were allowed to read the grand jury transcriptions of the witness testimony for themselves, which revealed that the all-important eyewitness account concerning the boy in the shower wasn't accurate, since Mike McQueary had not actually said that he had witnessed sodomy.

During those seven months, Sandusky tried to stay upbeat, despite the media mayhem and vilification heaped on him and the broken cinder blocks heaved through his house windows.

Free on bail, Sandusky tried to act as if nothing were wrong. He smiled and waved at people as he shopped or worked out at the gym, wearing Penn State clothing. His street turned into a circus, and his neighbors told reporter Sara Ganim that they felt "betrayed," though it wasn't clear by whom. "Once a quiet street that even veteran pizza delivery drivers had trouble finding, Grandview (where the Sanduskys lived) has become crowded with unmarked news vehicles and rubber-neckers who just can't resist taking a peek at the football legend's modest two-story brick home, where several children have alleged they were molested," Ganim wrote. "An aerial map of the neighborhood went viral last week when people realized Sandusky's backyard was adjacent to a playground and within walking distance from an elementary school."

Home is where the heart is.

A photo of the Sandusky home, with this caption, is from a 2010 Sandusky Christmas booklet.

When Jerry Sandusky played with his dog, a Saint Bernard named Bo, in that backyard, or sat on his back porch, people were appalled. "Sandusky being free has caused his neighbors to feel like they are the ones locked up in a jail," Ganim wrote. She spoke to one neighbor who was initially supportive of the Sanduskys, but after the Presentment came out, she changed her mind. "I don't feel safe," she said. "I'm nervous about the fact that this could go undetected for so long with such extreme behaviors."[1]

On November 14, 2011, Sandusky's lawyer, Joe Amendola, made his first media appearance on CNN, where he expressed concern for his client's "well-being and health." Sandusky was devastated. People were throwing bricks through the windows of his home. Amendola said that Sandusky was just a "big, overgrown kid," and said that he believed in his innocence. But then he equivocated. Would he himself ever take a shower with a boy? No. But that's just the way Jerry was. "Either way you go, if Jerry really did these horrible things, it's tragic that he's victimized these kids. But if he didn't do it, it's tragic, because he's ruined forever the reputation of just an outstanding person not only in Penn State history but nationally, Joe Paterno." He didn't mention Sandusky's reputation or potential imprisonment.[2]

Amendola had given the interview on CNN with the understanding that the network would air it that evening, because he had promised NBC to give that network an exclusive first interview later that same day, but CNN rushed it to air, which upset Kim Kaplan, the NBC producer who accompanied Amendola on his flight to New York City. When Amendola arrived at the NBC studios, he found that the media people considered Sandusky to be "above people like Adolf Hitler [in terms of] the most despised people in the world." He had an inspired idea—he would make it up to NBC by offering them an exclusive telephone interview with Sandusky himself. So now, with fifteen minutes' notice, he asked Sandusky to talk by phone to Bob Costas live on the air. "We have to try to get our side out," he told Sandusky. "I think you should do it. All you have to do is say you're innocent."

Otherwise, Amendola did not prepare Sandusky for the interview, as he would have done for any witness prior to testifying. There was no rehearsal for what kinds of questions he might get and what answers he planned to give. Amendola regarded this as a "golden opportunity" for Sandusky to reach a national audience with his side of the story. He assumed that because Bob Costas was a sports commentator, he would go easy on his client, a football icon.[3]

Instead, Costas asked direct, pointed questions about the alleged abuse, as any good journalist would. Recalling it later, Sandusky said that he was "absolutely surprised" by the tenor of the questions. "I was not in a very good emotional state, based on all the things that had happened to all the people who were dear to me," he said, not to mention what was happening to him, of course.

On air, during the phone interview, he stumbled badly. "I could say that I have done some of those things," he said of the accusations against him. "I have horsed around with kids. I have showered after workouts. I have hugged them and I have touched their legs without intent of sexual contact." In other words, he squeezed their knees while he was driving.

When Costas asked him about the McQueary rape-in-the-shower story, Sandusky answered mildly, "I would say that that was false." Why would McQueary lie? "You'd have to ask him that." Costas asked about the police assertion that after the 1998 shower incident with Zachary Konstas, he supposedly told the boy's mother, "I wish I were dead." Sandusky answered, "I didn't say, to my recollection, that I wish I were dead. I was hopeful that we could reconcile things." On it went. What about the janitor's shower story? No, that hadn't happened, Sandusky said.

"It seems that if all of these accusations are false, you are the unluckiest and most persecuted man that any of us has ever heard about," Costas concluded. Sandusky laughed. "I don't know what you want me to say. I don't think that these have been the best days of my life." Costas asked Sandusky how he felt about Joe Paterno being fired and Penn State's reputation torn in tatters. "How would you think that I would feel about a university that I attended, about people that I've worked with, about people that I care so much about? How do you think I would feel about it? I feel horrible," Sandusky said. But did he feel that it was his fault? No, but "I obviously played a part in this. . . . I shouldn't have showered with those kids."

Costas closed in. "Are you a pedophile?" No. "Are you sexually attracted to young boys?" Sandusky repeated the question rhetorically, as if he had to think about it, or as if it were a surprising question. "Am I sexually attracted to underage boys?" Yes, Constas said. Sandusky paused for a few seconds in what would become a famously long time. "Sexually attracted? You know, no. I enjoy young people. I love to be around them. I love to be around them . . . um . . . I . . . I, but no, I'm not sexually attracted to young boys."[4]

It was a disastrous interview. Ganim headlined her coverage with the quote, "I Shouldn't Have Showered With Those Kids," by which Sandusky simply meant that, in retrospect, he recognized that people would take it the wrong way. Sandusky had a way of laughing and smiling to diffuse tension, but when he laughed during the interview, people were appalled that this monster was making light of the situation. And his bumbling pause before saying that he wasn't attracted sexually to boys was a death sentence. Later he would say that he truly was taken aback by the question, that he couldn't believe anyone would ask him that, that it had never occurred to him—which, under the circumstances, seemed hard to believe.[5]

As a result of the interview, attorney Andrew Shubin told reporter Sara Ganim that several new alleged victims had approached him, and lawyer Ben Andreozzi said he'd heard from "close to half-dozen to a dozen," though it seemed odd that he couldn't give a precise number. A nineteen-year-old came forward, claiming that Sandusky had plied him with whiskey and molested him once when he was twelve years old. "He's had a difficult life," his new lawyer said. "And we have reason to believe that much of it was caused by that incident."[6] An Oklahoma prison inmate wrote a letter to the Pennsylvania Attorney General's office claiming abuse by Sandusky. Other calls lit up the victim hotline.[7] Most of these claims must have been too improbable even for Linda Kelly or the sex abuse lawyers, since they were not called to testify at the trial.

For anyone familiar with repressed memories, the lawyers used telltale vocabulary, such as saying that the Costas program "triggered" abuse memories. Ganim wrote that Shubin "has also teamed up with psychologists, social workers and a national child sex abuse organization so that these people can seek mental help along with possible legal recourse. . . . All are seeking to heal, and their pain was re-triggered by Sandusky's interview Monday night with NBC's Bob Costas." Shubin said that "these folks are being retraumatized" and added: "It's an extremely daunting process—getting prepared in their mind to deal with this."[8] He would help, though, by getting them into therapy so that they could prepare their minds better, quite possibly through repressed memory therapy.

Defense attorney Joe Amendola, who was known for negotiating good plea bargains for his clients, hinted that he might try to do that for Sandusky. "People who maintain innocence sometimes plead guilty because of the overwhelming evidence against them," he said. "So there's a lot of reasons why people decide to do certain things." Still, he added that Sandusky was adamant about his innocence and that he wanted to defend himself, "and I'm trying to give him that opportunity."[9]

When Amendola raised the possibility of a plea bargain to him, Sandusky said, "Plead guilty to what?" Either he was in complete denial of the reality of the abuse he had committed, or Sandusky really was innocent. Even Mike Gillum, the therapist who helped Aaron Fisher become "Victim 1," observed: "In a case like this, chances are that someone would have accepted a plea bargain or pleaded guilty and waived their right to trial."[10]

But Amendola's ace in the hole vanished. Allan Myers, the unidentified Victim 2, had come to Amendola's office with his mother on November 9, 2011, to assert clearly and adamantly that Sandusky had never molested him and that he was in fact a trusted father figure for him.[11] Yet two weeks later, Amendola got a fax from Andrew Shubin, saying that he now represented Myers. "I thought it was to protect Allan Myers from the Commonwealth," Amendola later recalled, "never dreaming it was to say that Allan Myers had now become a victim." So when he saw Shubin in the back of a courtroom shortly afterwards, he said, "Hey, Andy, it's great that you're representing Allan. I'd like to get together with him," because he needed to get his statement notarized.

"Oh, no, you're missing the point," Shubin said. "He's a victim. He's probably the worst victim. He's been victimized by Jerry for years." Amendola said, "I about fell over."[12] It turned out that Myers's mother worked for Shubin, who was also representing the young man for a recent charge of "driving under the influence" in a roll-over crash that occurred on September 3, 2011.[13] But how Myers could have changed his mind so quickly and develop his own abuse narrative remained a mystery, especially because he never testified, never gave the police any details about alleged abuse, and remained silent in public.

On December 7, 2011, when Sabastian Paden (Victim 9) and Ryan Rittmeyer (Victim 10) were added to the official body count and new charges were filed, police swooped in and arrested Sandusky again, dragging him from his home in handcuffs. He was wearing a Penn State track suit, sneakers, and a sweatshirt at the time, all of which became newsworthy. Bail was set at $250,000 cash, and since he couldn't raise that amount right away, he had to spend the night in jail. Then, having taken out a loan on his mortgage, he was released, but he had to remain under house arrest wearing an ankle monitor. In addition to the forty counts he already faced, he was now charged with further counts of "involuntary deviant sexual intercourse, indecent assault, unlawful contact with a minor, corruption of minors and endangering the welfare of children."[14]

Now Sandusky's wife, Dottie, was hauled into the spotlight. Sabastian Paden, Victim 9, was saying that he was kept a virtual prisoner in the Sandusky basement, where Jerry Sandusky had allegedly raped him more than sixteen times. He supposedly screamed for help in the small, non-soundproofed house, but Dottie had not come to his aid. Ganim now implied in the *Patriot-News* that Dottie, who stood by her husband and maintained his innocence, might have known about the abuse and chosen to ignore it. "I am so sad anyone would make such a terrible accusation which is absolutely untrue," Dottie Sandusky wrote in response. "We don't know why these young men have made these false accusations, but we want everyone to know they are untrue."[15]

But Jerry and Dottie Sandusky's proclamations of innocence just proved that they were guilty, according to lawyer Andrew Shubin and his associate, Justine Andronici. Many of the alleged victims kept returning to be molested and raped repeatedly, without giving any hint of their abuse to anyone. They maintained friendly relations with Jerry Sandusky for years after the alleged abuse had occurred. Yet the lawyers felt that such behavior was due only to embarrassment, shame, or intimidation. "Our investigation reveals that Sandusky is an unrepentant child predator," Shubin said.

Andronici attacked Jerry Sandusky for continuing to maintain his innocence. "These statements play on the victims' worst fears— that if they stand up and tell the truth they will be called liars and victimized again. Pedophiles seek to silence their victims with the threat that no one will believe them if they come forward. Perpetrators of sexual abuse also maintain manipulative, long-term contact with their victims for the very purpose of continuing to silence them."[16] Sara Ganim quoted Shubin and Andronici approvingly.

Part of the provisions of Sandusky's house arrest was that he could not be in the presence of children. His grandchildren didn't understand, and their parents, who thought their father was innocent and wanted to shield their children from the tumult, had a hard time explaining the situation. So Sandusky requested that the court allow his grandchildren to visit, which was eventually granted, much to the consternation of many people. An employee of the Lemont Elementary School, just behind the Sandusky house, called the police after seeing Jerry Sandusky on his porch. She asked if he was allowed outside his home while under house arrest. The police chief replied that, unfortunately, he couldn't do anything about it. Sandusky couldn't walk in his own back yard, but he could sit on the porch.[17]

In a rare statement that his lawyer allowed him to make to reporters, Sandusky said, "Our home has been open for 27 years to all kinds of people—hundreds of people who have stayed there, and more than that who have visited. I have associated with thousands of young people over the years." With every word he uttered, he dug himself a deeper hole in the minds of those who *knew* he was a serial child molester. "And now all of a sudden, because of allegations and perceptions that have been tried to be created about me, I can't take my dog on my deck and throw biscuits to him." Many people thought, *You, Jerry Sandusky, the Monster, are expecting us to feel sorry for you because you can't play in the yard with your dog?* "Now, all of a sudden, these people turn on me, when they've been in my home with their kids, when they've been at birthday parties, when they've been on that deck, when their kids have been playing in my yard. . . . It's difficult for me to understand, to be honest."[18]

Sandusky may have been perfectly honest about his befuddle-
ment, but it was very easy for almost everyone else to understand.
Of course former friends and associates had turned on him. Sara
Ganim dubbed Jerry Sandusky "the most hated man in the world."
She may have been right.[19]

Sandusky's preliminary hearing was scheduled for December
13, 2011, only a few days after the two new alleged victims and
charges were added. Joe Amendola was afraid that the prosecution
would heap on new charges and throw Sandusky back in jail while
seeking much higher bail; indeed, prosecutor Joe McGettigan had
suggested raising it to $5 million, although the district magistrate
had rejected that figure. So Amendola called a meeting with McGettigan, Frank Fina, Jonelle Eshbach, and two judges—John Cleland, who would preside over the trial, and the district magistrate
judge. They met at the Hilton Garden Inn in State College, the evening before the scheduled hearing, and struck a tentative deal that
Amendola and Sandusky would waive the right to the preliminary
hearing if the prosecution promised not to seek higher bail in the
event that additional victims and charges were forthcoming.

Amendola thought that it was "critical to our defense that Jerry
not be incarcerated," he asserted later. "The preliminary hearing
was only going to be for Commonwealth witnesses to say what they
said happened." He wouldn't be able to question their credibility.
Not only that, but "the media from all over the country would have
heard only the one side of the case, all the gruesome details of the
accusers." He explained all of this to Sandusky after the meeting
and strongly urged that they waive his right to the hearing.

Codefense attorney Karl Rominger wasn't invited to the Hilton
Garden meeting, but when Jerry Sandusky called him to tell him
they weren't going to have a preliminary hearing, Rominger was
surprised and upset. "I told Jerry that I had written an article,
'Don't Waive Your Preliminary Hearing.'" The next day at the courthouse, Rominger argued vehemently against the waiver. For one
thing, some of the charges might not stick and could be tossed out.
Mostly, it was important to get testimony from the alleged victims
on the record so that the defense lawyers knew who and what they
were up against, and if the witnesses changed their stories at trial,
they could use that previous testimony to impeach them. At that
point, the media had already tried and fried Sandusky, so it was
hard to see that there was anything to lose. "If you have to get a dip
in the jail for a couple days while we straighten things out, that's

not so bad," Rominger said. Better that than to spend the rest of your life in prison after the trial.[20]

But by then, the decision had been made. The eight alleged victims were at the courthouse, ready to testify, but they were dismissed. Instead, Joe Amendola held an hour-long press conference outside the courthouse, explaining that it made "absolutely no sense" that Joe Paterno and the Penn State administrators would merely ban Sandusky from bringing boys to the campus if Mike McQueary had told them he witnessed him sodomizing a child. Yes, there were multiple allegations, but some involved only hugging or knee-squeezing, he said. Besides, some of the alleged victims knew one another, so maybe they had colluded on their stories. He insisted that he was ready to defend Sandusky and that there would be no plea negotiations. "This is a fight to the death."[21]

THE ELUSIVE ALLAN MYERS

By the time of the trial, eight accusers had been "developed," as Jonelle Eshbach put it. But Allan Myers, the boy in the shower in the McQueary incident, had been so public and vehement in his previous defense of Sandusky that the prosecution did not dare call him to testify. When police inspector Joseph Leiter first interviewed him on September 20, 2011, Myers had emphatically denied that Sandusky had abused him or made him uncomfortable in any way.

After the Grand Jury Presentment was published on November 5, 2011, with its allegations that Mike McQueary had witnessed sodomy in a locker room shower, Myers realized that he was "Victim 2," the boy in the shower that night, but that the sounds McQueary heard were just snapping towels or slap boxing. Myers then gave a detailed statement to Amendola's investigator, Curtis Everhart, denying that Sandusky had ever abused him (*see Chapter 1*).

But within two weeks, Myers had become a client of Andrew Shubin. For months, Shubin refused to let the police interview Myers without Shubin being present, and he apparently hid Myers in a remote Pennsylvania hunting cabin to keep them from finding him.

After a February 10, 2012, hearing, Shubin verbally assaulted Anthony Sassano outside the courthouse, cursing him roundly. "He was very vulgar, critical of me," Sassano recalled. "Let's call it unprofessional [language], for an attorney." Shubin was angry because the Attorney General's office wouldn't interview Myers, who, he claimed, had stayed at Sandusky's house "over 100 times" where he had been subjected to "both oral and anal sex." But the police still refused to allow Shubin to be present during any interview.

Soon afterwards, Shubin relented, allowing a postal inspector named Michael Corricelli to talk to Allan Myers alone on February 28, 2012. But during the three-hour interview, Myers never said Sandusky had abused him. On March 8, Corricelli tried again, but Myers again failed to provide any stories of molestation. On March 16, Corricelli brought Myers to the police barracks for a third interview in which Anthony Sassano took part. Asked about three out-of-state trips, Myers denied any sexual contact and said that Sandusky had only tucked him into bed.

"He did not recall the first time he was abused by Sandusky," Sassano wrote in his notes, nor did Myers recall how many times he was abused. "He indicated it is hard to talk about the Sandusky sexual abuse because Sandusky was like a father to him." Finally, Myers said that on a trip to Erie, Pennsylvania, Sandusky put his hand inside his pants and touched his penis. Sassano tried valiantly to get more out of him, asking whether Sandusky had tried to put Myers's hand on his own penis or whether there had been oral sex. No.

Still, Myers now estimated that there had been ten sexual abuse events and that the last one was the shower incident that McQueary overheard. "I attempted to have Myers elaborate on the sexual contact he had with Sandusky, but he refused by saying he wasn't ready to talk about the specifics," Sassano wrote. Myers said that he had not given anyone, including his attorneys, such details. "This is in contrast to what Shubin told me," Sassano noted.

On April 3, 2012, Corricelli and Sassano were scheduled to meet yet again with the reluctant Allan Myers, but he didn't show up, saying that he was "too upset" by a friend's death. "Corricelli indicated that Attorney Shubin advised him that Myers had related to him incidents of oral, anal, and digital penetration by Sandusky," Sassano wrote in his report. "Shubin showed Corricelli a three page document purported to be Myers' recollection of his sexual contact with Sandusky. Corricelli examined the document and indicated to me that he suspected the document was written by Attorney Shubin. I advised that I did not want a copy of a document that was suspected to be written by Attorney Shubin." Sassano concluded: "At this time, I don't anticipate further investigation concerning Allan Myers."[22]

That is how things stood as the trial was about to begin. Karl Rominger wanted to call Myers to testify as a defense witness, but

Amendola refused. "I was told that there was a détente and an understanding that both sides would simply not identify Victim Number 2," Rominger later recalled. The prosecution didn't want such a weak witness who had given a strong exculpatory statement to Curtis Everhart. Amendola didn't want a defense witness who was now claiming to be an abuse victim. "So they decided to punt, to use an analogy," Rominger concluded.[23]

MORE INVESTIGATIONS, MORE LAWYERS, MORE MONEY

Meanwhile, seven different investigations spun off of the Sandusky allegations, and the money began to flow. In November 2011, Penn State hired former FBI director Louis Freeh to head an investigative panel to look into the sex abuse scandal.[24] The Second Mile organization, in an attempt to distance itself from the scandal, paid former Philadelphia district attorney Lynne Abraham to do an internal investigation.

The National College Athletic Association (NCAA) demanded that Penn State answer questions about compliance with regulations, and eventually stripped Penn State of all its 112 football victories from 1998 through 2011.[25] Internal NCAA emails later revealed that officials were concerned they didn't really have the authority to impose such sanctions, calling them a "bluff," but Kevin Lennon, the NCAA's vice president of academic and membership affairs, was correct that Penn State would accept the association's punishment because the university was "so embarrassed they will do anything."[26]*[27]

The US Department of Education sought to find evidence that Penn State might have failed to comply with the Clery Act, the federal law requiring colleges to report crimes, and sent officials to paw through years of Penn State security records. Agents with the Pennsylvania Office of the Attorney General had to investigate every new alleged abuse victim. Pennsylvania Children and Youth Services opened two new cases of alleged child sex abuse against Sandusky from purported victims who were still minors.

The Second Mile struggled to raise money and to continue to help troubled youth. Sandusky, who founded the organization, had cut his ties with it back in 2008 when the Aaron Fisher allegations

---

* Under a settlement agreement reached in January 2015, the football wins were restored to Penn State.

first arose, but the organization's close association with Penn State and its sports made it vulnerable, and the allegations that Sandusky had used the charity to fish for boys to molest had given it a terrible image. CEO Jack Raykovitz resigned, and his wife, Katherine Genovese, left as well, along with other staff, because of budgetary woes.[28]

The new director, David Woodle, tried to negotiate a merger with a similar organization, in order to shift its programs and ditch its name, but Volunteers of America Pennsylvania and the Centre County Youth Services Bureau wanted nothing to do with the tainted program. "I think the programs are very helpful to kids," a Second Mile board member said. "My preference would be in some way, shape or form that these programs would continue to exist." Second Mile programs had served 100,000 at-risk children in 2011, and many parents were desperate for it to continue, but its future looked uncertain, charitable donations were shriveling up, and there would be no more fundraiser themes such as "A Salute to Linebacker U," or inspirational sports cards featuring Penn State football players.[29]

More lawyers, smelling money, kept coming on board on a contingency fee basis. Michael Boni and Slade McLaughlin were now representing Aaron Fisher, Victim Number 1, who had changed schools in his senior year in high school because of purported bullying.[30] Howard Janet was the new lawyer for Zachary Konstas, Victim 6. When Amendola pointed out that Konstas had a friendly dinner with Jerry and Dottie Sandusky the previous year, Janet shot back: "It is grotesque that Sandusky or his lawyer would suggest that a victim of molestation attending a dinner Sandusky invited him to is somehow a defense to the indefensible actions of which Sandusky has been accused."[31] Tom Kline came aboard to represent Michal Kajak, Victim 5.[32]

In the run-up to the trial, two civil suits were filed against Sandusky seeking money for anonymous Second Mile graduates who were not called to testify at the criminal trial—presumably because they were not deemed sufficiently credible by the prosecutors. One young man, represented by Marci Hamilton and Jeffrey Anderson, claimed that Sandusky had sexually assaulted him more than one hundred times from 1992 to 1996. The other, with help from lawyer Charles Schmidt, said that Sandusky, a teetotaler, had plied him with whiskey before raping him in his Penn State football office in 2004.[33] There were at least ten other lawyers planning to file suits against Sandusky, the Second Mile, Penn State, and anyone else who might be named in testimony, after he was convicted.[34]

Joe Amendola, Sandusky's lawyer, hired a private investigator to try to find exculpatory evidence, though that seemed a hopeless task, with so many alleged victims telling their stories.[35] While the narratives would shift and contradict one another, and while Sandusky couldn't possibly have had time to commit all of the purported horrors, the ten official alleged victims and the intense negative publicity meant that he was unlikely to get any kind of fair trial, particularly not from a Centre County jury.

At the suggestion of investigator Curtis Everhart, Joe Amendola had added lawyer Karl Rominger, who practiced far to the south in Carlisle, PA, to his team to defend Sandusky, while prosecutor Joe McGettigan found a second banana in Frank Fina. And the preceding list of attorneys doesn't include the lawyers prosecuting or representing former Penn State administrators Tim Curley, Gary Schultz, and former president Graham Spanier, or helping with the other ancillary investigations.

The Penn State administrators and board, under the new president Rodney Erickson, made it clear that they would bend over backwards to appear to be sympathetic to proclaimed Sandusky victims. In January 2012, Erickson announced that Penn State planned to "lead the way in preventing and treating child abuse, planning to raise $527,000 for the Rape, Abuse, and Incest National Network (RAINN).*[36] He promised that Penn State would create the Center for the Protection of Children.

The Penn State board of trustees issued a statement on March 12, 2012, that echoed the most sanctimonious, politically correct dogma of the "Believe the Children" advocates of the daycare cases of the 1980s:

> We remain committed to remembering the children who were allegedly assaulted over the last 10 or more years, many on Penn State's University Park campus, and whose lives may well be scarred for years to come. The University has offered and will provide counseling and related health care services. We have contributed financially to organizations dedicated to protecting victims of sexual assault and child abuse.

---

* The RAINN website featured mythical "body memories" as one of the after-effects of sexual abuse. "Physical problems that can come of these somatic memories include headaches, migraines, stomach difficulties, light headedness/dizziness, hot/cold flashes, grinding of teeth, sleep disorders, etc." So-called body memories were one of the mechanisms to convince people that they had repressed memories of abuse. The website also claimed that child rape could produce multiple personality disorder, now renamed dissociative identity disorder—another version of repressed memories.

The National Center for Missing & Exploited Children, joined by the Pennsylvania Coalition Against Rape and the National Sexual Violence Resource Center, have agreed to join with the University to co-sponsor a national forum at Penn State on child sexual abuse. We plan to invite representatives from our 24 campuses, as well as from other Pennsylvania colleges and universities. We hope to turn this tragedy into an important teaching moment. We hope such a forum would bring together the nation's experts to inform all on recognizing early signs of child sexual abuse, the long-term effects on child sexual assault victims, and the legal and ethical responsibility to report even suspicions of such abuse.[37]

It would be difficult to find a clearer public presumption of guilt, along with the implication that sexual abuse invariably scars people for life in a way that other trauma does not. Two weeks later, newly appointed board member Karen Peetz (an investment banker for BNY Mellon) announced: "Immediately, we will reach out to the victims we know of and seek to pay for their abuse-related health costs, to pay for related counseling they have had to date, and to pay for counseling going forward related to the abuse." She reiterated: "There is no higher priority for us than to help the abuse victims get justice. The criminal legal process will take its course, and it would be wrong to pre-judge its outcome, but let me be clear: We and President Erickson will find a way to make sure that Penn State helps the victims of this tragedy." Of course, it would be impossible to interpret such a statement as doing anything other than prejudging Sandusky's guilt.

Penn State had already pledged $1.5 million to the Pennsylvania Coalition Against Rape and paid $5 million in legal and public relation fees and other expenses. Aside from free counseling, the university would also pay for things such as higher cell phone bills from talking to police and counselors, and some legal fees. Penn State had also hired Texas-based Praesidium, Inc. to set up yet another hotline for potential victims. "Praesidium will ask whether a person seeking counseling believes they are an abuse victim of Jerry Sandusky and a few, brief questions, but no one will be asked to prove anything and there is no investigation," the Praesidium spokesman promised.[38]

It is little wonder that by April 2012, Penn State had spent $7.5 million on the Sandusky case, and that was clearly just the beginning.[39]

— CHAPTER 14 —

Lurching Towards Trial

JOE AMENDOLA and Karl Rominger, the attorneys for Jerry Sandusky, faced a virtually insurmountable task in preparing for the trial, which Judge John Cleland was clearly intent on holding as soon as possible. Cleland was perhaps sensitive to media criticism questioning why it had taken three years from the time Aaron Fisher, "Victim 1," first made allegations, to the time of Sandusky's arrest.[1] As we have seen, it took those three years to grow memories, find other alleged victims, and convince the grand jury and Office of the Attorney General that there was sufficient evidence to recommend an indictment, but in the hysteria over the case, no one acknowledged that reality.

Cleland initially set the court date for May 14, 2012.[2] Then, in response to Amendola's increasingly anguished complaints that he had not even received the transcripts of the grand jury testimony, Cleland delayed the trial by a mere three weeks, until June 5.[3] Astonishingly, Pennsylvania law specified that prosecutors didn't have to hand over testimony given during secret grand jury proceedings until each witness testified at trial.[4] The grand jury had essentially amounted to a kangaroo court. Not only was Amendola not allowed to cross-examine witnesses there, he was not even allowed to be present. Judge Barry Feudale, presiding judge of the 30th grand jury, ruled that the Sandusky defense team could have access to the grand jury transcripts only ten days before the first witness was scheduled to testify.

Amendola and Rominger had to speed-read through the thousands of pages of discovery material that they *did* get, in large dumps, beginning only four and a half months before the trial began. "Right up until trial, we were getting boxes of material," Amendola later recalled. For a while, they couldn't even get the prosecution to give them the names and birthdates of the alleged victims, along with the exact dates on which they were supposed to have been abused by Sandusky. Amendola also wanted the names of anyone who had come forward to claim abuse but who "did not fit the Commonwealth's profile and/or the report was deemed to be false," but that was not forthcoming either.

Neither was information on whatever the prosecution had discovered on Sandusky's computer, probably because they had found nothing incriminating whatsoever—no child pornography, which was surprising if Sandusky was the compulsive pedophile he was supposed to be.*[5] "We're really being pushed to kind of decipher this stuff," Amendola said in February 2012 about the reams of material. "We'll be prepared to try the case whenever the judge says, but we're playing a lot of catch-up right now."[6]

Amendola kept complaining. He threatened to file a motion to dismiss the case, since it was very difficult to prepare a defense without exact times and dates of alleged offenses. "All we are asking is [for prosecutors] to go back to these accusers and say, 'You went to football games—which ones?' Give us at least something that we could check," Amendola begged.

Prosecuting attorney Joe McGettigan responded that "many of the alleged victims were abused several times a week, or month," so it wasn't possible to pin down a particular time. Besides, "They didn't want to remember what happened and were even encouraged by Sandusky to forget," he said. Here was another red flag that the alleged victims may have been in therapy searching for repressed memories, but no one picked up on it. When the prosecutors said they wouldn't provide the information, Judge Cleland commented, "I think the answer is they can't." He thus declared that it was "futile" to demand such details. According to reporter Sara Ganim, "The state Attorney General's Office countered that Sandusky is accused of abusing boys who are now men, who were pressured into forgetting what happened and many times abused weekly for many years."[7]

Despite Amendola's strenuous objections and repeated requests for a continuance, Cleland denied the requests and stuck to his promised June 5 trial date, which would take place in Centre County, where State College and Penn State were located. Incredibly, Jerry Sandusky had instructed Amendola to oppose a change in venue, assuming that his local reputation would benefit him.[8] Instead, the

---

* While there was no pornography on Sandusky's computer, his investigators were sending "graphic and raunchy" pornography by email to one another. See Chapter 19 for detailed coverage.

last place on earth that he was likely to get a fair trial was in Penn State territory, where the case had received a huge amount of horrendous publicity, and Penn State fans were bitter and angry at the impact on Coach Paterno and their beloved institution.

On May 30, in a private unscheduled meeting with the judge and prosecutors, Amendola pled for a delay of the trial to allow him time to prepare for it properly. He wanted to call a psychologist as an expert witness, but the psychologist had been unable to prepare his reports because he hadn't been given access to the grand jury testimony. His jury consultant was in Puerto Rico on vacation. One of Amendola's investigators was having surgery. Amendola and Rominger didn't have enough time to review all the evidence. They couldn't call Gary Schultz or Tim Curley because they were criminally charged themselves and had exercised their fifth-amendment rights. Cleland again denied the requested continuance, saying, "No trial date is ever perfect, but some days are better than others."[9]

In retrospect, there are many things Amendola should have done. He not only waived the preliminary hearing where alleged victims would have testified, he made no attempt to interview any of them before the trial, other than Allan Myers, who came to him, nor did he seek to talk to Mike McQueary or Ronald Petrosky.

Amendola could have asked for a continuance based on the need for a "cooling off" period, to allow for the incendiary atmosphere to subside somewhat, but he didn't, because "if we weren't getting continuances on all the other legitimate reasons that we had, we certainly weren't going to get it on that basis," as he later testified.[10]

That same day, in an official pre-trial hearing, Amendola asked Cleland to throw out three of the ten alleged victims before the trial. Victim 2, the unnamed Allan Myers, should be thrown out because Mike McQueary's version of the shower incident kept changing, including the date on which it was supposed to have occurred. Victim 8, the Phantom Victim supposedly witnessed by the janitor who now had dementia, should be thrown out because it was pure hearsay. And Victim 6, Zachary Konstas, should be thrown out because the district attorney had decided in 1998 that there wasn't enough evidence to prosecute, so to try it again amounted to a kind of double jeopardy. Cleland denied all of Amendola's requests. All ten alleged victims would be presented to the jury.[11]

On June 5, just before the process of picking a jury commenced, Amendola tried one more tactic. He filed a motion to withdraw as Sandusky's lawyer, "based on the lack of preparation of all the things that are going on, most notably the absence of our experts and jury consultant." A "key witness" was unavailable. "My office is still copying materials which we cannot send out to anybody because they're all confidential. They're all grand jury materials. My staff is ready to quit." He said that "some day when people talk to my staff and get a real flavor for what was going on in my office for the past 30, 60 days, they'll have a better understanding that this is not lawyering." The reality was that "we have been so far behind, just keeping up with the discovery materials and trying to do due diligence . . . but we're at a loss." They hadn't even had time to serve subpoenas to potential witnesses. He concluded that "we're not prepared to go to trial at this time."

Cocounsel Karl Rominger added that he had called the Pennsylvania Bar Ethics Hotline the day before, and they had called his attention to Rule 17.1, a lawyer's "duty of competency," and that Rule 1.16 called upon a judge to ask lawyers to withdraw if the judge could tell that they were completely unprepared. The lawyer who answered the hotline said that they would normally render a formal opinion in such cases, but since they knew it was the Sandusky case, they didn't want to get involved.

Amendola said that he was "fully cognizant of the fact that the Court will deny but at least there will be a record."[12] And he was right. Cleland refused to allow him to withdraw from the case, and jury selection began.

PICKING A JURY IN CENTRE COUNTY

As a pool of 220 local citizens, called for possible jury duty, waited at the Centre County Courthouse in Bellefonte, Pennsylvania, on June 5, 2012, they chatted nervously with one another. But, as reporter Sara Ganim observed, "When Sandusky walked into the room, silence fell, and there were then audible whispers as potential jurors waited for the judge to enter."[13]

In his introductory remarks to the pool of potential jurors, Judge Cleland struck a folksy tone. Instead of wearing his robes and sitting on the high bench, he came down to their courtroom level wearing regular clothes. "I wanted to do this a little more informally," he said, "just come in and talk to you and tell you a little bit about this case." He told them he would not be sequestering them by keeping them in isolation in hotel rooms. "With all this media, with 240 some reporters that are credentialed here and 30-some trucks, why are we not going to sequester you?" he asked. "I'm trusting you. I hope you'll trust me and that you will agree that you will not read the newspapers. You will not watch television news. You will not read the laws. You will not put posts on your Facebook page. You will not tweet. You will not read anybody else's tweets."

This level of trust seemed absurd, given the level of media hysteria and intrusion. Perhaps Cleland figured that it was too late for sequestration anyway. He as much as acknowledged that reality. "Well, today who knows nothing about this crime? Right. We don't live in a cave. So we don't ask you to say 'I know nothing,' but we do ask you to say, 'I can keep an open mind. I have heard stuff. I have read stuff. I have heard it discussed. I have argued about it, but I don't have an opinion, and I won't have an opinion until the Commonwealth proves to me beyond a reasonable doubt.'"

In his remarks, Cleland let drop a few of these subtle indications that he assumed the jury would find Sandusky guilty. "The State cannot bring its power to punish this defendant until twelve of you give them the permission to do that," he told the potential jurors. He did not say "*unless* twelve of you," but "*until.*"[14]

The jury selection, which took only two days, went remarkably swiftly compared to most major criminal cases, in which the process often consumes weeks. It quickly became apparent that many people in the jury pool had either attended or worked at Penn State University—not surprising in Centre County, where a third of the population had a direct Penn State connection—and many potential jurors knew or worked with various people involved in the case.[15]

It also became apparent that Joe Amendola really needed that jury consultant who was out of the country. A young Penn State graduate who was also a Second Mile volunteer said that he had discussed the case with coworkers. He had heard about "more accusations coming forward. It's more than one or two. It seems like where—a case where there's smoke, there's fire." Incredibly. Amendola said, "I find him acceptable, Judge." It was prosecutor Joe McGettigan who objected to him becoming a juror.[16]

Not surprisingly, several potential jurors admitted that they had already predetermined Sandusky's guilt. "I think I would have a very hard time being impartial," one man said. "I have read all that stuff. I think I kind of have my mind made up."[17] Another woman was married to a physician who worked with Dr. Jonathan Dranov. She knew both Mike McQueary and Gary Schultz. Yet when Amendola moved to strike her, Judge Cleland refused, observing: "We're in rural Pennsylvania. There are these kinds of social interactions and contacts that just can't be avoided, and in some ways I think there is a positive aspect of that, too, because people know each other in more than merely superficial ways."[18] This assertion seemed quite astonishing, given the kind of small-town prejudices and pressures that were likely to come into play. At any rate, the woman became a juror.

Another man, an engineer in his seventies who had retired from Penn State's Applied Research Lab but still worked there part time, said that "this whole thing has created some real problems . . . because you're the guy from Penn State . . . that kind of crap. And it's difficult to deal with sometimes." He said that he had begun to "form some opinions" about the case because of the "scope and breadth and duration of it. . . . This isn't like an isolated incident." He said that his wife was "totally convinced of Mr. Sandusky's guilt," and that if he found him not guilty, "I would have to do a lot of explaining." Yet when Amendola moved to strike this juror, Judge Cleland said, "I'm not going to grant that one. I think he was extremely candid and obviously wrestling with this." Amendola then exercised a peremptory challenge, an option he could have exercised seven times.[19]

Another engineer who was picked as a juror said that although he read a number of blogs, he avoided reading stories about the Sandusky case. "I reached a saturation point about two and a half months ago."[20] A different juror said he taught physics and chemistry at Bellefonte High School, but Amendola gave an early indication that he was either hard of hearing, inattentive, or both, by subsequently asking him, "Did you say you teach elementary school?"[21]

A rising senior at Penn State admitted to having "some opinions" about the case. "Being a student I just hear everything, you know . . . the whole outrage of everything." He followed Penn State and football-related websites. When Amendola asked him whether he could face his friends if he voted not guilty, the young man said, "I wouldn't tell them if that's how I felt because that's not how I feel." In other words, that wouldn't be a concern because he had already decided that Sandusky *was* guilty. Amendola moved to "strike him for cause," not because of this attitude, but because the lawyer mistakenly heard that he knew Trooper Scott Rossman, when it was a different Rossman. Judge Cleland refused to grant his motion to strike the juror, and, incredibly, Amendola failed to exercise a peremptory strike. The Penn State student became a juror.[22]

So did an older retired woman. By this time, Judge Cleland had taken over a good deal of the questioning, apparently because Amendola was so ineffective. "Do you have any strong fixed opinions about the Defendant's guilt or innocence?" Cleland asked her. "Yes,

I do. I drove school bus for seventeen years, and my responsibility was to take care of those kids and make sure that nothing happened to them. . . . I just can't see our children hurt. That's all there is to it." Cleland persisted. "The question is whether or not you think you could be fair in determining whether children were hurt." She answered, "I don't know. I really, I probably could be. I probably could be fair." Amendola accepted her as a juror without a murmur.[23]

And so it went. A retired Penn State soil science professor was accepted as a juror, even though he said that it would be "somewhat difficult, especially with my wife," if he found Sandusky not guilty, and he said that he was more likely to believe the testimony of a police officer than other witnesses—a belief that most of the jurors espoused.[24] In the end, the twelve jurors—five men, seven women—were a Walmart employee, a housewife, an engineer, two college students, a high school teacher, an employee at the Apartment Store, a retired bus driver, a Penn State professor, a retired Penn State professor, a Penn State administrative assistant, and a dance instructor who taught courses at Penn State.

Regardless of the jurors who were picked, Juror No. 1431, who was excused, expressed honestly what was probably true for anyone who lived in Centre County. "I think it's very difficult to be fair after you read what you have read and you make your own decision in your mind."[25]

Nonetheless, just before the trial began, Judge Cleland addressed the jury and assured them that he would trust their judgment. "You are men, women, older, younger, Penn State faculty, Penn State students. You may know people involved in this case or people who know people involved in this case. You have all read and heard things about the case." Nonetheless, he was "absolutely confident" in their ability to be balanced and to be the "conscience of this community."[26]

OPENING STATEMENTS

On Monday, June 11, 2012, Joe McGettigan opened with an impassioned speech to the newly picked jurors about the "serial predatory pedophile" whom they should convict. McGettigan, then sixty-four, a native of Philadelphia, had carved out a reputation as an aggressive, successful prosecutor. "He is smart, tenacious, and well-prepared," wrote one journalist, who also called him a pugnacious street brawler. "He will steamroll over anyone who gets in his way," another lawyer observed, adding that McGettigan was a "true believer" who thought "all criminals deserve life sentences." He was known as "Hollywood Joe McGettigan" because of his penchant for dark glasses, garish ties, and his serving as a legal consultant and writer for a one-season television series. In the press, he had already called the Second Mile "a victim factory."[27]

Now McGettigan told the jurors that the young men who would testify had endured "years of victimization," and that, although the molestation had occurred years ago, "the past is never dead. It's not even past." For a few alleged victims, the sexual abuse had taken place "in an escalating fashion, escalating to the point of . . . deviate sexual intercourse, oral sex." Others were "less invasive and less lengthy," and two involved only one alleged contact.

McGettigan asked the jurors to think of the witnesses not as young adults, but as helpless children. "You'll see them and understand them as the children they were." In order to prepare them for this leap of the imagination, he showed enlarged pictures of each alleged victim as a child, one at a time, on a twelve-foot high screen. "That's Brett," he said, showing the photo from Sandusky's book, *Touched*. "Do you know whose hand that is on his shoulder? The defendant's." In the picture of Michal Kajak, "the defendant is right behind Michal," McGettigan said, of course implying sodomy, although it was blown up from an innocuous group photo. McGettigan said that Zachary Konstas was "so innocent he wasn't even sure what part of a man's body should look like and why he should be touching him," even though Konstas never accused Sandusky of molesting him. McGettigan explained, "Here's a young boy who bore him no ill will because he wasn't even aware of what happened."

McGettigan never used the phrase "repressed memories," but he repeatedly implied them. He warned jurors that he would have to "press these young men for the details of their victimization" because "they don't want to remember." He instructed jurors to "imagine the age at which they were abused, the years that it was in the past, and the efforts which they had tried to bury [the memories]," which would "cause them to have difficulty in remembering with great specificity." But that lack of recall should not disturb them. Indeed, "sometimes the honest admission of a lack of memory about . . . minor detail gives the clearest indication of the absolute truth of the painful events they will never forget." In other words, the absence of detailed memory could be taken as proof that the recovered memories were true.

He explained that "the investigation was slow because doors were closed. Just like the doors of people's minds, they don't want to talk about anything. They were closed. . . . In many instances you will hear even when they spoke to the police the first time, they wouldn't fully disclose." With sufficient encouragement, however, they did.

Finally, McGettigan said that humiliation, shame, and fear were the reasons that none of the alleged victims had told anyone about the alleged abuse for years. He did not mention that some of them had not recalled the abuse until prompted by therapists, police, or lawyers.

According to reporter Sara Ganim, all jury members were "listening intently, wide-eyed." One juror shook her head in sympathetic disgust as the prosecutor described the abuse that each child had allegedly endured.

The rest of McGettigan's opening statement summarized the various witnesses he planned to call, including Mike McQueary, who would, he said, describe "how he saw that defendant in a shower pressed up against the wall, with a small boy beneath him . . . his front to this little boy's back moving back and forth."[28]

After McGettigan's opening statement, Amendola told the judge that his team had some objections to place in the record. "We didn't want to interrupt Mr. McGettigan," he explained. "We had an agreement." Amendola apparently wanted to be friendly, to be liked, so he agreed not to voice objections during opening or closing statements. Karl Rominger demurred, but because Amendola was in charge and was personal friends with Sandusky, he remained silent. "On many occasions, I disagreed with Mr. Amendola," he recalled. "However, I did not voice my disagreement because I did not want to undermine Mr. Amendola, who had the relationship with Mr. Sandusky." Because Amendola had taken few major cases to trial, Rominger said, "I felt I would be able to assist with trial objections and evidentiary issues more ably than Mr. Amendola."[29]

Thus, Rominger belatedly objected to McGettigan's photo array of the alleged victims, which were "stylized and cut for maximum emotional impact." He asked for a mistrial or a limiting instruction to jurors not to consider the images as evidence. Cleland curtly denied his motions. Rominger objected that "the prosecution wrongly kept referring to the complaining witnesses as victims." Cleland regarded the term as acceptable as a "matter of convenience" and would let the jury know that "we're using the terms *victims* as a shorthand, [it] obviously means alleged."

Rominger objected to McGettigan's use of the words *humiliation, shame,* and *fear.* "What they're doing is essentially explaining why the witnesses said nothing." This amounted to argument, not a presentation of facts. Similarly, McGettigan should not have argued that there was a huge amount of evidence for guilt. "There is no overwhelming evidence of anything at this point." Cleland denied these as well as all the rest of his objections.[30]

Then it was defense attorney Joe Amendola's turn. Early in 2009, upon learning of the Aaron Fisher allegations, Sandusky had first hired Amendola, a local State College practitioner. A former prosecutor, Amendola had switched to defense, taking on driving-under-the-influence and rape cases. He had a reputation for negotiating favorable plea bargains but had not argued many cases in the courtroom. He and McGettigan were the same age, but they were stark contrasts in many ways. McGettigan was abrasive and only recently engaged, for the first time, to be married. Amendola had a friendly, smiling demeanor that had seen him through several failed marriages, the most recent the result of an affair in which he impregnated his seventeen-year-old intern in 1997 when he was forty-eight.

Many observers, including Amendola himself, were surprised that Sandusky stuck with the hometown lawyer. Before Sandusky's arrest, Amendola said, "I'm sure some big-name attorney is going to volunteer to represent him."[31] But Sandusky, who was known for his sometimes-naïve loyalty to friends and colleagues, stuck with Amendola, and besides, no big-name attorneys wanted to take on the toxic case.

After McGettigan's masterful performance, Amendola's opening statement was embarrassingly lame. "This is a daunting task," he began. "I'll be honest with you, I'm not sure how to approach it. The Commonwealth has overwhelming evidence against Mr. Sandusky." It's difficult to imagine a worse defensive posture than talking about the "overwhelming evidence" against his client, particularly when his colleague, Karl Rominger, had just objected to McGettigan's use of that phrase. Rominger winced, since Amendola had just "cast Mr. Sandusky as guilty in the minds of the jurors," he thought.

"I never had a case like this in my life," Amendola continued, "and I can assure you I never will again." But, he said, he had to make an opening statement, even though it seemed hopeless. "We can pack it in now and say, 'Gee whiz, we don't have a chance.'" He compared his task as "similar to climbing Mount Everest from the bottom of the hill." He said that he was David to the government's Goliath, and he complained about the "boxes and boxes of materials to go through."

Finally, Amendola said that he needed to "figure out how we can present Mr. Sandusky's case to you so that you will understand that he's innocent." If he expected to convince the jury of his client's innocence, he certainly had a strange way of approaching it. He asserted, without much conviction, that "There are no victims in this case . . . because victims only come about after you twelve determine they're victims." He noted that Sandusky had "always said he's innocent" and that it had only been seven months since the Grand Jury Presentment had been made public and Sandusky was arrested, whereas "the Commonwealth had over three years to investigate these allegations."

"So how did it start?" It began with Aaron Fisher's allegations. "Jerry Sandusky fondled him above his clothing one time." What Amendola undoubtedly meant to say was that Fisher *alleged* at first that Sandusky had fondled him above his clothing, but instead he told the jury that he had indeed fondled him. Then he talked about the 1998 shower incident and said that Zachary Konstas would say that "there was no sexual touching. . . . They fooled around in the shower and they played."

Amendola admitted that Sandusky "got showers with kids," and that "many of us think that that in and of itself proves that he's guilty of horrendous crimes." But "Jerry's culture growing up in his generation where he grew up, he's going to tell you later it was routine for individuals to get showers together." In other words, he put the jury on notice that he planned to call Sandusky to the stand to testify.

He warned the jury that they would hear graphic descriptions of grotesque sexual abuse. "The testimony you are going to get is going to be awful, but that doesn't make it true." He wondered aloud, "How do we get to the end of this case, and how do we try to establish that Jerry Sandusky is not guilty, that there's a real reasonable doubt here?" He apparently had no idea.

He then talked about the McQueary shower incident. "What we think is that he saw something and he made assumptions." Amendola did not point out that McQueary did not in fact *see* much of anything. He *heard* slapping sounds. Then the defense attorney made it worse by alluding to "when he (McQueary) went into the shower and saw Jerry Sandusky with a young-looking person." In reality, McQueary never went into the shower, and he didn't initially say that he saw Sandusky with a boy in the shower. He told Dr. Dranov that night that he saw a boy, and that an arm reached out to pull him back into the shower. That was all he saw.

Amendola then alluded to this boy in the shower, Victim 2, and said, "I suspect [he] is not going to be a witness according to the Commonwealth because he hasn't actually been identified." Amendola didn't say that he *had* been identified as Allan Myers because he didn't intend to call him to the stand either, since Andrew Shubin had taken him as a "victim" client.

Finally, Amendola made a salient point. Dranov and McQueary's father advised Mike McQueary to tell Joe Paterno about his concerns. "It's not the kind of advice I would have given if someone said, 'I just saw Jerry Sandusky having anal sex with a ten-year-old boy in the shower.'"

But most of Amendola's opening statement could not possibly have convinced jurors that Sandusky was likely to be innocent. "When you hear this testimony," he said, "think about the logical sense [that] just doesn't make any sense," which, of course, made no sense. "The accusers. You saw those eight photos. Cute kids. Why would they lie?" Amendola's only explanation was financial motivation. "Money is the root of all evil." Also, because they were Second Mile kids, "they had issues." He did not allude to the influence of therapists (about which he had no clue) or leading police interviews, though he later noted that "the accusers were questioned multiple times. . . . The government went back until they got an answer they wanted to hear."

"After all this abuse occurred," Amendola said, "all these horrific things happened, they (the alleged victims) maintained relationships with Jerry and Dottie Sandusky." What he meant to say, of course, was that after all this *alleged* abuse and all these horrific things *allegedly* occurred, many boys remained friendly with the Sanduskys. But that's not how it came out.

"Jerry Sandusky didn't pick the time or place to be arrested," Amendola noted, as if this had any relevance to his innocence or guilt. Then, once again, he damned his own client. "Jerry, in my opinion, loves kids so much that he does things that none of us would ever dream of doing."

Desperately trying to salvage his ineffective opening statement, Amendola asserted, without conviction, "At the conclusion of [all the] evidence, we suspect that you'll find him not guilty." He ended by saying, "Thank you folks, for listening. I know it's been a long morning. I know you'll do a great job for both sides." For Amendola, it had indeed been a long morning.[32]

CHAPTER 15

The Prosecution Makes Its Case

THAT MONDAY afternoon of June 11, 2011, Joe McGettigan led off the prosecution's case with Brett Houtz, labeled Victim 4, who was the strongest, most compelling, articulate, and believable witness, as we have seen in Chapter 7.* He was accompanied by his civil lawyer, Benjamin Andreozzi. The twenty-eight-year-old Houtz recounted how when he was thirteen, he had met Sandusky in the Second Mile program. The coach had taken him under his wing, inviting him to a family picnic, playing racquetball and basketball with him, giving him gifts, and generally treating him like a son. "Basically like he was my dad is how he acted." He told the jury that "horsing around" and engaging in soap battles in the shower led to hugs, caresses, oral sex, and attempted sodomy. He recounted these instances without much emotion or credible detail, as we have seen.

Oddly, Houtz seemed most emotional about his distaste for Sandusky's habit of putting his hand on Houtz's knee when Sandusky was driving. Indeed, at one point Houtz hit Sandusky with an empty soda bottle when he kept putting his hand on his knee. (Recalling that Houtz did indeed hate the knee-squeezes, Sandusky later said during a prison interview, "I did it to irritate him. My name is Gerald Arthur Sandusky, and I used to say the A was for Aggravation.")[1]

McGettigan introduced many of the gifts Sandusky had given Houtz, including golf clubs, snowboards, shoes, sweat suits, "all from Penn State," Houtz said, "like memorabilia-type things. Like,

---

* Each of the alleged victims' cases has already been covered in detail, including their evolving testimony, culminating with this trial. To avoid too much duplication, this section covering the trial summarizes relevant testimony while conveying a sense of the trial, including the lawyers, judge, and jury.

he gave me a watch from the Orange Bowl, a football that was from Ohio State."*[2]

Houtz explained that as he got older and had a girlfriend, he tried to distance himself from Sandusky. He would agree to an activity but then wouldn't show up. McGettigan then introduced portions of several letters Sandusky had written to Houtz (some unsent), which were heartfelt pleas for Houtz to shape up, take responsibility, and be a good student.

Houtz also admitted that he had gone to visit the Sandusky family in 2010, when he was twenty-six, to introduce his girlfriend and their three-year-old son. He explained this friendly gesture by asserting that she had complained that he had never taken her to see his old mentor. He said that she had become "suspicious" that maybe something sexual had happened between them. So he took her there "so she could see that it was normal and nothing bad had happened." According to Houtz, it backfired, because Sandusky was "trying to rub my shoulders and horsing around kind of thing again and she just—she knew."

At the end of his testimony, McGettigan asked Houtz leading questions, to which Amendola failed to object. "Did it (Sandusky's behavior), in fact, involve him placing his penis in your mouth dozens of times, more than 40 times?" *Yes.* "And trying to insert his finger into your anus on at least a couple of occasions?" *Yes.* "And his erect penis into you?" *Yes.* "Any reason you'd say that other than the fact that it's true?" Houtz: "No. No reason whatsoever."[3]

At the beginning of his cross-examination of Houtz, Amendola revealed for the first time—but not the last—that he had a hearing problem, despite his hearing aids. "I've had some difficulty over here hearing everybody on the other side." Remarkably, he had not objected or said anything. Nonetheless, he made an effort to show that Houtz had a reputation for lying and that he was motivated by the prospect of making money from a subsequent civil suit mounted by his lawyer, Benjamin Andreozzi.

Amendola questioned why Houtz could hit Sandusky with a bottle in the car because of a hand on the knee, but that he couldn't prevent him from forcing him into oral sex in a shower. "You seem like a relatively forceful person," Amendola said. "I get the impression that if you don't like something, you don't mind telling people." Houtz agreed but said he went along with it because "I kind of

---

* Sandusky later noted that he had gotten most of these items as donations, so they were free. "It is interesting to me that Brett saved all those gifts, when experts say those abused want no reminders of their abuse."

looked at Jerry as a father figure" and besides, he got to be cool and hang out with football players.

Then Houtz offered a broad hint that some of his allegations may have stemmed from repressed memory therapy. "I have spent, you know, so many years burying this in the back of my head forever." Amendola did not follow up on the clue.

The defense attorney did question Houtz about his father arranging for sex abuse lawyer Benjamin Andreozzi to contact him, but Amendola failed to ask Houtz about why his allegations had grown and changed over time. On his own, Houtz offered a confusing account, saying that the first time he told the police and lawyer that "something actually happened to me was just before I was going to the grand jury." He said that he had told policemen Joseph Leiter and Scott Rossman very little in their first two interviews. That was not, in fact, the case, since in his first formal interview, which was tape-recorded, he alleged many shower abuse incidents, though that did not yet include oral sex. At any rate, by the time he testified before the grand jury, he said that he provided a detailed account, "as much as I could remember it" at that point. Again, Amendola paid no attention to the hint of repressed memories.

Amendola did get Houtz to reveal that the new Lasch building shower, in which he alleged that multiple sex abuse incidents occurred, had no shower curtain, so that anyone walking by could see the occupants. Nor did it require anyone to punch a code to get into the locker room. Yet Sandusky had not worried about being caught, nor did he ever ask Houtz not to tell anyone, according to Houtz's testimony.

When he recounted how Sandusky had tried to help him with school and had him sign a contract promising to give him $1,000 towards college tuition if he fulfilled it, Houtz was contemptuous, saying he signed it just to get Sandusky to stop pestering him about his responsibilities. Amendola got Houtz to read parts of a letter in which Sandusky had written, "You like to express yourself in a straight-forward manner," so the coach was doing the same, complaining that Houtz didn't keep his commitments. "You seek happiness through control, domination, and what satisfies." Ironically, that's what Sandusky himself was now being accused of doing.

Amendola's cross-examination did not make a dent in Houtz's sex abuse allegations. The jury members were horrified by the images of soapy coerced 69 positions on the shower floor. That was the crux of the matter. It was irrelevant that Sandusky would have been taking insane chances in a college locker room where anyone could walk in on him. It was also irrelevant when Houtz told Amendola that he had never known what to do with his life. But now his life clearly had new meaning.[4]

DAY TWO: AARON FISHER'S TEARFUL TESTIMONY

On Tuesday, June 12, 2012, Aaron Fisher, "Victim 1," took the stand. By this time, the eighteen-year-old had been in therapy with Mike Gillum for three years, had been interviewed and influenced repeatedly by the police and lawyers, and had testified three times before grand juries, as covered in Chapter 4. On the stand, Fisher explained that he had grown up in public housing in Lock Haven, Pennsylvania, and had never known his father. He met Jerry Sandusky in the Second Mile program when he was ten years old. When he was twelve, Sandusky began to have him stay at his house overnight on Saturdays, where he could play pool, shuffleboard, darts, or air hockey in the basement. Fisher's mother encouraged him to go, thinking that it would be good for him (and also to give her time to party). Sometimes Fisher slept in an upstairs guest room, sometimes in a basement bedroom.

Sandusky would put his hand on his knee while driving and kiss him on the forehead at bedtime. He would also crack his back sometimes by hugging him, something Fisher had learned to enjoy during wrestling warmups, when his coach cracked his back by crossing his arms and lifting him up. "I didn't honestly think it was anything wrong," Fisher said. McGettigan repeatedly had to ask Fisher leading questions to fit the script they had clearly already rehearsed. "Did he do anything else in the way of having physical contact and touching you? And tell us the first thing he did."

Fisher said that Sandusky would "rub underneath my shorts in the back" after cracking his back, and that he used to blow on his stomach, "like you do to a little baby to get them to laugh." Finally, breaking into tears, Fisher said that "he put his mouth on my privates." When that happened, "I spaced . . . I just kind of blacked out."

McGettigan moved on to the next item on the agenda. "Mr. Fisher, at some point after he did this, did he do something else to you or cause you to do something to him?" Fisher didn't immediately comply. "He took me out to do stuff. We had fun activities. We came back to the house. We ate. We played games." But then, after the back cracking, "he made me put my mouth on his . . . his privates." How did that make him feel? "I froze like any other time. My mind was telling me to move, but I . . . I couldn't do it." He didn't tell his mother because "she might not believe me."

Fisher then said that "after I started staying with him, it changed noticeably," a suspiciously adult-sounding phrase from the eighteen-year-old. "I acted out. I started wetting the bed." But, as we have seen, he had begun wetting the bed *before* he began to stay overnight at the Sandusky home.

McGettigan continued to lead Fisher, getting him to talk about how Joe Miller, his elementary school wrestling coach, had walked into the middle school weight room one day. They had been lifting weights, then Fisher was climbing on a rock wall but fell off, as Sandusky caught him. The boy laughed, and he and Sandusky were wrestling around on a mat there when Miller came in. Fisher now made much of this incident by saying that Sandusky had "hopped up like a rabbit" when Miller came in, though when Miller testified later, he said Sandusky didn't get up but just said they were practicing wrestling moves.

Fisher claimed that in 2008, when he was in the ninth grade, he began to "hide underneath the pool table, in closet spaces" at Sandusky's house to avoid him and that he began to spend less time with him because he joined the Big Brother program. Sandusky, who was a volunteer football coach at his high school, allegedly called him out of his history class to talk about it, though Sandusky claimed that this one-time event occurred during a school assembly. Sandusky asked why Fisher was avoiding him and not answering his phone calls, and he wanted him to commit to Second Mile programs he had promised to help with. Later that day, Fisher found that the retired coach was in his front yard talking to his mother and grandfather.

Then Fisher recounted the story of how he had asked his mother about a sex offender website to see if Sandusky was on it, and she set up a meeting with the guidance counselor at the high school, who asked him "if Jerry ever did anything wrong to me." At that point, "I broke down and cried and said yes." Fisher's motivation, he said, was that "I just thought that it would keep him away from me." The school counselor and principal called his mother, but, according to Fisher, "They said that we needed to think about it, and he (Sandusky) has a heart of gold and he wouldn't do something like that, so they didn't believe me."

His mother took him to Children and Youth Services, where social worker Jessica Dershem interviewed him, but "I didn't tell her very much of anything," nor did he tell a policeman, because

"I kind of just wanted to forget it ever happened. I just . . . I didn't feel comfortable."

McGettigan then tried to skip directly to Fisher's grand jury testimony, thereby avoiding any discussion of therapist Mike Gillum's enormous influence over his memory and testimony. For once, Fisher took the initiative to say, "Before that I actually talked to a Children and Youth psychologist, Mike." McGettigan brushed this topic aside. "Okay. And do you remember the first time you talked to the grand jury?"

Finally, McGettigan got tired of trying to get Fisher to repeat what they had agreed on, so he went right at it himself. "I'm going to ask you now—did the defendant put his penis in your mouth more than 25 times over the course of 2007, 2008?" Fisher answered, "It was—yeah." And did Sandusky also "place his mouth on your penis that many times or more during 2006, '7, and '8?" Yes, even more times.

Then, somewhat anticlimactically, McGettigan got Fisher to identify various photos and gifts, such as golf clubs and clothing, that Sandusky had given him. These were items that donors had given to the Second Mile.

When Joe Amendola cross-examined Aaron Fisher, the young man admitted that Sandusky had given him the nice clothes so that he could wear them to church. "That was the first time I ever went to, actually, a church." Fisher denied that he had ever told a neighbor that he and his mother would get rich from the Sandusky allegations, able to buy a big house and nice cars. Amendola also reviewed Fisher's contradictory, changing story. Fisher said he had initially said that he and Sandusky were fully clothed when he cracked his back and had denied that he had touched his privates. "Yeah," Fisher said, "it's a tough subject to talk about." The accommodating Amendola said, "I understand, and I would be embarrassed, too," apparently accepting that Fisher really *had* been molested.

The defense lawyer did, at least, get Fisher to admit that he had changed his claims about oral sex repeatedly, denying, asserting, denying again, and then reasserting its occurrence, as well as changing the claimed dates and extent of the alleged abuse. The teenager complained that "with everything that I was trying to forget," it was hard to remember exactly what happened, how often, in what years. "I don't remember all that I testified to or what I said. . . . I may have white-lied, you know, trying to cover the embarrassment."

Fisher volunteered that therapist Mike Gillum "believed that something more did happen and we talked," later bringing up Gillum again, "who I've been talking to for quite some time now." (In fact, three years.) "I [still] go and see him every Thursday."

Fisher also revealed that the police had encouraged him to tell them more, saying that other Second Mile alums were claiming abuse. "They said that I'm not alone." [5]

The prosecution called several more people to the stand during this second day of the trial. Donald Fisher, Aaron's grandfather, testified that he used to sit in the bleachers with Sandusky at Aaron's wrestling tournaments. He talked about the front lawn confrontation about Aaron's backing out on his commitment to help out at a Second Mile golf event.

The director of housekeeping at the Hilton Garden Inn talked about how Sandusky had thrown a football around in the inn's swimming pool with her two grandchildren and another kid. The children had a great time. [6]

Jessica Dershem, the case worker for Clinton County Children and Youth Services, testified at some length about her meeting with Aaron Fisher before she handed him off to therapist Mike Gillum. She also reviewed her subsequent interview with Jerry Sandusky. Fisher had told her about the wrestling and back-cracking but had said both of them were fully clothed. Dershem asked him several times "if there was anything else Mr. Sandusky did or any other actions that made him feel uncomfortable," and he said there weren't. When Dershem later asked to videotape her second interview with Fisher, policeman Joseph Cavanaugh wouldn't allow it because taped interviews "help out the defense lawyers."

When Dershem interviewed Jerry Sandusky, she said, he stated that he wanted to make Fisher feel "significant and important." He confirmed that he wrestled with Fisher, cracked his back, blew raspberries on his stomach, hugged him, and kissed him on the forehead, as he did other Second Mile *protégés*. Sandusky had attended his sporting events and had given him a used computer someone had donated, to help him academically. The last time he saw Fisher was on his fifteenth birthday, November 9, 2008, when he gave him a homemade card featuring a photo of the boy at a track meet.

When Joe Amendola cross-examined Dershem after lunch, he tried to be self-deprecating but instead sounded ineffectual: "It's going to be tough enough going through this right after lunch," he said. "People may be tempted to take a nap. They usually do when I'm speaking." Prosecutor McGettigan, on the other hand, aggressively put words in Dershem's mouth. Didn't Sandusky give her "just self-serving statements?" Yes, she agreed. McGettigan pursued: "To you, as a trained professional, [does Sandusky's story] indicate right there an inappropriate relationship between a middle-aged adult and a small child?" Yes, Dershem concurred. Amendola made no objections.[7] After the trial, Dershem told a reporter that Sandusky had "admitted to everything except the sexual contact. To me, that meant it was all true." In the face of such logic, it is little wonder that the caseworker thought Sandusky was guilty.[8]

Mike McQueary then took the stand to tell his latest version of the shower incident with "Victim 2" (i.e., the unnamed Allan Myers), where he heard "showers running and smacking sounds, very much skin-on-skin smacking sounds." (Later in his testimony, he said he heard only two or three slapping sounds that lasted two or three seconds.)

He had reframed and reexamined his memory of the event "many, many, many times," he said, and he was now certain that he had looked into the shower three separate times, for one or two seconds each, and that he saw "Coach Sandusky standing behind a boy who is propped up against the shower. The showers are running and, and he is right up against his back with his front. The boy's hands are up on the wall." He saw "very slow, slow, subtle movement." After he slammed his locker, McQueary said, they separated and faced him. Surprisingly, he said that Sandusky did not have an erection.

When Amendola failed to object, Judge Cleland inserted himself, obviously fearful of future appeal or post-conviction relief issues. "Wait, wait, wait, just a second," he warned McGettigan. "I think you have to be very careful for you not to lead this witness." A few minutes later, the judge asked both lawyers to approach the bench. "I don't know why you're not getting objections to this grossly leading [questioning]," he told McGettigan, who said, "I'm just trying to get through it fast."

McQueary recounted how he had met with Joe Paterno. "I made sure he knew it was sexual and that it was wrong, [but] I did not go into gross detail." Later, he said, he met with Tim Curley, the Penn State athletic director, and Gary Schultz, a university vice president. In an email quoted during his testimony, McQueary had written, "I had discussions with the police and with the official at the university in charge of the police." He now explained that by this he meant just one person, since Schultz oversaw the university police department.

With only an hour's warning, Joe Amendola asked Karl Rominger to conduct the cross-examination of McQueary and handed him the file. Rominger did the best he could, asking McQueary why in 2010 he had told the police that he'd looked into the showers twice but had now added a third viewing, and he questioned him about his misremembering that the shower incident occurred in 2002. Rominger also noted that McQueary had told the grand jury, "I was nervous and flustered, so I just didn't do anything to stop it." Now he was saying that he slammed the locker, which allegedly ended the incident.

Without meaning to, McQueary indirectly helped Sandusky's case by explaining the demanding work schedule of a Penn State football coach, typically reporting to work Sunday through Tuesday at 7:00 a.m. and working until 10:00 p.m. or later. Then, Wednesday through Friday, it was 8:00 a.m. to 8:00 p.m. If Sandusky kept the same hours, it was difficult to see when he would have managed to molest all those boys, at least during pre-season training and football season.

Finally, McQueary revealed that he had filed a whistleblower lawsuit against Penn State for having removed him from his football coaching job in the midst of the Sandusky scandal. "I don't think I've done anything wrong to lose that job."[9]

Day Two of the trial ended with Joe Miller, the middle school wrestling coach, who had walked in on Jerry Sandusky and Aaron Fisher when they were wrestling around in the weight room. "I was always a big fan of what Jerry did with the Second Mile," he said. "I thought it was a great thing, because Aaron needed a father figure." When he walked in on them, Sandusky did not jump up, but just propped himself up on one arm and said, "Hey, Coach, Aaron and I are just working on some wrestling moves." Miller thought nothing of it, other than, "Well, it's Jerry Sandusky. He's a saint, you know. What he's doing with these kids, it's fantastic."[10]

DAY THREE: RECOVERED MEMORIES AND JANITOR TALES

The third day of the trial featured three more alleged victims, a few ancillary witnesses, and janitor Ron Petrosky presenting his double-hearsay evidence about the Phantom Victim. The prosecution led with the father of Mike McQueary, who added no new information. In one remarkable exchange, Karl Rominger tried to ask John McQueary about contradictory statements he had made in a previous hearing, but when McQueary said he didn't remember being at the hearing, Judge Cleland refused to allow him to proceed.[11]

Then Ryan Rittmeyer, "Victim Number 10," took the stand to assert that Sandusky had performed oral sex on him in his basement and in a silver convertible. We have already covered his case in some detail in Chapter 8, so will just summarize it here. Jerry and Dottie Sandusky did not know Rittmeyer, who approached the police after the case had created a media firestorm. The young man had been imprisoned twice and may have seen his newly claimed victimhood as a way to make money.

There is no evidence that his allegations involved repressed memories, but it was replete with contradictions. Rittmeyer's story allowed for no grooming behavior whatsoever. According to him, Jerry Sandusky went right to work on him: "Well, we were wrestling, and the defendant pinned me to the ground. He pulled my shorts down and started performing oral sex on me." He used those exact same words to questions from both McGettigan and Amendola. Despite being freaked out and scared, Rittmeyer said that he kept coming back for more.[12] McGettigan then called to the stand Rittmeyer's former foster parent, Cheryl Sharer, who affirmed that he had said nothing to her about any sexual abuse, but she was now sure that it must have occurred.[13]

Dustin Struble, "Victim Number 7," testified before lunch. As we have seen in Chapter 6, he as much as announced that his accusations were based on abuse memories recovered in therapy, but Amendola didn't understand. "The more negative things, I had sort of pushed into the back of my mind, sort of like closing a door."

It isn't clear how much the hard-of-hearing defense attorney actually heard. "You said a lot of things today, Mr. Struble," Amendola said, "and I just caught a few of them." He did ask Struble why he had told the grand jury that Sandusky had never touched his privates but now was saying that Sandusky had fondled his penis. "That doorway that I had closed has since been reopening more," Struble explained. "More things have been coming back and things have changed since that grand jury testimony. Through counseling and different things, I can remember a lot more detail." When he testified before the grand jury, he had "a little different mind-set."

Still, Amendola didn't pursue the impact of repressed memory therapy. "But today you're telling us no blurry memory any more, correct?" he asked Struble. That's right, the young man said. He had remembered more abuse during his therapy. "Different things triggered different memories." Previously he had blocked out the negative memories, and he was just starting the process of recovering the memories when he had testified before the grand jury.

Nor did Amendola realize that Struble and Zach Konstas had been encouraging one another to recall more abuse in therapy, even though Struble told him: "He (Zach) had asked me if I remembered anything more, if counseling was helping." The only thing Amendola focused on was a financial motive for a false allegation. He didn't understand that Dustin Struble had truly come to believe in his new-found "memories."*[14]

Amendola got Struble to read from his 2004 application for a scholarship to the Second Mile, in which he had written that Sandusky was "a kind and caring gentleman" who had helped him in many ways. The defense attorney asked whether this was the same man Struble had been describing to the jury for the last hour. "Not to me, no," Struble said. Instead of following up, Amendola gave up. "That's all I have, Your Honor." It was McGettigan, in a brief follow-up, who got Struble to explain: "I wasn't mad at [Sandusky] or feel hostile or anything towards him until fairly recently."[15]

After lunch on that Wednesday, Michal Kajak, "Victim Number 5," took the stand. We have already reviewed his case in detail in Chapter 6, including the police records showing that he, alone among the initial accusers, appears to have made sex-abuse allegations during his initial interview. Yet the police routinely used leading questions and methods and did not tape-record this interview. Also, by the time he spoke to the police, the abuse allegations against Sandusky had been publicized in the media. And Kajak may have spoken with his friend Dustin Struble, who was "remembering" his own abuse and might have helped him with his own shower story.

In his testimony, Kajak said that he had first met Sandusky after seeing him in a Second Mile skit playing a Polish gangster. "I approached him and told him that I was Polish, and it was just cool to meet the camp director." Sandusky had said, "I'm Polish too," and then said something in that language, though Kajak, whose parents were native Poles, said Sandusky's linguistic attempt wasn't very good. After that, Sandusky invited Kajak to go to Penn State football games, where he played with other kids and ate food during tailgate parties before the games.

---

* Joe McGettigan failed to disclose to Amendola that Dustin Struble had been in memory-enhancing therapy, nor did he tell the defense team about the evolving testimony of other alleged Sandusky victims, which amounted to "Brady violations," referring to a 1963 US Supreme Court ban on prosecutorial suppression of evidence material to guilt.

Like many other Second Mile alums, Kajak said that Sandusky put his hand on his knee while driving, but it didn't bother him. "My father would always squeeze my knee to help me relax," he said. Before his only shower with Sandusky, Kajak said they had gone into a sauna, where the defendant had "sat down on his towel and he sat back and exposed himself to me." But that's what people do in saunas, so it is hardly necessary to accuse him of "exposing" himself. Kajak didn't enjoy the experience, at any rate. "It felt like forever. It was really hot."

Then, in the shower, Sandusky's penis was "enlarged" but he didn't know what that meant. Kajak was thirteen years old in August 2001, when he said this shower occurred. (As we have seen, Kajak's story had changed over time, with more severe abuse claims moved forward by three years to another location.) Now, eleven years later, he related a detailed, well-rehearsed memory. Sandusky had thrown soap on him and lathered his shoulders, then pressed against him. "I just felt his penis on my back. I kind of turned away and I felt his arm move forward and he touched my hip, my genitalia. And then he took my hand and he placed it on his. That was . . . I don't know how long that was, but I was able to just round around the corner and get away. I just remember just drying off."

He never told anyone about it. "I wanted to forget, and I was embarrassed." It is not clear whether Kajak had sought counseling at this point, whether this abuse memory was enhanced, whether he had always remembered it, or whether his story had been influenced by police or lawyers.

Amendola's cross-examination was predictable. He hadn't been able to hear much of what was said. Mostly, he questioned Kajak about the discrepancy between 1998, the year he originally said the shower occurred, and the new claimed date of August 2001. But Amendola failed to remind the jury that in February 2001, Sandusky had been told not to bring any more Second Mile kids to Penn State facilities, so it is unlikely that he showered there with Kajak after that.* Nor did the defense lawyer point out that the claimed abuse—almost immediate during the first and only time in the shower—didn't fit the pattern of gradual grooming that Sandusky allegedly practiced.[16]

---

* Although Sandusky was forbidden to bring children on campus, it is still possible that he did so without anyone's knowledge. He denies having done so (and says he never showered again with another teenager at any location), and no one saw him with a child on the Penn State campus after February 2001.

Nor did Amendola point out that the infamous photo of Kajak and other alleged victims with Jerry Sandusky had been published in Sandusky's book, *Touched*, in 2000. Since Kajak was claiming that the abuse in the shower happened shortly after Sandusky befriended him, the date a year after that photo made little sense.

After Michal Kajak left the stand, McGettigan let the jury hear a ten-minute tape of Sandusky's stumbling interview with Bob Costas, televised on November 14, 2011, in which he hesitated before saying that he was not sexually attracted to young boys. Indeed, they heard that stumbling answer *twice*, because the tape had been erroneously edited.[17]

Then, with the jury in recess, Judge Cleland discussed whether he should allow the hearsay evidence from janitors Ron Petrosky and Jay Witherite about what fellow temporary janitor Jim Calhoun had allegedly witnessed. There was much controversy over whether Calhoun's alleged statements amounted to "excited utterance" that would be admissible in court. Assistant Prosecutor Frank Fina argued that it fit "a clear pattern of conduct" already introduced by other shower allegations. "I don't know that you can buttress it with other conduct," Cleland said. "The question was whether or not this statement is sufficient standing alone."

Cleland went on to raise further objections. "The proof of the exciting event can't be the excited utterance. . . . We're presented with the troublesome situation in which the excited utterance itself is being used to prove than an exciting event did, in fact, occur. This circuitous reasoning is unacceptable."

Yet, in the end, Cleland contradicted himself and said it *was* acceptable, overruling Karl Rominger's defense objections. He allowed the hearsay testimony, perhaps because the prosecution had assured him that there would be two janitors testifying. For reasons no one ever made clear, however, Jay Witherite did not testify.[18]

On the stand, as recounted in Chapter 8, Ron Petrosky presented his lurid secondhand testimony that Calhoun had seen Sandusky with "the boy up against the shower wall licking on his privates," a well-practiced phrase that prosecutor Joe McGettigan had just used during the discussion while the jury was recessed. Petrosky recounted how upset Calhoun was. His fellow janitors, he said, thought Calhoun was going to have a heart attack.

Then Petrosky said that he saw Sandusky driving slowly around the parking lot twice, around 11:00 p.m. and 2:00 a.m., though it was an inexplicable thing for him to have done.

After Amendola's ineffectual cross-examination, Cleland ad-journed for the day.[19] Calhoun himself did not testify, because he was allegedly suffering from dementia, though the defense did not ask to see any medical proof. And because Amendola had appar-ently not listened to the taped police interview with Jim Calhoun, he didn't know that the janitor (presumably aware enough at that time) had denied that it was Sandusky he'd seen in the shower.

DAY FOUR: THE PROSECUTION WRAPS UP

The prosecution planned to wrap up its case on Thursday, June 14, 2012, to be followed by a long weekend, since Friday was a day off for some reason. McGettigan led off with Zachary Konstas, who reviewed the shower he and Sandusky had shared in 1998, which led to his mother, Deb McCord, contacting the police, as covered in Chapter 2. While Konstas had not found the shower objectionable (or sexual) when he was interviewed soon afterward, he now revised his memory to recall that he found Sandusky's chest hair was "icky" and that Sandusky had lathered his back and shoulders, which "escalate[d] the uncomfortableness of it." Yet Konstas had said soon after the shower in 1998 that he had soaped himself.

Although Konstas still could not come up with any overt abuse memories, he said that after Sandusky lifted him up to wash his hair off, "it's just kind of black. . . . I don't even remember being put down. . . . I got home somehow and everything else is just blackout. I just don't remember it." It is likely that in therapy Konstas had been told that his failure to recall details indicated some kind of repressed traumatic memory. Still, McGettigan asked, "If it hadn't been for the police, would you even remember today what hap-pened in the shower?" Konstas said, truthfully, "I doubt it."

During his cross-examination, Amendola once again revealed that he couldn't hear well, asked repetitious questions, and then acted more like a prosecutor by asking, "Did he (Sandusky) have an erection?" Konstas said he didn't know because "I tried my very best not to look down."

At least Amendola explored how Konstas had remained friends with Sandusky in the ensuing years, soliciting a donation from him to help pay for a Christian mission trip to Mexico, and going to many football games together. Sandusky loaned him a car at one point. The lawyer also read a text message Konstas had sent Sandusky for Thanksgiving in 2009, saying "You are an awesome friend. Love you." In the summer of 2011, Konstas had a friendly lunch with Dottie and Jerry Sandusky. Later, Sandusky called to ask him for Dustin Struble's contact information, hoping that the Second Milers he had mentored would give him good character references—not suspecting that they would turn on him and become accusers themselves.

Dustin Struble had already testified that he and his friend Zach had discussed whether therapy was helping to uncover new memories. Konstas denied that they had discussed the Sandusky case, but Amendola did not follow up on that contradiction and possible perjury. Instead, he asked, "Do you have private counsel?" Konstas said that he had, but then asked, "Are you talking about a psychologist?" In other words, he thought the lawyer was asking him about therapy. Amendola ignored this clue. "No, no, no, legal—an attorney?" Yes, Konstas said, he had a lawyer as well.

Konstas explained that "my perceptions changed" about Jerry Sandusky and the shower incident after January 2011, when the police contacted him. "I feel violated," he said. "I've gone through a lot of emotional roller coasters since then."[20]

The next witness was Ronald Schreffler, the Penn State criminal investigator who had set up a sting operation in Konstas's home after the 1998 shower. Deb McCord, the mother, called Sandusky to ask him to come over. Schreffler and another State College policeman had hidden in the bathroom and bedroom to overhear the conversation, but when McCord said her son seemed troubled following the shower incident, Sandusky asked, "Do you want me to talk to Zach?" That didn't incriminate him, so they set up a second similar sting, during which McCord emphasized how upset she was and how her son had been acting "really weird." According to Schreffler, Sandusky then said, "I wish I could ask for forgiveness. I know I will not get it from you. I wish I were dead."

Schreffler presented the comment as an incriminating confession. The policemen did not record this conversation, so it is hearsay. Sandusky vehemently denies ever saying "I wish I were dead," but it's likely that he did say he was really sorry that Zach was acting strangely and that McCord was so upset. Even though the boy had denied during the leading interview that any kind of sexual act had occurred in the shower, Schreffler remained unconvinced. "I felt there was more that Zachary hadn't told me."

Then Schreffler described his subsequent interview with Sandusky, who denied that anything inappropriate had taken place in the shower. "He was concerned about the effect it would have on Zach as far as if he did anything to upset Zach." Given the conversations he had had with Deb McCord, such concern was natural, though Zach Konstas was *not* in fact upset by the shower, only by all the subsequent attention to it. Schreffler ended, he said, by advising Sandusky not to shower with boys any more, and he promised "he wouldn't do it again."

If Sandusky made that promise, he must not have taken it seriously, since he did continue to take showers sometimes after exercise with Second Mile boys such as Allan Myers until February 2001, as we have seen. Sandusky later said that he thought he was not supposed to shower again with Zach Konstas, because of his mother's concerns, so he didn't. But that didn't apply to other Second Mile boys.[21]

Jason Simcisko, "Victim Number 3," next took the stand, recounting that as a child he didn't get along well with his single mom because he was "in trouble all the time." When Jerry Sandusky took him under his wing, he became "like a father to me." Although Simcisko had initially told the police that Sandusky had not abused him, he now recounted how he molested him at bedtime, grabbing his penis and giving him an erection when he was twelve years old. He had not understood "what was happening," he said, because "I was a kid," but he added, "I'd obviously saw, like pornographic videos."

It was only after sex abuse attorney Andrew Shubin sought out Simcisko and became his lawyer that the young man came up with abuse memories. It is likely that Shubin sent him to repressed-memory therapy, as he did several other clients. Simcisko explained why he had then claimed abuse before the grand jury and that such claims had expanded since then. "I told some of it to the grand jury, what I recalled back then." Now he had "thought about it more. I tried to block this out of my brain for years."

As we have seen in Chapter 6, Simcisko's real problem with Sandusky was that as a boy he had felt "unconditionally loved" and accepted as part of Sandusky's extended family, and he was bitter that in later years, when Simcisko entered group homes and foster care, Sandusky lost touch with him. That is what made him "infuriated" and "enraged," not any alleged abuse.[22]

Before the lunch break, the judge discussed plans for the rest of the day. Joe Amendola, apparently trying to be funny and accommodating, promised to be quick, "unless Mr. Rominger cross-examines him. It might be little longer [then], Judge." Amendola obviously thought that his colleague took too much time, but that was apparently because Rominger was more thorough and careful.

Then they discussed a problem with the NBC audio of the Costas interview that the jury had heard, in which the question and answer about whether Sandusky was sexually attracted to children had been repeated. Judge Cleland planned to give the jury the real transcript to use instead. The judge hoped that wouldn't be grounds for requesting a mistrial. "Judge, believe me when I say the last thing I want is a mistrial," Amendola said. "Then I'm caught between a rock and a hard spot." It isn't clear what the defense attorney meant. Given his abysmal preparation and his attempt to back out of the trial just before it commenced, it would seem that he would have been delighted with the delay and chance to prepare that a mistrial would have permitted.[23]

After lunch, Anthony Sassano, an agent with the Pennsylvania Office of the Attorney General, took the stand. He was primarily a narcotics agent, but he had been assigned to the Sandusky investigation early in 2009. "It was a daunting task to try to get other victims to come forward," he testified, and "to get them to admit to having been sexually abused." Sassano claimed that Sandusky had been at it for "a long period of time. It was kept very secretive, of course." He said that "hundreds of thousands" of children were involved in the Second Mile program every year.

At that point, Judge Cleland intervened, calling Frank Fina, the assistant prosecutor who was questioning Sassano, to the bench. "Let's not blow this case at the end," he said, apparently referring to Sassano's derogatory comments about Sandusky and absurd figures. "Judge, I hear you," Fina said. Then, with the microphone turned off, he cautioned the witness about his testimony. When they resumed, Sassano explained how they had searched for Second Mile victims within an hour's radius of State College, sought the boys from the photos in *Touched*, Sandusky's book, and "canvassed quite a few janitors" to try to get them to say something. The agents pursued every lead, but "it wasn't always fruitful."

In searching Sandusky's home, Sassano had found a list of Second Mile children, with some names highlighted with an asterisk, including several of the alleged victims. He also read from Sandusky's letters to Brett Houtz, asking him to behave better and promising to "always care" about him.

During the cross-examination, Joe Amendola failed to ask Sassano how many Second Mile alums his team had interviewed who had insisted that Sandusky was a wonderful mentor and had never abused them, nor did he ask the agent to explain that he had found no pornography in Sandusky's home, office, or computer.

Then McGettigan called his final witness of the day, Sabastian Paden, "Victim Number 9," who recounted his experience as a sex slave in the Sandusky basement, which was covered in detail in Chapter 8. Paden was the only witness who claimed to have been sodomized as well as subjected to oral sex. He screamed for help, he said, to no avail. Perhaps the basement was sound-proofed, he suggested. (It wasn't.) He was kept there for three days without food. And yet, he returned there "almost every weekend," perhaps 150 times.

"Who placed his penis in your mouth and placed his penis in your butt?" McGettigan asked in his dramatic conclusion. "I won't look at him," Paden demurred. When urged, however, he pointed. "Who are you pointing at?" McGettigan asked. "Jerry," Paden murmured.[24]

After the long weekend, on Monday morning the prosecution called Paden's mother, Angella Quidetto, a bar manager who lived in a trailer park, as its final witness. She added little meaningful information. Sabastian had "a lot of stomach problems" and "behavior issues." Sandusky gave him athletic clothes and sneakers and a racquetball set, but she claimed that her son's underwear went missing, implying that Paden's claims about rectal bleeding from anal sex were true.[25] And with that, the prosecution rested.

The jury never heard about another development that had occurred on Thursday afternoon. At 3:00 p.m., at the end of Anthony Sassano's testimony, the judge declared a twenty-minute recess because of a "technical problem." He then told the lawyers that McGettigan and Fina had made a "very unusual request for an ex parte conference," meaning that they wanted to talk to the judge without the presence of the defense attorneys. "I don't know that I am in a position to reveal the substance of that right now," Cleland said, but it involved "possible new evidence." He promised that Frank Fina would call Joe Amendola that night to explain "as soon as they are able to confirm the veracity and reliability of this information." Amendola went along, saying, "Your Honor, we trust you. We trust Mr. Fina." He added: "It lets us have something exciting to look forward to, since we're not in court tomorrow."[26]

This new development turned out to be Matt Sandusky's flip, in which he went to the police with his story of having just remembered being abused by his adoptive father, as related in detail in Chapter 10. It would have a dramatic impact on the case, even though Matt would not end up testifying.

— CHAPTER 16 —

The Short Case for the Defense

ON THURSDAY night, June 14, 2012, Joe Amendola called Jerry Sandusky to tell him about Matt's allegations. As Sandusky recalled, he was "completely unstrung" and said, "I don't know whether I can go on." But Amendola eventually settled down and tried to face the new reality. After a frenetic long weekend, Amendola drove on Monday morning, June 18, from State College to the courthouse in Bellefonte, a fifteen-minute trip, with Sandusky in the front seat and his sons Jon and E. J. in the back. They were planning to testify in their father's defense. As he turned a corner, Amendola said, "I don't think any of you should testify."

Amendola feared that the prosecution could call Matt Sandusky as a rebuttal witness. Because Matt wasn't on the list of alleged victims who would testify at trial—indeed, he was on the defense's list of witnesses—the prosecution couldn't otherwise call him to the stand. Jerry Sandusky wanted desperately to testify in his own defense. "But there is so much we could say to refute Matt's testimony!" he said, pointing out that Matt had chosen to be adopted at the age of eighteen and had testified, under oath, before the grand jury, strongly asserting that his adoptive father had never abused him. No, no, Amendola said. "We don't have time, we have no time to prepare for that." And, in fact, Amendola never even reviewed Matt's grand jury testimony. Sandusky acquiesced. "Everything was in a state of chaos," Sandusky later recalled. "He was so emotional about Matt Sandusky testifying that I assumed, I believed that he knew a lot more than I did about this whole matter, and I had trusted that to him."[1]

When the trial recommenced that day, Karl Rominger presented several motions to dismiss some charges because they were too vague. "It's very difficult to defend when the charges include long periods of time without specific information about when and where they occurred," he complained. He also wanted to throw out charges related to the janitor's alleged hearsay victim and from Zachary Konstas, who claimed no sexual abuse during his 1998 shower.

Frank Fina explained why he thought all the charges should remain, citing a case in which a man was found guilty of sexual abuse for massaging teenagers' feet. "The child would remain fully clothed," Fina said, "and he would simply massage the feet of the child. The Court found in that case that that met the definition of indecent assault, that the jury could determine that he was doing that for his own sexual gratification." Thus, if the jury found that Sandusky was grooming Konstas for potential abuse, that should be sufficient.

Judge Cleland agreed, denying all of Rominger's motions.[2]

After the prosecution wrapped up with Angella Quidetto's brief testimony, the defense called Dick Anderson, a retired football coach, as its first witness. Anderson said that he had played football with Jerry Sandusky as a Penn State student in the early 1960s and then coached with him from 1973 to 1984 and again from 1990 until Sandusky retired in 1999.

Anderson recounted the busy schedule of a Penn State football coach. Other than three weeks of vacation in July, they worked long hours, as Mike McQueary had also testified. During August preseason, "you kind of live almost with the players," often from 6:00 a.m. until 11:00 p.m. Once the season began, Sundays through Wednesdays called for fifteen-hour days. Thursdays were somewhat lighter, with families eating together at the training table. Friday was either a travel day for away games or was filled with meetings. Games were on Saturdays. And then there were long scouting and recruiting trips to high schools in the off-season, plus spring training. Jerry Sandusky had to do all of that and more, because of his commitment to the Second Mile, giving speeches at fundraising banquets around Pennsylvania.

Anderson said that he considered Sandusky a close friend. Amendola then asked him whether Sandusky had a reputation for being truthful, honest, law-abiding, and nonviolent, a list of adjectives reminiscent of the Boy Scout code that Amendola would repeat *ad nauseum* to each of his character witnesses in a formulaic way that virtually guaranteed that jurors would yawn and stop paying attention. Yes, Anderson said, "Jerry had a great reputation."

In his cross-examination, Joe McGettigan proved himself a master of sly innuendo. "You would say the defendant was a driven kind of coach, right?" Anderson responded that Sandusky was indeed a committed coach. "Tireless worker, correct?" Yes. "And he would work to find time to get things done what he needed to; wouldn't you say that? . . . In fact, spent a great deal of time at the Second Mile? . . . Working with young boys?" Yes, he did, Anderson said.

McGettigan concluded by asserting that Sandusky must have been "an expert at getting inside boys' heads and motivating them and move them in the right direction; wouldn't you say that?" Anderson didn't see where the prosecutor was headed. "I don't know if we are experts in that, any of us, but we try."

The retired coach also said that he still showered frequently with young boys at the YMCA, though he didn't hug them. McGettigan persisted, asking about Sandusky bringing Second Mile kids to bowl games. "So he would take little boys in airplanes across state lines to go to bowl games at various places?" Yes, Anderson said, "with his family, as part of his family."[3]

Amendola then called Clint Mettler, a thirty-year-old Second Mile alum, to testify. Mettler had stayed overnight several times at the Sandusky home, gone to church with the family, and had gotten free football tickets from him. He later helped Sandusky with a local Second Mile fundraiser. Amendola asked Mettler if Sandusky had a reputation "for being honest, truthful, law abiding, nonviolent, a good person."[4]

That's all he asked, which took only a few minutes, as did his subsequent questioning of other supportive Second Mile alums. They were on the stand so briefly that these character witnesses made little impression. Amendola did not elicit any compelling warm memories or anecdotes that would have brought their relationship with Sandusky alive, nor did he ask them whether Sandusky had hugged them, squeezed their knees while driving, kissed them on the forehead at bedtime, or how they had felt about any such ways that Sandusky may have shown physical affection.

The next witness, Booker Brooks, was another retired college football coach who had worked at various times with Sandusky. "Jerry and I were almost like rookies of the league on the staff together," he said. "When you work with a person 14-hour days, seven days a week over years, you get to know him." Amendola went through his honest-truthful-law-abiding-nonviolent list. Yes, Brooks said, Sandusky's reputation was "exemplary, top-notch."

He, too, said he had showered with children. "Now, since I am a grandfather, I take my grandchild to the local YMCA and since she's not old enough to go into a room by herself, we go in and we shower together and I put dry clothes on her and so forth." That was it. Amendola didn't ask Brooks about Sandusky's relationship with his football players or Second Mile kids or about his marriage or children.

During cross-examination, McGettigan got Brooks to admit that he found it "puzzling" that Sandusky would hug a child in a shower. And yes, he had indeed read the damning Grand Jury Presentment but asserted that "everything that happens in the grand jury room is only one-sided." McGettigan mocked this attitude, dismissing Brooks as "basically an old friend of the defendant" who thought he was a good guy. "I think he's a great guy," Brooks answered. "Do you?" sneered McGettigan. "Thank you very much," and dismissed him.[5]

The next witness, Linda Caldwell, ran the golf program to which Sandusky referred Brett Houtz and had "no recollection whatsoever about it," so it is not clear why Amendola wasted time on her.

Then Brent Pasquenelli, a fund-raiser for the Second Mile from 2007 to 2009, said that Sandusky's office was next to his and that they took at least fifteen trips together to visit potential donors in every corner of Pennsylvania. "Jerry was a local hero," he said. Amendola asked how he would describe Sandusky's activities with kids. "I saw a mutual admiration between Second Mile youth of boys and girls with Jerry. I saw a lot of goofing around. Jerry had a very unique way, and many of us were inspired by this, how he could relate to youth of all ages and really get to their level and communicate."

McGettigan asked Pasquenelli whether he thought that "the only regret he (Sandusky) appeared to have was that it (fundraising) took him away from spending time with the children he loved to interact with so much," his sarcasm scarcely concealed. "I'm not sure," Pasquenelli said.[6]

Next up was Brett Witmer, a second-grade teacher who had worked at the Second Mile and the Centre County Youth Service Bureau as an AmeriCorps volunteer in 1999 and 2000. As part of his job, he oversaw activities at the Snow Shoe Youth Center, where Brett Houtz sometimes came after school. He knew that Sandusky and Houtz spent time together and that "Jerry certainly seemed to be an important part of his life." Sandusky would check in with Witmer periodically to see how Houtz was doing, to make sure "the kid was moving in the right direction."

Witmer recalled one particular day when Sandusky drove to Snow Shoe to pick Houtz up, but he didn't show. "You know, driving out to Snow Shoe is a pretty long distance" from State College, which he knew because that was his daily commute. Yet Sandusky didn't seem too upset and explained to Witmer that in dealing with "kids who are coming from a difficult situation, that sometimes they're not going to want to meet with you, not want to talk to you." Other times, they will want to do fun activities, so "you always have to be there for them." Witmer said he carried that lesson with him, to go "a step further . . . to make sure the best interests of kids is being served."[7]

That was the last witness for a short trial day that ended before lunch. After the jurors left, the judge and lawyers discussed other issues, including whether the grand jury testimony of former Penn State officials Gary Schultz, Tim Curley, and Graham Spanier could be used in the defense's case. Amendola and Rominger wanted to be able to cite their testimony that Sandusky had apparently been engaged only in "horseplay" in the shower when Mike McQueary overheard slapping sounds. But since they had been charged with alleged perjury for those grand jury statements, the judge said that might create a problem. He deferred a final ruling until later. Ultimately, he did not allow reference to that grand jury testimony.

DAYS SIX AND SEVEN: A BUSY WITNESS STAND

Tuesday, June 19, 2012, was a packed day in court, with nineteen witnesses taking the stand. Then on Wednesday morning, the jury heard testimony from only four more people, and that was it. The defense rested, having taken the equivalent of only two full days to present its case.

Rather than dealing with the rest of the witnesses in strict order, as we've been doing, let us first look at six more Second Mile alums, then other character witnesses such as Sandusky's friends, neighbors, and colleagues. Next, we'll examine the testimony of witnesses more central to the case—a lawyer, two police investigators, and others related to alleged Sandusky victims. Finally, we'll hear the testimony of two opposing forensic psychologists who examined Sandusky and came to different conclusions, with Dottie Sandusky's appearance as a witness tucked between them.

Three female Second Mile alums said nice things about Jerry Sandusky. Tanessa Inhoof attended the program for six years and "enjoyed every minute of it." She went to the Sandusky home for picnics with football players, played in their backyard, and spent the night a few times. "I learned to cook dinner, thanks to Dot." Amendola got her to endorse his honest-truthful litany, and that was it.[8]

Megan Rash had attended the Second Mile for four years. "It was an amazing summer every year that I went." She knew Brett Houtz as her older brother's best friend and said, "He [Houtz] was dishonest and embellished stories." But Amendola did not elicit any supporting evidence of Houtz's alleged lies.[9]

Kelli Simco was a camper at Second Mile for eight years and went on to college. "Thanks to Jerry half my tuition was paid." Yes, he was truthful, honest, peaceful, and the rest, with an "amazing" reputation.[10]

Three more male Second Milers also testified. Josh Green attended for three years and had visited the Sandusky home twenty times, spending the night there several times. Yes, Sandusky was honest, peaceful, law-abiding, nonviolent. That was it. Amendola asked no questions about bedtime at the Sandusky home, what Green had done there, or anything about possible sexual abuse. Green was on the stand for only a few minutes.[11]

Chad Rexrode was a five-year camper at Second Mile, then moved to Pittsburgh, but Jerry Sandusky kept in touch, "seeing how I was doing and just kind of making sure that, you know, everything was good, because I never had a father in my life, and he was like a father figure to me." Sandusky asked about his grades and took him to various sporting events. He stayed at the Sandusky home "many times," but Karl Rominger, who was taking a turn instead of Amendola, asked him nothing about his experience there. Instead, the defense lawyer repeated the familiar truthfulness-honesty list, which must have had jurors rolling their eyes by this point. Sandusky had a reputation, Rexrode said, for being "someone that reaches out to people and goes way out of his way."

It was Joe McGettigan, during cross-examination, who asked Rexrode in more detail about his experience at the Sandusky home and then asked if there was "anything else you recollect about your contact with the defendant," obviously fishing for something incriminating. "I just want to thank him for everything he's done for me . . . and for so many other people. That's why I'm here today."[12]

David Hilton, the last Second Miler to testify, said he had been in the Sandusky home more than fifty times, and he had also gone with Sandusky on a trip to San Francisco. "He was definitely a father figure. He's helped me out with a lot of things academic-wise [because] both of my parents are deaf. So I was always behind in school." Sandusky had bought him a membership at a local fitness center and helped him get a part-time job.

After the Sandusky scandal broke, the police came to Hilton's house three times and gave him a subpoena to force him to go to Harrisburg for another interview. By the "second or third time, like, I felt like they wanted me to say something that wasn't true. Like, they would ask me the same questions and ask it a different way to, I guess, to see if I would slip up or whatever." They clearly wanted him to say that Sandusky had abused him. "They said if I was lying that I could get in trouble and [it would be] like a felony."

McGettigan began his cross-examination by asking the twenty-one-year-old, "Mr. Hilton, how are you doing?" to which Hilton replied, "Hi. How are you doing?" McGettigan ignored him. "Are you okay?" he inquired, trying to establish that somehow he was troubled. Then he asked whether Hilton had been "a little blond guy" as an eleven-year-old when he met Sandusky. This was part of McGettigan's tactic to imply that Sandusky was particularly attracted to slightly built, blond boys.

The prosecutor then tried to discount the pressure the police had put on the boy to say that Sandusky had abused him. "Anybody handcuff you? . . . Anybody mace you? . . . Anybody give you anything to read and say, say this?" No. Well, then, "did you get the feeling somebody was trying to make you tell a lie?" Yes. "I felt like they wanted me to say something that wasn't true."

McGettigan went on to ask about Hilton's uncle, who lived in Maine and who had contacted the police to suggest they speak to his nephew, because he suspected Sandusky must have abused him. Indeed, the uncle had called Hilton to tell him he would pay for a lawyer (who would presumably seek monetary compensation for alleged abuse). Hilton declined the offer.[13]

OTHER CHARACTER WITNESSES

Amendola called seven more friends or acquaintances to say nice things about Jerry Sandusky. Given the awful stories the jurors had heard, it was unlikely that such testimony would make much difference, but it did provide more background information. Joyce Porter and her husband, who lived in State College, had fourteen children, five of whom were adopted, so they had a lot in common with Dottie and Jerry Sandusky and their six adopted children. The couples had known one another for forty years. Because Jerry was so busy with football, Joyce and Dottie spent the most time together, but sometimes their husbands would join them. As usual, Amendola asked if he had a reputation for being truthful, honest, peaceful, lawful, nonviolent. Yes, "he's a wonderful man," Porter said.

That's all Amendola asked. It was McGettigan who found out that the Porters had a son with Down Syndrome, and that Jerry and Dottie had been "very kind and wonderful" to him, taking him out to dinner and helping to celebrate his birthday. If you asked the boy "Who's the best?" he would answer, "Jerry." This son had just been selected as the best Down Syndrome representative in the United States.[14]

A neighbor, Phil Mohr, a retired Penn State microbiology professor, took the stand. He had known Sandusky for thirty-five years, attended the same church, St. Paul's United Methodist, and had played the organ at Sandusky's parents' funerals. Yes, his accused friend had a great reputation. McGettigan snidely asked about all the boys Sandusky had brought to church through the years, and that was it.[15]

Another neighbor, Jack Willenbrock, had retired from Penn State as a civil engineering professor and also attended the same church. Their children were in and out of each other's houses all the time. "Among our children, among our grandchildren, Jerry Sandusky is a father figure, and he's also respected for what he did professionally." McGettigan asked if, since the allegations arose, some opinions had changed. Yes, Willenbrock said, but "when people started talking about it, we decided that we didn't want to hear it." They were Christians and were not going to judge Sandusky.[16]

Lance Mehl came from Ohio to testify. He had been a Penn State linebacker for Sandusky in the late 1970s, then gone on to play eight years for the New York Jets. Now he was a probation officer. He had stayed in touch with Sandusky through the years, helping with the annual Second Mile golf tournament. Did Jerry have a reputation for being peaceful, honest, truthful, law-abiding, nonviolent? Yes. "We all looked up to him. He was a class act."[17]

High school guidance counselor and football coach John Wetzler, of Bellefonte, Pennsylvania, had attended Penn State football clinics and summer camp, where he usually stayed in the same dorm as Sandusky. "I never heard anyone have any negative things to say about Coach Sandusky." After the charges were filed, Wetzler called Sandusky to offer his support. McGettigan asked whether the high school counselor had ever asked Sandusky about the alleged abuse. He had not. "Just kind of took it on faith, hey, it's Jerry Sandusky, couldn't have done anything wrong?" No, Wetzler said. "My opinion was based upon what I saw from him in working with him at those camps and those clinics."[18]

A former Penn State wrestler named James Martin, now an orthopedic physician, said that he and Jerry Sandusky had become "very good friends" when he lifted weights in the same locker room area. During medical school, when he served a month-long rotation at Penn State, he stayed at the Sandusky home. Sandusky had given him a Fiesta Bowl watch and made him a photo album featuring Martin and his wife. At the end of the album, Sandusky had handwritten a corny poem he had found or made up: "Thanks for having a special touch. / Thanks for the feeling of caring so much. / Thanks for making a smile on that frown. / Thanks for being there when we were down," and so on. It was signed, "Love, Dottie, Jerry, E.J., Kara, Jeff, and Jon."

During his cross-examination, McGettigan made the point that Martin had wrestled in a low weight class and implied that Sandusky must have befriended him because he was slender, blond, and attractive. And he got Martin to say, "Jerry had a lot of Second Mile kids around him with a lot of things he did."[19]

Elaine Steinbacher, who had moved from Pennsylvania to North Carolina in 2010, testified that she had known Jerry and Dottie Sandusky for forty-seven years. As a special education teacher, "I always used him as my motivator and inspiration." Then, when she worked for Pennsylvania Migrant Education, she would bring students to Penn State and stay at the Sandusky home eight to eleven times a year.

Steinbacher happened to be there the summer day in 2009 when Brett Houtz brought his girlfriend and their infant son to visit. She contradicted Houtz's version of the visit, in which he had said that Sandusky acted strangely towards him and his girlfriend could tell something was not right. "Jerry and Dottie made a big fuss over his son," Steinbacher recalled. "I would say he stayed for two or three hours . . . It was very amicable. Just a lovely afternoon. I remember commenting to Dottie, 'Wow, you're going to see a lot of them because obviously he's looking for some foster grandparents.'" She knew how welcoming that home was. "There were always people in and out of the Sandusky home."

Steinbacher recalled talking to Jerry for four hours one day about troubled children they each worked with. "I was, like, amazed that I could talk so long to one person. I had so much in common with him, when I can't even talk to my own husband for four minutes."[20]

THE ACCIDENTAL TAPE INCIDENT

At least Amendola did explore more substantive issues involving the inadvertent tape recording the police made during a break in the interview with Brett Houtz in April 2011, which Amendola played for the jury. This tape, covered in detail in Chapter 7, featured a conversation between Houtz's civil attorney, Benjamin Andreozzi, and police investigators Scott Rossman and Joseph Leiter. It included incriminating, leading quotes from Leiter, such as, "We need you to tell us this [presumed oral sex] is what happened."

Amendola then called Andreozzi, Rossman, and Leiter to the stand, in that order. Andreozzi acknowledged that Houtz had signed a contingency fee agreement with him, so that if he represented him in a future lawsuit, he would earn a substantial percentage of any settlement. The agreement "included getting him counseling," Andreozzi said, though Amendola didn't understand its significance. "Did you ever suggest to Brett anything that he should say?" Amendola asked. "I have never suggested anything to Brett," he asserted, even though such suggestion was apparent on the tape, when Andreozzi had said, "I've got to get him. . . . It seems like we're getting a little bit more, and I was in a hurry, I only had an hour. Now we have more time." Now, on the stand, Andreozzi said that Houtz had been "extremely uncomfortable talking about this from day one." He had regarded Sandusky as a father figure, so getting him to say he was abused was not easy.[21]

Scott Rossman and Joseph Leiter had actually testified briefly a bit earlier in the day, but they were now recalled after the playing of the tape. Karl Rominger asked Rossman if he had talked to Leiter about the case after they had gotten off the stand the first time. Yes, they had, but not about their testimony. But when Leiter, who had been waiting outside, was called, he contradicted Rossman, saying they *had* conferred about their testimony in the hallway. So was Rossman lying? Judge Cleland interrupted, saying "That's for the jury to decide," dismissing the issue, even though Rossman appeared to have perjured himself.

Under cross-examination, Joe McGettigan asked Leiter, "Did you feel or were you attempting to communicate to this victim anything that you expected him to repeat, embellish, add to, or change?" No, the policeman felt that he had used "appropriate technique," even though the tape clearly showed that he *did* want Houtz to add to and embellish his abuse narrative.[22]

A NICE BIG HOUSE IN THE COUNTRY

Josh Fravel, a neighbor in the other half of the public housing duplex where Aaron Fisher and his mother Dawn Daniels lived, next took the stand. He said that he had been outside on the lawn one afternoon in late 2008, when he overheard an argument between Fisher and his mother. The teenager wanted to hang around with his friends instead of going with Sandusky. "She (Daniels) would frequently send her children off to several different places so she could have a weekend here and there."

After this argument, mother and son went inside for a while, and then Daniels came back out. According to Fravel, she came over and asked, "How do I find out if somebody is a registered sex offender?" He asked why she wanted to know. "Because I was just told that Aaron was touched by Jerry Sandusky." She was excited about the prospects of a lawsuit, Fravel said, and she exclaimed, "I'll own his (Sandusky's) house." She also said that "when this all settles out, she'll have a nice big house in the country with a fence and the dogs can roam free." Fravel said that Aaron later told him that he would buy "a nice new Jeep."

Under cross-examination, Fravel admitted that he didn't like Dawn Daniels, whom he considered a bad person and bad mother. Under pressure from McGettigan to quote her exact words, Fravel said she had told her son, "You're going to the Second Mile because you're not going to fuck up my weekend."[23]

WHAT MIKE MCQUEARY TOLD DR. DRANOV

In his brief appearance for the defense, physician Jonathan Dranov recalled the night (which we now know was probably December 29, 2000) that his friend and employee, John McQueary, had called to ask him around 9:00 p.m. to come over, because his son Mike was upset by something that had happened in a Penn State locker room. When he came in, Mike was sitting on the couch, "visibly shaken and upset." The younger McQueary said he had gone to the locker room to put away some new sneakers and "he heard what he described as sexual sounds." Dranov asked him what he meant. "Well, sexual sounds, you know what they are," McQueary said. "No, Mike, you know, what do you mean?" But he didn't explain. "He just seemed to get a little bit more upset. So I kind of left that."

McQueary told him that he looked toward the shower "and a young boy looked around. He made eye contact with the boy." Dranov asked him if the boy seemed upset or frightened, and Mc-Queary said he did not. Then, as Dranov recalled, McQueary said that "an arm reached out and pulled the boy back."

Was that all he saw? No, McQueary said "something about going back to his locker, and then he turned around and faced the shower room and a man came out, and it was Jerry Sandusky." Dranov asked McQueary three times if he had actually witnessed a sexual act. "I kept saying, 'What did you see?' and each time he (Mike) would come back to the sounds. I kept saying, 'But what did you *see?*' "And it just seemed to make him more upset, so I back[ed] off that."

Karl Rominger asked Dranov, "You're a mandatory reporter?" Yes, he was, meaning that he was legally bound to report criminal sexual activity to the police. He did not do that, since he obviously didn't conclude that it was warranted. He only told Mike McQueary to report the incident to his immediate supervisor, Joe Paterno.[24]

As a follow-up witness, a Second Mile administrator named Henry Lesch explained that he had been in charge of the annual golf tournament, in which Mike McQueary had played in June 2001 and 2003. The implication was that this seemed strange behavior, supporting an activity in which Jerry Sandusky was a leading sponsor and participant, if McQueary had witnessed sodomy in the shower.[25]

JERRY SANDUSKY'S ALLEGED PERSONALITY DISORDER

Karl Rominger called psychologist Elliot Atkins as an expert witness. By way of background, Atkins revealed that he had been a painter and sculptor but "I wasn't good enough to support myself or my family," so he got a master's in clinical psychology, followed by a doctorate in school psychology. He worked primarily with teenagers with drug problems but had also begun to testify in court cases, mostly for the defense.

Atkins had talked to Jerry Sandusky for six hours, then read his book, *Touched*, and the letters he had written to Brett Houtz. Sandusky also filled out multiple-choice answers for the Minnesota Multiphasic Personality Inventory (MMPI) and the Millon Clinical Inventory. From all of this, Atkins concluded that there was indeed something drastically wrong with Sandusky. It wasn't that he was a pedophile, but that he suffered from "histrionic personality disorder."

As Atkins explained, according to the fourth revised edition of the *Diagnostic and Statistical Manual of Mental Disorders* (*DMS-IV-TR*, 2000), people could be diagnosed with histrionic personality disorder if they displayed five or more of eight characteristics. Such people sought to be the center of attention, displayed "sexually seductive or provocative behavior," expressed shifting, shallow but extreme emotions, tried to draw attention to themselves by their physical appearance, spoke in an "excessively impressionistic" manner without detail, were dramatic and theatrical, were suggestible and easily influenced by others, and thought their relationships were more intimate than they really were.

The diagnosis was actually the direct descendent of what Sigmund Freud and others of his era labeled "hysteria," and it was mostly applied, in quite a sexist way, to women. As Atkins acknowledged, the *DSM* was undergoing revision for a fifth edition that would come out in 2013, in which histrionic personality disorder was nearly eliminated but ended up being subsumed in "Cluster B" with other dramatic, emotional personality symptoms.

A writer for *Psychology Today*, reviewing the changes in 2013, observed:

> Because of their history, their inherent difference from clinical syndromes, and a mystique that developed around many of their names (e.g. "Psychopath," "Histrionic," "Borderline"), the personality disorders were always particularly difficult to diagnose. You might be diagnosed as having Narcissistic Personality Disorder by one mental health professional, only to be told by another that you were actually Histrionic. . . . In the process of revising the DSM-IV-TR, the personality disorders panel developed a number of alternative models to get away from the categorical diagnostic system. The most extreme was to dispense with the named categorical diagnoses entirely. However, this idea was dispensed relatively early in the process because many commentators, viewing the information on the DSM-5 website, believed that the categories had inherent value. The DSM-5.0 Work Group members then proposed a compromise in which six would be retained.[26]

In short, the *DSM* is a political as well as psychiatric document, subject to the opinions and compromises of psychologists who are often unscientific and swayed by cultural norms. Many critics have made this observation. For instance, homosexuality was considered a mental disorder until 1980.[27]

What is astonishing is that Amendola and Rominger thought it would help Sandusky's defense to assert that he was mentally ill with some kind of personality disorder, thus implicitly endorsing Brett Houtz's characterization of Sandusky's writings to him as "creepy love letters" rather than an understandable attempt to reach out and get Houtz to behave better. As an indication of his lawyers' lack of communication with their own client, Sandusky had only a vague idea of what Atkins was going to say, and he was appalled as he sat in the courtroom and heard himself characterized this way. "I assumed that Dr. Atkins would be supporting me," he later said, "would be giving documentation and information that I wasn't a pedophile . . . that I wasn't the monster that I was made out to be. That's what I assumed."

As he sat in the courtroom, next to defense investigator Lindsay Kowalski, "I became extremely upset, emotional," Sandusky remembered later. He whispered urgently to her, "This isn't me! This isn't the person I am." Kowalski had to calm him down and keep him quiet.[28]

In fact, in contrast to what Atkins testified, Sandusky didn't usually seek to be the center of attention. He didn't behave in a flirtatious, sexual way. His emotions didn't shift quickly, and as we have seen, he impressed many friends and colleagues as being self-effacing and genuinely caring. Atkins said that people with histrionic personality disorder "may have difficulty achieving emotional intimacy" and "often have impaired relationships," but Sandusky had a long, successful marriage and career and many close friends.

Atkins admitted that "the field of psychology is not at the state of science where we can be confident that our diagnoses are accurate. There's a lot of subjectivity." The MMPI test did *not* identify Sandusky as having any personality disorders, though the shorter Millon test gave some such indication, mostly because Sandusky's answers appeared to be "defensive"—hardly surprising for someone accused of being a pedophile.

Prosecutors Joe McGettigan and Frank Fina were delighted with Atkins's testimony. "It's opened the door," McGettigan said in a sidebar conversation with the judge, since now he could call his own expert and look for an alternative diagnosis involving pedophilia. "That has not only opened the door," Fina said. "This has obliterated the door. There is no more door. This has gone directly into the issue of his broader behavior, including his sexual behavior."

In his cross-examination of Atkins, McGettigan pointed out that Sandusky had no previous psychiatric treatment or diagnosis. "A need for attention, approval, respect, admiration, and intimacy," McGettigan said, listing some characteristics the psychologist had given for those with histrionic personality disorders. "That sounds like a lot of people, doesn't it?" Indeed it did, Atkins admitted, adding, "I have a need for every one of those things."

McGettigan bored in. "Some elements that you found that you say underlie this histrionic personality disorder also underlie a psychosexual disorder, isn't that correct?" Pinned down, Atkins replied, "Anything is possible. This [diagnosis of histrionic personality disorder] does not preclude any other diagnosis." But he said that in Sandusky's case, there was "no clear diagnosis of a psychosexual disorder," because Sandusky denied those behaviors. "If, in fact, the things that he is accused of are true, *then* he would have a psychosexual disorder." Clearly squirming on the witness stand, Atkins added, "I found nothing to support that that's the case."

But didn't the psychological tests indicate that Sandusky tried to minimize problems and to "conceal an element of himself?" Atkins answered evasively. "I wouldn't say it exactly like that." Didn't the tests reveal that it was important for Sandusky to appear virtuous? Yes.

Under redirect questioning by Rominger, Atkins dug himself further into a hole. "If we all identified with seven or eight of [the characteristics listed in the *DSM-IV-TR*], we may have a histrionic personality disorder. I come pretty close. I really do."

When Rominger asked about the letters to Houtz, Atkins said, "His behavior [in writing the letters] was inappropriate. His behavior was not typical behavior for someone his age. His behavior caused him to be viewed with suspicion at different points in his life. It led to where he is right now." The expert witness for the defense had turned into a complete disaster. He further asserted that Sandusky's ability to "sustain normal adult relationships was limited."[29]

THE DEVOTED DOTTIE

Immediately afterwards, Dottie Sandusky, who had been sitting in back of the courtroom listening to this testimony, was called to the stand. Atkins had just declared her husband incapable of having good, long-term relationships, when they had been married for forty-five years. It was a solid marriage, she said, but as a football coach, "he was not around a lot." She verified what Dick Anderson had said about a coach's busy schedule. Still, "Jerry always came home for dinner . . . but he would go upstairs and work after that." Yes, he brought Second Mile kids to the house, and sometimes they slept overnight. And after he retired, his work schedule didn't lighten up. "He just became more involved in the Second Mile," fund-raising, speaking, and mentoring.

Dottie acknowledged that she was sometimes called Sarge. "I'm strict and I like for things to run a certain way, and we expect a lot of our kids." Amendola asked if she knew the various accusers. She did, but she only vaguely recalled Michael Kajak, and she had no idea who Ryan Rittmeyer was. She didn't go down to the basement much, other than to get food out of the freezer, but no, the basement wasn't sound-proofed.

She had never seen any inappropriate behavior between her husband and any child and was confident that he was innocent. She remembered the last dinner they had with Zach Konstas in 2011 at a Cracker Barrel. "We talked about . . . how his life was changing because of his values and the Bible school that he was going to [and] his mission trip that he had taken," which they had helped to fund. She also remembered the day Brett Houtz came over with his girlfriend and baby. "It was good to see him and, you know, think he had gotten his life together and things were going really well for him." When he was younger, Dottie recalled Houtz as "very demanding and he was very conniving. He wanted his way and . . . didn't listen a whole lot."

She said that Aaron Fisher was "very clingy to Jerry. Aaron would never look people in the eye." But she really liked Dustin Struble, who was "very nice." Sabastian Paden was "a charmer. He knew what to say, when to say it."

Amendola failed to ask her about her feelings for her husband, about their sex life, or about what she thought about his spending all that time with Second Mile kids. Then, when McGettigan cross-examined her, he asked, "Can you think of any reason why any of . . . those boys, those young men, or Mike McQueary would lie about anything?" Disastrously, she answered, "I don't know what it would be for." McGettigan hastily dismissed her. "I have nothing further, Your Honor." [30]

THE PROSECUTION'S EXPERT

McGettigan then called psychiatrist John O'Brien in rebuttal to Elliot Atkins. O'Brien said that the two tests Atkins had administered to Sandusky showed a tendency for Sandusky to "portray himself in overly positive terms," but that was understandable, since "the outcome of the trial could be very damaging to Mr. Sandusky and he's aware of that."

O'Brien didn't think Sandusky had a personality disorder that caused him any distress or impairment. "I spent . . . three hours with Mr. Sandusky on Sunday, and I didn't detect any distress in him whatsoever other than pertaining to this circumstance." The retired coach had been "extremely high functioning over the years." Indeed, O'Brien was far kinder to Sandusky than the defense's psychological expert. "He was a very committed worker. He was a committed father. He took time out on a nightly basis to have dinner with his family. He was an individual who kept all the balls in the air." Nothing indicated a personality disorder that caused him problems.

Far from needing to be the center of attention, Sandusky had been content to remain on the sidelines as an assistant coach while head coach Joe Paterno got all the glory. Nothing about Sandusky's childhood indicated that he was developing histrionic personality disorder. "What he talks about . . . is the selfless commitment that his parents had to the recreation center and their commitment to kids, to the disabled, and to developing and maintaining a program for kids who had very little else. That's a far cry, almost a polar opposite, to someone who's histrionic." In creating the Second Mile program, Sandusky was "fulfilling a desire to follow in his parents' footsteps and give back and to give to others."

O'Brien didn't think the letters to Houtz were so terrible. They were written "to reflect disappointment and emotional upset." Yes, Sandusky expressed personal hurt, but he also referred to "other football players, other people that the recipient has known. . . . There's all these people here that are interested in you."

The psychiatrist did think that the letters were written "in a very adolescent way," conveying "this illusion that Sandusky and the child are on the same plain." O'Brien considered them "highly manipulative" in the sense that they were trying to sway Houtz to behave better. "I don't see them as anything more than that."

McGettigan asked the psychiatrist how he and other psychological experts arrived at a diagnosis. "You are basically looking for information to support your conclusion," he answered, perhaps inadvertently revealing that such confirmation bias was all too common in his profession.

O'Brien said that the evidence could point to "another diagnosis being present," but it took McGettigan's leading question to name it, asking if that could be "a psychosexual disorder with a focus on adolescents or preadolescents." Yes, O'Brien said. But he added, "you're considering evidence that hasn't [yet] been proven." In other words, he could make such a diagnosis *after* Sandusky was convicted, a form of circular logic that didn't seem to bother him.[31]

A STAB TO THE HEART OF THE DEFENSE

The jury was dismissed late on Wednesday morning, with instructions to come back the next day for closing arguments. The lawyers retired to the judge's chambers, where they discussed Amendola's decision not to call Jerry Sandusky to the stand to defend himself, despite Amendola's repeated references to his imminent appearance. When Matt Sandusky flipped mid-trial to accuse his father of abuse, it was "so nuclear to his defense," Amendola said, that "from that point on we were very concerned whether or not Mr. Sandusky could testify."

McGettigan initially agreed not to call Matt Sandusky but reserved the right to call him as a rebuttal witness if Jerry Sandusky testified. Then the prosecutor promised not to call Matt even if his adoptive father did testify, but he could still question the defendant about his son's accusations. After discussions with his client, Amendola decided that he couldn't risk calling him to the stand, which "took the heart out of our defense," he said, "because our defense was going to be Mr. Sandusky testifying." Not only that, "Matt Sandusky had been a part of our defense and actually had told us he would testify for his dad." He had also planned to call three other Sandusky sons to testify, but he couldn't do that now, since that, too, could trigger Matt's appearance.

Amendola then asked for a mistrial (though he had previously stated that the last thing he wanted was a mistrial), based on this untenable situation, along with the botched Costas interview tape, in which one part had been repeated. To no one's surprise, Judge Cleland denied the request.[32]

— CHAPTER 17 —

Guilty

"HOW COULD eight individuals and other individuals, like Mike McQueary and the janitor who you heard from last week, how could they all come into court and say these awful things happened if they didn't happen?" asked Joe Amendola to introduce his closing argument the morning of Thursday, June 21, 2012. Having posed such a damning question, he failed to answer it.

"Over a 14-year period, from 1994 to 2008, [there were] allegations, hundreds of times these kids say, 'He did this to me. He did that to me,'" Amendola continued, driving nails further into Sandusky's coffin. Finally, he offered the lame defense that "there is absolutely no direct evidence" for the abuse, other than these multiple accusations. Many of the alleged victims knew one another, he pointed out. Also, "if you believed their testimony, [Sandusky] was a very busy man. How in the world did he work?"

Before he went on, Amendola stressed that "what I recollect from the testimony of folks—I think there's over 50 witnesses—doesn't matter. If your recollection of the facts is different from mine . . . it's your recollection of the facts that count." He went on to repeat this assertion like a mantra throughout his rambling hour and twenty minute closing statement, serving to undermine himself still further by implying that he didn't really know the facts of the case very well.

He soon proved this to be so, saying that Aaron Fisher had at first said that "Mr. Sandusky fondled me above the clothes." Fisher did *not* initially say that Sandusky had "fondled" him, only that he had cracked his back when they were both fully clothed. Amendola did note that therapist Mike Gillum "kept prompting Aaron," which made it even more appalling that he never called Gillum to the stand.

"Over time, did you see Mr. Sandusky? He's not a lawyer," Amendola inexplicably stated. Yes, the jurors saw him sitting in the courtroom, but they didn't hear him testify. "I have told him a number of times. I told him he used stupid judgment. He wanted to fight that." Telling a jury that your client used "stupid judgment" without explaining exactly what you're talking about is not perhaps the best strategy. Maybe Amendola meant that Sandusky shouldn't have showered with teens, or that he was wrong to insist on maintaining his innocence rather than seeking a plea bargain.

By June of 2009, when the first grand jury convened, "they only had two victims," Aaron Fisher and Zach Konstas. Amendola should have said *alleged* victims, and in fact Fisher was the only person claiming sexual abuse at that point. "After the case went public through the media, other people came forward," he said. This statement implied that when others heard about the alleged abuse, they spontaneously came forward, but that was not true except for Ryan Rittmeyer and Sabastian Paden, who made their abuse claims after the Grand Jury Presentment was sensationally released. Until then, the police and civil lawyers had to seek out Second Mile alums and induce them to say that they were abused, sometimes with the help of repressed memory therapy.

Amendola went over various witnesses, including Megan Rash, who had said Brett Houtz had a reputation for dishonesty. "Again, it's your recollection that counts, not mine," he added gratuitously.

He emphasized that there was a financial motive for the abuse claims, through contingency fee agreements with civil attorneys. Then he bumblingly undercut himself again: "Everyone says, well, okay. They can have lawyers. I understand that, but Mr. Sandusky can still be guilty. So the financial part of it doesn't make sense. We can buy that."

The police searched for more victims, he said, including contacting the Second Mile kids in the photographs in *Touched*. All right, he said, "Let's assume they went out, they talked to these kids, and the kids said, 'Oh, my God, yes, Jerry did abuse me.' That could be, that could be." But that is *not* what happened, as we have seen. Most Second Milers denied that Sandusky had abused them, at least initially, and the vast majority never succumbed to police pressure. Amendola urged jurors to use their common sense. "Jerry Sandusky took these kids everywhere. Is that what a pedophile does?" Well, yes, that could very well be what a pedophile does.

Amendola went on and on. He talked about Gus instead of Bob Costas before correcting himself. He repeated the horrible Costas interview nearly verbatim, then said, "Folks, what more could that man say? He went on national TV with a guy who probably was every bit as tough as Mr. McGettigan." This non-sequitur must have raised the question in the jurors' mind: If Sandusky didn't mind standing up to tough questions, why didn't he testify?

"Jerry is a monster. Such a monster, why didn't you arrest him in 2008? Take him off the streets?" Of course, that's exactly what many people were asking themselves. "If you believe what happened to these other kids after that, if you believe that, then you have to believe there's responsibility elsewhere. I submit that this stuff didn't happen." It was anyone's guess what Amendola was trying to say, or why he thought this would convince anyone that "this stuff didn't happen."

The defense attorney went over the 2001 shower incident, saying that Mike McQueary could have called the police instead of his father. "They get the young boy. They get Jerry Sandusky. Case over. They figure out what happened." It sounded as if Amendola thought his client was guilty. He failed to point out that McQueary had changed his story and memory, that he had not told Dranov and his father that he saw Sandusky in the shower with the boy, only that he had heard slapping sounds. Instead, "I submit to you he saw something," but it wasn't really sodomy.

During part of his talk, Amendola clearly relished the notoriety of the Sandusky case and how he, a small-town lawyer, had been catapulted into the spotlight. "This has gone international, folks. This isn't Centre County. This isn't Pennsylvania. This isn't eastern United States. This is international." Later, he said, "Think about this. He's arrested. This is going global . . ."

Amendola eventually realized he couldn't take up the entire morning. "You heard from Chad Rexrode—and before I forget because I'm running out of time. Before I forget. Did Zach Konstas who's Accuser No. 6—he's the one from 1998. . . . And you heard from Ron Schreffler and his opinion was he would have prosecuted. That's fine."

It is painful to read Amendola's closing argument, but it must have been truly confusing for a juror who tried to listen to it. He did go on to make the point that Konstas had continued to have a friendly relationship with Sandusky for many years following the 1998 shower incident. "What did he tell you about when he started thinking this was inappropriate? After all these years? I think— again your recollection counts, not mine. But I think he's the one who also said he had sent Mr. Sandusky text messages. . . . 'I'm so thankful you are in my life.' Does that sound like a victim?"

He went over the janitor's story briefly, complaining that it was hearsay testimony. Then, as he wound down, he said, "Nobody wins in this case. This is awful no matter what happens. This is awful if Jerry Sandusky did this, and I'll be the first to tell you if he did this, he should rot in jail for the rest of his life. That's my feeling."

Lamely, he then added, "But what if he didn't do it?" but his heart didn't appear to be in it. "He's touchy. He's feely. He's sensitive. He loves kids," Amendola said. Then, at Sandusky's request, he read "Do It Anyway," a poem by Mother Teresa, with lines such as "Forgive them anyway" and "Be kind anyway." Amendola concluded by saying, "My heart is heavy. I'm sure your hearts are heavy, but thank you very much for your attention."[1]

THE DENYING PEDOPHILE AND HIS VICTIM POOL

Joe McGettigan began his closing argument for the prosecution by mocking what he called the defense's "conspiracy theory." Were police investigators Scott Rossman and Joe Leiter conspiring to get Brett Houtz and other victims to make false allegations? No! The troopers "weren't the best witnesses in the world," McGettigan admitted, but they were merely "trying to find out what was true." Yes, Leiter was "really looking to make something out of this case," but it was an admirable thing to tell Houtz, "You're not alone."

The police had not used leading methods; more victims were "uncovered by thorough and reasonable investigation." Nor were the civil lawyers and other accusing Second Mile alums part of some grand conspiracy. "Well, if you conclude there's a conspiracy," McGettigan said, "somebody bring in handcuffs for me and Mr. Fina and everyone involved in this. . . . Bring us all along and lock up the lawyers and lock up some victims because you always have to accuse the victims."

McGettigan acknowledged that the alleged victims' stories shifted and grew over time, and that it was hard to pin down exact days or even years that the abuse had occurred. "This is not a discussion and argument that is susceptible to real close and linear organization." Nor was it a surprise that none of the victims had given any hint of their abuse until Aaron Fisher's therapy sessions with Mike Gillum. "Humiliation and shame and fear and what they equal is silence."

The prosecutor said, "I'm not wrenching your heart strings," then proceeded to do just that. "They were boys," he said, throwing up his enlarged photos again. "It's what happened to those boys. [And] you know what? Not just those boys, [it happened] to others unknown to us, to others presently known [only] to God but not to us, but we know what the defendant did to them because adults saw them and adults told you about them."

He was referring to the testimony of Mike McQueary and janitor Ron Petrosky. His claim that only God knew the identity of the boy in the McGettigan shower incident wasn't true, though. McGettigan knew that this boy was Allan Myers, who had insisted that no abuse had taken place—at least, he had done so before becoming a client of civil lawyer Andrew Shubin. But the jury had no way of knowing this fact. Even though McGettigan himself knew the identity of Allan Myers, he went on to hammer at Sandusky for failing to name him during the Bob Costas interview. "He had the complete capacity to exonerate himself at the time and just say who was there [in the shower with him] . . . Why not remember the name of the little boy you're soaping and just being innocently cleansing to? But he didn't provide that name to anybody, ever, certainly not to Bob Costas, no. He forgot that."

That assertion was not true, since Sandusky had told his lawyers that Allan Myers was the boy in the shower, and Myers had said the same thing. Not only that, but McGettigan came very close to saying that Sandusky could have testified at the trial but didn't. That would have abrogated Sandusky's legal right to remain silent without an implication of guilt.

"That's the person who did it, the defendant, sitting right there," McGettigan said, pointing at Sandusky. "This case is about *him* and what he did to them."

Sure, the victims' memories seemed to change. "You see younger people who come up and are affected in different ways. Their recollective capacities are not as great. Sometimes, because of age even, their perception of things isn't even that great." That's why Zach Konstas "didn't know what was happening" in the 1998 shower incident. He didn't identify it as grooming for abuse. And Aaron Fisher had "difficulty in speaking because of the emotional response."

McGettigan never used the term "repressed memory," but he alluded to the supposed phenomenon. "Oh, yeah, the conspiracy, but think about the capacities and the abilities of each of the witnesses as they try to tell you something that they tried to bury; that they had, in fact, buried."

Then McGettigan denigrated the defense witnesses. Retired coach Booker Brooks, for instance—"Did he say he showered with his granddaughter? Is that what he said?" The prosecutor implied that Sandusky really *had* molested Chad Rexrode, David Hilton, and James Martin, who had come forward to defend Sandusky. They were, he told the jurors, "little blondies" when Sandusky met them. "Did you notice his demeanor on the witness stand, Mr. Rexrode? . . . When I asked him if he had anything more to tell us, he said he had been to the defendant's house fifty times."

And David Hilton, whose parents were deaf, and who had such nice things to say about Sandusky? This wasn't a case of Sandusky caring for troubled kids. "He was preying on those that were most vulnerable—kid with the deaf parents, the kid with the parents who didn't speak English, never knew their fathers." Sure, Sandusky may have done some good for such children, but "does that give you a dispensation from being a molester?"

Oh yes, McGettigan said sarcastically in describing pedophiles. "They *love* children. Children respond positively to them. They would never do anything that would cause harm to a child. . . . They would never make a child do anything the child doesn't want to do. They have a special relationship with children. They're always around them."

That's the rationalization pedophiles make, McGettigan said. "That's what's known as the denying pedophile . . . Love children . . . Want to be around them all the time. Why not? They're a victim pool. They are a victim pool."

And that is how he described Sandusky—"a serial predatory pedophile gliding through the victim pool to select the most vulnerable, the weakest, those most in need of a father figure at the expense of the child, the child who's looking for a father figure, a mentor, indecently assaulted, anally raped, orally raped, abused." Just look at those photos of the boys. "You see some of the looks on their faces sometimes reveal more pain than you can imagine."*[2]

McGettigan wrapped up his closing argument with a dramatic, poetic image. "I've been doing this a long time. I tried a lot of murder cases." After so many cases, he needed a break because he felt that he had "too many souls in my pocket," lives that were gone. "And now I feel like I have eight—no, not eight, ten, pieces of ten

---

* One of the methods that repressed memory therapists frequently used to get people to believe that they had repressed memories of sexual abuse was to tell people to examine their childhood pictures closely for signs of abuse. This proved to be remarkably successful, because once you have the idea that there may be hidden signs of abuse in a child's photo, it is easy to find evidence.

souls in my pocket, pieces of childhoods ravaged, boys' memories destroyed, incinerated by this pedophile."[3]

THE JURY REACHES A VERDICT

Judge John Cleland charged the twelve jurors before sending them off just after 1:00 p.m. to deliberate. He noted that the trial had been much shorter than he had anticipated "due to the professionalism and organization of counsel." In fact, it was short because of the terrible job Amendola had done, lodging few objections, questioning his own witnesses inadequately, and failing to call others who could have helped.

Before the closing arguments, Cleland had given a legal lecture to the jurors, which normally would have occurred just prior to the charge to the jury. The defense wanted the judge to tell them that "failure to make prompt complaint" was an issue in the case, but Cleland refused, because "in my view the research is such that in cases involving child sexual abuse delayed reporting is not unusual and, therefore, is not an accurate indicia of honesty and may be misleading." He later admitted that he could cite no such research, but that was his impression from "handling child sexual abuse cases in a variety of contexts."[4]

During his legal lecture, he gave a garbled instruction about assessing Sandusky's character witnesses. "Evidence of good character may by itself raise a reasonable doubt of guilt and require a verdict of not guilty," he said. "However, if on the evidence you are not satisfied beyond a reasonable doubt he is guilty, you should find—that he is guilty, you should find him guilty." Cleland had probably intended to say, "If you are not satisfied beyond a reasonable doubt he is guilty, you should find him *not* guilty." But he left out that crucial second "not," so that he said precisely the opposite of what he meant.[5]

By the time they adjourned to make a decision, the jurors had probably forgotten all about such technicalities anyway, having just heard McGettigan's stirring argument. During their deliberations, the jurors sent a note asking for a list describing each exhibit, then another asking: "What distinctions are there between repeated counts of involuntary deviate sexual intercourse for a single victim?" Cleland commented that the confusion apparently arose because the first charge for Victim 1 (Aaron Fisher) was for Sandusky allegedly performing oral sex on Fisher, and the second identical charge was for Sandusky forcing Fisher to fellate him.

Indeed, the four dozen charges covering ten alleged victims were all redundant variants of this sort of thing, as Judge Cleland had explained earlier to the jurors. "Involuntary deviate sexual intercourse" meant oral or anal sex with a child over twelve but under sixteen. "Indecent assault of a child" involved "indecent contact" with a child less than thirteen years old. "Unlawful contact with a minor" meant intentionally contacting a minor (in person, print, or electronically) for the purpose of committing sexual offenses. "Corruption of minors" meant harming the morals of a child through sexual contact. "Endangering the welfare of a child" meant that Sandusky had been someone caring for a child and knowingly abusing him.

Finally, "attempted indecent assault on a child" could cover grooming activity. "A person may be found guilty of attempting to commit a crime," the judge said, "even if the crime is not actually committed." So if the jury concluded that he *intended* to molest Zach Konstas, that was enough to find him guilty. And if they found Sandusky guilty of these other crimes, they could also find him guilty of abusing the Phantom Victim of the janitor's story. "You must be satisfied that there is other evidence that supports that a crime had been committed besides Mr. Calhoun's hearsay statement," the judge advised. That could include circumstantial evidence, which Cleland likened to seeing deer tracks in the snow without actually seeing a deer.

At 5:00 p.m., the jurors requested a list of victim birthdays, but Cleland refused, saying that "the law does not permit me to provide a summary of any information—any evidence testified to." At 7:40 p.m., Cleland got a note: "We wish to review the testimony of Mike McQueary and of John Dranov." The judge summoned the jury and suggested they retire to the sequestered Holiday Inn for the night.

The next morning, Friday, June 22, 2012, before the jury was brought in, Cleland noted that the news about Matt Sandusky's new allegations had been leaked and was all over the news, so "last night I instructed the deputy sheriffs to assure that newspapers were removed from the racks in the jury's hotel. Televisions had been disconnected, as have telephones," and jurors were not allowed to have cell phones or laptops.

Then, with the jury as an audience, Frank Fina played the role of Mike McQueary, reading his two hours of testimony, followed by Joe Amendola reading the brief testimony of Jonathan Dranov.

Cleland received several more jury queries. At 2:45 p.m., they wanted to hear again what the judge had said about circumstantial evidence and deer tracks, so he read it aloud again. During the jury deliberations Joe Amendola gave an interview saying that if Sandusky were found not guilty, he would have a heart attack—an unbelievable statement for a defense attorney to make. Amendola later defended this statement, saying, "At that point it didn't matter anymore. The jury was not in the room." But his statement certainly conveyed an unfortunate message to the media and the public.[6]

Finally, at 9:53 p.m., the jury reached a verdict. Jerry Sandusky stood to listen as the foreman read off "guilty" for forty-five of the forty-eighty counts against him. The only three for which he was found not guilty involved the alleged sodomy in the shower, since Mike McQueary hadn't actually claimed to witness the act, only the "slow, subtle movement" of Sandusky's midsection, as well as two "indecent assault" accusations for Zachary Konstas and Michal Kajak, though Sandusky was found guilty of other charges for them, such as "unlawful contact with minors" and "endangering welfare of children."

"Mr. Sandusky, you have been found guilty by a jury of your peers," Judge Cleland announced. Sentencing would take place within ninety days. Until then, Amendola requested that his client be allowed in-home detention, but the judge refused, and Sandusky was taken in handcuffs to the Centre County Correctional Facility.[7]

Outside the courthouse at 10:30 p.m., Pennsylvania Attorney General Linda Kelly stood before a cheering, whistling crowd, giving a triumphant press conference in which she said that this was a historic moment, "capturing the attention of the eyes of the world, mesmerizing us until it plays itself out and its stardom begins to fade. . . . The eyes of the world have since then (since the Grand Jury Presentment) been upon us." The attorney general praised the accusers for their persistence, digging for memories they had evidently forgotten when they first spoke to authorities. "It was incredibly difficult for some of them to unearth long-buried memories of the shocking abuse they suffered at the hands of this defendant."[8]

Joe Amendola also gave a press conference outside the courthouse, where he managed to inflict further harm on his own client. "We always felt that Jerry's fairest shake would come from a Centre County jury, and we still believe that," he said. Was the guilty verdict a surprise? "No, it was the expected outcome because of the overwhelming amount of evidence against Jerry Sandusky." He praised McGettigan and Fina for handling the case "in an exemplary manner. They are professionals. They presented their case in solid fashion. We congratulate them." Judge Cleland had been "marvelous . . . the ultimate jurist," fair, firm, and reasonable. "The only disagreement we had was our request for a continuance. . . . We believe he did an outstanding job."

Just afterwards, in a remote televised interview with reporter Anderson Cooper of CNN, Amendola was practically giddy to be on the show, grinning broadly and commenting about Cooper's associate, "Come on, Anderson, he knows I love you." What was next? "Tomorrow, I gather my wits and we start thinking about sentencing because that's the next step." He emphasized that Sandusky claimed to be innocent, but he hedged on whether he, Amendola, really believed his client: "For better or worse, none of us were there when any of these things happened, but he always maintained he was innocent." When Cooper thanked Amendola for speaking with him, the lawyer fawned, "Any time, Anderson, I watch you all the time." As one reporter observed, "He was glowing. The 64-year-old [lawyer] had just lost the most notorious and high-profile case he'd ever snagged, and he was beaming."[9]

Three days later, two jurors explained to CNN reporter Soledad O'Brien what had persuaded them that Jerry Sandusky was guilty. Joshua Harper, a young high school science teacher who was chosen as the jury foreman, said, "I didn't see anything in the victims that would lead me to think that they were not credible"—an astonishing observation, given the ever-shifting nature of much of their testimony, from initial denial of abuse, with many saying that Sandusky was a mentor and friend, to incrementally "unearthed" abuse memories and then fully formed narratives of oral sex and rape. Harper said that he had watched Sandusky's face and posture carefully during the trial. "I took a look at Sandusky while he was watching the victims testify, and it seemed to be that he was kind of reminiscing of the victims. . . . He would kind of lean in towards them and pick his chin up a little and just kind of like he was thinking about the victims and his behavior with them." He found that "a little creepy."

Harper's observation is a classic example of confirmation bias, in which his opinion of what he saw was influenced by what he had been led to believe. Sandusky may very well have been "reminiscing" about all the time he had spent trying to help these young men, and how he had once regarded them as members of his extended family.

The second juror, Ann van Kuren, said that she was influenced by the fact that Sandusky didn't testify. "We had to see all the victims and witnesses on the stand and tell their stories. It would have been nice for Jerry Sandusky to be on that stand as well and go through that same interview." She found the victims' testimonies to be "very compelling" and said that "there were moments when some of the jurors, including myself, would leave the courtroom for recess and have to deal with some very strong feelings."

Harper was impressed with the victims' consistency. "We saw a common thread throughout what was happening to all the victims." The inconsistency within each of the victim's stories apparently didn't register with him, nor did the testimony of the Second Mile alums who said that Sandusky had been a mentor and had never abused them. Harper was particularly swayed by the testimony involving the two unidentified victims. "Michael McQueary's testimony and Ron Petrosky, the janitor, his testimony, because they weren't victims themselves and so I didn't feel they had a reason to lie. So if they observed this behavior from Sandusky, then you know, he was capable of these things, so that gave more credibility" to the other testimony.

It is alarming that Harper apparently thought that Petrosky said he had witnessed oral sex in the shower, when it was secondhand hearsay from Jim Calhoun, who never testified, and whose taped interview, saying that Jerry Sandusky was *not* the man he saw in the shower, was never entered into evidence.[10]

SENTENCING

The day before his sentencing hearing, which took place on October 9, 2012, Jerry Sandusky released a jailhouse audio tape that was played on CNN and other media outlets. In introducing it on CNN, reporter Anderson Cooper said that at the forthcoming hearing, "there will be no expressions of remorse for recruiting, grooming, and ultimately raping all those boys," because Sandusky wouldn't take responsibility for any abuse. On the tape, Sandusky said: "They can take away my life, they can make me out as a monster, they can treat me as a monster, but they can't take away my heart. In my heart, I know I did not do these alleged disgusting acts."[11]

The next day, Sandusky was brought from jail in handcuffs, wearing a red jumpsuit, to the sentencing hearing. Joe McGettigan submitted a report by psychologist Robert Stein, a member of the Pennsylvania Sexual Offenders Assessment Board, stating that Sandusky was a "sexually violent predator." Then McGettigan let loose, complaining that in his tape the previous day, Sandusky had "defamed his victims once again, victimized them yet again, calling them liars." Sandusky's statement was "an insult to common sense and to human decency." He was "the most insidious and depraved of criminals," McGettigan asserted. What appeared to be a successful career as a football coach and founder of a charity was "just disguise, a cloak for his real life of rampant degradation of children." The Second Mile was just a "victim factory."

The prosecutor's invective continued. "His depravity spread across the spectrum of human behavior from touching and washing to massaging and kissing to genital grabbing and finally to oral and anal penetration." And after all that, Sandusky just discarded his victims. And now "he goes on the radio and whines of his own pain." Just look at him sitting there in the courtroom! "He smirks at those he defiles." The accusers who were there "wish never to see the face of their victimizer again, and I will not blame." He didn't want to have to "ask for one more tortured word from those boys," even though the young men sitting in court were not boys.

Joe Amendola had to speak in the wake of this excoriating hellfire sermon. It was a "sad day," he noted, regardless of which side you were on. He hoped Judge Cleland would take into account the letters that Sandusky's supportive children had written, recalling family outings and unconditional love. As an organization, there was no question that the Second Mile had helped thousands of needy children, some of whom had testified about the positive impact Sandusky had had on their lives. Amendola then essentially admitted his client's guilt by asserting that these good deeds were part of "another side to Mr. Sandusky." He hoped that such "mitigating circumstances" would induce the judge to be as lenient as possible, despite the mandatory minimum sentence of ten years for some offenses.*

Then Joe McGettigan took the floor again to read two statements. The first had purportedly been written by Aaron Fisher, "Victim 1," though it is likely that his therapist, Mike Gillum, actually composed it. Fisher was present in the courtroom but didn't want to read it himself. So McGettigan read of "ultimate betrayal and disgusting deeds" that had "humiliated me beyond description" and left Fisher with deep wounds. "My psychologist describes it as post-traumatic stress disorder which involves intense and chronic anxiety, conversion disorder, and depression." This left him with "memories I don't want to remember."

McGettigan followed with a letter from Angella Quidetto, the mother of Sabastian Paden, "Victim 9." She blamed all of her son's

---

* In 2013, the following year, Pennsylvania's mandatory minimum sentences were struck down as unconstitutional.

problems on Sandusky. "He lost weight, was sick a lot, didn't sleep, was getting in trouble at school, had strange behaviors." Because of Sandusky, she wrote, she had to move three times in one year and had to quit her job. "How embarrassing for me as a mother to know something so disgusting happened to my son." She appeared to be full of more self-pity than worry over the alleged abuse. "You have caused me to have so many problems both as a mother and a person," she complained. "My son and I are both in therapy likely for years, for the rest of our lives."

Zachary Konstas followed with his own statement about his 1998 shower with Sandusky. Though he had never managed to remember any sexual abuse, he had now reinterpreted this shower so that it had assumed a monumental, negative significance. "My personality changed for the worse and I became somewhat of a social outcast," he asserted, because of this shower. "I have been left with deep, painful wounds that you caused and had been buried in the garden of my heart for many years." He felt violated. "But through the storm, I have cried out to Jesus for help, relied on the Holy Spirit for comfort, and have now begun my journey to healing and recovery."

"Victim 5," Michal Kajak, spoke next about how Sandusky had once "lured" him into a shower and forced the boy to touch him. "This behavior to be called horseplay, it was [only] later in life that I realized that it was sexual assault," he said. "I am troubled by flashbacks of his naked body, something that will never be erased from my memory," Kajak added, lapsing into therapy-speak. "I continue to be haunted by the incident and [it] has forever negatively altered my life. For years, I have been struggling with anxiety, posttraumatic stress disorder, depression, nightmares and sleeplessness, embarrassment, and guilt."

Then Kajak revealed that Sandusky was "a man who I trusted, respected, and admired." It was a shock when he learned that his mentor had molested other boys, which apparently made him reinterpret his own experience. Kajak concluded with a statement familiar to anyone who has studied sex abuse stereotypes. "He took away my childhood the day he assaulted me" during that single shower.

Brett Houtz, "Victim 4," was the last accuser to speak. As the star victim who had alleged that Sandusky had subjected him to oral sex and attempted sodomy, he was oddly subdued compared to the others. "You were supposed to be teaching me things like honor, respect, and accountability," Houtz said. "Instead, you did terrible things." (As we have seen, Sandusky *did* try to teach Houtz precisely those virtues, without success.) "Because of you, I trust no one, and I will not allow my own child out of my sight."

Finally, Jerry Sandusky stood to speak, denying that he had molested anyone and saying that he was full of emotion and determination. He had spent his time in jail trying to find some purpose in what had happened. "Maybe it will help others. Some vulnerable children, who may have been abused, might not be as a result of all the publicity, but I'm not sure about it." He hoped that "some way something good will come out of this."

It had been painful for him to hear these young men make these false allegations, which they apparently truly believed. "These are people I cared about and still do. I used to think of ways to praise them, to help them, to have fun, improve their self-esteem."

He spoke of his life in prison, where he was kept in solitary confinement. "I meditate, read, write, exercise, eat, all in that small room." Sometimes other inmates screamed. He longed to be with Dottie. "My wife has been my only sex partner in life, and that was after marriage. . . . Our love has continued."

The hardest thing for him was pondering the future. "I think about not being with her (Dottie), not being there for our children, not being there to see our grandchildren mature." It would mean "helping people less, laughing less, maybe crying a little more." He said that he tried to get through, in part, by remembering all the good times in his life. "I see loved ones carrying the light. I see family and friends. I see those who overcame huge obstacles. I see all the people who thrived with just a little of our help and a little of our hope." Despite the allegations of child abuse, "I see me throwing thousands of kids up in the air, hundreds of water balloon battles, happy times, people laughing with us, maybe at us sometimes." He apparently referred to himself in the plural.

Sandusky quoted from a supportive letter from a Second Mile alum. "You have impacted my life in so many ways. You were my lifeline. . . . In my eyes, you are Touchdown Jer. I remember staying at your home and how good it was and how good you and your family were to me."

Sandusky said that he loved underdogs who never gave up. "I have been comfortable with black, white, brown, yellow, young, old, large, small, whatever, gifted or handicapped, mentally or physically." He remembered visiting Second Milers who landed in prison, "and now I stay in one." He had been in ghettoes and trailer parks to seek out Second Mile kids. "I have been to many celebrations and weddings, graduations of Second Mile success stories."

He struggled to find meaning in what was happening to him. "Today is a difficult day. I'm being labeled and sentenced." To prepare himself, he had been reading books about people who had endured extreme suffering and persecution. "They certainly put my struggles in perspective. No way have I reached the level they reached."

He had a card in his room that had the word *Hope* on it. "I cling to that card." He was determined to endure. "I have always smiled through the pain." It was that smile that prosecutors, jurors, and accusers had taken as a smirk.

In looking back at his life, Sandusky said, "I have been blessed. I have been to the mountain top. I have seen the valley of the shadow of death. I have been in a locker room hugging and crying out of joy as national champs. I have been in a locker room crying with devastation after a very difficult loss." Now he was in another contest that he compared to being down in the fourth quarter of a football game. "It's like all the suffering it takes to win an athletic contest. This experience helps you realize how temporary life is and we're just briefly passing through."

In conclusion, Sandusky said, "It would be unmanageable without God's light and without God's hope and love."

Then Judge John Cleland spoke to Sandusky. "It cannot be disputed that you have done much positive work in your community, in your church, not only for Second Mile but for other organizations as well." But "you abused the trust of those who trusted you." His crime wasn't just what he had done to boys' bodies. "Your crime is also your assault to their psyches and to their souls." Sandusky had stolen their innocence. "Their lives have been irrevocably altered."

Cleland said that this case should serve as a lesson to communities to be more vigilant. "Where pedophiles are concerned, it is very often the case, as you were, that they are trusted community figures." In other words, Sandusky's prominence was considered as further evidence of his guilt. "It is this remarkable ability to deceive that makes these crimes so heinous."

Cleland then sentenced the sixty-eight-year-old Jerry Sandusky to thirty to sixty years in prison, observing: "That has the unmistakable impact of saying very clearly for the rest of your life."[12] The next day, Penn State revoked Sandusky's right to collect his pension of $59,000 a year.[13]

— CHAPTER 18 —

Piling on the Vitriol

THE CONVICTION of Jerry Sandusky as a serial child molester had enormous repercussions that would ultimately lead to an estimated $1 billion flowing as a direct result of the case, in addition to changed regulations and laws, political maneuvers, numerous related lawsuits, impacted lives, and a spate of books, documentaries, and reports. A week after the guilty verdict, Governor Tom Corbett signed a hastily (and unanimously) passed bill to allow sex abuse "experts" to testify in trials to explain why delayed and incremental disclosures of abuse were admissible and normal, despite a lack of extensive research to indicate that this was true. It essentially allowed trauma theorists to tell jurors that, despite repressed memory therapy and leading police interviews, they should believe allegations, even though alleged victims initially denied that abuse had occurred and the allegations grew over time like mushrooms.[1]

Paterno, a biography by Joe Posnanski, had been in the works before the scandal erupted, but of course it included material on it when it was published in August 2012. Hard on its heels came *Silent No More: Victim 1's Fight for Justice Against Jerry Sandusky*, ghostwritten by Stephanie Gertler in the names of Aaron Fisher, his mother, and therapist Mike Gillum. In 2014, Jay Paterno would publish *Paterno Legacy: Enduring Lessons from the Life and Death of My Father*, and Sylvia Kurtz wrote her stereotypical effort, *To Believe a Kid: Understanding the Jerry Sandusky Case and Child Sexual Abuse*. In 2016, Matt Sandusky chimed in with *Undaunted: Breaking My Silence to Overcome the Trauma of Child Sexual Abuse*, and Ronald Smith published *Wounded Lions: Joe Paterno, Jerry Sandusky, and the Crises in Penn State Athletics*.

Two documentaries covered the case. *365 Days: A Year in Happy Valley* was released at the end of 2013. "Our film explores how individuals [in State College] came together to grapple with unresolved issues in the wake of the Sandusky crimes," the director said. "It looks at the crimes' reverberations in this small, high profile community." Nearly a year later, the *Happy Valley* film featured Matt Sandusky as a self-proclaimed victim.

In 2017 HBO announced that Barry Levinson (*Rain Man; Wag the Dog*) would direct a made-for-TV movie about the Sandusky scandal, starring Al Pacino as Joe Paterno—perfect casting for the abuse narrative.[2]

These books and films presented various viewpoints on the Penn State scandal and on Joe Paterno's involvement. But they all shared one unvarying presumption: Jerry Sandusky was a pedophile, a sexual predator, a monster.

THE FREEH REPORT AND ITS ALLEGATIONS

One more document had a huge impact on the case in the aftermath of the guilty verdict. On July 12, 2012, former FBI director Louis Freeh issued his long-awaited report on his law firm's investigation of the case, for which he charged Penn State $6.5 million. Its official title was *Report of the Special Investigative Counsel Regarding the Actions of The Pennsylvania State University Related to the Child Sexual Abuse Committed by Gerald A. Sandusky,* but it was universally called the Freeh Report.

After his investigative team had conducted over 400 interviews and analyzed over 3.5 million pieces of electronic data and documents, Freeh came to a scathing conclusion: "The most saddening finding by the Special Investigative Counsel is the total and consistent disregard by the most senior leaders at Penn State for the safety and welfare of Sandusky's child victims." The report vilified Graham Spanier, Gary Schultz, Tim Curley, and Joe Paterno, who "failed to protect against a child sexual predator harming children for over a decade."[3] Freeh accused them of concealing Sandusky's activities from the Penn State Board of Trustees and the authorities.

The most compelling new evidence Freeh's investigators had uncovered were emails between Spanier, Curley, and Schultz during the 1998 and 2001 shower incidents, as well as handwritten confidential notes Schultz had kept. "Behavior – at best inappropriate @ worst sexual improprieties," Schultz had scribbled on May 4, 1998, the day after Sandusky's shower with Zachary Konstas. "Is this opening of pandora's box? Other children?" Once that case had been investigated, however, with both Konstas and Sandusky insisting that no sexual abuse had taken place and with no charges brought, on June 9, 1998, Schultz emailed Curley and Spanier, saying that Sandusky had been "a little emotional and expressed concern as to how this might have adversely affected the child. I think the matter has been appropriately investigated and I hope it is now behind us."

Then came Mike McQueary's reports in December 2000 and February 2001 that he had overheard what he thought were sexual sounds in the Penn State locker room and that Jerry Sandusky and a young boy had been in the shower. Recalling the 1998 shower incident, Schultz was alarmed. In his notes on February 12, 2001, he wrote, "Unless he (Sandusky) 'confesses' to having a problem, TMC (Curley) will indicate we need to have DPW (Department of Public Welfare) review the matter as an independent agency concerned w child welfare."

Tim Curley was charged with informing Jack Raykovitz, the Second Mile chairman, about the incident and with contacting the Department of Public Welfare, but it bothered him that no one had even talked to Sandusky about what had happened in the shower or asked for his version of the event. After talking it over with Joe Paterno, Curley emailed Schultz and Spanier on February 27, 2001: "I am having trouble with going to everyone, but [except] the person involved. I plan to tell him we are aware of the first situation [the 1998 shower]." He wanted to tell Sandusky that "we feel there is a problem" and offer to help him get "professional help." If Sandusky was cooperative, they would talk to the Second Mile together and might not need to go to the Department of Public Welfare. "Additionally, I will let him know that his guests [Second Mile boys] are not permitted to use our facilities."

Spanier, the Penn State president, emailed back to agree that the approach Curley suggested was "humane and a reasonable way to proceed." But he added, "The only downside for us is if the message isn't 'heard' and acted upon, and we then become vulnerable for not having reported it. But that can be assessed down the road." Schultz agreed that this was a "more humane and upfront way to handle this" and that they could "play it by ear to decide about the other organization [i.e., whether to inform the Department of Public Welfare]."

On March 5, 2001, Tim Curley met with Jerry Sandusky and explained that someone had reported him for showering with a boy about a few months ago. At first, Sandusky couldn't recall what he was talking about, which makes sense if the shower took place on December 29, 2000. But then he remembered the exercise session and shower with Allan Myers and called Curley a few days later to say he *did* remember it, so they met again. There is no record of these conversations, but Curley apparently did not identify Mike McQueary as the complainant, nor did he indicate that McQueary had witnessed sexual abuse.

Curley and Sandusky had known each other since Curley played football at Penn State in the 1970s. Despite the strong wording in his email, saying that he would tell Sandusky "we feel there is a problem," and that he should seek "professional help," it does not appear that Curley told Sandusky that he had a "problem" and might be attracted to boys. Curley later testified that "I thought Jerry had a boundary issue, judgment issue that needed to be addressed."[4] They discussed the shower incident, and Curley did say that showering with boys wasn't a good idea. Had Sandusky spoken to anyone about it? Sandusky explained that he had just been slap boxing or snapping towels playfully in the shower and that it was no big deal, but he agreed to talk to psychologist Jack Raykovitz, the head of Second Mile.*[5]

When I asked Sandusky about this crucial conversation, he wrote back: "My memory is likely not perfect, but I don't think Tim had anybody in mind as a therapist and didn't come across ever in a way to make me think I had a problem."[6]

Sandusky knew that it had been Allan Myers in the shower and asked Curley if he would like to know his identity or wanted to talk to him. Curley, convinced that nothing serious had occurred, said that wasn't necessary. Still, he emphasized that the administrators were uncomfortable about the incident and that Sandusky must stop bringing Second Mile students to Penn State athletic facilities.

And there the matter was left, until the police came to talk to Mike McQueary in 2010. No one reported the matter to any child protective agency or the Board of Trustees. Jack Raykovitz, the head of Second Mile, concluded it was a "non-incident" and didn't think it was serious enough to talk to his board about either.

Spanier, Curley, Schultz, and Paterno were called to testify before the grand jury after McQueary gave his revised version of what he had seen in the shower. None of them appeared to take the allegations all that seriously. McQueary had not told them that he witnessed sodomy or any explicit sexual abuse, for that matter. They explained that they thought Sandusky was "horsing around" with a boy in the shower.

---

* Sandusky subsequently did speak to Raykovitz, who advised him to wear swim trunks in any future showers with kids.

It wasn't until November 5, 2011, when the Grand Jury Presentation was published, that they realized the extent of the case against Sandusky, and by then it was too late. Curley and Schultz were indicted for alleged perjury during their grand jury testimony. Five days later, Spanier and Paterno were fired.

Joe Paterno was apparently busy coaching and didn't do email, since he wasn't included in the email chain about either the 1998 or the 2001 showers. On May 5, 1998, two days after Sandusky showered with Konstas, Tim Curley wrote an email to Gary Schultz and Graham Spanier with the subject heading, "Joe Paterno," saying "I have touched base with the coach. Keep us posted. Thanks." Eight days later, Curley emailed Schultz, asking "Anything new in this department? Coach is anxious to know where it stands." He was apparently referring to Paterno rather than Sandusky, so the head coach was aware of the 1998 shower incident, even though he wasn't actively involved with it.

In 2001, after McQueary told him about the shower incident, Paterno reported it to his boss, Tim Curley, as he should have done. In his grand jury testimony in January 2011, Paterno didn't recall the 1998 shower incident. "I do not know of anything else that Jerry would be involved in of that nature, no." That isn't surprising, since he apparently knew of it only peripherally. Also, by the time he spoke to the grand jury, he was eighty-four years old, and the event had taken place thirteen years ago and had not led to any charges.

During his grand jury testimony, Paterno *did* remember Mike McQueary coming to see him on the Saturday morning of February 10, 2001, and telling him of his concern that Sandusky had been in the shower with a boy and that he had thought that something of a "sexual nature" had taken place. "I'm not sure exactly what it was," he said. Then Paterno said McQueary told him that Sandusky had been "fondling, whatever you might call it—I'm not sure what the term would be—a young boy in the showers."[7]

Louis Freeh pounced on this use of the word "fondling," and in his speech on the day his report was released, he quoted Paterno's saying that he had told McQueary, "You did what you had to do. It is my job now to figure out what we want to do." Freeh sneered at this. "Why would anyone have to figure out what had to be done in these circumstances?" He also faulted Paterno for delaying his reporting the alleged abuse to Tim Curley because he did not "want to interfere" with his weekend. (In fact, Paterno misremembered, since he did report it on Sunday.) Freeh at least gave Paterno credit for saying, on the day he got fired on November 9, 2011, "With the benefit of hindsight I wish I had done more." But he lambasted the deceased coach for "callous and shocking disregard for child victims."

But Freeh's damning report, apparently so well-researched, deliberately left out crucial information. Freeh ignored a 110-page report by John Snedden, a special agent for the Federal Investigation Service, which was completed on May 8, 2012. When Graham Spanier was fired as the Penn State president, he had a top-secret national security clearance, since he had helped the FBI, CIA, and Department of Defense with university liaisons. Consequently, Snedden was dispatched to State College to conduct a six-month investigation. After interviewing many Penn State officials, including Spanier, Curley, and Schultz, Snedden concluded that there had been no cover-up, because there had been nothing to cover up. McQueary had not observed or reported sexual abuse in 2000 or 2001. Snedden found that Spanier had been an outstanding, compassionate, moral, trustworthy leader and recommended that he keep his security clearance, which he did.

The federal investigator concluded that Curley and Schultz were indicted as part of a strategy to prevent their testimony during the Sandusky trial. "I sat with them for hours, talking to them under oath," Snedden recalled. "There was no indication that they had been given information by McQueary that Sandusky was a pedophile."

Snedden's deep background check revealed that Spanier's father was a Holocaust survivor who had physically abused him, which led to his study of sociology and child psychology. Spanier played racquetball and enjoyed kayaking and white-water rafting. He played the musical washboard, was an amateur magician, held a commercial pilot's license, and liked writing movie reviews. He had traveled extensively on university business to Europe, Asia, Latin America, and the Middle East.

The federal investigator concluded that Governor Tom Corbett, who had a seat on the Penn State Board of Trustees, despised Spanier because the university president had fought bitterly, publicly, and successfully to prevent severe budget cuts that Corbett had tried to impose earlier in 2011. The Sandusky scandal provided an opportunity for Corbett, who for the first time took an active role as a board member and pushed for Spanier's ouster. "The whole case was a political hit job," Snedden said later.*[8]

---

* The FBI also conducted extensive interviews with Second Mile personnel in 2012 and found no evidence of molestation or a cover-up.

Spanier told Louis Freeh about Snedden's report, but Freeh wasn't interested. He didn't try to access any information about it, nor did he mention it or Spanier's renewed security clearance in his own report. Indeed, anyone reading the Freeh Report would think that Graham Spanier was a deceitful, conniving, authoritarian leader who deliberately hid evidence of child sexual abuse. "If your goal in an investigation is to determine the facts of the case," Snedden later said, "you do that. You gather any and all facts and you evaluate them. I can't imagine why Louis Freeh ignored my report. Apparently it didn't fit the narrative he was going for."[9]

Freeh must have had access to the police interviews with Allan Myers and Myers's statement to Curtis Everhart that he was "Victim 2" and that he and Sandusky had been snapping towels in the shower, not engaging in sex. Freeh also must have read Jonathan Dranov's testimony about what Mike McQueary told him the night of the shower incident, which made it clear that McQueary had heard slapping sounds but had not actually witnessed any sexual activity. Yet none of this information appeared in the Freeh Report, and Freeh didn't even interview McQueary.

As already documented in Chapters 1 and 12, Mike McQueary's memory changed over the decade that intervened between the 2001 shower incident and his testimony, and his memory continued to evolve even then. It isn't necessary to believe that he was lying when he now remembered seeing Sandusky standing behind the boy in the shower, moving his hips. Eyewitness testimony is notoriously unreliable, especially when it is the recall of long-ago events and the memory has been influenced by current circumstances and attitudes. With rehearsal, false memories become as "real" as memories for actual events. What greater influence could there be than the police assurance that Sandusky was a serial child molester?

What Louis Freeh did not point out in his report was that the 2000 shower incident came down to one man's current version of events—Mike McQueary's—versus at least six other men—Jonathan Dranov, John McQueary, Joe Paterno, Tim Curley, Gary Schultz, and Graham Spanier—who all concluded, based on what McQueary reported at the time, that Sandusky had been "horsing around" in the shower with a Second Mile boy and that it may have been inappropriate but was not criminal.

It is inconceivable that McQueary told his father and Dr. Jonathan Dranov, then Paterno, Curley, and Schultz, that he had witnessed overt sexual abuse and that those men, as well as Spanier, wouldn't have turned the matter over to the police and child protective services. Joe Paterno was notorious for his straight-laced integrity. His unfortunate use of the term "fondling" in his grand jury testimony was his old man's guess, influenced by the current allegations, of what McQueary may have said. Paterno clarified, "I knew some kind of inappropriate action was being taken by Jerry Sandusky with a youngster." When the university lawyer, Cynthia Baldwin, had asked Paterno about the incident, he told her, according to her notes, that McQueary "saw Jerry horsing around with the kid."*[10]

When biographer Joe Posnanski asked Paterno, near the end of his life, whether he had ever heard any rumors that Sandusky was a pedophile, he said, "Absolutely not." When told that critics thought that he had allowed children to be molested in order to protect his own legacy, Paterno said, "They really think that if I knew someone was hurting kids, I wouldn't stop it? Don't they know me? Don't they know what my life has been about?"[11]

As Tim Curley testified before the grand jury, McQueary did not tell him anything about having witnessed sexual abuse. "I can't recall the specific conversation with Mike and exactly how he said it. My recollection was that Mike could hear there were people in . . . the shower area, that they were horsing around, that they were playful, and that it just did not feel appropriate." When asked whether McQueary had told him he had witnessed anal intercourse, Curley was appalled. "Absolutely not! That? He did not tell me that."[12]

All of the administrators, right up to the president of the university, would have been immoral to disregard such sexual abuse, and they would have been idiotic to have done so, because the truth was bound to come out eventually. They also had no reason to cover up abuse by Sandusky, who no longer worked for the university at that point.

Instead, as Gary Schultz testified before the grand jury, he thought Sandusky had engaged in "wrestling around activity" and that Sandusky perhaps had accidentally "grabbed the young boy's genitals or something of that sort." In fact, he was just speculating. McQueary had not seen or reported any such activity. He had only seen a boy peak around the corner, and a man's arm had pulled him back. That's all, according to Dranov's testimony.

Schultz explained why he thought that some sort of inadvertent genital contact might have occurred: "Jerry was the kind of guy

---

* Cynthia Baldwin, the university lawyer, initially represented and advised Spanier, Schultz, Curley, and Paterno during their grand jury testimony, but later she said that she did *not* represent them individually, so she felt free to testify against them.

that he regularly kind of like physically wrestled people. He would punch you in the arm. He would slap you on the back. He would grab you and get you in a headlock, etc. That was a fairly common clowning around thing." He concluded that McQueary's "allegations came across as not that serious. . . . We had no indication a crime had occurred."[13]

Graham Spanier had written in an email: "The only downside for us is if the message isn't 'heard' and acted upon, and we then become vulnerable for not having reported it. But that can be assessed down the road." If he were referring to a case of known sexual abuse, that comment from the university president would be sinister and unforgivable. But that wasn't the situation. Spanier was talking about Sandusky's showering with boys, not having sex with them. The message he wanted Sandusky to hear was that he couldn't bring boys to the Penn State showers any more.

On the advice of their lawyers, Curley and Schultz refused to speak to Freeh's investigative team, but Graham Spanier did. He explained that Curley communicated in "code" in sensitive emails because the Athletic Department was notorious for leaks.*[14] That's why Sandusky was referred to as the "subject" or the "person involved," while the Second Mile was "his organization" and the Department of Public Welfare was "the other organization." It certainly did appear that they were trying to hide something, though.

Spanier explained that he was concerned that Sandusky's shower with a boy "doesn't look good. I was concerned with what people will think, the visibility and the public relations aspects of it. I was not concerned with criminality. There was no suggestion of anything about abuse or sexual contact."

The ex-president didn't recall the 1998 incident, even though he had been copied into a few emails about it. He did remember the 2001 events well, however. He remembered asking two questions. "Are you sure that is how it was described to you, as horsing around?" Yes, Curley and Schultz had answered. "Are you sure that that is all that was reported?" Yes. They had all agreed that they were "uncomfortable with such a situation, that it was inappropriate, and that we did not want it to happen again." But there had been "no mention of anything abusive, sexual, or criminal."

Likewise, when Tim Curley wrote that Sandusky should admit that he had a problem and should seek professional help for it, he

---

* In subsequent testimony, Tim Curley confirmed that he used vague language because the athletic department was "rumor mill central."

wasn't referring to Sandusky being a pedophile, but to him romping with boys in the shower. He thought that this sort of juvenile behavior by a fifty-seven-year-old man was inappropriate. Yet after he talked to Sandusky about the incident, Curley's concerns were apparently allayed. Sandusky explained what had happened that night with Allan Myers and offered to identify him and let Curley talk to him, but Curley didn't think that was necessary.

In retrospect, given the snowball of allegations, it is clear that Curley should have said, "Yes, Jerry, I'd like to talk to that boy. Who is he, and how do I find him?" That would probably have prevented the cascade of events that culminated with the trial, conviction, and the Freeh Report.

The Freeh Report not only condemned the Penn State administrators but concluded that football-as-religion was at fault. "A culture of reverence for the football program . . . is ingrained at all levels of the campus community," he wrote. He claimed that there was an overemphasis on "The Penn State Way" and a resistance to seeking outside perspectives, along with a "lack of emphasis on values and ethics-based action." Given Joe Paterno's emphasis on precisely those values, this was another smear of the coach's reputation. "It is up to the entire University community—students, faculty, staff, alumni, the Board, and the administration—to undertake a thorough and honest review of its culture," the Freeh Report concluded.*[15]

IN THE WAKE OF THE FREEH REPORT

The reaction to the issuance of the former FBI director's report was dramatic and swift. "The Freeh Report was a very sad, sobering read," Penn State President Rodney Erickson said. "But we're taking accountability for it, and we're going to make sure that we put the processes, policies and practices in place so that something like this will never happen again at Penn State."

Scott Paterno, the lawyer son of the maligned coach, spoke for the family in defending JoePa while assuming Sandusky's guilt. "I

---

* Ironically, just four days after the Freeh Report was released, news broke that Louis Freeh himself was accused of a "massive cover-up" during his tenure as FBI director from 1993 to 2001, when he allegedly suppressed an investigation of flawed FBI forensic evidence that put innocent people behind bars. According to an ex-FBI whistleblower, "This man (Freeh) has no conscience and he is accusing Penn State managers of not taking any steps. He ought to be ashamed." As FBI director, Freeh had overseen the false allegations against Richard Jewell for the 1996 bomb during the Atlanta Olympics and for the disastrous attack on the Branch Davidian compound in Waco, Texas.

know my father did not know Jerry was a pedophile and did not suspect he was a pedophile," Paterno said, insisting that his father's legacy would be preserved, despite the scandal. "This is a tragedy, not because it's harming my father or his legacy, but because Jerry Sandusky was somehow able to do this for so long," Scott Paterno said, trying to tread the tightrope of condemning Sandusky while defending his father. "I understand why the public feels the way it does. . . . [but] I honestly believe that it was a situation where people who thought they were doing the right thing made mistakes."[16]

The Paterno family watched in dismay as a small airplane flew over State College on July 17, 2012, dragging a banner that read: "Take down the statue or we will." Four days later, the seven-foot statue of Joe Paterno was indeed removed from its honored place outside Beaver Stadium. The Paterno family objected: "Tearing down the statue . . . does not serve the victims of Jerry Sandusky's horrible crimes or help heal the Penn State Community." Scott Paterno noted "that Joe Paterno has never had a hearing; that his legal counsel has never been able to interview key witnesses, [and] that there has never been an opportunity to review critical evidence which has not been made public." He concluded that "selective evidence and the opinion of Mr. Freeh is treated as the equivalent of a fair trial."[17]

On July 23, 2012, in response to the Freeh Report, the National Collegiate Athletic Association (NCAA) announced extraordinarily severe sanctions against Penn State's football program. It imposed a $60 million fine, banned Penn State from the next four bowl games (depriving the university of about $13 million in conference bowl revenue), and put the team on five-year probation. In addition, Penn State had to create an anonymous hotline for reporting violations, and all student athletes and athletics employees had to complete an annual training course on integrity and ethics.

The kicker was that the NCAA retrospectively revoked Penn State's 112 football wins between 1998 and 2011, from the date of the shower incident with Zachary Konstas to the issuance of the Grand Jury Presentment. This was an egregiously unfair sanction, punishing the entire football team for thirteen years because of an unproven allegation against a formerly beloved coach. It meant that the deceased Joe Paterno was summarily toppled from his perch as the winningest college football coach in history to twelfth on the list.

The NCAA had made no investigation but relied solely on the Freeh Report in making its decision. Even though Penn State could have appealed the NCAA ruling, University President Rodney Erickson immediately signed a consent agreement and announced that the $60 million fine would fund a special endowment to pay for programs for the detection, prevention, and treatment of child abuse. Erickson announced that this "can never reduce the pain suffered by victims, but will help provide them hope and healing."[18]

The infuriated Paterno family issued another statement. While everyone agreed that sexual abuse was "reprehensible," that had nothing to do with JoePa. "The release of the Freeh Report has triggered an avalanche of vitriol, condemnation and posthumous punishment on Joe Paterno. The NCAA has now become the latest party to accept the report as the final word on the Sandusky scandal. The sanctions announced by the NCAA today defame the legacy and contributions of a great coach and educator without any input from our family or those who knew him best."[19]*[20] In an attempt to counter the influence of the Freeh Report, Scott Paterno commissioned reports from two experts on pedophiles.

THE DEMISE OF THE SECOND MILE

In his report, Louis Freeh called out the Second Mile CEO and two of its trustees for concluding that the 2001 Sandusky shower was a "non-incident for the Second Mile and that there was no need to do anything further."[21] The Freeh Report hammered the last coffin nail into the once-thriving Second Mile charity, which had helped so many disadvantaged children, because it was perceived as serving primarily as a hunting ground for Sandusky, the sexual predator. In an article in the *New Yorker* published on September 24, 2012, Malcolm Gladwell put the liberal intellectual stamp of approval on this concept. "We now know what Sandusky was really doing with the Second Mile," Gladwell wrote. "He was setting up a pipeline of young troubled boys. . . . Here was a man who built a sophisticated, multimillion-dollar, fully integrated grooming operation, outsourcing to child-care professionals the task of locating vulnerable children—all the while playing the role of lovable goofball."[22]

Jack Raykovitz, the child psychologist who had run the Second Mile from its inception, had quit in November 2011 after the Grand

---

* In January 2015, the NCAA finally restored the Paterno football victories, but the Paterno family continued its 2013 lawsuit against the NCAA, which asserted that "the NCAA has no authority to investigate or impose sanctions on member institutions for criminal matters unrelated to athletic competition at the collegiate level." But the Paternos eventually dropped the lawsuit in 2017.

Jury Presentment was published, and his wife, Katherine Geno-vese, left in the first round of layoffs, when donations to Second Mile evaporated. New Second Mile CEO David Woodle had hired former Philadelphia district attorney Lynne Abraham to conduct an internal investigation, but as the charity entered free fall, Abraham's team shifted to planning for some kind of future, ending up with a recommendation to shift Second Mile assets to Arrow Ministries, a Texas-based charity looking to expand to Pennsylvania.[23]

In a petition to the court, the Second Mile administrators wrote: "As a result of the Sandusky disclosures, donations to The Second Mile virtually ceased." The sad document noted that the statewide organization sponsored "nine different programs that reach more than 100,000 Pennsylvania children annually, with over 6,000 individuals receiving direct services," including the summer camps, a mentoring program to connect college students with needy kids, and a program to support foster families—all for free, and all grinding to a halt.[24]

Still, the Second Mile camp limped along in the summer of 2012, serving two hundred children. Alarmed that Second Mile money might slip out of their grasp, civil lawyers for alleged victims objected to the transfer of assets to Arrow Ministries, so that shift was put on hold. David Woodle said that this stay would "limit further stress on victims." Employing the stereotypical therapy-speak that had now become standard fare in dealing with the Sandusky scandal, he added: "Since the beginning of this tragedy, my objective has been to be a part of the healing process and given the circumstances, I believe this action is an important step toward that goal."[25]

MCQUEARY AND SPANIER LAWSUITS

As 2012 ground to an end, two more lawsuits spun off from the Sandusky fiasco. In October, Mike McQueary, who had lost his football coaching job as a result of his allegations about Sandusky's 2000 shower, filed a $4 million whistleblower suit against Penn State. During his trial testimony, he had said, "Frankly, I want to be a football coach at Penn State University. . . . I don't think I've done anything wrong to lose that job." He suffered for having done nothing to stop the alleged abuse in the shower, as a sportswriter observed: "He's a villain to some in his hometown, ostracized from old friends, the lawsuit alleges, going broke . . . and served up as a scapegoat piñata for every aggrieved party in this scandal—from apologist writers to desperate defense attorneys to Penn State fans bitter over NCAA sanctions."

McQueary's lawsuit claimed that when Graham Spanier expressed his "unconditional support" for Tim Curley and Gary Schultz, that implied that McQueary was a liar, which ruined his career and reputation.[26]

Meanwhile, Spanier came out swinging against the Freeh Report's attack on him. "Sadly it is now apparent that Judge Freeh was not an independent investigator . . . but a self-appointed accuser who in his zeal to protect victims from a monster . . . recklessly created new victims of his own," Spanier's lawyer said on August 22, 2012. "Among those, a dead man who couldn't respond, two under indictment who couldn't respond, and a former university president who welcomes the opportunity to respond."[27]

In a nearly two-hour interview on ABC News on August 22, 2012, Spanier denied any wrongdoing. He said he didn't recall the 1998 shower incident.

> I remember almost nothing about that. I wasn't involved in meetings or discussions. I have no specific recollection of it. I understand now that there was an email I was copied on, one of about 30,000 a year that I didn't respond to, just a piece of information saying someone was being interviewed, and a follow up email about five weeks later, saying the matter had been concluded. So my exposure to that was very tangential.

He reiterated that all he knew about the 2001 McQueary report was that it involved Sandusky horsing around with a boy in a shower. Spanier didn't know Sandusky, having had only one conversation with him, but he assumed that he was guilty. "He was a child predator who fooled a lot of people. He fooled the parents, he fooled teachers, he fooled his colleagues who were coaches." Spanier emphasized: "Never in my time as president of Penn State did I ever once receive a report from anyone that suggested that Jerry Sandusky was involved in any child abuse, in any sexual abuse, or in any criminal act. And it should be unthinkable to anyone who knows me and how I operate that I would ever turn my back on the welfare of a child." Spanier's father had physically abused him as a child, he said, which is one reason he studied the sociology of children, youth, and families.[28]

Nonetheless, on November 1, 2012, Graham Spanier was charged with conspiracy, obstruction, endangering the welfare of children, and perjury. At the same time, charges against Tim Curley and Gary Schultz were escalated from perjury and failure to report a crime to felony obstruction, endangerment, and conspiracy. In making the announcement, Pennsylvania Attorney General Linda Kelly asserted that there had been a decade-long cover-up. "This is not a mistake, an oversight, or a misjudgment," she said. "This was a conspiracy of silence by top officials at Penn State, working to actively conceal the truth, with total disregard to the suffering of children."

The three former Penn State administrators now faced potential prison time, though their trial date would be pushed down the road for years, in contrast to the rushed Sandusky trial.[29]

PENN STATE'S PAY-OUTS

On November 4, 2012, the anniversary of the leaked Grand Jury Presentment, Sara Ganim wrote a long article looking back on the eventful year. It was her valedictory summation, since she was moving to a new job at CNN in Atlanta. "The ramifications of the case have been far-reaching," Ganim wrote, "but one year later we had the first idea of how many victims might be out there when Penn State lawyers said they have been contacted by more than 20 men who say they were abused by Sandusky." The Penn State lawyers said they were looking at each case, and that the number of claimants might grow. "Since last November, at least one man who alleges abuse by Sandusky in the 1980s and another who says he was abused in the 1970s have hired attorneys," Ganim reported. In the last week, "investigators interviewed three men who say they were abused by Sandusky more than forty years ago at the Brownson House, a recreation center in Washington County that had been run by Sandusky's parents."[30]*[31]

By July 2013, when Penn State announced that it had set aside $60 million to pay alleged Sandusky victims in settlements, there were thirty-two claimants. Among them were Travis Weaver and Greg Bucceroni, who had appeared on the *Dr. Phil* television talk show. Weaver, a Second Mile alum, said that Sandusky met him when he was ten years old and abused him over one hundred times

---

* Only one of these alleged early victims spoke to the media. This man, who remained anonymous, claimed that Sandusky had raped him when he was eleven years old in the Brownson House basement in 1966, when Sandusky was twenty-two, while telling him, "Real men don't cry." Note that the story includes the now-stereotypical basement.

from 1992 to 1996, in all the places now familiar to alleged victims—the Penn State locker room, Sandusky's basement, and a trip to the Rose Bowl. The abuse allegedly started with a bear hug and blowing on the stomach and proceeded to oral sex. When he threatened to tell his parents or go to the police, Weaver said, Sandusky laughed at him and said that no one would believe him. So he never told anyone. Weaver didn't mention repressed memories but said, "I tried to put it in the back of my head and not think about it."*[32]

Greg Bucceroni, then in his late forties, said he was a victim of Philadelphia pedophile Ed Savitz, who died of AIDS in 1993 while facing child sex abuse charges. Bucceroni claimed that Savitz and Sandusky were in cahoots in a tri-state child porn ring and that, in 1979, Savitz arranged for him to have a sexual encounter with "The Coach" for $200. He said that he met Sandusky, who wanted to have sex with him, but that it didn't occur.[33] Sandusky says he has never met Bucceroni.

It's surprising that Bucceroni hadn't yet come up with a Sandusky sex abuse memory, because in 2015 he wrote: "That kind of therapy (repressed memory therapy) digs up horrible past memories for which the human mind conceals in a self survival effort in protecting the host of said horrible memories." When the Sandusky scandal broke, he wrote,

> My brain was scrambled in making sense of numerous incidents of child sexual abuse and exploitation that occurred between the years 1976-1980 involving Sandusky and a few of his wealthy friends from Philadelphia and other areas. . . . After receiving professional therapy I eventually was able to put together a painful timeline. . . . Now today 2015 a clear timeline of abuse and who was involved as abusers and/or enablers has established pertaining to my victimization tied to the whole Sandusky scandal during the early days of the 1970s.[34]

Penn State hired New York City arbitration lawyer Michael Rozen, who was involved with settlements for the 9/11 World Trade Center terror attacks, to negotiate settlements with alleged victims, who had to promise not to sue Penn State. By mid-August 2013, Rozen had reached tentative agreements with twenty-six claimants.

---

* Jerry Sandusky recalled Travis Weaver as an extremely troubled young man who once threatened to kill him because Sandusky insisted the sixteen-year-old stop watching a TV show he considered inappropriate. Sandusky would later visit him in jail.

He explained that there was a wide disparity in the settlement amounts, depending on the severity of the claimed abuse, its location, and timing. The premium dollars went to those who said they were abused on the Penn State campus after the February 2001 (actually December 2000) McQueary shower report. Thus, Michal Kajak, "Victim 5," who had shifted his alleged abuse date from 1998 to August of 2001, received multiple millions because his abuse "positively could have been stopped," Rozen said, if only Penn State administrators had acted decisively on McQueary's report.

The second tier of payments went to those supposedly abused between 1998, the date of the Konstas shower, and 2001, and the lowest amount went to pre-1998 claims, many of which were beyond the Pennsylvania statute of limitations, which required victims to file claims by the time they were thirty years old. Rozen said that he also took the credibility of the story into account, but it was clear that he and Penn State were willing to pay almost anyone who said they were a Sandusky victim. Kajak's lawyer, Tom Kline of Philadelphia, said that it was difficult to evaluate injury because "you're looking into the mind of a victim of sexual abuse." Rozen, who had known Kline for years, agreed that "it's like a 3-D chess match. There are multiple layers and lots of pieces." Kline, happy with his client's reward (of which he took a healthy chunk), praised Penn State: "It convinced me of what the university was trying to say to the victims."

Another Philadelphia lawyer, Joel Feller, had joined State College attorney Andrew Shubin to represent seven alleged victims (thus far), including Allan Myers, Jason Simcisko, Dustin Struble, Ryan Rittmeyer, Matt Sandusky, and two unnamed men. "No amount of money is going to take away what these young men are going to have to endure for the rest of their lives," Feller said. "But they are pleased to have this over with." Undoubtedly, he and Shubin were happy with their share, too.[35]

Astonishingly, it appears that no one really vetted the abuse claims. No lawyers deposed the alleged victims. None were examined by forensic psychiatrists. No evidence was submitted to substantiate their claims, nor were the claims investigated. Eventually, the university paid $93 million to thirty-three alleged victims.* Anthony Lubrano, a Penn State Board of Trustees member who voted against some of the payments, complained that "there was little to no vetting of claimants." The approach, he said, was to "pay and

---

* According to investigator John Ziegler, Frankie Probst, who had previously denied that he was abused, became the latest alleged Sandusky victim to receive a large settlement in 2017.

don't push back." Because of the Sandusky case, he said, "I have lost a great deal of respect for our justice system; it doesn't seem to be particularly just."[36]

According to court documents filed in the Court of Common Pleas in Philadelphia County—there were three separate Sandusky-related cases there, all expensive, lawyer-rich affairs—in which insurance companies refused to pay for various settlements, there were thirty-nine total claimants, of whom fourteen claimed abuse outside the statute of limitations. Penn State paid all but six of them anyway.[37]

In the coming years, other dubious claimants made headlines. For instance, Anthony Spinelli, a Massachusetts murderer, saw the breaking news of the Sandusky scandal on a prison TV in November 2011. In 1988, when he was sixteen, he had attended a Penn State football camp. Now he claimed that Sandusky had abused him there, and *that* was why he had turned to drugs and had beaten a man to death. When he was released from prison, his contingency fee lawyer, Steven Passarello, filed a claim against Kathleen Kane to force the Pennsylvania attorney general to allow an exception to the statute of limitations in his case, saying that Spinelli wanted to be a "voice for the voiceless." A year later, Spinelli stabbed a man in Boston. No doubt he could blame that on Sandusky, too.[38]

And there was Jesse Keith, a young black man who claimed to be a Sandusky abuse victim. In February 2017, he persuaded his friend, Mike Jackson, a reporter for an NBC-TV affiliate in Columbus, Ohio, to do a news segment on him, in which he said, "I'm an overcomer. A lot of the things with me was, nobody believed me while I was in foster care, that's the biggest thing, guidance counselors, nobody really believed what I was telling them." But Keith didn't actually say *what* he was telling them—nothing about how he met Sandusky, or when any alleged abuse took place. Mostly, the segment was a puff piece for a business Keith planned to launch.

It turned out that Keith's father, Ed Manigo, a janitor at Penn State, had been convicted of rape, though he maintained his innocence. In an article in *Ebony* magazine dated June 6, 2012, just before the Sandusky trial, Manigo claimed that these were trumped up charges in retaliation for his having reported that Jerry Sandusky had brought boys to work out in the gym. Yet Manigo denied that his son ever claimed that Sandusky had sexually abused him, and Jesse Keith was apparently not one of the settlement accusers. It appeared that Keith got the idea of using Sandusky as a convenient foil from his father.[39]

CHAPTER 19

John Ziegler's Lone Crusade

OME OF those who accepted that Jerry Sandusky was an evil pedophile were, nonetheless, outraged over the firing of Joe Paterno, who had coached at Penn State for sixty-one years. And when he died of cancer only two months after his abrupt dismissal, they felt that the calumny heaped on him had helped to kill him. Former Penn State and professional football running back Franco Harris came forward to defend Paterno, along with a group called Penn Staters for Responsible Stewardship. Harris hosted on-going meetings to discuss Paterno and the Sandusky case called "Upon Further Review."[1]

One critic, a conservative talk-show host and documentary filmmaker named John Ziegler, also thought that Paterno had been unfairly vilified, and he would become a loud, lonely voice in the wilderness, questioning the rush to judgment in the case. Because Ziegler became such an important gadfly for the Sandusky case, and because his research helped unearth some of the facts in this book, it is important to understand him and his background.

Ziegler then lived in Camarillo, California, but he had grown up, the son of a financial manager and stay-at-home mother, in Washington Crossing, Pennsylvania. His parents were devout Catholics, which accounts for his attendance at Pennsylvania's Holy Ghost Preparatory School, where he was an outstanding golfer. Living near Philadelphia rather than State College, he rooted for Notre Dame, but of course he was keenly aware of Joe Paterno's team and reputation.

At Georgetown University, Ziegler majored in government with a minor in philosophy and theology, but he became an agnostic and later referred to himself as a "recovering Catholic." Though he hadn't played the sport, Ziegler's first job was as a football coach at a high school in Ocean City, New Jersey. That led to a four-year career as a television sportscaster, including a stint in Steubenville, Ohio, where he got to know legendary local high school football coach Reno Saccoccia, who was the main character in Ziegler's first book, *Dynasty at the Crossroads: A Story of Kids, Fans and Values*, about the team's 1993 season.

But Ziegler, a critical thinker who suffered fools poorly, did not fit into that career niche. "The whole world of sports and local news is so disgusting," he observed. "Local TV news is half a step above prostitution." In 1995, he was fired from his sportscasting job in Raleigh, North Carolina, for saying on the air that former football star O. J. Simpson had murdered his wife.[2]

With his strong opinions, hatred of political correctness, and quick wit and tongue, Ziegler found a better fit as a talk-radio host, though he bounced from job to job in North Carolina, Tennessee, Pennsylvania, Kentucky, and California, after getting himself in various vats of hot water for things he said on the air. In April 2005, he was the subject of a long cover story in *The Atlantic* by famed writer David Foster Wallace, who clearly enjoyed Ziegler, despite himself. Wallace wrote: "John Ziegler, who is a talk-radio host of unflagging industry, broad general knowledge, mordant wit, and extreme conviction, makes a particular specialty of media criticism." That same year, Ziegler published *The Death of Free Speech: How Our Broken National Dialogue Has Killed the Truth and Divided America*, in which he lambasted mainstream media for prissy political correctness.

Ziegler described himself as "more libertarian than conservative, more conservative than liberal, and more cynical and skeptical than anything else." Restless in talk radio, he became a documentary filmmaker. He made *Media Malpractice*, which asserted that the mainstream liberal media had maligned Sarah Palin and helped elect Barack Obama. Matt Lauer invited Ziegler to appear on NBC's *Today* show to premier that film in February 2009.

JOHN ZIEGLER TAKES ON THE SANDUSKY CASE

With his cynicism about the media and sports commentators, his experience as a football coach, and his Pennsylvania childhood, Ziegler's antennae immediately went up when the Penn State scandal broke. The day after Joe Paterno was fired over the telephone on the evening of November 9, 2011, Ziegler wrote an article for *The Bleacher Report*, a sports news website, complaining: "Despite what you may have heard from the vast majority of the sports media, we still don't know for sure what exactly, if anything, Joe Paterno actually did or didn't do in order to suddenly get fired after 61 years of incredible service to a university he almost literally built."

Ziegler identified the hysteria fomented by the media, particularly sports programs, as the culprit. "ESPN has basically blown out its normal broadcasting schedule to go with virtual wall-to-wall coverage of this scandal. Almost all of that coverage has been focused on Paterno and whether he could possibly continue as the head coach." In fact, some people thought that it was JoePa who was being accused of child molestation because of the way the media covered the scandal.

Five days later, in another *Bleacher Report* piece, Ziegler wrote: "At this point, being perceived as defending Jerry Sandusky or even Joe Paterno is roughly about as ill-advised as appearing to say anything positive about Adolf Hitler." Nonetheless, he waded in. "Whenever there is this much pressure to accept one side of a highly controversial story, I get inherently nervous," he stated. "There is indeed a plausible scenario where Paterno has been largely railroaded and where Sandusky may not be quite the monster you currently think that he is."

He pointed out that most of the allegations involved "inappropriate touching," not severe sexual abuse, that two of the alleged victims were unidentified, and that Amendola claimed that Victim 2 (Allan Myers) said he had not been raped by the retired coach, as McQueary had asserted. But Ziegler emphasized, "I am NOT saying that Jerry Sandusky is innocent."[3]

Four months after the incendiary Freeh Report was published, Ziegler posted a thirty-two-minute mini-documentary, *The Framing of Joe Paterno*, on YouTube on November 9, 2012, the anniversary of Paterno's firing. He had ventured to State College, Pennsylvania, to interview Franco Harris as well as Penn State Board of Trustee member Anthony Lubrano, former prosecuting attorney and Penn State football player Christian Marrone, Sandusky defense attorney Joe Amendola, two Penn State professors, and two young former Penn State football players.

The video began with clips of inflammatory media coverage in the days after the scandal broke, epitomized by a TV sports commentator pronouncing: "You cannot watch a football game Saturday and be thinking about child molestation, and that's *exactly* what you'll be thinking about if you see that man (Joe Paterno) on the sidelines." Atop such footage, written comments appeared such as

"Facts don't matter?!" Ziegler, then forty-five, came on camera as an introductory commentator: "People think they know the story of the Jerry Sandusky scandal. But they don't. The media created a largely false narrative that fit their own agenda."

Then he let Harris, Lubrano, and the other commentators express their outrage over the way Paterno had been fired. "I couldn't believe what I was watching. I was shell-shocked. I'm hollering at the television," Lubrano said. (At that time he was not yet on the Board of Trustees.) Lubrano questioned Paterno's grand jury testimony that included words such as "fondling" and "sexual" that would not normally come out of his mouth. "It won't surprise me if we learn at some point that in preparation for his grand jury testimony, Joe spent some time with people to help him refresh his recollection."

Andrew Pitz, a young former player, claimed that Coach Mc-Queary had falsely accused him of bad off-field activities. "I did not find him (McQueary) to be trustworthy. . . . I was always a little concerned about his motivation with everything."

Penn State professor Gary Gray, who had played football for Sandusky, coached with him, and maintained their friendship through the years, said, "Jerry created a wonderful persona. It would have been unbelievable to believe that he was a pedophile. I thought I knew him very well. I spent a lot of time with him and couldn't conceive of him doing the things that he supposedly has done." Gray was clearly still confused, but at that point Franco Harris apparently accepted Sandusky's guilt, saying, "So he groomed a whole town. He got the whole town used to seeing him with boys, so it wasn't anything unusual, and as a matter of fact, people looked at it as a positive thing."

Ziegler's film heaped scorn on the idea that Paterno had covered up for Sandusky to avoid bad publicity. Rashard Casey, a black quarterback for Penn State in 1999-2000, talked about how he had been falsely accused of assaulting a police officer in 2000, and Paterno had stood by him, despite intense media pressure.*[4] "If he had feared bad publicity, he would have gotten rid of me at that time," Casey said. Instead, "he sacked two of the best players on our team because they didn't do well in school."

Ziegler appeared on screen to wrap up the video, explaining that the mainstream media didn't have the expertise or the will to

---

* Rashard Casey was eventually exonerated and he countersued, receiving a large settlement in 2003. About his case, Joe Paterno said, "People rush to judgment and they want to believe the worst," an observation that would apply all too aptly to what happened to him and Jerry Sandusky a few years later.

delve into such a complex story. "They don't care about details, they don't care about the facts." He said he hoped to make a full-length documentary but added: "This is the hardest thing we've ever done. We're going up hill into the wind on ice with lead bricks around our feet, because everyone's against us on this. The only thing we've got going for us is the truth. And I don't know if that's going to be enough or not. I hope it is. I actually have my doubts."[5] The film ended with a link to www.framingpaterno.com, a website Ziegler had created to post new information on the case.

Much to Ziegler's chagrin, the media ignored the film, and it didn't help that lawyer Scott Paterno was uneasy about Ziegler, even though the filmmaker was defending his father's honor and reputation. In a January 2013 email to Ziegler, Paterno complained that "your methods and guerrilla style is [sic] off putting." But Ziegler refused to drop the issue.[6]

A PRISON INTERVIEW WITH JERRY SANDUSKY

Ziegler decided to seek Sandusky's version of the story in person, though the talk-show veteran still believed that the former coach was indeed a child molester. When the Paterno family's two hired pedophile experts, Jim Clemente and Fred Berlin, published their reports on February 6, 2013, Ziegler pored over both of them.*

Berlin, a Johns Hopkins psychiatrist who specializes in the treatment of pedophiles, strongly defended the reputation of Joe Paterno against the "unsubstantiated inferences and innuendo" of the Freeh Report, which "presented no credible evidence whatsoever substantiating the claim that Joe Paterno had been involved in an effort to repeatedly conceal critical facts relating to Mr. Sandusky's child sexual abuse." Berlin was careful not to draw unwarranted conclusions, even about the convicted Sandusky, because "I have not clinically evaluated Mr. Sandusky." He cautioned: "In our legitimate effort to protect innocent children, the fair treatment of adults should not become a collateral casualty."

Still, the Second Mile founder might well be a molester, he wrote. "Persons with pedophilia can manifest a genuine concern for the well-being of children, and they often enjoy spending time with them," Berlin noted. "That is not the problem," but hiding

---

* The Paternos also hired former US Attorney General Dick Thornburgh to critique the Freeh Report, and the entire Paterno case was summarized by lawyer Wick Sollers of the King & Spalding law firm. See www.paterno.com.

the nature of their sexual desires was. "I have seen many such examples over the years in the course of my professional work."[7]*

Jim Clemente, a former FBI profiler for the Crimes Against Children unit, was far less restrained in his lengthy report, in which he proclaimed that Sandusky was a typical "nice guy" or "pillar of the community" offender. "This case is about . . . how [such pedophiles] groom, deceive, and defraud all of us right under our noses. This case is about compliant victimization and the shame, embarrassment, and guilt that drive victim behavior."

Clemente, himself a victim of child sexual abuse, was far more interested in vilifying Sandusky than in defending Paterno, though he did say that Sandusky completely fooled the head coach, along with everyone else, so Paterno should not be blamed. "Sandusky is a skilled and master manipulator, and in my expert opinion," Clemente wrote, "he is in the top one percent of effective 'groomers.'" Teachers, camp counselors, coaches, and clergymen were sometimes pedophiles, he wrote, who "typically seek out needy, isolated, or disadvantaged children."[8]

There is undoubtedly truth to these assertions in some cases, though there are no substantial studies that indicate what percentage of pedophiles are of the "nice guy, pillar of the community" variety.** The trouble with the stereotypes Clemente espoused is that any truly altruistic person who becomes a teacher, coach, or clergyman is likely to come under suspicion. Indeed, Jesus himself, who summoned children to come unto him, might find himself under such a cloud were he to appear today. And the more prominent he became, the more likely that people would believe the allegations.

John Ziegler thought that Clemente, the presumed expert on pedophiles, might be helpful, so he sought his advice before going to see Sandusky. How should he question him? "Tell him that you know he didn't intend to hurt these boys, that he's a good person, that you know he really loved them," Clemente advised. Then Sandusky was sure to confess.

---

* I interviewed Dr. Berlin, who told me that in his experience, it is very unusual for a serial child molester to maintain his innocence. Usually, such perpetrators rationalize what they have done, but they admit it. In the one case he knew of, in which the accused denied his guilt, he was eventually found innocent and exonerated.

** I contacted the Association for the Treatment of Sexual Abusers and asked for data on the prevalence of "nice guy" offenders. Katie Gotch, the Coordinator of Public Affairs for ATSA, wrote back to say that she had no such statistics. She added: "Such typologies were developed in the 1980s/1990s and are not often used within the professional arena anymore for several reasons—typologies were typically developed for criminal profiling/law enforcement purposes which does not reflect clinical knowledge or approaches and criminological research."

Thus prepared, Ziegler arrived at State Correctional Institution (SCI) Greene, a maximum-security prison in Waynesburg, Pennsylvania, on February 28, 2013, and managed to smuggle in a digital recorder (disguised as a pen). The transcript of his entire three-hour prison interview with Sandusky is available at www.framingpaterno.com, along with an astonishing array of other information about the case. Ziegler asked Sandusky what the worst thing in prison had been, and he said that it was being put on suicide watch, which meant solitary confinement with nothing to read and no bedding. Sandusky had told the prison officials, "I want to live, I want to fight. I am the furthest thing from suicidal," but they didn't listen. "Actually, I said to my wife if you're not suicidal going in, you are going out," he told Ziegler, laughing ruefully.

When Ziegler asked about the 1998 shower incident with Zachary Konstas, Sandusky said that no one from Penn State, other than Detective Ron Schreffler, had ever talked to him about it, and that "it was never made a huge deal to me from anybody at Penn State, including Mr. Schreffler." After it was labeled "unfounded," that was it, as far as he was concerned. They told him not to shower or work out with Zach Konstas anymore, so he didn't.*

He denied ever saying "I wish I was dead" to Zach's mother, but he explained that he was concerned when she told him that Zach "had nightmares and was all upset. . . . You know, it bothered me that he had that kind of perception. And I certainly felt bad." He had been told that Konstas had cancer and loved Penn State football, so he had given him Penn State shorts and Joe Paterno socks. And he *was* able to take him to football games in the years to come, along with his friend Dustin Struble, "Victim 7."

Zach Konstas "was not bashful about asking [for tickets]. We went out to dinner in July [2011], the July preceding the trial, while he was there with another young man (Allan Myers) that was in The Second Mile. The next day, I had a colonoscopy. He called me asking me about how that went. What in the world? Does that make any sense [if I abused him]?" Sandusky laughed. "You're getting me fired up."

They talked about Sandusky retiring in 1999, after Paterno told him that he wouldn't succeed him as head coach. Ziegler circled back to the 1998 shower, asking if that incident had made him more cautious. No, not really. "The way it's been portrayed was like

---

* Schreffler's report indicates that he told Sandusky not to shower with *any* boys in the future, but Sandusky took him to refer only to Zach Konstas.

I did all of this showering, and I did shower occasionally with kids after '98. There were times when they would come to activities, that I wouldn't shower with them. There were a few times that I did, [but] not nearly as many as was alluded to or presented by those who made the accusations."

Ziegler told Sandusky that a *Sports Illustrated* reporter had erroneously written that he'd been accused of raping the boy in the 1998 shower and had never corrected it. "After this experience, nothing surprises me," Sandusky replied. "So many monster-creating terms [have] been thrown out." Did that still anger him? "When you mention it, it's in my craw. The hurt, the pain, the anger, all of the emotions come out when you mention things like that, and I think about how all this transpired. But yeah, I'm beyond that. That's done. All I want is another chance [for a fair trial]."

In the long conversation, Sandusky asserted that Aaron Fisher, "Victim 1," was a "story teller" who made the first vague allegation and then embellished it. Then Sandusky talked about the infamous Bob Costas interview. "The world today is much different than the world I grew up in," Sandusky said. "To be asked by Bob Costas, the question I was asked . . . I never thought in terms of being attracted to kids like that, sexually. It was the furthest thing from my mind. . . . My world was athletics and what I could do there. My world was what I could [do to] help these kids, not [being] sexually attracted to them."

They discussed at length the 2001 shower with "Victim 2," Allan Myers, with its slap-boxing or towel-snapping, and about Tim Curley's conversation with him about that shower. "I offered to actually, if he (Curley) thought it was [necessary], to bring the young man in to talk to him." Sandusky recounted having grown up in a recreation center where he showered with men and boys.

He said that it never even occurred to him that the Grand Jury Presentment would involve this shower with Allan Myers. "That young man . . . asked me to be at his wedding. He asked me to stand as his father. He asked me to speak at his graduation. He lived with us practically. During the summer I got him a job. . . . He drove ten hours to come to my mom's funeral. You know, why would I think it would be of concern? I don't know . . . [*laughs*]. I was naïve, obviously. Oh boy was I naive. Some say stupid [*laughs*]."

Near the end of the interview, Sandusky discussed how he had felt when he was under house arrest, awaiting trial. "The [real] victims were all the young people in The Second Mile that were going to get hurt [*crying*]. All the people that I had been with who were going to get hurt. What happened to Tim Curley. What happened to Joe Paterno . . . If I hadn't showered maybe none of that would have happened. So I felt horrible. I felt horrible that all that transpired."

He had tried to maintain a brave front for his wife and family, so mostly he cried with his dog, Bo. "I spilled my guts out more to Bo than anybody else. He understood. I cried with him. I didn't want my family to think that I was going to get what happened. Until the very end, I didn't talk to them about if the worst scenario happened."

Bo - Our friend, our partner, our defender. We are his life, his love, his leaders.

Bo, the loyal St. Bernard, from Sandusky family 2010 Christmas booklet.

Sandusky had apparently read the Clemente report and objected to "the FBI person coming forward with stating that I was such a secretive person, that these are people to watch out for. If you look at [me] being sneaky you would see: No alcohol involvement with these kids. No videos. No child pornography. No seductive conversations. No warning, no threats. None of the things that some people like this will do." Sandusky asked, if he were a pedophile, would he have put his victims' photographs in his book?[9]

Ziegler followed up with two fifteen-minute taped phone interviews with Sandusky. At the end, he tried out Clemente's advised approach. "You never intended to harm these boys," he said. "In your mind, you never did harm them. I think you loved them. I think you did great things for them and with them. I think they loved you back. But I also think that things may have gone further than what, you know, you have said that they have gone. And I think people would be more forgiving and remember you better if you go and tell the full truth. And this might be your last real chance to do that, Jerry. Why don't you come clean and admit that you did touch some of those boys inappropriately?"

But Sandusky still denied any sexual abuse. "Yeah, I hugged them. Maybe I tested boundaries. Maybe I shouldn't have showered with them. Yeah, I tickled them. I looked at them as being probably younger than even some of them were. But I didn't do any of these horrible acts and abuse these young people. I didn't violate them. I didn't harm them."

After Sandusky talked about "testing boundaries"—a term therapists use frequently in talking about molesters, and a term Tim Curley may have employed in questioning him about the 2001 shower—Ziegler asked him to clarify. "I mean some people feel that showering with kids was a test of a boundary. I didn't think that at that time." In retrospect, he recognized that showering with boys was breaching a societal boundary, but it had been the way he was raised, and at the time he thought nothing of it.[10]

GOING PUBLIC ON NATIONAL TELEVISION

When he heard about the Sandusky prison interview, Scott Paterno went ballistic and called Ziegler, alarmed that he might post the interview on the website, FramingPaterno.com, which had his family name on it. Paterno had fully embraced the Sandusky-as-monster narrative and wanted nothing whatsoever to do with debunking McQueary or hearing Sandusky's version of events. "Do you think anybody believes a word Jerry has to fucking say?" he yelled. "I can't have my name giving Jerry a voice!"

Ziegler became convinced that Scott Paterno *needed* Sandusky to be guilty, or else the destruction of his father would have been his fault for the way he handled himself and his father during the media blitz as the scandal broke. Scott had thought that they had to distance themselves from Sandusky and support McQueary's sex-in-the-shower story, but that strategy backfired.

At any rate, armed with his taped Sandusky interviews, John Ziegler, who had appeared on NBC's *Today Show* in 2009, was invited back by host Matt Lauer to talk about the case on March 25, 2013. Lauer immediately asked, "Do you believe he was wrongly convicted?" Ziegler, who had begun to doubt the extent of Sandusky's guilt, tried to sidestep the question, saying, "Jerry Sandusky already had his day in court. . . . My focus here has been on Joe Paterno." But Lauer persisted, forcing Ziegler to say: "I have no doubt that Jerry Sandusky was guilty of many of the things if not all the things that he was accused of, but I do believe that there were due process problems with the trial."

Lauer played short excerpts from the Sandusky interview, but the chosen segments were neither compelling nor informative. Ziegler focused primarily on the McQueary incident. "I don't know that Mike McQueary is lying," Ziegler told Lauer. "I think a large part of what has happened here is that over ten years, your memory changes." The most important thing he learned from his Sandusky interview, he said, was the identity of Victim 2. He had in fact intended to name Allan Myers, but the NBC team strictly forbade him to do so. Waving the redacted version of the Curtis Everhart interview with Myers, Ziegler said, "I have it in my hand, this is an interview he gave to an FBI-trained investigator, a former police officer, saying that nothing happened in the shower that night."

But Ziegler never got to read from that astonishing document, which clearly exonerated Sandusky, nor was any portion of it blown up to appear on television. Instead, Lauer read a message from civil lawyer Andrew Shubin, which *was* shown on-screen: "Jerry Sandusky is a convicted child predator giving interviews from prison. Our clients, including Victim 2, have heard enough from Jerry Sandusky. They are focused on healing and holding Penn State accountable for choosing to protect Jerry Sandusky and themselves instead of protecting children from years of horrific sexual abuse."

Ziegler told Lauer that perhaps Sandusky *had* abused Myers, just not that night in the shower, so "Joe Paterno was railroaded here," because there was no actual sex abuse to report from that McQueary incident.

Then, as the words appeared on the TV screen, Lauer read a message from the Paterno family attorney: "They (the Paternos) feel that it is important to make it clear that they had no role in obtaining or releasing this recording. . . . They believe that any attempt to use this recording as a defense of Joe Paterno is misguided and inappropriate." Scott Paterno thus effectively negated any impact Ziegler's appearance might have had.[11]

Later the same day, Ziegler had a disastrous interview on CNN with British host Piers Morgan. Ziegler was forced to repeat that he thought Sandusky was indeed a pedophile, but Morgan didn't want to hear any defense of Paterno or to give any credence to what Sandusky might say. "Joe Paterno might not have known the whole scale of it," Morgan said, "but he knew damn well that Sandusky was having naked showers with these boys. That's why he got fired." Ziegler shot back: "You know nothing about this case."

It degenerated from there, with the two men talking over one another. Once again, Ziegler waved the redacted Allan Myers interview on camera, to no avail. Morgan read the Paterno family statement. "Those are the words of his family. They don't want you doing this." To end the fray, Morgan brought Sara Ganim (now a fellow CNN reporter) on camera. "I think that the only thing we should be focusing on at this point is helping those victims, helping all the victims of sexual abuse," Ganim preached. As Ziegler sputtered off-camera about Ganim's "agenda," Morgan cut him off and abruptly ended the interview. "Mr. Ziegler, if I were you, I would take the Paterno family's advice and just disappear."[12]

COULD HE REALLY BE INNOCENT?

But Ziegler did not disappear. In July 2013 he published an online eBook, *The Betrayal of Joe Paterno*, on his FramingPaterno. com website, making his case thus far for Paterno's exoneration. In the book, he acknowledged, "I am a loud, in-your-face, shoot-first-and-ask-questions-later, kind of person." His response to being ignored and vilified was to become more strident, dig deeper, and to call people names. Scott Paterno was a "moron," reporters were a "swarm of media jackals," and CNN's Piers Morgan was "extremely rude, arrogant, and ignorant."

In introducing the book, Ziegler wrote, "Here is what I think probably *really* happened in the most amazing, depressing, fascinating, troubling, perplexing, frustrating, unpredictable, and, ultimately, significant saga with which I have ever been intimately familiar." In *The Betrayal of Joe Paterno*, Ziegler continued to maintain that Sandusky was probably a guilty pedophile, but "he could easily be a pedophile and yet still be 'innocent' of some specific allegations." Or perhaps he was even a "chaste" pedophile, someone who was sexually attracted to boys but who didn't act on it—hence, the inappropriate showers and hugs. But those were not criminal acts. The manuscript critiqued McQueary's testimony, the media rush to judgment, the Freeh Report, and Aaron Fisher's changing story. For the first time, Ziegler noted that repressed memory therapy may have contributed to some false allegations, though he continued to believe that money was the prime motivator.

Ziegler's writing style was a combination of solid factual research and surmise, with phrases such as "My gut tells me," "I really believe," and "I can't help but think," and the author could sometimes lose readers by going off on interesting tangents—perhaps hangovers from his talk-radio days. But for readers with an open mind, Ziegler's eBook would have raised compelling concerns about the case—if they had read it. But by and large, they didn't.[13]

In late January 2014, Ziegler visited Sandusky in prison again, this time with Dottie Sandusky, and he came away convinced that Sandusky was in fact innocent. "When was the first moment you thought this might not turn out OK for you?" Ziegler asked. Breaking down, Sandusky said that it was when he heard the verdict. Dottie, also in tears, said the same thing. Until then, Sandusky said that he had had faith in the legal system and God's protection, and that they really thought he would be found not guilty. As Ziegler later told a radio interviewer, he became convinced then that there was "no consciousness of guilt on their part."[14]

On March 12, 2014, Ziegler convinced Dottie Sandusky to break her public silence and appear on the *Today Show* with Matt Lauer, who came to State College to interview her in her home, where she took Lauer on a tour of the now-infamous basement, where her husband was supposed to have abused multiple Second Mile boys, including Sabastian Paden, "Victim 9," who said he had screamed for help, to no avail. Lauer noted that it was a small house and that such screams would definitely have been heard in the nearby kitchen or living room.

Dottie Sandusky strongly defended her husband, asserting his innocence, explaining that such showers seemed normal for many men in his generation. "But have you allowed yourself to think of the possibility that somehow you have blocked this out?" Lauer asked, implying that perhaps she had repressed the memories herself. He also read from a *Washington Post* editorial by Melinda Henneberger, who wrote, "It's a shame that Dottie Sandusky doesn't have a cell of her own next to her notorious husband. We know that predators prey on the more vulnerable. They also tend to choose spouses who can be counted on to suppress any unpleasant ideas that might occur to them."

"I'm not a weak spouse," Dottie replied. "They call me 'Sarge' because Jerry said I kept everybody in line. . . . I know who I am. And I know who Jerry is. And I know he did not do the horrible crimes that he's convicted of." Then why did all those young men accuse him? "They were manipulated, they saw money, once lawyers came into the case." At the end of the interview, Dottie said that she had planned to grow old at her husband's side, but that she trusted that what had happened was "the plan that God has, and something good will come out of it," though she couldn't say what that might be.

Dottie Sandusky at Christmas 2010.

John Ziegler, sitting next to Dottie on the show, said that he, too, now thought that Sandusky was innocent. Sandusky may have had "boundary issues," but he didn't molest any boys. He reiterated that "Victim 2" had clearly stated that he was not abused in the shower or anywhere else, and that the entire case against Paterno therefore collapsed. "That was the snowball that turned into an avalanche." At the end of the interview, Ziegler emphasized that he had made no money from the two years he had spent on the case. "I'm fully aware that doing this interview with you today is going to destroy whatever's left of my career," but this had been "the worst case of media malpractice and injustice that I have ever seen." He concluded: "I'm going to put myself on this grenade and I'm going to dedicate my life to people understanding what really happened here."[15]

After Dottie Sandusky's television appearance in support of her husband, a flood of viewers posted horrific comments on the Yahoo Sports site about her being in denial and deserving to be imprisoned or killed, showing the visceral emotion the case still evoked, and the level of vitriol that perfect strangers could unleash against the pleasant-looking grandmother. Among them:

- "Since she knew all along what her husband was doing, she should have been charged, tried, and convicted just like her pervert husband. Sadly though, since this country doesn't use the death penalty properly, they will both be able to live out their sorry lives."

- "A sicko married a sicko. It's not the first time, unfortunately."

- "She also raped the children, she stood and could hear the screams of the boys being raped, and giving her the opportunity to speak those boys were raped again."

- "I could NOT care less what this delusional, disgusting, HAG has to say. Listen up hag, your husband is a repulsive pedophile who destroyed the lives of scores of boys. One can only imagine the emotional damage and pain these men have suffered."[16]

DIGGING FOR DIRT

The case against Sandusky was built on two pillars—the 2001 Mc-Queary shower incident, which Ziegler first focused on, and the allegations of Aaron Fisher, "Victim 1," which had started the snowball rolling in 2008. Over the next year, Ziegler delved into the Aaron Fisher story and turned his attention to other alleged victims. In May 2015, a *Philadelphia Inquirer* feature on Fisher noted that he had turned being "Victim Number 1" into a vocation. After a speech, "he boasts about a new truck and the home he is building in Mill Hall, Pa. He tells total strangers intimate details of his personal life, like a split with the mother of his children—Nikolai, 1, and Mia, 4. He pauses occasionally to spit tobacco juice into a soda can." This article also quoted John Ziegler. "They have gotten no scrutiny for their story," Ziegler said of the Fishers. "I would go away in a heartbeat if Aaron answered just a couple of questions for me." In response, Aaron Fisher told the reporter, "If he has questions about me, he should just ask them directly—reach out and shake my hand like a man."[17]

Yet Fisher and his mother never took Ziegler up on his offer to pay $10,000 to a charity of their choice if Fisher passed a lie detector test, nor would Fisher meet with Ziegler for a one-hour interview for a similar offer of $3,000. Instead, Fisher made a public death threat against Ziegler.

In August 2015, after another trip to Pennsylvania, Ziegler posted a smorgasbord of information. He had spoken to numerous friends or acquaintances of Aaron Fisher who thought he was lying about being abused by Jerry Sandusky, although some of them refused to go on the record. One who *did*, in a video posted on Ziegler's website, was long-time friend Jamon Gharet, who contradicted Fisher's claim that he was harassed at school and cut himself. He knew

Fisher as "happy-go-lucky and proud." Fisher was "an out-spoken person [with] no filter" who would have reported any abuse. Fisher had instead bragged about having sex with various girls from an early age, keeping a list of some three hundred women he claimed to have slept with. Gharet said that Fisher was now threatening to run people over with his truck if they questioned his abuse story.

Ziegler also posted a video interview with Josh Fravel, the Fishers' former next-door neighbor who had testified at the trial. Fravel was there one day in November 2008 when Fisher's mother, Dawn Hennessy, insisted that her son should go with Sandusky because she planned to party. Fisher, who wanted to hang out with his friends (or girlfriend), told his mother that he didn't want to go with Sandusky because "he makes me feel weird." She said, "You need to tell me more than that," and took him into the house to talk. When Hennessy came back out, she told Fravel, "I'm gonna own that mother-fucker's house," referring to Sandusky.

"I just thought Aaron was saying what he needed to say to get out of going with Jerry," Fravel said, adding that Hennessy was unemployed and living on welfare. In subsequent conversations, she talked about how she would buy a house in the country, while Aaron would dream of buying a sportscar and Jeep. Fravel said that Dawn could not have checked the sex offender list online that day, as she later claimed, because she couldn't pay for Internet service and had to use his. Fravel was sure that Aaron Fisher was lying about having been abused.

Another of Fisher's high school friends, Sierra Nicole Foster, told Ziegler in a taped interview that Fisher was "money hungry" and that she did not believe he had been abused, nor that he would have kept going back for more and never said anything about it. She said he was untrustworthy because he lied to her about having broken up with his girlfriend so that Foster would sleep with him.

In July 2015, a family member posted a Facebook picture of Aaron Fisher lying on a bed, with cash strewn all over him, smiling broadly and gesturing with his middle finger, in an apparent message to John Ziegler, who promptly posted it on his FramingPaterno.com website (see image on facing page).

Ziegler also posted Dawn Hennessy's 2015 Facebook comment about the Penn State millions they had received: "It's ours, we made it, we spend it however the hell we want." He published photos of her Porsche and Mercedes, Aaron Fisher's souped-up Mustang, and Fisher's large new under-construction home, as well as pictures of fancy sportscars bought by Dustin Struble, Ryan Rittmeyer, and

Mallory Foster was with Aaron Scott Fisher and Dawn Renee Hennessy.

Michal Kajak. Of course, the fact that these young men loved their new cars, bought with the windfall settlement cash, did not prove that they had been lying. Still, Ziegler found it unseemly.

Ziegler kept digging. He found Aaron Fisher's girlfriend from 2009, when Fisher was in therapy with Mike Gillum and telling the police that Sandusky had abused him. "He and his mom never stopped talking bout how much money theyd get how excited they were," she wrote to Ziegler on Facebook. "I believed in part of it (the abuse story) but I knew it was exaggerated for the money. . . . do u ever think u say something sooo many times for soo long u actually start to believe it[?] i think that's what happened with aaron i think his mom drilled it into him."

Ziegler also dug up another tantalizing lead. Dawn Hennessy's brother, Donald J. Fisher, had apparently been one of the alleged victims in the case against Dr. Barry Bender, a Pennsylvania general practitioner accused in 2001 of having offered drugs and cash to teenage boys in return for sex. The investigator was Anthony Sassano, the same narcotics agent who became a lead investigator in the Sandusky case. "These were kids from the wrong side of the tracks who, instead of going to school, would do booze and cocaine," Sassano told a reporter at the time.

Bender had practiced in Lock Haven until 1997, and Ziegler guessed that this case gave Aaron Fisher's mother the idea that sex abuse claims might be lucrative, if the accused had deep pockets. "Dawn claimed (to multiple people) that she helped police find her brother Donald (who is at least friendly with Aaron) in the Dr. Barry Bender sex abuse case," Ziegler wrote. So perhaps she was motivated in part to get a huge settlement in the Sandusky case to avenge her brother and help pay for his house, which she apparently did.

Bender initially took a plea bargain but tried (unsuccessfully) to take it back. Thus, like Sandusky, he maintained his innocence, according to his first lawyer, even as multiple low-income young male accusers came forward.[18]

Ziegler also called attention to Stacy Park Miller's involvement in the Sandusky case. As the Centre County district attorney, she would have handled the case initially if it had not been transferred to the state attorney general's office. She was the one who received the anonymous email tip about McQueary on November 3, 2010, which lit the fire under the case. As a private lawyer, she had also once represented Brett Houtz, "Victim 4," in a criminal matter. Was it possible, Ziegler asked, that Miller had told Houtz about the Sandusky investigation? "It certainly doesn't seem to be a stretch that Miller simply went through her memory for any males she knew who were closely associated with Jerry Sandusky and then contacted 'Victim 4' to alert him that something was up."[19]*[20]

"BILLY DOE" AND THE SLADE MCLAUGHLIN CONNECTION

Another alarming Pennsylvania case caught Ziegler's attention when he learned that attorney Slade McLaughlin was involved. McLaughlin represented Aaron Fisher, along with eleven other alleged Sandusky victims.[21]

In January 2009—just as the Sandusky investigation was getting underway with Aaron Fisher's first tentative allegations—Danny Gallagher, a twenty-year-old who had been arrested six times for theft and drugs, and who had been in and out of twenty-three different drug rehabs for using marijuana, mushrooms, LSD, and

---

* As part of the tangled web of scandal involving Pennsylvania legal affairs and politics, in 2015 Stacy Parks Miller was accused of forging a judge's signature, which she denied.

heroin, made grotesque child sexual abuse allegations against two priests and an elementary teacher. He told Philadelphia social workers that when he was a fifth grader, the Reverend Charles Engelhardt had plied him with sacramental wine and then sodomized him in the church sacristy for five hours and threatened to kill him if he ever told anyone.

Danny Gallagher ("Billy Doe")

That same year, he said, Edward Avery, another priest, knocked him out with a blow to the head, and he awoke to find himself naked, his hands tied with altar boy sashes. Avery anally raped him, after which he "made him suck all the blood off his penis," and if he ever told anybody, Avery said he would "hang him from his balls and kill him slowly."

In sixth grade, Gallagher continued, as the appalled social workers furiously took notes, his homeroom teacher Bernard Shero offered him a ride home, then hit him in the face, tried to strangle him with a seat belt, and performed oral sex on Gallagher, who was then forced to masturbate Shero.

In 2010, when Gallagher testified at a grand jury hearing, he changed his story to remove most of the violent, lurid elements and threats. Instead, he now said that he had been forced to perform a strip tease and took part in oral sex and mutual masturbation with the same three men. That was the story the 2011 grand jury presentment about the case told and that Philadelphia District Attorney Seth Williams uncritically accepted, which led to two trials and avid coverage from media that lapped up the predatory Catholic priest narrative about poor "Billy Doe," as Gallagher was called to protect his privacy as an alleged victim. *Rolling Stone* published a 2011 article about the case by Sabrina Rubin Erdely, who described Gallagher as a "sweet, gentle kid with boyish good looks," though as an adult he wore dark glasses, muscle shirts, and gold chains and enjoyed giving the finger to the camera.

Erdely was married to an assistant district attorney in the Philadelphia DA's office. In 2014, she wrote another article about what turned out to be false allegations by "Jackie," who claimed that she had been gang-raped by seven fraternity boys at the University of Virginia.[22]

Investigative reporter Ralph Cipriano, who helped uncover the extent of *real* sexual abuse by Catholic priests, has written extensively about the outrageous "Billy Doe," pointing out twenty errors in its grand jury presentment and revealing that Danny Gallagher had a long history of ever-shifting stories about being sexually abused. He had said he was molested by a family friend at age nine. No, he was sexually abused by a friend at age six and a teacher at age seven. Come to think of it, he was raped in third, fourth, and sixth grades. It is little wonder that one of the defense attorneys called Gallagher "a lying sack of shit."

The police detective who questioned Gallagher was alarmed at all the contradictions. Yet the case went ahead, and not only were the three alleged abusers found guilty, but so was Monsignor William Lynn, who supervised the priests. Lynn's conviction was twice overturned by the Pennsylvania Superior Court, but he was returned to prison by the DA's appeal. Rev. Charles Engelhardt died in prison in November 2014 at the age of sixty-seven, after being handcuffed to a hospital bed and denied a heart operation.

In a civil suit Danny Gallagher brought against the Catholic Church, his lawyer, Slade McLaughlin, claimed that in addition to the alleged rapes, Gallagher suffered from "post-traumatic stress disorder, manifested by physical ailments and complaints, including, but not limited to, sleeplessness, loss of appetite, pain in his testicles, and uncontrollable spontaneous gagging and vomiting." In addition, he suffered "embarrassment, loss of self-esteem, disgrace, humiliation, and loss of enjoyment of life, and has suffered and continues to suffer spiritually."

McLaughlin sent Gallagher to therapist Mary Gail Frawley-O'Dea, who reported that Gallagher "acknowledged that he originally embellished the overt violence and the extent of what happened to him." But that was because he was "so ashamed; so guilty that he 'did not do something,' that he 'did not stop [the attack],' so self-blaming that he tried to make himself appear more overpowered, physically helpless, and unable to fight back than he actually was."

The case was settled out of court by the Catholic Church, which paid Gallagher an estimated $5 million. When John Ziegler interviewed reporter Ralph Cipriano about the case on his podcast, Ziegler observed: "The similarities to the Penn State case are extraordinary . . . and the reaction to them by the prosecutors and by the media have been almost identical."[23]

THE PORNGATE SCANDAL

Ziegler also wrote about the "Porngate" scandal that broke in late 2014, eventually revealing that Frank Fina, one of the Sandusky prosecutors, had been emailing pornographic images back and forth with his buddies in the Office of the Attorney General and elsewhere in state government during the entire Sandusky investigation, between 2008 and 2012. The emails, sent on state computers on state time, were not only pornographic but racist, misogynistic, and homophobic, while making a joke out of domestic violence and drunken rape.

The saga of how they came to light is intimately tied to the Sandusky case and illustrates the way Pennsylvania's "incestuous, dysfunctional political system" worked, as one reporter put it. It should come as no surprise that in 2015 the Center for Public Integrity gave Pennsylvania an "F" grade, ranking it 45th in the nation in terms of corruption prevention, and 47th in judicial accountability, with an "entrenched culture of malfeasance."[24]

In November 2012, Attorney Kathleen Kane won the race to become the state's attorney general, based largely on her allegations that then-Governor Tom Corbett had delayed Sandusky's prosecution when *he* was the attorney general, because he received donations for his gubernatorial campaign from leaders of the Second Mile organization. Once in office, Kane appointed special investigator Geoffrey Moulton to delve into the way the Sandusky investigation was handled. In his June 2014 report, Moulton found no evidence that Corbett had delayed the investigation. Instead, it was clear that it had stalled because Aaron Fisher was the sole, unreliable witness for over two years. Among other things, the Moulton report revealed that many Second Mile alums had denied that Sandusky had abused them.

But in the course of his research, Moulton also came across this trove of pornographic emails, including a photo collection entitled "Blonde Banana Split," showing two women stuffing bananas into each other's orifices. A close-up of a champagne bottle inserted into a vagina was captioned: "Thank you, Mr. Daniels. Thank you, Mr. Guiness. Muchos Gracias, Señor Tequila," apparently in gratitude for rendering the woman unconscious. A photo of a woman with a black eye was entitled "Irish Sunglasses," and promised a "free pair when you forget dinner."

Frank Fina, who had left the attorney general's office to work for the Philadelphia district attorney (who had prosecuted the Billy Doe case), alleged that Kane had dropped the ball by failing to prosecute a bribery case against six black legislators. In return, Kane not only made more of the pornographic emails public but leaked information about a grand jury investigation in which Fina had been involved, making *him* look bad for a stalled investigation of a local NAACP leader. This eventually resulted in Kane's disbarment and conviction for perjuring herself about the grand jury leak, which led to time in prison.

It did not escape John Ziegler's notice that it was incredibly ironic that Sandusky, who had no pornography on his computer or in his home or office, was prosecuted by a man who sent and received such grotesque pornographic images. In addition, no one was ever prosecuted for the leaked Sandusky grand jury information to reporter Sara Ganim, which probably came from somewhere within the attorney general's office. But such a leak brought down Kathleen Kane.[25]

EVICTED FROM MATT SANDUSKY'S SPEECH

In addition to the alleged victims who testified at trial, John Ziegler was particularly contemptuous of Matt Sandusky, the adopted son who had "flipped" in the middle of the trial. He had offered to give $10,000 to Matt's Peaceful Hearts Foundation in return for an hour-long videotaped interview, which Matt declined. Ziegler posted a long email from Matt's former girlfriend (whom I called "Anne" in Chapter 10) about their mutual suicide attempt, explaining that it had nothing to do with any alleged abuse by Jerry Sandusky.

On April 27, 2016, Matt Sandusky gave his first speech in Pennsylvania at the Lewisburg High School auditorium, during Sexual Assault Awareness Month. Entitled "Triumph After Oppression," the poster noted that tickets were free but registration was required. Ziegler dutifully registered for a free ticket and showed up.

But Matt Sandusky refused to speak if his chief critic was there, so the local police dragged the protesting Ziegler from his seat. "I was sitting at a public event at a public school, with a ticket in my own name," Ziegler recalled. "Yet they dragged me out of the arena, threw me to the ground, jumped on my back, and I sustained knee and arm injuries and cuts on my hand when they pulled my hands behind me and handcuffed me hard." He was kept in solitary confinement for two hours before his arraignment and ended up taking a plea bargain and paying a $100 fine for disturbing the peace. "My lawyer was terrible. It would have cost more than that to come back [from California] for the hearing."[26]

TAKE THIS BURDEN AWAY

By the time he appeared on the Glenn Beck Show in March 2017, Ziegler was clearly tired of dealing with the Sandusky case. "I will pay money, please prove me wrong. I want this off my back. This has been the worst thing that's ever happened in my life, and I've had a lot of bad things happen. Please, take this burden away," he implored Beck.

Ziegler still had his own self-produced weekly talk show, "The World According to Zig," at FreeSpeechBroadcast.com, and wrote a regular column for the news website Mediaite.com, but otherwise he lived off of his savings, real estate rental income, and his wife's salary as a middle school teacher. They had a five-year-old daughter, born just before he took on the Sandusky case, and another child on the way.

In the two-hour radio interview, Ziegler insisted, "I'm 100% convinced he is innocent, and it's not even close," despite the fact that he didn't particularly like Sandusky. "Jerry's a goofball, he's a weirdo, he's a dolt, but he's not a pedophile. He's incredibly naïve, and he's innocent."

Ziegler talked about a purposely fake accuser, a Second Mile alum who had asked what he could do to help Sandusky's cause. Ziegler sent him to one of the lawyers who had made a killing by representing alleged Sandusky victims. This lawyer had, Ziegler said, overtly molded the fake accuser's story to conform to what Penn State would want in a settlement case, and then sent him to a therapist who had helped others recover memories of abuse. "We have incredibly damning audio," Ziegler said, but he couldn't currently play the tapes due to a variety of concerns.

In conclusion, Ziegler emphasized that the road to Jerry Sandusky's hell, littered with the corpses of Joe Paterno, Penn State administrators, the deceased Second Mile program, and other detritus, truly was paved with the best of intentions. "A lot of people in this case thought they were doing the right thing. That's when people become really dangerous. Everyone thinks they're fighting the monster."[27]

— CHAPTER 20 —

Legal Grind

THE GEARS of the Pennsylvania legal system continued to grind slowly but inexorably following Jerry Sandusky's 2012 conviction. On January 3, 2013, Philadelphia attorney Norris Gelman worked on an appeal of the decision, submitting arguments that Sandusky had received an unfair trial. In Pennsylvania, as well as many other states, the trial judge—in this case John Cleland—decide such issues. Since a ruling for the defense would be tantamount to admitting that he had presided over a flawed proceeding, it was unlikely that such a judge would favor the appeal.

At the end of January, Cleland ruled against all seven of the appeal points. The most compelling issue presented was the fact that Cleland had denied all of Amendola's motions for a continuance so that he could deal with the "vast amount" of discovery material before going to trial. Indeed, Amendola had received over 12,000 pages of material in addition to tapes and other evidence. Cleland now dismissed this claim, citing Amendola's outrageous statement at a January 10, 2013, hearing that "he had discovered no item he would have used at trial if he had had it; and he discovered nothing that would have altered his approach to the trial."

Why Amendola made such a damaging statement is anyone's guess, or why Gelman failed to follow up with cross-examination to show that Amendola had not even gone through all of the discovery material. It is a certainty that he had not read all 12,000 pages at that point, and it is difficult to conceive that he would not have used the taped interview with janitor Jim Calhoun if he had listened to it.

The appeal asserted that it was a judicial error to allow janitor Ron Petrosky to give hearsay testimony about what fellow janitor Jim Calhoun had allegedly witnessed in a locker room shower, because "an excited utterance, standing alone, cannot be used to prove the exciting event occurred." In his opinion, Cleland wrote that "other facts" to which Petrosky testified, along with "a second witness, Jay Witherite," supported the conclusion that the shower incident took place. Incredibly, Cleland failed to note that Witherite had not, in fact, testified at the trial. He added that even if the accounts involving "Victim 8," the phantom victim, were set aside, it wouldn't make any difference because of all the other charges. Thus, "it cannot be said that the introduction of hearsay statements as to this one victim was anything other than harmless error."*

The judge also defended his decision not to issue a standard instruction to the jury about "Failure to Make Prompt Complaint in Certain Sexual Offenses." During the trial, Cleland had denied a request that he issue this standard instruction to the jury because he said that research showed it wasn't unusual for people to delay reporting child sexual abuse. He now admitted that he knew of no such research but was relying on his extensive experience as a judge with other sex abuse cases. At any rate, he denied any error.

Nor was Cleland concerned that in the closing argument, Prosecutor Joe McGettigan had improperly commented on Sandusky's failure to testify at trial. McGettigan had said that the defendant "had wonderful opportunities to speak out and make his case," as he had done with Bob Costas. But "I only heard him (Sandusky) on TV. Only heard him on TV." Although this statement clearly referred to Sandusky's failure to testify, Cleland dismissed it as a non-issue, since he had instructed the jury repeatedly that the defendant had no obligation to take the stand.

And so it went for the other issues raised on appeal, including the point that it was difficult to defend against allegations without knowing exactly when they were supposed to have occurred. The Commonwealth admitted that it was "unable to provide specific dates because there were numerous offenses over the course of several years. The victim, a child at the time of the crimes, is unable to provide exact times and dates."[1]

Norris Gelman appealed this decision to the Pennsylvania Superior Court, which affirmed Cleland's ruling on October 2, 2013, and the Pennsylvania Supreme Court rubber-stamped it without further comment on December 18, 2013.[2]

The next step for Sandusky was to file for post-conviction relief, in which a defendant can ask for a new trial based on ineffective

---

* The phrase "harmless error" sets defense attorneys' teeth on edge, since it is frequently used by judges in denying appeals.

assistance of counsel, or new evidence found after the trial that would have had an impact on the jury's decision, or constitutional violations. For this task, Sandusky hired Al Lindsay, then sixty-seven, a former prosecutor and veteran defense attorney with over four decades of experience, who officially took on the job on June 16, 2014. "I was probably destined to be a lawyer," Lindsay told a reporter. "My father was a lawyer, my grandfather was a lawyer." Lindsay had successfully defended the Rev. Richard Rossi, accused of attempting to murder his wife, and John Vojtas, a former police officer accused of killing a man during a traffic stop. But the Sandusky case would represent the biggest challenge of his career.[3]

THE FIGHT FOR A NEW TRIAL

It took Al Lindsay nearly a year to prepare his Post-Conviction Relief Act (PCRA) Petition, in part because Joe Amendola was slow to turn over the massive amount of discovery material, but mostly because it took a long time to read through the trial transcript, the sealed grand jury testimony, police reports, and thousands of pages of documents, in addition to listening to taped interviews. On May 6, 2015, Lindsay filed his 111-page brief claiming that Joe Amendola and Karl Rominger had provided ineffective counsel and that several issues violated Sandusky's constitutional rights.

Lindsay wrote that Sandusky's right to a fair trial was "crushed under a stampede of vitriol, rage and prejudice that mandate a new trial in this case." On multiple grounds, Lindsay condemned Amendola for the horrendous job he did in defending Sandusky, concluding that he had "essentially abandoned Sandusky, leaving him without any defense, and, in reality, trial counsel (Amendola) acted more like another prosecutor instead of defense counsel."

Lindsay started with Amendola's failure to follow legal ethics and quit rather than go on with a trial for which he was admittedly unprepared. Amendola did not demand a continuance based on the "highly prejudicial pretrial atmosphere," to allow a cooling down period. Not only that, but Amendola had *opposed* moving the trial outside Centre County, where there was a lynch-mob mentality against Sandusky, who was blamed for Paterno's death and a possible NCAA "death penalty" against the Penn State football program. Amendola had waived Sandusky's right to a preliminary hearing and had never attempted to interview any of the alleged victims prior to trial.

In his opening statement, Amendola had inexcusably talked about the "overwhelming evidence" against his client and had repeatedly promised the jury that Sandusky would testify, when it turned out he did not. Amendola had not sought a pre-trial hearing where an expert witness could explain why the testimony should be disallowed from alleged victims who had been influenced by improper suggestive interviews or psychotherapy. He had not issued subpoenas to gain access to contingency fee agreements with civil lawyers to prove financial motivation for allegations, nor had he sought Penn State records of Sandusky's football schedule to develop an alibi defense.

Amendola had failed to demand proof that former janitor Jim Calhoun was incompetent to testify, had not listened to the police tape in which Calhoun denied that Sandusky was the abuser he saw in a shower, and had failed to appeal the resulting conviction for abuse of the fictional Victim 8.

Not only that, but he called Elliot Atkins as an expert witness to label Sandusky with "histrionic personality disorder," thus opening the door to the prosecution's expert saying that he might instead have a "psychosexual disorder." In addition, "the testimony of Dr. Atkins was irrelevant to Mr. Sandusky's defense that the charged conduct did not occur," and Amendola had not explained to his client what Atkins would say.

Amendola had not objected to caseworker Jessica Dershem proffering unwarranted expert opinion from the stand. He had not objected to the prosecutor leading his own witnesses. In fact, Amendola had made hardly any objections to anything. He had no discernible trial strategy and was overwhelmed and disorganized. He had ill-advisedly told Sandusky, without any preparation, to submit to an interview with Bob Costas. He had told reporters during the jury deliberations that he would have a "heart attack" if Sandusky were acquitted.

Finally, Amendola had testified after the trial that nothing in the vast amount of discovery would have changed the way he conducted the defense, even though he had never reviewed all of the discovery material. The Superior Court had cited this testimony as its reason for declaring that Sandusky had not been prejudiced by the lack of a continuance prior to trial.

In the PCRA, Lindsay asserted several issues that violated Sandusky's constitution right to a fair trial. In his closing argument, Joe McGettigan had prejudicially referred to Sandusky's failure to testify, even though the defendant had a right to remain silent. Amendola had idiotically agreed not to object to anything in the closing argument unless it was "egregious," but this issue *was* egregious, as was McGettigan's reference to Victim 2 as being "known to God but not to us," when he knew full well that Allan Myers was that boy in the shower.

Lindsay claimed that the leak of grand jury information to reporter Sara Ganim, whose coverage on March 31, 2011, had a major impact on the case, was "a deliberate act by the prosecution and its agents" in order to "shake the tree" to find more alleged victims, because the case was stalled. Thus, "the investigating grand jury system was abused so fundamentally that the only proper remedy is to exclude all evidence derived from the grand jury, including all the witnesses who came forward after the leak to Sara Ganim," which would require a new trial involving only Victims 1 and 2. The Presentment also contained a crucial inaccuracy by stating that McQueary had actually witnessed sodomy.

The prosecution had performed "late-hour 'open file' document dumps in discovery . . . on the eve of trial," hoping that Amendola, buried under the avalanche, "would not find relevant Brady [exculpatory] material." Lindsay wrote that the charges filed against Penn State administrators Tim Curley and Gary Schultz were brought in "bad faith" just to prevent their being called as witnesses during the Sandusky trial. Curley and Schultz had still not gone to trial, over three years later. "The Commonwealth apparently had no intention of actually prosecuting these cases," Lindsay scoffed.

In summary, Lindsay wrote: "The Commonwealth's entire case was a house of cards resting on testimony that trial counsel should have exposed as incompetent, unreliable, and inadmissible."[4] He asked for hearings in which he would call most lawyers and investigators in the case, including Amendola, Rominger, McGettigan, and Fina, as well as reporter Sara Ganim, police inspectors Sassano and Leiter, hidden "Victim 2" Allan Myers, former attorney general Tom Corbett, and psychologist Philip Esplin, who would testify about repressed memories and suggestive questioning.

It took Deputy Attorney General Jennifer Peterson six months to respond to Lindsay's PCRA Petition on September 1, 2015. Mostly, her answer complained that Lindsay had not provided sufficiently detailed proof of his claims or said that they had already been denied on appeal or waived because Amendola had failed to ask for a mistrial at the time of the prosecutorial misconduct.

But Peterson's answer regarding repressed memory therapy was astonishing. Lindsay's petition had provided little concrete evidence for the involvement of repressed memories in the case. That term had never been used at trial, even though, as we have seen, there were strong indications for it, particularly in Dustin Struble's testimony. Rather than claiming new post-trial evidence in the form of Mike Gillum's and Aaron Fisher's revelations in *Silent No More*, or my interview with Struble in which he talked about his repressed memories, Lindsay had asserted that Amendola should have known to ask for a pre-trial hearing on such influences on the memory of alleged victims. Lindsay also conflated the concern with leading police questioning and misguided psychotherapy.

In her response, Peterson didn't even mention therapists, the crucial memory influencers. "In his continued attack on the credibility of the victims," she wrote, "Sandusky now suggests that the witnesses testified regarding 'repressed memories' and that there was a question as to whether these memories were the product of serial suggestive interviews by law enforcement and Children and Youth [Services]."

Rather than arguing that repressed memories were not involved in the Sandusky case, Peterson apparently believed in recovered memories and proceeded to defend their validity. She cited a 2000 South Carolina case that regurgitated all the old bromides and myths about repression and dissociation: "To cope with the horror of their experiences, many child sexual abuse victims develop dissociative defense mechanism. . . . Dissociation can take a number of forms, including traumatic amnesia—more commonly known as repressed memory." So the sexually abused child would completely forget the abuse because the event was "so traumatic, that, in a desperate effort to cope, one's mind . . . shuts the memory out." In other words, "the victim keeps a secret, even from herself" or himself, as the case may be.

Peterson then cited the 1998 Pennsylvania *Crawford* case in which the crucial accusing witness, John Reed, had allegedly recovered memories of Franklin Crawford drowning a woman in 1971, and subsequently "hallucinatory visions or voices" had urged him to come forward. Dr. Himmelhoch, the psychiatrist who examined the accuser for the defense, questioned the validity of such repressed memories in his written report. The trial judge refused to allow Himmelhoch's expert testimony. The jury found Reed's recovered memories to be believable, and Crawford was found guilty. The Pennsylvania Superior Court overruled the decision, saying that Himmelhoch's testimony should have been allowed.

The case went to the Supreme Court, which reversed the Superior Court and reaffirmed the original guilty verdict, but the Supreme Court's convoluted reasoning held that repressed memories were not an issue, because "no expert testimony was offered by the Commonwealth to explain that revived repressed memory was recognized by the scientific community." Therefore, the defense was not entitled to introduce an expert witness on the issue, even though repressed memories were central to the case. "We do not address whether expert testimony regarding revived repressed memory would be admissible into evidence," the opinion noted.

Thus, Peterson did not deny that repressed memory therapy influenced some of the alleged victims in the Sandusky case. Instead she appeared to believe that repressed memories were accurate and should be used to convict people. She said that Lindsay had no right to raise the issue because "the prosecution did not introduce any expert testimony on revived repressed memory, nor make it an issue."[5] But of course the prosecution would not have wanted to highlight the fact that some of the "memories" of abuse were shaped by suggestive, misguided psychotherapy.

LEGAL MANEUVERS

Before Judge Cleland could rule on the issues raised, a flurry of legal briefs and maneuvers intervened. On September 29, 2015, Lindsay filed a request for further discovery material, which could be granted in PCRA matters only under "exceptional circumstances." The defense attorney observed wryly that "this case is exceptional to say the least." Lindsay requested authority to issue subpoenas to Allan Myers, Joe McGettigan, and others, along with confidential documents pertaining to Myers, on the grounds that McGettigan had lied during his closing arguments about not knowing the identity of Victim 2.

Lindsay also wanted to subpoena witnesses in relation to the grand jury information leaked to reporter Sara Ganim, including Ganim herself, Aaron Fisher and his mother, Mike Gillum, Debra McCord (Zachary Konstas's mother), attorneys Frank Fina and Jonelle Eshbach, and James Reeder, who had been appointed by Grand Jury Judge Barry Feudale to investigate the leaks, but whose report (if ever completed) was never made public. He also wanted all correspondence, including emails, between the judiciary and the attorney general's office staff during the time of the Sandusky grand jury.[6] Given the recent furor over Kathleen Kane's unrelated grand jury leaks, Lindsay asserted that "these leaks were part of the systemic breakdown of the grand jury process over time by the Attorney General's Office and supervising Judges."

Finally, Lindsay requested copies of contingency fee agreements that any alleged victims had signed with civil attorneys.

The day after Lindsay filed these requests, an Associated Press story quoted a spokesman for Kane saying that she had "strong suspicions that the [Sandusky grand jury] leaks came from people associated with this office."[7] Lindsay pounced, demanding that Kane reveal any evidence to support these suspicions. In writing, Attorney General Kane, whose legal license had just been suspended, wrote to Judge Cleland, saying that she hadn't been referring to the Sandusky case, but to Grand Jury Judge Barry Feudale's leak of sealed Supreme Court documents, all part of Pennsylvanian's convoluted politics. About those leaks, Kane wrote, "Make no mistake, Judge Feudale's overriding concern was how to leak sealed documents without getting caught."

In 2013, Kane had used her influence to remove Feudale from his grand jury judgeship. In a series of July 2013 emails to newspaper reporters, Feudale had complained that "the OAG's 'sneak attack' . . . gripes my butt." His comments on the Sandusky case revealed extreme bias towards Sandusky, who was "a SEXUAL PREDATOR WHO WILL PROBABLY DIE IN JAIL," as well as Curley, Schultz, and Spanier, who "turned deaf eyes and ears to such a horrible thing. Just like some in the catholic church and boy scouts." He said he would "not abandon those kids," referring to the young adult alleged victims, because he had observed the "pain and shame" on their faces as they testified.

Cleland ordered Kane to appear before him for a private hearing on November 5, 2015. The beleaguered attorney general, who would be convicted of perjury and removed from office the following year, repeated that she didn't know whether Feudale had leaked any grand jury documents, but neither had she read all 3,300 of Feudale's emails on the Office of the Attorney General's servers.

On November 12, 2015, Judge Cleland refused to grant Lindsay the power to subpoena witnesses to force them to testify, nor did he grant him the right to review the Sandusky grand jury communications, which he characterized as a "fishing expedition." But at least Cleland would review the contingency fee agreements with civil lawyers "in camera"—i.e., privately.

An obviously frustrated Lindsay then filed a request on November 25, 2015, to subpoena James Reeder and Kenneth Brown, who had been assigned as special prosecutors to investigate the Sandusky grand jury leaks, since Reeder refused to speak to the defense lawyer or to reveal whether he had completed his report. If they hadn't finished the job—which was apparently the case—Lindsay requested that Cleland assign another special prosecutor to investigate the leaks and file a complete report. The defense attorney asked for a hearing on the issue. Cleland didn't even respond, and so things stood as the Christmas season came and went.

ANDREW SALEMME ON THE CASE

As 2016 arrived, Al Lindsay hired a bright, young lawyer named Andrew Salemme, who had written *Guilty Until Proven Innocent: A Practitioner's and Judge's Guide to the Pennsylvania Post-Relief Act*. Salemme had previously worked for the Pennsylvania Superior Court, helping to research and write appellate decisions. He quickly reviewed all of the Sandusky case material and helped Lindsay write a revised PCRA petition, which was submitted on March 9, 2016, to supplement the post-conviction argument.

Lindsay and Salemme were a good fit, with Salemme helping to shape the new petition as a compelling narrative: "This is a story of how the media, overzealous law enforcement, a biased grand jury judge, an abused grand jury process, prosecutorial malfeasance, a discredited and pseudoscientific type of therapy, greed, and serial instances of ineffective assistance of counsel resulted in transforming an innocent man into one of this country's most infamous 'child predators.'" To prove it, in the 158-page document, the petition raised 34 distinct issues that justified a new trial.

In particular, Salemme apparently recognized the extent to which repressed memory therapy had influenced the Sandusky case, citing Harvard psychologist Richard McNally's statement that the theory of repressed memories "is a piece of psychiatric folklore devoid of convincing empirical support." The PCRA petition reviewed the ever-shifting, ever-growing allegations of the alleged victims. For the first time, the defense team claimed "after-discovered evidence" of repressed memories involving Aaron Fisher, Dustin Struble, and Matt Sandusky, in addition to the claim of ineffective counsel for Amendola's failure to present expert testimony on the pseudoscience of repressed memories.

"The Commonwealth knew that many of the victims' stories evolved based on their therapy," the petition stated, "yet never disclosed that the victims had no independent recollection of sexual abuse." Amendola failed to recognize the reference to repressed memories in Struble's or others' testimony. Thus, the state had committed a Brady violation by failing to reveal that Fisher, Struble, Houtz, and Simcisko (at minimum) were undergoing repressed memory therapy. There was no way the defense could have known about the therapy because of therapist-patient privilege.

While Pennsylvania's Supreme Court had not ruled on repressed memories, it *had* banned hypnotically refreshed memories in a 1981 decision in Commonwealth v. Nazarovitch. That case involved the 1976 murder of a twelve-year-old girl. On the third anniversary of her death, Pamela Wilfong, who had known the girl, had a nightmare about her and concluded that perhaps she held information about the murder in her subconscious. The excited police then had her hypnotized, after feeding the hypnotist facts about the case. Wilfong then "remembered" three men who had allegedly committed the murder.

Wilfong's testimony was ruled inadmissible under the 1921 "Frye" precedent that a concept has to be generally accepted within the relevant scientific community before it could be used in court.* The Nazarovitch decision noted that "the [hypnotized] subject may intercept and internalize any suggestions about the desired answer."[8] That is true not only of hypnosis, but of any psychotherapy in which the "desired answer" is that subjects should recall repressed memories of abuse by a particular person, whether it be through hypnosis, dreams, panic attacks, bodily sensations, or just plain old suggestive "thinking about it more."

The Sandusky petition also included strong language about the leading nature of the police interviews, in which the investigators "all but begged the accusers to make ever more serious allegations and were egged on in at least one case by a civil attorney seeking significant remuneration."

The way Amendola and Gelman had handled the phantom victim of janitor Ron Petrosky, supposedly relating the story of Jim Calhoun, was "simply mind-boggling," Salemme and Lindsay noted, and they quoted from the tape-recorded interview in which Calhoun denied that Sandusky was the abuser in the shower.

In conclusion, they wrote: "If a text book were to be written on how not to try a sex offense case involving overwhelming media attention, this case would provide the model."[9]

---

* The more stringent Daubert/Kumho (1993, 1999) standard has replaced Frye in most states, demanding scientific proof of a theory—but Pennsylvania still relies on Frye.

THE MEDIA LOVES THE ABUSE NARRATIVE

Remarkably, reporters covering the Sandusky case did not write about the two most revelatory parts of the new PCRA petition: the repressed memory evidence and the exculpatory Calhoun tape. At that point, I wrote to these reporters, explaining the importance of this information and sending the link to the PCRA petition, citing page numbers, just in case they had been too lazy to read the lengthy document. But it became apparent that no one in the media was interested in questioning the abuse narrative, even when there was new, compelling evidence.

Instead, the media quickly latched onto anything that smacked of sensational Sandusky abuse claims, no matter how absurd. In May 2016, as part of yet another spin-off Sandusky lawsuit, they got what they wanted. Penn State had brought suit against its insurance companies to force them to reimburse the university for the $93 million settlements with thirty-three alleged Sandusky victims. The insurance companies refused to pay for claims when university officials had allegedly known about the abuse. That included a settlement to someone claiming that Sandusky had abused him in 1976. In one sentence of a pretrial ruling, Judge Gary Glazer in the Court of Common Pleas of Philadelphia County mentioned the claim. An alert reporter wrote a piece, headlined "Child Told Paterno of Sex Abuse in 1976." This finding also included allegations that two different assistant Penn State coaches had witnessed Sandusky molesting children in 1987 and 1988. Judge Glazer apparently accepted these anonymous cases as true in his order.

Reporter Sara Ganim, having moved to CNN, followed up with a truly unbelievable story of an anonymous man who claimed that, when the alleged victim was fifteen, Sandusky picked him up hitchhiking in 1971, gave him beer and marijuana, and then raped him as he was standing at a urinal in a Penn State bathroom. And when he told Joe Paterno on the phone, the coach wouldn't believe him because Sandusky had done "so many good things." Every element of this story is absurd. Sandusky never drank or took drugs. He was never accused of assaulting strangers. And he hadn't done "many good things" at that point, six years before he started the Second Mile program. Nonetheless, Penn State gave this accuser settlement money as one of Sandusky's supposed victims. Regardless, the stories of the 1970s victims took off nationally.

Penn State President Eric Barron, who had replaced Rodney Erickson in 2014, blasted the news coverage, saying that he was "appalled by the rumor, innuendo, and rush to judgment," adding that the allegations were "difficult for any reasonable person to believe." Finally, a Penn State leader displayed some backbone, although the same rush to judgment had occurred with *all* of the Sandusky allegations. Joe Paterno's widow, Sue, complained of "this endless process of character assassination by accusation."[10] It was implausible that Paterno heard any complaints about Sandusky's alleged pedophilia in 1976, since the next year, he promoted Sandusky to defensive coordinator and agreed to be an honorary board member of the new Second Mile.

Two months later, when the court documents were unsealed, it turned out that "John Doe 150," the alleged 1976 victim, had said that Sandusky had stuck his finger into his rectum during a shower, and that when he told the head coach about it, Paterno supposedly ignored him, saying, "I don't want to hear about any of that kind of stuff, I have a football season to worry about." Even though such anonymous allegations were clearly fabricated to milk Penn State's settlement millions, the *Washington Post,* renowned for its careful journalism, regurgitated them without question, along with more anonymous allegations that various assistant coaches had supposedly witnessed Sandusky's child abuse through the years.[11]

Jay Paterno, who had coached with his father, snapped. In an open letter, he noted that "coaches turned over cell phones, e-mail accounts, computers and iPads, and what did they find to reveal some vast conspiracy spanning decades? Nothing." And of course, his father would never have ignored child abuse. The real story, Paterno observed, was "how Penn State failed to vet these claims properly and overpaid to make them all go away. But that story doesn't move product and that story wasn't fed to the writers who jumped on this."[12]

THE QUEST FOR A NEW TRIAL PUSHES AHEAD

Meanwhile, the post-conviction relief effort ground on. In a May 2, 2016, hearing, Judge Cleland questioned the need for any evidentiary hearings.[13] In response, a week later Lindsay filed a request for Cleland to recuse himself from the case, based on the judge's participation in the off-the-record pretrial meeting at the Hilton Garden Inn in December 2011, making a deal to waive the Sandusky preliminary hearing. Because that made Cleland a witness to one of the PCRA issues, he faced a conflict of interest. But Cleland refused to step down.

He did, however, grant three evidentiary hearings in August 2016, limited to ten of the thirty-four issues raised in the PCRA petition. He wouldn't allow any testimony about repressed memories, the Jim Calhoun tape, the flawed jury selection process, and many other issues.

Nonetheless, Cleland opened the door for calling some witnesses in support of the claim for a new trial and allowed them to be subpoenaed. On August 12, 2016, Jerry Sandusky was finally able to take the stand for the first time, where he vehemently denied that he had sexually abused anyone. About oral or anal sex, he said, "That idea is totally foreign to me. It's disgusting and dirty." He then testified how Amendola had given him fifteen-minutes' notice, without preparation, for the interview with Bob Costas, and how his lawyer had advised him to waive the preliminary hearing. Sandusky also related how desperate Amendola had been after Matt Sandusky's mid-trial flip and how he told Sandusky he shouldn't testify. "Everything was in a state of chaos," he recalled. Sandusky said that he didn't understand what psychologist Elliot Atkins would say and was infuriated by his testimony.

Why hadn't Sandusky questioned Amendola's tactics? "I was very new to this entire process," Sandusky said. "I trusted Mr. Amendola. He was the expert on this."

Then Karl Rominger took the stand. At that point, he had surrendered his license to practice law after he was caught misappropriating a client's funds. Indeed, five days after he testified at this hearing, Rominger pled guilty to the charges and was sent to prison.[14] Ironically, he had been far more competent at Sandusky's defense than Amendola. Now, on the stand, he explained why he thought waiving the preliminary hearing was a terrible idea, how Amendola had told him that there was an "understanding" that neither side would call Allan Myers as a witness, and that it was "obvious" that someone at the Office of the Attorney General had leaked grand jury information to Sara Ganim.

Next, Joe Amendola testified, seeking to justify his defense of Sandusky. He said that he had "no idea" that there were accusers other than Aaron Fisher until he read the Grand Jury Presentment. He figured that since Sandusky was already so vilified, it was a "golden opportunity" for him to do an interview with Bob Costas. He defended his decision to waive the preliminary hearing. He said that he "about fell over" when Shubin told him that Allan Myers was claiming to be a Sandusky victim, and that Matt Sandusky's mid-trial flip was a "nuclear bomb" to his defense efforts that convinced him not to put Jerry Sandusky on the stand.

About the ill-advised decision to have Elliott Atkins testify that Sandusky had a histrionic personality disorder, Amendola said that Atkins was a third last-minute choice of experts and admitted that his testimony hadn't worked out so well.

Had Amendola considered introducing the grand jury testimony of Tim Curley, Gary Schultz, and Graham Spanier that they thought the 2001 shower involved only "horseplay" and that Mike McQueary had not told them about observing overt sexual abuse? Yes, but he decided against it because the prosecution would then say they were facing charges of perjury. He denied having made a deal that neither side would call Allan Myers.

The final witness of the day was Lindsay Kowalski, who had been hired three weeks before the trial to review and organize the case files. She recalled that Sandusky, who had been calm throughout most of the trial, was "almost shaking with anger" during Elliot Atkins's testimony.[15]

Ten days later, on August 22, 2016, Andrew Shubin, Mike Gillum, Scott Rossman, Joe Leiter, and Anthony Sassano testified at the second day of hearings.

Civil Attorney Shubin verified that he represented Dustin Struble, Jason Simcisko, Ryan Rittmeyer, Matt Sandusky, and Allan Myers, and that Myers was indeed Victim 2, the boy in the 2001 shower. He had represented Myers twice for driving under the influence of alcohol, the last of which was just before the Grand Jury Presentment came out. Yes, Myers had gone to Amendola, identified himself as Victim 2, and told his investigator Curtis Everhart that Sandusky had never molested him. But then two weeks later Shubin took him on as a client with a contingency fee agreement. Yes, he had refused to let the prosecution interview Myers without Shubin being present, but Shubin refused to say whether he had hidden Myers in a remote cabin. Because the judge would not allow any testimony about repressed memories, Shubin was not asked about whether he sent his clients to therapy to help them recall abuse.

Similarly, when Mike Gillum next took the stand, Lindsay couldn't ask how the therapist had gotten Aaron Fisher to reveal buried sexual abuse memories. Instead, he asked only about leaked grand jury information and how Sara Ganim had found Fisher's address and name, which Gillum thought indicated "a major leak from the top," as he had written in *Silent No More*. But Gillum had nothing to add other than surmise. Nor did investigators Scott Ross-man, Joe Leiter, or Anthony Sassano shed any new light on leaked information, though Sassano recounted how Andrew Shubin had been "very vulgar" towards him when he insisted that his client, Allan Myers, had been severely abused over a hundred times, and that Shubin had hidden Myers in a hunting camp. He also said that when he finally was able to interview Myers in March 2012, he had drawn an inaccurate sketch of the Lasch building showers.[16]

During the third day of hearings, on August 23, 2016, prosecution lawyers Jonelle Eshbach, Frank Fina, and Joe McGettigan testified. Eshbach admitted that she had written the Grand Jury Presentment about the boy "being subjected to anal intercourse by a naked Sandusky" and she insisted that during his grand jury testimony, Mike McQueary had really said that's what he saw, even though McQueary had *not* said he had actually witnessed an act of sodomy. Otherwise, she added no useful information.

Nor did Frank Fina, though he admitted that many alleged victims "had given dramatically inconsistent statements." Both Fina and Eschbach acknowledged that there had been grand jury leaks but didn't know who had committed them. And since the judge had refused to let Lindsay see internal emails or other communications during that time, there was nothing further the defense attorney could do.

Joe McGettigan proved to be a very hostile witness. Lindsay said he would read from the prosecutor's closing argument, politely adding, "if you don't mind." McGettigan snarled, "And if I do mind?" McGettigan admitted that he had referred to Victim 2 as if he were known only to God, even though he knew that Allan Myers had identified himself as Victim 2. McGettigan had never spoken to him or even met him. Nonetheless, the prosecutor asserted now that he didn't believe Myers was Victim 2, the boy in the shower, because his shower drawing was inaccurate—not too surprising, given the ten years since he had been in that shower.

One last hearing took place three months later, on November 4, 2016, when Allan Myers finally took the stand. He had evaded all subpoena attempts for the August hearings. Jerry Sandusky could hardly recognize the overweight, bearded, sullen twenty-nine-year-old, who clearly didn't want to be there. He wouldn't use Sandusky's name, referring to him as "your client" in response to Al Lindsay's questions. Yes, he had gone to the Second Mile camps for a couple of years "until your client hand-picked me," he said. He admitted, however, that he had regarded Sandusky as a father figure and that he had lived with the Sanduskys the summer of 2005, before he attended Penn State. "I left because he was controlling," Myers said.

Lindsay had him read the notes of his September 2011 police interview, in which he said that Sandusky never made him uncomfortable and had not abused him, and that he didn't believe any of the allegations. "That would reflect what I said then," Myers said, "not what I would say now." That would become his refrain during his testimony, which appeared to be well-rehearsed, along with "I don't recall." Yes, he had told Curtis Everhart that "Jerry never violated me while I was at his home or anywhere else. . . . I felt very safe and at ease at his home, whether alone with Jerry or with others present." Yes, he had denied any anal or oral intercourse or any abuse at all. "That's what I said then."

Yes, Shubin was Myers's lawyer for his DUI charge, and then he represented him as a claimed Sandusky victim, and yes, he had received a settlement from Penn State. And yes, he said, he was Victim 2.

During her cross-examination, Jennifer Peterson asked Myers, "And you told him (Anthony Sassano) that you were sexually abused by Mr. Sandusky, right?" Surprisingly, he didn't agree. "I don't remember exactly what I said in the meetings. I know then I was more forthcoming, but not all the way coming, because still processing everything and dealing with it." It sounded as if he might have been in repressed memory therapy.

Peterson asked again, "Were you sexually abused?" This time he answered, "Yes," although he didn't actually say that it was Sandusky who had abused him. And there the matter was left.

GETTING OUT OF DODGE

Ten days after Allan Myers testified, Lindsay and Salemme filed a "Brief on Evidentiary Hearing Issues," reviewing the hearing testimony and using it to strengthen arguments they had already made. Among them was the issue of the meeting at the Hilton Garden Inn in December 2011 in which a deal was made to waive Sandusky's preliminary hearing. In a footnote, the defense attorneys again suggested that John Cleland should recuse himself from the case because he had been present at this off-the-record meeting. They had initially made this request in May 2016, when Cleland had brushed it aside. They now made a stronger case, citing case law that a judge should disqualify himself if he might be called as a material witness in the proceeding.

The next day, Cleland ordered the defense lawyers to notify him by 10:00 a.m. on November 17, 2016, whether they intended to call him as a material witness. If not, he demanded that they formally withdraw that argument. Lindsay and Salemme refused to delete the footnote but noted that as long as Cleland was the judge for the PCRA, they could not legally call him as a material witness.

The following day, Friday, November 18, 2016, Cleland issued an extraordinary opinion and order, recusing himself from the case, sounding more like a petulant child than a judge. He complained that Lindsay and Salemme had questioned the competence and integrity of most of the prosecutors and judges involved in the Sandusky grand jury and trial. "Now they have chosen to impugn the integrity of the court itself." By "the court," he meant himself, John Cleland.

He was particularly upset that the defense attorneys had written that Cleland had been "involved in the negotiation of waiver of important rights." He hadn't had anything to do with that negotiation; he had simply been present while the deal was negotiated. He complained that the way Lindsay and Salemme had put it had "nefarious undertones." They had made the Hilton Garden Inn meeting appear "somehow sinister," and by doing so, they had "created a cloud over these proceedings." The only way to remove that cloud was for him to recuse himself. But in doing so, he suggested that Lindsay and Salemme be called before the legal Disciplinary Board.

As a parting shot, Cleland wrote, "In my view, having studied all 34 issues raised in the petition and the applicable law, no grounds raised in the petition merit relief." In other words, he was offering his unsupported opinion that Sandusky did not deserve a new trial—an extraordinarily unprofessional, prejudicial statement, given that he was now handing over the decision to another judge.[17]

After six years presiding over the Sandusky case, Cleland finally revealed his hand. He had carefully presented himself as an objective, fair arbiter of the proceedings, but he had made crucial rulings in favor of the prosecution during the trial and its aftermath, and at Sandusky's sentencing hearing, he had told him, "Your crime is also your assault to their (victims') psyches and to their souls."

Now Sandusky's quest for a new trial had to await the appointment of a new judge, but Lindsay and Salemme were glad to be rid of Cleland. Asked why the judge had finally recused himself,

Lindsay opined that Cleland didn't want to have to rule on the post-conviction relief application, because it was so strong that he couldn't have easily denied it. But he absolutely didn't want to grant a new trial. "So he decided to get out of Dodge," Lindsay said.[18]

MORE SANDUSKY-RELATED CASES, DECISIONS

Meanwhile, several Sandusky-related legal decisions came down, all of them relying on the truth of the abuse narrative. Three weeks before Cleland's recusal, Mike McQueary won his whistleblower lawsuit against Penn State, with the jury awarding the former Penn State coach $7.3 million. At the end of November 2016, Judge Thomas Gavin ruled that that amount wasn't enough, so he added another $5 million. In doing so, he cited Prosecutor Jonelle Eshbach's testimony during the trial that McQueary had been a terrific grand jury witness: "He was rock solid in his testimony as to what he had seen," Eshbach said. "He was very articulate. His memory was excellent."

Eshbach, the author of the notorious Grand Jury Presentment, was correct that McQueary had been articulate, but his "rock solid" testimony had morphed from what he told his father and Jonathon Dranov in December 2000—that he heard sounds but witnessed no sexual abuse—to his grand jury testimony ten years later. And he kept modifying his story and memory after that. Nonetheless, the judge ruled that McQueary had suffered "humiliation" when Graham Spanier publicly supported Curley and Schultz, which by implication impugned the assistant coach. Gavin later added another $1.7 million to pay for McQueary's lawyers' fees.[19]

On November 3, 2016, a week after the McQueary verdict, the US Department of Education released its report on its investigation into Penn State's Clery Act violations, fining the university $2.4 million. The 1990 Clery Act requires universities benefitting from federal financial aid programs to disclose information about crimes on campus. The investigation had been sparked by the Sandusky scandal, with its alleged coverups, and it therefore looked at the fourteen-year span between 1998, the date of the first Sandusky shower incident, and 2011, after the Grand Jury Presentment was published. Although the fines involved many alleged extra-Sandusky infractions, they would never have been imposed if not for the scandal.[20]

In February 2017, the name Sandusky once more made national headlines with new sex abuse allegations, this time against Jerry and Dottie's adopted son Jeff, then forty-one. "Sandusky's Son Charged with Sexually Assaulting Children," the headline read in the

New York Times. The real story was that Jeff Sandusky had sent an incredibly stupid text message to his live-in girlfriend's sixteen-year-old daughter in the spring of 2016, apparently requesting that she send him a nude photo of herself. His odd explanation was that he was "role playing" and wanted to warn her *not* to do such things with her boyfriends, as she had allegedly done in the past. They all lived in the same household. Nothing came of it at the time, but in November 2016, the girl got mad at Jeff about something and forwarded the text message to her father, who promptly turned it over to the police.

With the enticing name of *Sandusky* before them, the police went into overdrive, labeling the girl "Victim 1" and calling in her older nineteen-year-old sister for questioning, along with her mother, Jeff's girlfriend. They had lived together for five years and were engaged to be married. The police got the older girl to say that Jeff had sent *her* an inappropriate text message three years prior to that, when she was sixteen, thus making her "Victim 2," even though there was no evidence in the form of an actual message.

In the criminal complaint, the police charged Jeff Sandusky with multiple counts of felonious sexual assault, asserting that he had "engaged in deviate sexual intercourse" with Victim 2, and then saying that he had "solicited, encouraged, and requested" Victim 1 to send him a nude photo to his cell phone. Jeff lost his job as a prison guard and was himself locked up in solitary confinement.

His local lawyer, Lance Marshall, decided not to say anything and to hope that the national headlines would die down. At the time, Jeff's fiancé was still supportive of him. The older daughter, "Victim 2," apparently said that nothing had happened, that Jeff sent no inappropriate email to her, and that the police were putting words in her mouth. Nonetheless, Marshall thought it was best not to get her to speak out but to keep Jeff Sandusky's name out of the press.

Yes, he said, it was true that the charges of "deviate sexual intercourse" were absurd, since no one claimed that Jeff had even touched either girl. The real charges, he felt, would be for "solicitation." And no, he couldn't get the charges knocked down, because he advised Jeff to waive his right to a preliminary hearing, which also meant that he couldn't yet even see the evidence, the actual offending text message. His reasoning was that a preliminary hearing would only keep the case in the news, and he hoped that when the case went to trial, the jurors would think, "Oh, is that all he did?" instead of the way the police and media had portrayed it.[21]

It appeared that once again, as with Jerry's Sandusky's faith in Joe Amendola, a Sandusky put his naïve trust in a local lawyer who made questionable decisions. Jeff Sandusky ended up taking a plea bargain for all fourteen counts against him, with sentencing due in December 2017, apparently for up to eight years. Otherwise, if found guilty at trial, he faced up to twenty-five years in prison. At the same time, ex-Congressman Anthony Weiner was sentenced to a mere twenty-one months in prison for sending sexual text messages to a fifteen-year-old girl.

It was ironic that Jeff, the only Sandusky child who had publicly supported his father's claims of innocence—he had "Sandusky 4 Life" tattooed on his arm after his father's trial—was now himself accused and imprisoned. He could easily have "flipped" to accuse his father and garner sympathy, as had Matt Sandusky, but he did not.

Although Jeff Sandusky was never diagnosed with a learning disability, he struggled in school, and when I met him in 2014, he seemed like a sincere, big man of somewhat limited intellect. His parents knew that he had been hit with an ashtray as a baby before they adopted him and had always wondered about its long-term effect. Before this incident, Jerry Sandusky had written of him: "Life has never been perfect for Jeff, but he has a good heart."[22]

A month after the charges against Jeff Sandusky made headlines across the country, the long-delayed trials of Tim Curley, Gary Schultz, and Graham Spanier were finally scheduled for March 2017. Because Curley and Schultz had been charged first, they would be tried separately from Spanier. On the eve of their trial, facing possible felony convictions that could have put them in prison for two decades, Curley, sixty-two, and Schultz, sixty-seven, opted for plea bargains for the lesser misdemeanor charge of "child endangerment," though neither of them had come close to harming any children. They were guilty only of believing that Sandusky had been "horsing around" with a boy in the shower, rather than foreseeing the story that McQueary would tell ten years later.[23]

Graham Spanier maintained his innocence and went to trial on Tuesday, March 21, 2017. Prosecutor Patrick Schulte told the jury in his opening statement that because of Spanier's failure to report McQueary's concerns in 2001 to a child protective agency, "evil in the form of Jerry Sandusky was allowed to run wild" for another decade as Sandusky used Penn State's showers as his "sanctuary for child molestation."[24]

Over two days, fourteen witnesses testified for the prosecution, including Mike McQueary, Jack Raykovitz (former Second Mile CEO), and Michal Kajak (Victim 5). Contrary to expectations, Tim Curley and Gary Schultz, who had taken plea bargains, did not turn on Spanier, the former Penn State president. They both insisted that McQueary had not told them that he had seen Sandusky sexually abusing a boy in the shower. They all thought the retired coach was just horsing around.

Kajak provided emotional testimony, breaking down on cue. He asserted that Sandusky had abused him in a Penn State shower in August 2001 (or maybe it was 2002), which was an all-important date because it showed that Sandusky had purportedly ignored Schultz's order that he not bring Second Mile kids to the athletic facilities after February 2001. (As we have seen, Kajak originally said that this shower took place in 1998.)

McQueary repeated his well-rehearsed testimony about seeing Sandusky apparently committing sodomy on a boy in the shower. But he inadvertently slipped up when he said that someone from the Attorney General's office (apparently Jonelle Eshbach) had called him on November 4, 2011, and said, "We're going to arrest folks and we are going to leak it out," thereby providing more fodder for Al Lindsay's post-conviction relief case.[25]

Surprisingly, the defense rested without calling any witnesses. Ex-Penn State President Graham Spanier, a confident, well-spoken man who had eloquently defended himself on television and elsewhere, never took the stand. In his closing argument Spanier's lawyer, Sam Silver, argued that the prosecution had "no evidence at all" of any cover-up or failure to report known child sexual abuse. But co-prosecutor Laura Ditka (the niece of famed Coach Mike Ditka), in her closing remarks, asserted that the Penn State administrators "took a gamble. They weren't playing with dice. They were playing with kids."

After deliberating for much of Thursday and all of Friday, March 24, 2017, the jurors came to a compromise verdict. They cleared Spanier of the felony charges but found him guilty of the same "child endangerment" misdemeanor that Curley and Schultz had taken in their plea bargains.

Over two months later, Pennsylvania Judge John Boccabella sentenced Spanier to four to twelve months, the first two to be spent in jail and the remainder under house arrest. Despite their plea bargains, Schultz and Curley got nearly two years each, with two or three months of that time behind bars. "All three ignored the opportunity to put an end to [Sandusky's] crimes when they had a chance to do so," the judge said, then added a gratuitous stab at the deceased Joe Paterno, saying he "could have made that phone call without so much as getting his hands dirty. Why he didn't is beyond me."

Spanier's lawyers filed an appeal, which Judge Boccabella rejected in July 2017; Spanier appealed that decision. Curley, suffering
from lung cancer and liver damage, asked the judge to allow him to
serve all of his time under house arrest, as did Schultz, who wanted
to care for his wife, who has multiple sclerosis. The judge denied
both pleas but left the door open for "work release." Both men served
several months in prison and were then put under house arrest.

In the meantime, Penn State was suing Spanier, claiming that
he should return about $6 million he had received as part of his
retirement package, and Spanier was counter-suing. Spanier was
also suing Louis Freeh for defamation because of his report.

In other legal action, the Paterno family had filed a lawsuit
against the National Collegiate Athletic Association for its alleged
misuse of the Freeh Report. Son Jay Paterno and a fellow assistant
football coach were also suing, claiming that the Freeh Report had
prevented them from finding comparable coaching work.[26]

Finally, in September 2017, Penn State belatedly announced
that it planned to sue the remains of the defunct Second Mile
program.[27]

NEW JUDGE, NEW HEARINGS

Jefferson County Judge John Foradora, then fifty years old, was
assigned the Sandusky post-conviction relief case on February 13,
2017. In his unsuccessful run for the Pennsylvania Supreme Court
two years beforehand, his campaign literature claimed that "Judge
Foradora has always taken on big challenges, has never shied away
from the tough cases," and that he would not "cave to insider political pressure."[28] Perhaps once he got up to speed on the Sandusky
case, he would have the courage to grant him the right to a new trial.

The new judge was willing to hold hearings on all thirty-four of
the issues Lindsay and Salemme had raised, including the alleged
use of repressed memory therapy, and he read through the transcripts of the trial and previous hearings to get himself up to speed.
Foradora quickly called a new hearing for March 24, 2017, at which
Joe Amendola, Mike Gillum, Joe Leiter, and Scott Rossman testified again, but this time the judge permitted more latitude in the
issues Al Lindsay could explore.

Incredibly, Joe Amendola claimed under oath that he was merely being "satirical" in his opening statement at trial when he said
that there was "overwhelming evidence" against Sandusky. Equally
outrageous was his claim that the reason he didn't introduce janitor

Jim Calhoun's taped interview, in which the janitor said Sandusky was not the man he saw in the shower, was that Calhoun was "basically incompetent." He claimed that he had listened to the Calhoun interview but chose not to introduce the evidence at trial. That seemed unbelievable. If true, it meant that Amendola was not only ineffective but incompetent.

Lindsay continued to hammer Amendola on why he had not called an expert witness on the hazards of repressed memories, why he had not sought a cooling off period before jury selection, why he had not refused to handle the case for ethical reasons because he was unprepared, why he had not objected to the prosecution's failure to notify him of new abuse claims, and why he had not questioned alleged victims more aggressively about their ever-growing abuse stories. Amendola couldn't remember a great deal about the trial, so much so that at one point Jerry Sandusky threw his shackled arms in the air and shook his head in disbelief. Lindsay asked Amendola why he hadn't moved for a mistrial for assorted prosecutorial infractions. "Because we were flying by the seat of our pants," Amendola admitted.[29]

When Mike Gillum took the stand, he would not admit to using repressed memory therapy and said that it was a "very dangerous game" to use methods such as hypnosis because "if one talks about something that might have happened to somebody, they could develop what's called an artificial memory, or a false memory." Yet he also talked about how the process of extracting Aaron Fisher's memories was "kind of like peeling an onion," and that abuse victims "tend to give it to you in layers if they trust you." He admitted that he believed it was possible to repress traumatic memories.

Still, Gillum stressed that "you don't want to lead them by saying, 'Oh, so maybe this happened to you.'" Yet it was clear that Gillum presumed from the outset that Sandusky had molested Fisher, and that it was his job to peel the onion layers to get him to say what he wanted. "We're talking about boys that have been made to perform oral sex on men, have been chronically raped orally, anally, whatever, over a long period of time."

Lindsay got Gillum to explain how the therapist had influenced Fisher to reinterpret Sandusky's concern and kindness as "grooming" behavior, and Gillum admitted that he had crossed over the line from counselor to advocate, partnering with the prosecution and police to get Aaron Fisher to testify against Sandusky.

But Lindsay unaccountably failed to quote anything from Gillum's book, *Silent No More*, even though he held the book aloft as he questioned the therapist. Thus, he did not challenge Gillum's assertion that he didn't lead Fisher. He didn't quote from passages in which Gillum explained to Fisher how he must have "dissociated" to forget his abuse. "With Sandusky's help," Gillum had written, "Aaron managed to disassociate himself from the grim reality of abuse, as victims do."[30] In *Silent No More*, Gillum told Fisher during their first therapy session, "Look, I know that something terrible happened to you." He further informed him, "I really think I know what you must be going through even though you won't tell me.

Nor did Lindsay quote from Gillum's description in the book of his outrageous method of guessing what abuse had occurred and asking leading questions to which Fisher could just answer *Yes* or *No*. In the book, the therapist admitted that he pressured Fisher. "If not for my pushing him along, he (Aaron) might have backed out a long time before this."[31]

Lindsay thus missed a golden opportunity to show Judge Foradora exactly how leading Gillum's methods were, and how he did in fact practice recovered memory therapy. On the stand, Gillum denied delving for repressed memories, apparently because he didn't hypnotize Fisher. Gillum told the Commonwealth's attorney, "I don't employ those techniques with anyone I work with," and Lindsay allowed that statement to stand without questioning him further.[32]

But Lindsay was more effective in questioning police investigators Joseph Leiter and Scott Rossman, the last witnesses in that day's hearing, getting them to admit that they used leading rather than open-ended questions, that they told Second Milers about other accusers and pressured them to say similar things, and that they had interviewed up to six hundred young men but only managed to come up with eight accusers. Even though the policemen denied knowing anything about repressed memories, they admitted encouraging accusers to seek "mental health assistance" and to contact them if they remembered more abuse.

Leiter and Rossman admitted that neither had any training or experience in sex abuse investigations prior to their search for Sandusky victims. They had never heard of "confirmation bias," in which people tend to seek selective confirmation of the preconceived theories they already hold. Yes, Rossman said, some of the abuse allegations grew over multiple interviews, but that was because they had to build "rapport." He was only trying to uncover the truth.[33]

At the end of the hearing, Judge Foradora asked if Lindsay planned to call John Cleland, the original trial judge who had held the initial post-conviction relief hearings before recusing himself, while Cleland asserted that "no grounds raised in the petition merit relief." Foradora was apparently appalled. "I don't understand why he wrote what he did." He was considering calling Cleland himself, but he had found that he was in Florida. "I mean, there's part of me that doesn't want his order hanging out there. His order sounds more ominous than what it is."

Foradora said he hoped to complete all necessary hearings in May and that, because he was an avid hunter, he intended to rule before hunting season of 2017 on whether Sandusky would get a new trial.[34]

Foradora held a final hearing on May 11, 2017. He announced there that he had decided not to call Cleland as a witness. "Why cross that bridge?" he said. "I'll let you guys do your work. I don't want to try your cases for you."[35]

Dustin Struble, "Victim 7," took the stand to talk about his growing abuse memories after seeking psychotherapy to help him recall them. His testimony included reference to my 2014 interview with Struble and follow-up emails, in which he acknowledged that he was in repressed memory therapy and wrote: "Both of my therapists have suggested that I have/had repressed memories and that's why we've been working on looking back on my life for triggers."

Struble acknowledged that he had spoken to me "about seeking counseling for help and through that, kind of reaching deeper into my memory." He said that he had explained to me "why for so long it was mostly a positive experience with Mr. Sandusky. . . . And then I was able to, unfortunately, recall some of the not-so-good events." Struble admitted that his therapist said that he might have repressed memories and that by "going back and recounting events step by step that possibly it can bring more things to light." But he insisted that he had already begun "the process of opening the door" of his memory by himself before he sought therapy.

When Sandusky defense lawyer Andrew Salemme asked Struble what methods his therapist had discussed with him, he said, "One involved something with headphones and beeps. . . . And it was supposed to, I guess, stimulate, you know, past experiences and help, I guess, bring things out." He was apparently referring to one of the stranger variants of EMDR (Eye Movement Desensitization and Processing), which usually involves people moving their eyes back and forth. According to Teagan Darnell, a California therapist who specializes in trauma, eating disorders, and spiritual issues, "Clients participate in EMDR by holding paddles and wearing headphones that vibrate and make quiet beeping noises. This is done while they process through traumatic memories."[36] It wasn't clear whether Dustin Struble actually participated in this exercise, because Salemme didn't pursue the topic, instead asking about things that "triggered" his alleged abuse memories.[37]

Struble was followed on the witness stand by Norris Gelman, Sandusky's first appeal lawyer, who had worked with Joe Amendola on Sandusky's post-sentence motion. His testimony revealed little, other than Gelman's failure to raise the issue of the hearsay janitor testimony. "That was a studied and strategic omission," Gelman claimed, because he didn't think it would make any difference.[38]

Then, as the last witness, Elizabeth Loftus testified by telephone. One of the world's leading memory experts, she explained that she was a distinguished professor of both psychology and law at the University of California at Irvine, the recipient of seven honorary doctorates, the author of twenty-two books and over five hundred scientific articles and chapters, and that her specialty was the study of human memory and its malleability. She had consulted for and lectured to the US Secret Service, the FBI, and the CIA and had testified in over three hundred trials.

Asked for a brief overview of human memory research, she emphasized that memory "doesn't work like a recording device," but is "much more constructive and reconstructive." We take bits and pieces of our experiences (or what we've heard about) and come up with a likely scenario. "People are sometimes exposed to other experiences later that can contaminate or distort or supplement a person's memory." Experiments by Loftus and others have proved that "you can plant entirely false memories into the mind of people for events that never happened," including being lost in a shopping mall, nearly drowning, being attacked by a vicious animal, and committing a crime as a teenager.

She said that she had studied the Sandusky case extensively, and that "it seems pretty evident that there were dramatic changes within the testimony of some of the accusers." She had written a report focusing on three of them, Dustin Struble, Aaron Fisher, and Brett Houtz. "One of the major reasons why someone's testimony changes from one point to another is they have been exposed to suggestive information that causes a change in their memory."

Such suggestive information could come in a number of forms, Loftus said. "When you have either suggestive interviewing or suggestive psychotherapy, it can sometimes cause people . . . to visualize things differently. . . . And these [visualizations] can solidify and come to feel as if they're actual memories." Over time, they can become quite convincing. "People can be very emotional and detailed and confident about them, even when they're false." Loftus explained that no one could completely disprove the Freudian theory, but "there is no credible scientific support for this idea of massive repression" of traumatic memories.[39]

A DISAPPOINTING DECISION

True to his word, Judge John Foradora made his decision on October 18, 2017, in plenty of time for hunting season. Despite the strong case for a new trial, he denied it in a 60-page opinion that universally took the prosecution's side. Foradora assumed, for instance, that Joe Amendola really had been "satirical" in his opening statement when he said there was "overwhelming evidence" against his client, that Amendola really had listened to the tape with Jim Calhoun and was justified in not using it, that Dr. Atkins' testimony about histrionic personality disorder was not so bad, and that Joe McGettigan really didn't believe that Allan Myers was Victim 2. Yes, there were Brady violations, he admitted, but they didn't warrant a new trial.

Foradora dismissed any concerns about repressed memory therapy, taking Mike Gillum's word that he had not practiced it (though Gillum clearly had encouraged Aaron Fisher to come up with new abuse memories) and asserting (erroneously) that Dustin Struble claimed not to have been in such therapy before the trial. Struble said only that he had not been hypnotized or subjected to beeps while wearing headphones. He had indeed recovered new memories of abuse during the time he was in psychotherapy before the trial, as he told me quite clearly.[40]

Foradora's decision should have come as no surprise. All judges in Pennsylvania are elected, and for Foradora to have approved the need for a new Sandusky trial would have almost certainly ended his career.

Nor was it likely that the Pennsylvania Superior Court, where the post-conviction relief application would go next, would vote for a new trial, and the state's Supreme Court is not even mandated to consider the matter. That would leave one final chance—a federal habeas corpus petition. There, outside of the state, Jerry Sandusky should logically win a new trial. But it is likely to be 2019 or 2020 by that time.

— SECTION III —

THE REAL JERRY SANDUSKY

— CHAPTER 21 —

A Big Kid

THUS FAR in this book, we've examined the incredible media firestorm and moral panic that engulfed Jerry Sandusky, but who is he as a real person rather than the stereotypical predatory monster portrayed in the abuse narrative?

Gerald Arthur Sandusky was born on January 26, 1944, the only son of Art and Evie Sandusky. As he wrote in his autobiography, young Jerry was very close to his parents, whom he loved and admired. He was also close to his paternal grandparents, Edward and Josephine Sendecki, Polish immigrants whose last name was misspelled as "Sandusky" by someone at Ellis Island. They settled in Washington, Pennsylvania, south of Pittsburgh, where "Jaja" (his nickname as a grandfather) worked in the local tin mill. Sandusky's maternal grandfather worked in a southwestern Pennsylvania coal mine. After he died, his widow moved in with the Sanduskys, and young Jerry became fond of Grammie.[1]

Art Sandusky was a trolley conductor, while Evie worked in a glass factory. They also ran Art's Ice Cream Stand, an afternoon and evening gathering place in their local neighborhood of Tylerdale, where many other Poles lived. "[My parents] taught me the meaning of respect toward all people—young or old; rich or poor; black or white," Jerry Sandusky recalled. As an only child, he learned to play alone. He would stage fantasy baseball games with his Louisville Slugger bat, in which he was the pitcher, batter, radio announcer, and crowd. But he also formed the Tylerdale Recreation Club with neighborhood friends David Schieck, Benny Lucas, Ron Kubovcik, Paul Pchinow, and Johnny Kazarik.

His father, hardworking Art Sandusky, found time to coach a neighborhood baseball team, which won the Pony League World

Series in 1955. That same year, town leaders asked him to revive the Brownson House, a town recreation center that had been closed because of damage by juvenile delinquents. Art Sandusky quit his trolley conductor job and threw himself into making the recreation center work. Evie, no longer working at the glass factory, ran a nursery school at the rec center. They soon sold their small home and moved into the second floor of the Brownson House, when their son Jerry was twelve. A handyman, Art Sandusky fixed up the place. He also painted houses, dug ditches, dragged baseball fields, cut grass. At holidays, Art and Evie prepared fruit baskets and turkeys for the poor, and they threw an annual Christmas party at the recreation children for hundreds of kids.

"To Art and Evie," Sandusky recalled, "honoring family was a way of life. They never turned their back on a family in need, and they made it clear to everyone that theirs was a house of sharing." But they allowed no alcohol in that home, and their son would be a teetotaler as well.

As a growing teenager, Jerry Sandusky loved life in the Brownson House rec center. "The Bug House, which is what we called it because of all the 'buggy' people who ventured through its doors, was an ideal place for me to grow up, because it helped me to meet so many people and take part in so many different activities." He played sports on its fields, and in the basement were pool and ping-pong tables and a boxing mat. On the first floor were offices, a rehabilitation clinic for handicapped children and adults, and a small gym, with the building's only shower, where Sandusky took communal showers after exercise. "There were always pickup basketball games, football games; ping-pong contests, pool tournaments, and dart and card games." There were dances and play rehearsals. "And to think, this was all held right under the very roof where I lived," Sandusky reminisced. "Kids came and went every day. They were the brothers and sisters I never had."

An enthusiastic competitor, Jerry Sandusky threw himself into the rough-and-tumble games at the rec center, running into a gym pole and knocking out two front teeth "because I wasn't watching where I was going." Another time he whacked the back of his head and required five stitches. His father just laughed. "Jer," he would say, "you could mess up a free lunch."

The young Sandusky enjoyed pranks. "I allowed myself to be mischievous, but I didn't let it get to the point that someone would be intentionally hurt. . . . And I swore I would tell the truth if I was every caught doing something wrong." Thus, when he and his friends were arrested for heaving water balloons out of their car in nearby Canonsburg, Sandusky cheerfully told the town mayor, "Guilty! I did it!"

Various disabled people worked at the Brownson House, and Sandusky learned to respect them, including "Big Ern," one of three mentally challenged brothers, Shirley, a wheelchair-bound secretary, and Chico, who was physically disabled. Art Sandusky had a sign in his office, "Don't give up on a bad boy, because he might turn out to be a great young man," and he acted on that principle, serving as a father figure for many troubled kids.

A scrappy child, Jerry Sandusky didn't mature physically until his sophomore year in high school, when he became a blocking back on the football team, as well as an outstanding basketball and baseball player. "Football was everything to me," he observed later, "but I still tried my best at other sports." He did well enough to be actively recruited to play football at several colleges, including Penn State, where he entered as a freshman in 1962. He mostly played defense under Head Coach Rip Engle but also caught a few passes for Offensive Coach Joe Paterno. He also hit his head on a desk while wrestling in his dorm and needed fifteen stitches.

In the summers he returned to Washington, PA, to work at the local Coca-Cola bottling plant and to work with kids on the Brownson House playground. He decided he wanted to be a teacher and coach. During the summer before his senior year at Penn State, Sandusky met Dottie Gross, whose parents had moved from Washington, PA, to Chicago, but she was back visiting friends. A year older than Sandusky, she and Jerry spent a lot of time together that summer. "She enjoyed playing with the kids as much as I did" on the playground, he remembered, and she drove with him in the rec center pickup truck to take children to a Pittsburgh Pirates game.

Dottie Gross was the young Sandusky's first serious girlfriend. In high school, he was shy around girls, and at college, he was busy with studies and sports, though he had dated a bit there, and more frequently when he came home on breaks. Now he found himself smitten.

After she went home, he wrote Dottie Gross a love letter. "As I sit here staring at Mount Nittany . . . I see only your face. Amidst all this violence and brutality we call football, I feel no pain or hatred. I feel only love for you." They were married in September 1966, a few days before Sandusky started grad school in physical education at Penn State, where he would serve as an assistant football coach under Joe Paterno, who had coached at Penn State since 1950 and was appointed head coach in February 1966.

Although he was an excellent athlete, Sandusky was a complete klutz in many other ways. When Dottie asked him to change a bathroom lightbulb in their small attic apartment, for instance, he stood on the toilet seat, which tilted over. As he fell, he grabbed the medicine cabinet off the wall. Dottie ended up changing the bulb. But Sandusky enjoyed teaching phys. ed. classes and coaching the freshman football team. "I liked helping young men at that age," recalling how homesick he himself had been as a freshman. There were "some very special moments, and I had a wonderful woman like Dottie to share every one of them with me."

STARTING A FAMILY

The young couple, with a mutual love of children, planned to start a family after Jerry got his first coaching job at Juniata College, a small liberal arts college in Huntington, PA, in 1967. But Dottie never got pregnant. It turned out that Jerry had low testosterone and an inadequate sperm count—ironic, given all the sex abuse allegations that later arose, since people with low testosterone generally have relatively low sex drives.[2] "It was a devastating blow," Sandusky recalled, but he kept in mind what a coach had once told him. "It's not what happens to you in life that's important. It's how you react to it." So they decided to adopt children, just as Jerry was offered an offensive line coaching job at Boston University, which he took in 1968. But they hated the big city and put off adoption until the following year, when Joe Paterno invited Sandusky back to Penn State as the offensive line coach.

In 1969, they adopted an infant son and named him Edward Joel Sandusky, though they always called him E. J., and they eventually adopted a total of five boys and one girl. Three—E. J., Kara, and Jon—were adopted as newborns. Jeff, whom they took in as a foster child when he was nine months old, had been physically abused and hospitalized. They officially adopted him when he was seven years old. Matt and the last son (who does not want to be named, but who supports his father) were adopted when they were eighteen. The Sanduskys also took in several temporary foster children.[3]

Despite his hectic schedule as a football coach, Jerry Sandusky managed to eat breakfast and dinner with Dottie and the kids most days, unless he was traveling to scout other teams or recruit promising high school seniors. Home life was cheerfully boisterous. Jon and Jeff would get into fights in the living room, while their father was playing fierce basketball outside with E. J.

Jerry and Dottie also took the kids on family trips, stuffed into their hatchback so tightly that the children started calling themselves the Sardinskys, while Dottie sang songs she had learned at Methodist church camp, or Country Western favorites she knew from her Tennessee childhood.*

On summer weekends, they often ended up at a state park, where the football coach, his children, and any other kids who had come along, romped in the swimming area. "I always loved to fool around in the water, often to Dottie's embarrassment, because it usually took a lifeguard or park ranger to tell me to straighten up or get out," Sandusky recalled, citing one afternoon when a lifeguard blew his whistle and announced, "No volleyballs in the water." Next, he banned beach balls. "Then I began to pick up one child after another and toss them a few feet into a safe spot of the pool. The kids were laughing, splashing, and having a great time." The whistle blew again. "No throwing children in the water!"

Daughter Kara recalls an idyllic childhood, with her father its Pied Piper, especially during their improvised Fourth of July parades:

> We'd load little red wagons with dogs, grab instruments (or anything that made some sort of noise) and all the neighborhood kids, and we'd march the streets singing at the top of our lungs. The leader of this one-of-a- kind, wonderful childhood memory was my Dad. It's who he was, and he loved the absolute chaos of it. We all did. The smiles, the joy, the silliness will forever remain unique to those of us who participated.

In the winter, she remembers standing with her sled at the top of a steep hill. "My Dad would stand beside me with a huge smile on his face, encouraging me to just let go of my fear and have fun. 'You can do it, Kara! I know you can!'"[4]

E. J. Sandusky, who lost his college football coaching job as a result of the scandal, echoed his sister's observations about their upbringing. "There was no molestation going on, I can tell you. We grew up in a family that loved each other, cared for each other, were there for each other." His father was always full of energy and

---

* Dottie Gross grew up in Tennessee until her father's job took the family to Pennsylvania and Illinois.

enthusiasm, calling himself a "playground director," encouraging kickball games in the backyard for as many as thirty kids. "He grew up with a 1950s Leave-It-to-Beaver mentality. He could never really fathom that people could take advantage of his generosity, when he was just trying to help people out. He's very naive."

His brother Jon says almost exactly the same thing. "My parents gave me morals, taught me how to live my life, with a good work ethic, mixing in pleasure too, with trips to Bowl games, kickball in the backyard, trips to the lake. They modeled things I'm striving to be as a parent myself."

Jeff Sandusky—who is now in prison for sending a questionable text message to his fiancé's teenage daughter—recalled that "Dad was a touchy-feely guy," but there was nothing sexual about it. Every morning, he would wake his children by rubbing their backs, often singing "Wakie, wakie, rise and shine, another great day is dawning." His father was there for most meals, Jeff said, but his mother was the constant support system. "There are not enough wonderful things to say about that woman." When it came to discipline, his father never laid a hand on him. Instead, he just shook his head and said, "What were you thinking?" Some people talk about the Bible, Jeff said, but "my parents *live* the Good Book, that's how they live their lives. When people say, 'Angels walking among us,' yes, and I have two of them as parents."

In his autobiography, Jerry Sandusky gave full credit to Dottie for mostly raising the children. "Dottie has always been there to look after them when I was away, and usually from the minute I was back in town, I became another big kid for her to supervise as well." Although there was never a dull moment, he thought none of them would have wanted it any other way.[5]

LINEBACKER U

Sandusky spent his first year back at Penn State coaching offensive tackles, which meant he was under the direct supervision of head coach Joe Paterno, who was not an easy boss for the easy-going younger man. "Coach Paterno often got upset with me, and he came charging down the hall . . . so he could scream at me," Sandusky wrote in his autobiography. "I think I got moved to the defense simply because I upset Coach Paterno enough with my constant questions about why we did certain things on offense." For the next seven years, he served as a linebacker coach before being promoted to defensive coordinator, a position he held until his retirement.

He was credited with making Penn State a defensive powerhouse that contributed to the team's outstanding record during Paterno's long reign, including a 1986 national championship and many Bowl game victories, so that Penn State football became known as Linebacker U. In 1995 Sandusky published *Coaching Linebackers*, explaining how to develop players who could think on their feet and react quickly, defending against either a run or a pass. But the major responsibility of the coach, Sandusky emphasized, was "to help young men to mature and develop as people and football players." Joe Paterno wrote a foreword, calling Sandusky "a man of high standards and deep-seated beliefs in hard work, dedication, and honesty."[6]*

But this public praise hid a deep-seated conflict between the two coaches, who were polar opposites in personality and approach, as Paterno biography Joe Posnanski observed. Paterno was a stickler for rules and conformity. Sandusky was a goofball who loved practical jokes. Paterno enjoyed hard liquor. Sandusky was a teetotaler. Football players feared and sometimes loathed Paterno, who yelled and screamed and belittled them at practice. Only later in life did they look back and see that Paterno instilled discipline and self-respect. As Posnanski wrote, "Sandusky connected with them in ways Paterno never could. He joked with them, hugged them, taunted them, and often inspired them." Thus, it is not surprising that, as Posnanski noted, "Paterno often fired Sandusky, and Sandusky often quit, and the two men clashed so violently in team meetings that other coaches expected a fight to break out."[7]

Sandusky admits that he and Paterno had their conflicts, but he insists, "I didn't hate Joe Paterno. We worked together for 35 years. In many ways he was like a second father to me. His teams reflected his class, his toughness, his determination, and his sportsmanship. Joe wasn't perfect, never claimed to be, but nobody did it better as a coach. He was a fierce competitor, very persistent, and I was stubborn too. So yes, we clashed at times."[8]

GOING THE SECOND MILE

The conflict between Paterno and Sandusky was exacerbated after the assistant coach started a program for troubled youth. In 1977, Sandusky incorporated the Second Mile, naming it after a passage

---

* This 1995 publication was a revision of Sandusky's self-published book, *Developing Linebackers the Penn State Way*, published in 1977 in order to raise money for the Second Mile program, which was launched that year.

in Matthew 5:41, "And whoever compels you to go one mile, go with him two," just after Jesus's admonition to turn the other cheek. "I was happy beyond my wildest dreams to be known as a Penn State football coach, but I wanted my life to be remembered for something else," he explained. "I wanted to do something similar to what my parents did in that recreation center when I was a kid." So he planned to open a foster home for needy children. In 1981, the home opened, but it wasn't easy to find good house parents for the long-term, and there were predictable behavioral and disciplinary challenges.

Under the leadership of executive director Jack Raykovitz, Second Mile morphed into a service organization, opening several summer camp locations for troubled children, for ages 8 to 15, along with other programs that eventually involved more than 100,000 Pennsylvania children annually, with over 6,000 directly served. The summer camps were the heart of the program, where children played games, sang, swam, canoed, and hiked. Sandusky and other leaders stressed the importance of cooperation and teamwork. In lectures, they sought to instill values and build confidence. "We talk about being *somebody* and what that takes," Sandusky wrote. "We talk about happiness, about reaching out and extending themselves to others."

Sandusky himself gave many of those talks as well as taking part in many camp activities, and he wrote letters to Second Mile kids four times a year. "Especially at the summer camps," he wrote in his autobiography, "I've enjoyed wrestling and swimming with the kids. I even had to have knee surgery in the summer of 1991 because of my fooling around." He reached out to particularly challenging children, such as Brett Houtz, Matt Heichel (now Sandusky), and Aaron Fisher, encouraging them to do better in school, sports, and life. He became a surrogate father, treating them as family members who would sometimes spend the night and attend football games.

As we have seen, Sandusky was incredibly naïve about the hazards of showering alone with these boys, hugging them, or telling them he loved them. His help was also sometimes rejected as the boys grew older and didn't want to spend much time with the older man and listen to his lectures about schoolwork, when they preferred to hang out with friends, sometimes engaging in drug-taking and sex with girlfriends.

Sandusky desperately wanted to help these young men to mature into responsible young adults, but many came from dysfunctional homes and ended up in detention centers or other institutions. "A lot of the kids I grew close to and spent a lot of time with spent some time in psychiatric clinics," Sandusky wrote. "I tried to visit them, and there was one young boy who had a lot of problems at home but still had so much good in him." He thought that if only he could influence him, he might turn out well. "When he got away from home, he was fine, but when he was at home, his problems multiplied."

Some of his Second Mile boys turned out well. Others did not. "We throw out the rope and hopefully, the kids will take hold," he wrote in his autobiography. "We try to motivate, mentor, and provide memories. If nothing else, there will always be memories."[9] Given the type of psychotherapy that would distort those memories and turn hugs into sexual abuse through the concept of repressed memories, these words turned out to be highly ironic.

NEVER A HEAD COACH

Jerry Sandusky always wanted to be a head coach, but that never happened. In the early 1970s, he nearly took that position at Marshall University in West Virginia. But a foster child named Christopher was staying with them, and Sandusky turned down the offer because he couldn't bear the thought of abandoning him. He later had other interviews with Boston College, University of North Carolina, and Temple University, which made him an offer in the late 1980s. But he turned it down. "I couldn't leave the things that were so near and dear to me: The Second Mile, Penn State football, and the State College atmosphere."

By 1999, Sandusky had been an assistant coach at Penn State for thirty years, and many considered him the obvious heir apparent to Joe Paterno. But the previous year, Paterno had made it clear to Sandusky that he would not endorse him as the next head coach. Paterno focused solely on his team, driving his players to excel, and it drove him crazy when Sandusky brought Second Mile kids to sit on the sidelines at games. In 1993, Paterno had written what his family called the "Why I Hate Jerry Sandusky Memo," complaining that the assistant coach seemed constantly distracted and was more interested in the Second Mile than football.[10] Among Paterno's papers was a handwritten note, apparently relating to a 1998 conversation he had with Sandusky:

> If there were no 2nd Mile then I believe you believe that you probably could be the next Penn State FB Coach. But you wanted the

best of two worlds, and I probably should have sat down with you six or seven years ago and said, "Look, Jerry, if you want to be the Head Coach at Penn State, give up your association with the 2nd Mile and concentrate on nothing but your family and Penn State."[11]

Sandusky consequently decided to take advantage of a "30-and-out" window that Penn State was offering as a special early retirement package. Paterno, then seventy-two, clearly had no intention of retiring anytime soon anyway. So in 1999 Sandusky negotiated an attractive retirement package, taking a lump sum of $168,000 along with emeritus status that included a campus office and rights to use Penn State's athletic facilities.

Twelve years later, when the sex abuse scandal exploded, and the 1998 shower with Zachary Konstas became a focal point, many people concluded that Sandusky must have been forced into retirement because of that incident, but that was clearly not the case, as even Louis Freeh concluded. Sandusky went out in triumph following the 1999 Penn State win over Texas A&M at the Alamo Bowl, carried off the field on the shoulders of his jubilant players.

In the ensuing years, especially after the Penn State football team had two dismal seasons in 2003 and 2004, many observers thought that Paterno just wasn't the same without Sandusky. As former player Mac Morrison told a reporter, "I don't think people understand the impact Jerry Sandusky had. He's not just an assistant coach. He has the best defensive mindset and defensive knowledge that I've ever known." As Paterno biographer Joe Posnanski wrote, "There was a powerful groundswell within the [State College] community to convince Paterno to retire, finally, and to bring Sandusky back as head coach."[12]

A year after his retirement, in December 2000 Sandusky was very nearly chosen as the head coach at the University of Virginia. After a first interview, he was given an agreement but hesitated to sign it until he verified that he could start a Second Mile branch in Virginia. After a second interview with Sandusky, UVA alum Al Groh was chosen instead, leaving his position as coach of the New York Jets, where Groh has just lost three straight games and probably bailed out before getting fired.[13]

So Sandusky threw himself into promoting the Second Mile program and helping to mentor troubled youth, and he also volunteered to help coach the football team at Central Mountain High School in Lock Haven, PA, where Second Mile teenager Aaron Fisher, "Victim 1," was a student.

AS OTHERS SAW HIM

Despite the numerous alleged victims, people who thought they knew Jerry Sandusky well—childhood friends, fellow coaches, Second Mile alums, and others—had a hard time accepting that he might be a pedophile. For instance, Bruce Heim, a Second Mile board member, wrote:

> Nobody at the Second Mile knew anything about Jerry doing anything other than wonderful things with and for at-risk kids until 2008 [when the Aaron Fisher allegations arose]. . . . Even at that time it was hard to believe for many in this community that Jerry would have done anything wrong. In 30 years of working with disadvantaged and at-risk children, to our knowledge Jerry had not had a single allegation of even the slightest inappropriate behavior toward children.[14]

I spoke to Dick Cameron, eighty-seven, who was the Coca-Cola bottler in Washington, PA, and good friends with Sandusky's father, Art, with whom he played golf hundreds of times. "Artie and Evie ran the Brownson House with an iron fist. I used to play volleyball there and coached basketball for a while. I didn't know Jerry all that well, but he seemed like a nice kid, and we later gave money to the Second Mile program. We were all shocked and in disbelief when these allegations first came up."

Gary Johnson, seven months older than Jerry Sandusky, also grew up in Washington, PA, and got to know him as a competitor and baseball teammate from age ten to seventeen. "Jerry was a pleasant kid to be around, always laughing, having a good time. He was a prankish kid. He would run up behind someone and snatch their baseball cap and toss it to someone else, kind of impishly, but not in a mean way at all." Johnson, who went on to become the Director of Services for the Developmentally Disabled in Washington-Greene Counties for thirty years, remembered how Art Sandusky adopted Ernie Ruscello, a mentally challenged boy, as a kind of team mascot, including him in all activities. Swimming at the YMCA in the 1950s, he recalled that men and boys all had to swim naked in the pool, which didn't bother anyone.

Sandusky's college roommate, Tom Frederick, wasn't a great student:

Jerry had a great work ethic, wonderful study and health habits. We were very different, but he never judged me. I never met a person who was more committed to simply being good and sticking to his values and beliefs. In the two years that I was roommates with him, I never saw any behavior that was even remotely unusual. Because of Jerry, my grades improved and I graduated. I became a high school history teacher for 33 years and remained good friends with Dottie and Jerry ever since.

Retired Penn State coach Dick Anderson has also known Jerry Sandusky since 1962, when they were football teammates. "He was the same then as he was as an adult," he recalled, "a good, hard-working guy, a fierce competitor, but with an outgoing personality, a fun-loving guy. There was always a smile on his face. I don't think anyone disliked him." The same was true when Anderson and Sandusky coached together (one for offense, the other defense). "The players really liked Jerry. He could be stern but he was also out-going and would kid around. He could have a good laugh on the field with them. Jerry took a real interest in his players. I did, too, but I had a different style."

Buddy Tesner was a Penn State linebacker from 1971 to 1975, early in Sandusky's coaching career. "Jerry and I really hit it off. He was a happy-go-lucky goofball, a touchy-feely guy, and I was like that, too." I asked Tesner, now an orthopedic surgeon, if Sandusky appeared to be attracted to boys. "No, he didn't seem to be overly interested in boys. He was a man's man, a great football player in his time, and he worked with high-level athletes to develop them. There was nothing 'off' about him. Nothing like that."[15]

Donald Steinbacher entered Penn State as a fellow freshman with Jerry Sandusky in 1962. "We competed for the same position on the football team," he recalls. "Jerry won." He considers Sandusky "a very good friend and role model for myself and my sons. I have so much respect for him that I find it intellectually impossible to accept the charges." He recalls once stopping by to see Jerry and Dottie after a Penn State football game. "Jerry told us his vision of the Second Mile and his burning desire to create an outreach effort to help the lost kids—those kids from poor families for whom life had passed them by." He concluded that "Jerry was nuts. There was no way that an assistant football coach in a small town in central Pennsylvania could create something like this." But he did. "I have been in Jerry's company in social situations where he thought nothing about excusing himself because someone called him and needed help. Jerry was single-minded in his commitment to help-ing those that could not help themselves."

His wife Elaine Steinbacher, who has known Jerry and Dot-tie for over fifty years, worked in King of Prussia, PA, directing a program that served at-risk, low-income, minority students and their families, partnering with the Second Mile program, where she served on the board. She said:

> I am not the type that would take child abuse lightly. I was so successful in my job because Jerry Sandusky was my role model and mentor. I wanted to be just like him and patterned myself after him. I saw the way Jerry interacted with kids, even some of the "alleged victims." We helped each other and shared ideas. He gave me advice, and I helped him find federal monies for low-income students to attend college. I knew the real Jerry Sandusky very well.

She also knew Dottie Sandusky, who "had her finger on the pulse of her family. She would never have allowed anything to hap-pen as the so-called victims and media describe. She was in charge and always knew what was going on. She was a mother and house-wife only and always watching all their activities closely."

In 1973 Jerry Sandusky recruited Guy Montecalvo, from his hometown, as a defensive back for Penn State. After his college ca-reer, Montecalvo served as a Penn State graduate assistant football coach from 1977 through 1979, before becoming the head football coach back at Washington High School for twenty-three years. He recalls Sandusky as "an affable gentleman and beloved coach. He liked to clown around, joking and shadow boxing with players all the time. He had a very compassionate heart. But he was a me-ticulous defensive coach and the heir apparent to Joe Paterno, it seemed."

SECOND MILERS SPEAK

Many Second Milers said similar things. Chad Rexrode (who testi-fied briefly at the trial) grew up with a single mother, so Sandusky became a father figure for him. "Jerry would make sure I got to pic-nics at their house. I would go on trips with his family, and he would take me to Second Mile banquets. He was always there for me." San-dusky helped Rexrode secure a college scholarship. "He has done so much for me. He made me who I am today." Yes, Sandusky obviously enjoyed spending time with children. "Kids were always climbing on him, jumping on him. They would never leave him alone. He was just a big kid himself, with a personality that kids identified with. He made them feel cared about and special."[16]

Another young man, who preferred to remain anonymous, told me: "Jerry took me under his wing, as he did for quite a few participants in Second Mile." Yes, when driving, Sandusky might put his hand on his knee, and they wrestled around sometimes. And he'd call and leave messages, saying, "I have football tickets. Love ya, bye." But there was "nothing that made me uncomfortable at any time. Nothing icky." Similarly, Second Miler David Hilton said that Sandusky was a "nice, caring, giving guy. Touchy, but not in a sexual way. He enjoyed rough-housing with me, stuff like that. Sure, I stayed in their basement overnight. It was just an ordinary room, with a pool table, air hockey, darts. Yeah, of course I liked it, or I wouldn't have gone back again."[17]

Same with Second Miler Jason Smeal, who considered Sandusky "a caring, wonderful, honest human being." He said that Sandusky was a "grandfatherly type of guy" who would put his arm around you and put his hand on your knee, but never in a sexual or threatening manner. He considered Sandusky to be instrumental in his life, even though he has had some ups and downs.

Kevin Wynn, a young African American, said that Sandusky helped him to choose a college. "Jerry checked around before I made my decision to see what coaches would be a good match for me." Sandusky helped Wynn secure a Second Mile Scholarship to attend Holy Cross in Massachusetts, where he played football. "I will never deny all the positive things that happened to me because of the Second Mile and because of Jerry Sandusky. I still cannot believe what has happened to him because of the accusations. Jerry was such a great friend to me."

Matt Granite, who met Sandusky at a Penn State football camp in 1988, spent a lot of time with him from age thirteen to sixteen. "I was the classic kid that Jerry would identify and want to help. During that time I got into trouble. I stole beer and broke into houses in ninth and tenth grades. He would give me advice, and I knew him as a friend, father figure and someone I knew really cared about me." Yes, they would work out together in locker rooms. "I even spent time with him in his motel rooms that he rented while recruiting. He'd pick me up at my house or my school dozens of times. He would have had plenty of opportunities to abuse me and *nothing* ever happened."

Nor did Sandusky help only boys. Kelli Simco was both camper and counselor at Second Mile. "I would often go to their house to sing Christmas carols. Jerry and Dottie came to my graduation parties and my wedding and baby shower. Many times I was with Jerry with other kids playing in a pool. He would always pick up kids and throw them in the water. In all that time that I was a camper and friend, I never saw a red flag."

Ellen Kunkle, a staff member for the Second Mile program from 1999 through 2006, got to know Jerry Sandusky extremely well. "Instead of standing on the sidelines, he would show up at summer camp in sweatpants and play tag, tell the kids funny jokes, and basically interact with them as if he was a big kid himself." She considered him an inspiring role model. "He always made sure that the staffers never made promises to the kids that they couldn't keep. He stressed honesty and always tried to build the kids up."

Kunkle said that she had counseled children for many years and has learned to identify behavior indicating that they feel uncomfortable. "I never saw a kid recoil, stand erect or act like they were scared around Jerry. His interaction with the children was always positive, and they reacted that way."

Like his father, Jerry Sandusky was particularly compassionate towards people with handicaps. In 1999, he met Todd Reed, then thirty-four, at a Special Olympics event. A Vietnamese refugee whose childhood polio had left him disabled and weighing less than a hundred pounds, Reed became another Sandusky protégé, with the retired coach often taking him for medical appointments. He knew four of the Sandusky accusers, whom he called "backstabbers," and he later visited Sandusky in prison.

In one of Sandusky's letters quoted during the trial, he wrote: "I'm not good at hiding my feelings. I have many Forrest Gump qualities . . . I cried at that movie." He said that he identified with the Gump character because he was "so naïve, oblivious to the world. . . . He was so happy because he wasn't caught up in being anything other than a caring person. I wish I had [even] more of that in me."[18] Yet, it was precisely that naiveté that helped put Sandusky in prison.

— CHAPTER 22 —

Enduring Prison

S ANDUSKY'S EXPERIENCE in prison has been predictably difficult. He has been kept in solitary confinement twenty-three hours a day for most of that time and subjected to abuse and persecution by many prisoners and guards, although since his move in March 2017 to a new prison, State Correctional Institution (SCI) Somerset, conditions have improved somewhat. Regardless, he has maintained a remarkably positive outlook and has even managed to stick to a regular exercise regimen.

He also had time to write a 155-page manuscript that he called *Will We Endure?* The plural refers to his family as well as himself, but Sandusky (maddeningly) sometimes calls himself "we," as in "We've never been one to moan about life's circumstances." He is not a great writer, tending to lapse into generalizations and the passive voice. But the manuscript is revealing, along with dozens of letters I have received from him, a few phone calls, and my two in-person prison visits.

After his conviction, Sandusky was locked in the Centre County Correctional Facility while he awaited sentencing. "It was the end of June 2012," he wrote, "and I sat in solitary confinement in a jail cell. I was on what they refer to as suicide watch, though I had given no indication that I wanted to kill myself. There was a guard watching me 24 hours a day, and the lights remained on at all times. I was fed three times per day, but nothing else, no contact with the outside world. There was no bedding, sheets, or blankets. They strap you in a one-piece outfit made of a woolen material. Other than exercising three times a day, I meditated, clung to fond memories, and reflected on what had happened." As part of his exercise regime, he would run in place, but "it was clear I wasn't going anywhere."[1]

He thought back over the last three-and-a-half years. "First, I looked at myself. I saw my vulnerability, my naiveté (some say stupidity), and trust in people to see who I really am. Many of my experiences led me to want to help those who didn't have the same opportunities I had as a child. It bothered me when I saw young people who didn't have a chance. I had seen lives changed with that chance, with love, guidance, structure, and commitment."

As Sandusky fell asleep in his cell on September 2, 2012, he pondered that the next day would be his forty-sixth wedding anniversary. "Just before I awakened, in my thoughts, I was going to give Dottie a hug and good wishes. Crack! My head hit the cinder block wall." For him, that symbolized the many walls he had encountered in the past few years, as the allegations and number of accusers mounted and the media frenzy enveloped him.

In an effort to occupy himself, Sandusky created homemade playing cards out of small strips of paper and enjoyed a few games of solitaire before a guard saw him and confiscated the paper. A new inmate screamed and cursed continually, saying terrible things to Sandusky. But there were a few interactions with more friendly inmates, including a former Second Miler, who told Sandusky he thought the charges were "bullshit." Later, Sandusky would encounter three more Second Milers—another inmate, a guard, and a police officer. [2]

Through his window, the former coach watched other inmates playing football, until a guard spotted him and told him he couldn't look on. "He delighted in his authority to make life more difficult," Sandusky concluded.

On October 23, 2012, Sandusky was moved to SCI Camp Hill for eight days of psychological and medical evaluations. The cell was filthy and cold. One of the doctors who examined him was Arif Shaikh, a Pakistani immigrant, who was impressed with Sandusky's decency and intelligence. "As a physician, I really look at my patients," he recalled. "I really see them. I believe the accusations against Jerry have been blown out of proportion. People want to see evil in others, even in the likes of a Mother Teresa. In Jerry's case, people have gone for the drama, not for the reality." Shaikh gave Sandusky a copy of his book, *Healing Tips for the Mind, Body & Soul*, one of the many inspirational books that have helped him endure prison.[3]

Sandusky was designated a Level 2 offender, for inmates deemed to be generally non-violent. Yet, he was then transferred west, fifty miles south of Pittsburgh, to SCI Greene, a maximum-security facility that houses Level 5 prisoners, the most violent offenders, many on death row. When he asked the prison Program Review Committee why he had been placed there, Sandusky was told that the order came "from Harrisburg," presumably originating with John Wetzel, the Secretary of the Department of Corrections, who reported to then-Governor Tom Corbett.

In January 2013, Sandusky wrote a letter to Dr. Shaikh, telling him how much his book had meant to him and summarizing the messages he got from it: "We are all important; Be grateful; Find purpose through suffering; Take care of the moment; Judge yourself first; We control our reaction to circumstances," and more. Sandusky also included an acronym-like admonition he had made for himself, with the first letters spelling **ENDURE**: "**E**mbrace each day as a gift. **N**ever surrender except to God. **D**on't let your situation get the best of you. **U**nderstand God's purpose and presence. **Re**main as positive as possible. **E**xercise your mind, body, and spirit."

When Shaikh opened it, he said, "I felt like I received a letter from a saint," and he later visited Sandusky in prison. So did Dottie Sandusky, who drove over six hours once a week to and from their home in State College to visit her husband in a cubicle, where they could see one another through glass and speak through a bad sound system.

LIFE AT SCI GREENE

Sandusky's experience at SCI Greene, over the next four years, was miserable. At my request, in January 2017 he wrote a nineteen-page single-spaced summary, handwritten on yellow legal paper, which he entitled "My World of Incarceration." He lived in various 13-by-7-foot cells, moved at times without explanation. "At some locations, I was tortured around the clock with pounding and verbal abuse. My neighbor was eventually sent to a mental health unit."

Each cell contained a small metal table and stool, metal bed, sink, and toilet. Some cells had a small window to see outside. Each was part of a "pod" containing twenty-four cells. The cell door had two tiny windows to look into the pod, and an opening for food, mail, and enough room to be handcuffed prior to any exit.

Sandusky described a Kafka-esque nightmare world where rules shifted by whim and few showed any humanity or compassion. "Most days in prison I awaken in the neighborhood of 4:30 a.m.," he began. "I have a pulse. I have been given another day." He would empty the water from his C-Pap machine (for sleep apnea), replacing it with distilled water if the guards had permitted him to have it, then stretch (mostly for his bad lower back) and exercise for an hour, doing squat jumps, push-ups, jumping jacks, leg raises, and the like.

Breakfast arrived at 6:30 a.m. If Sandusky was not standing at his door at the right time, he would not get his meal. At some unspecified morning time, inmates were supposed to get "Yard" privileges, taken to adjacent 18-by-16-foot enclosures (known as "dog cages") for an hour of exercise five times a week. "Inmates are strip searched, handcuffed, and escorted by two guards every time they leave the cell."*4 In the cage, Sandusky would do chin-ups, walk, and run short sprints.

Since this Yard time was his only regular contact with other prisoners, he sometimes tried to start a conversation. "Once, one [inmate] spit at me." He would respond to such provocations by saying, "You are entitled to your opinion, but it is wrong. I know who I am and what I did not do." That sometimes quieted them, though Sandusky, who never cursed, was appalled by the ever-present obscenity. "Profanity is the norm. The 'F' word is constant. It seems like these people have a hard time completing a sentence without using it." He couldn't trust anyone. "It's totally foreign to my whole way of life," he wrote, "and hard to get used to."**

Often, Sandusky didn't get Yard as scheduled. It was denied for various fabricated reasons, such as his not being at the cell door in time, wearing the wrong clothing, or no reason at all. Guards were often overtly hostile and resented extra effort. "Many of the guards appear very miserable. They work for a paycheck; do not seek or find fulfillment; have little purpose. Doing the minimum seems to be the goal—just do, begrudgingly, what you must." The guards often reminded inmates, "This is prison, it ain't supposed to be pleasant or fair."

Sandusky had trouble with medical issues as well. For several years before prison, for instance, he had taken Androgel, prescribed for his low testosterone, to prevent osteoporosis. It was denied him for quite some time, and he also had trouble getting sterile water

---

* A 2015 Pennsylvania legal document described the strip search, which requires an inmate to "lift and shake his genitalia, . . .bend over, spread his buttocks in the direction of the officer so that he may look at [the inmate's] anus, then made to squat and cough, and afterwards [the inmate] is handcuffed behind his back."
** But Sandusky maintained his sense of humor. On the day of the 2013 NFL draft, he did linebacker drills during yard time, singing "Hit a little harder now, run a little faster now, fight a little longer now," to the amusement of the other inmates.

for his sleep apnea machine. "Some of the nurses refuse to address any concerns and have made condescending or arrogant remarks. I shake my head in wonder, questioning why they chose to do this work. Many could care less about your health."

Showers, as we have seen, were important to Sandusky after exercise, but he was only allowed to shower (in handcuffs) three times a week, when the water could be either frigid or scalding. Sometimes he didn't even get a shower. "Life is full of unexpected occurrences," he wrote. "Actually, the unexpected becomes the expected."

One day an inmate decided to flood the pod. "Angry inmates do this as a way of retaliation for their treatment or to grind another inmate." Sometimes inmates threw urine or excrement or smeared human waste all over their cells. "This inmate must have clogged his toilet that backed up the sewer system," so when Sandusky flushed his toilet, it erupted. "I didn't think it was going to stop, so I pressed the emergency medical button but got no response. It entered my mind that I might drown." Finally the flow of water and waste stopped, but his property on the floor (no cabinet in the cell) was ruined.

The guard who ignored the emergency button apparently had it in for the famous inmate and later falsely alleged that Sandusky had sworn at him. Sandusky was put on cell restriction and then told to prepare for being sent to Disciplinary Custody, otherwise known as The Hole. "I was told by inmates they would take my property, which they did. The inmates were shouting, 'Don't go!'" Sandusky foolishly decided to stand his ground. "As a matter of principle, I refused to go for two days." As a result his property was confiscated and destroyed, including over $100 worth of commissary items (the only food or other items prisoners can purchase). He was kept in The Hole for over 100 days in 2016, for much of that time denied visits, phone calls, Yard, showers, commissary, and television.[5]*

And so it went for Jerry Sandusky at SCI Greene. Yet he actually came to regard it as home and wanted to return there rather than be held for weeks at another facility every time he was taken to a hearing for his post-conviction relief effort. On the bus rides, during which he saw trees for the first time in months, he was kept

---

* As one indication of just how insane Pennsylvania prison regulations are, my wife and I sent Jerry Sandusky a Christmas card on December 17, 2016, which came back stamped "REFUSED: Greeting card in a colored envelope." We had committed the crime of sending a card in a grey envelope.

in a small cage, handcuffed and shackled. On one trip, another inmate screamed obscenities at him for two hours, and the guard did nothing to stop it. "Returning to SCI Greene always presented challenges. I would be treated as a transfer, indoctrinated, as if I hadn't been there. I never knew if I would get my property, including medication, C-Pap machine, sheets, pillow, blanket, towel, washcloth, legal and reading material." Upon one return, Sandusky was greeted by the overtly hostile guard, who refused to give him his medications, sheets and blanket, or even toilet paper.

In his "World of Incarceration" document, Sandusky summarized his frustration with an apt sports analogy. "It is stressful for me, trying to figure out how to play their game, on their field, with their referees." On January 2, 2017, Penn State played the University of Southern California Trojans in the Rose Bowl, and Sandusky badly wanted to watch the game. At the same time, he was offered a rare chance to use the law library (a cage with a computer and a few books), but turned it down because the pod officer said he would put the game on TV. But the officer didn't, which might have been just as well, because in a dramatic, high-scoring game, Penn State lost, 49-52. Worse, a banner hung from a freeway near the game, stating, "**Shame. JoePa knew**," as Trojans fans smashed two large Joe Paterno and Jerry Sandusky piñatas during their Rose Bowl tailgate party.[6]

THE IMPACT OF SOLITARY CONFINEMENT

Jerry Sandusky was placed in "Administrative Custody," supposedly for his own protection, though he had to battle for privileges such as getting a television or being able to buy stamps or food items. "I did not and will not understand what more phone calls, commissary items, and a TV and radio had to do with my protection," he observed. He hated solitary confinement, yet he recognized that if he were placed in the general population of violence-prone inmates at SCI Greene, he might be killed. He thought, however, that at a Level 2 facility, the other inmates would get to know him and he would probably be fine. Pennsylvania Secretary of Corrections John Wetzel disagreed. "Those high-profile inmates [like Sandusky] really become targets," Wetzel said. "We have a responsibility to protect both inmates and staff." Convicted child molesters were at particular risk. "You're a dad. You're sitting in prison. You're not in a place to protect your child," Wetzel said. "Then you hear about someone with these charges. It's a scary population."[7]

It was a particularly scary population at SCI Greene, where in 2015 reporter Jan Murphy wrote that "150 men between the ages of 24 and 74 sit in solitary confinement waiting for the day they will either die or win a court appeal that frees them from the possibility of being executed by lethal injection." It was, she observed, "a facility that houses what some regard as the worst of the worst inmates in the state." In her article, Murphy praised how clean, calm, and quiet the facility was. Perhaps she should have spent a few nights in Sandusky's pod.[8]

In 2013, US Department of Justice (DOJ) investigators wrote a scathing report about the treatment of mentally ill patients at SCI Cresson in Pennsylvania, saying that their solitary confinement violated the Eighth Amendment's ban on "cruel and unusual punishment." Prisoners held in such conditions suffered "physical and psychological harms, such as psychosis, trauma, severe depression, serious self-injury, or suicide." The report gave numerous examples. One prisoner tore open his scrotum with his fingernail. Another ate plastic bags and a syringe. A third banged his head on the cell wall and smeared feces all over the cell. A fourth was found "lying in a fetal position in his cell, mumbling incoherently." In response, Pennsylvania closed SCI Cresson later that year, but as the DOJ report concluded, "We identified system-wide policies and individual instances that may reflect inappropriate placement of prisoners with serious mental illness into prolonged isolation."[9]

In February 2017, the US Court of Appeals for the Third Circuit issued a ruling on two Pennsylvania prisoners who had been kept for over twenty years in solitary confinement. The convicted murderers had both been on death row (one at SCI Greene), which meant automatic isolation, but they were still kept there, even after their sentences were changed to life without parole. In a strongly worded precedential opinion, the judges ruled that there was no justification for keeping them on death row after their death sentences were vacated.

Beyond that, however, the opinion reviewed the horrific implications of prolonged isolation on human beings. "Numerous studies on the impact of solitary confinement show that these conditions are extremely hazardous to well-being," the judges wrote. If you weren't mentally ill before such treatment, your odds of going crazy in isolation were high. "In the absence of interaction with others, an individual's very identity is at risk of disintegration." They quoted a psychiatric researcher who found that such inmates "experience a degree of stupor, difficulties with thinking and concentration, obsessional thinking, agitation, irritability, and difficulty tolerating external stimuli."[10]

Such observations are not new. After his 1833 tour of a US prison, Alexis de Tocqueville wrote:

> In order to reform them, [the convicts] had been submitted to complete isolation; but this absolute solitude, if nothing interrupts it, is beyond the strength of man; it destroys the criminal without intermission and without pity; it does not reform, it kills. The unfortunates on whom this experiment was made fell into a state of depression so manifest that their keepers were struck with it; their lives seemed in danger if they remained longer in this situation.

And in 1842, after visiting Eastern State Penitentiary in Philadelphia, where Pennsylvania was pioneering in solitary confinement, Charles Dickens wrote:

> I believe that very few men are capable of estimating the immense amount of torture and agony which this dreadful punishment, prolonged for years, inflicts upon the sufferers. . . . I am only the more convinced that there is a depth of terrible endurance which none but the sufferers themselves can fathom, and which no man has a right to inflict upon his fellow creature. I hold this slow and daily tampering with the mysteries of the brain to be immeasurably worse than any torture of the body. . . . I denounce it, as a secret punishment which slumbering humanity is not roused up to stay.[11]

In 2015, Supreme Court Justice Anthony Kennedy noted that cells such as the one that held Jerry Sandusky were "no larger than the typical parking spot." In their 2017 opinion, the Third Circuit judges were appalled that such prisoners were allowed to leave their cells "only five times a week for two-hour intervals of exercise in the open air," after being strip searched. Yet, Sandusky endured worse treatment, with only one hour for Yard, which was frequently denied. The judges stated that "courts have recently started recognizing inmates' due process right to avoid solitary confinement as clearly established." Nonetheless, over 80,000 American prisoners are kept in such conditions. And despite the fact that Jerry Sandusky was labeled a non-violent offender who was not deemed to be a threat to himself or others, he remained in solitary.[12]

FINDING A PURPOSE

Thus, it is all the more remarkable that Sandusky managed not only to retain his sanity but to maintain a sense of his own dignity and worth. In his manuscript, he strove to find some kind of meaning in his imprisonment. "It was difficult to see a purpose. The best one could be that some vulnerable children may be helped . . . [but] I am not sure." He also wanted "to be a little candle for other inmates," but that was impossible in solitary confinement. Sandusky rehearsed and cherished his precious memories of family and friends, of team celebrations, of Second Milers he had helped. "God has been good to us," he concluded. "Maybe that is the purpose of prison. It helps your memory. You hold on to what's left."

At Thanksgiving, during Yard exercise, he considered how utterly isolated his fellow prisoners were. "The other inmates were so alone, not just in their cages, but alone in life. I've gained respect for some of society's lowest when I realize how blessed and armed I am and how unprotected they have lived. I've had a wonderful life and remain connected to much support, as I try to adjust, learn from, grow from, and endure the struggle."

Maybe all the injustice and pain would make him a better person. "Our ultimate hope is somehow all this suffering will lead to a better life for all when the last breath comes. It's like all the suffering it takes to win an athletic contest. If that's the case, the pain makes sense."

While in prison, he read books about people who had suffered and survived worse fates than his, he thought. He read *Night*, Elie Wiesel's Holocaust memoir, and *Left to Tell*, Immaculée Ilibagiza's story of how she and seven other women hid for three months in a 3-by-4-foot bathroom during the 1994 Rwandan genocide, during which her faith in God grew stronger, even as the rest of her family was slaughtered. If such people could keep going, so could he. Sandusky was particularly struck by Ilibagiza's lament: "How could my dearest friend turn against me? We'd loved each other like sisters once. How could she be so cruel now? How was it possible for a heart to harden so quickly?" He wondered the same thing about his accusers and some of the friends who had abandoned him. Yet, as he observed, "She was able to forgive the killers and go on helping others. I'm hoping to do the same, but it will be difficult."[13]

He also read *A Small Price to Pay*, by Harvey Yoder, about the persecution and imprisonment of Mikhail Khorev in the Soviet

Union during an era when to profess Christianity was a crime. Sandusky identified with Khorev's wry observation: "It was interesting to see what lengths the state officials had gone to prove to themselves that I was a criminal."[14] Then he read *Just Mercy*, by Bryan Stevenson, about false convictions of many black men in Alabama. "When I closed it, once again I realized others have had it worse. We are all human and vulnerable to being broken."[15]

Sandusky tried to remain philosophical. "We are all just passing through. As difficult as this journey is, as much as it doesn't make sense, we must endure!"

HOW DID IT HAPPEN?

Nonetheless, Sandusky couldn't stop torturing himself, wondering how his efforts to help troubled children could have ended with his imprisonment. "I always looked for and believed in the good in everybody. Trust was always a big part of my life. Now I sit in a cell and look back. I have witnessed betrayal, dishonesty, cruelty, hurt, pain, and sorrow. . . . I battle to hold on to trust, trust in people, trust in God."

As Sandusky saw it, he had spent his life trying to do good. "I did whatever I could to help many attend college with a little of my personal money and help from others. Through life's twists and turns, elations and disappointments, victory and defeat, laughter and tears, we felt our calling was to help. . . . We would visit nursing homes, prisons, and hospitals. Wherever we would go we would make an effort to help people be happy." He donated money to his church, Volunteers in Medicine, Park Forest Day Nursery, the Second Mile, Bethel Home in Chattanooga, United Methodist Children's Home, Children and Youth, Penn State, the Brownson House, and many health charities. "This wasn't done for show. However, people obviously don't know."

Through the Second Mile, he had witnessed and participated in many success stories. "I didn't want to be accepted because I was a 'Big Shot' person or coach. All I wanted to be was Jer, a person who really cared about them, a person who would be there for them."

He had tried to provide a positive, fun-filled part of their childhoods that they had otherwise missed. "Yes, I played games with them, horse played in the shower, threw them in the swimming pool, tickled them, hugged them, squeezed their guts out, cracked a few of their backs. They were greeted with hugs in public. I said goodbye with hugs. I told many I loved them." Was that bad? "My time was short. I didn't get to see them that much. I felt I was doing what they wanted. Everybody kept coming, didn't complain. You would think with all the allegations, somebody would have said something."

He concluded that he had tried too hard. "I tried to force my caring (what I thought they needed and missed) on them." He thought that if he tried hard enough, even the most rebellious teenager would respond. "I was naïve enough to believe they would all care, connect, and be as loyal as some had been. I had seen 'change,' witnessed young people overcoming big obstacles. It wasn't that simple, that easy, and it has gotten me to where I am [in prison]."

Sandusky was frustrated that the jurors hadn't taken into consideration the background of the alleged victims. "These accusers were not poor, little, innocent kids, as portrayed. They were adults who chose to fabricate allegations." And in some cases, he thought "they may have gotten to the point where they didn't think or know they were lying."

They all came from troubled backgrounds.

> One must realize the accusers didn't come forward out of isolation (a vacuum). They were influenced by many factors. They were products of their experiences, their issues, their guidance, their biological families, their circumstances, and many vested influences. . . . Some were dragged into it by family, the media, investigators, psychologists, attorneys. Some had their own financial problems. Many have been or are on probation. Over half have gotten into trouble for drugs.

By becoming alleged victims, "they received attention, a sense of power, an opportunity to get out of poverty, and an excuse for any shortcomings they might have had."

At this point, it's worth quoting from a long-time foster parent who prefers to remain anonymous:

> Most foster children will game the system if an opportunity arises. They are all different, of course, but there is a common tendency. The kids are horribly abused at an early age—hardly anybody realizes what a horrible, horrible start in life almost all of these kids had. All the adults who were supposed to care for them have betrayed their trust. By the time they get to our house, they hate the system more than they hate their original abusers in their birth families. Of course, they'll game it for whatever they can get from

it. Those of us who care for them have a fine line to tread. On the one hand, they have a lot of disadvantages that are certainly not their fault. On the other hand, they have to learn that this does not entitle them to be coddled for the rest of their lives.

These kids aren't hopeless, but many need extra help. Statistically, about half are likely to end up in jail or otherwise institutionalized as adults. I'm proud to say that of the dozen or so we've spent much time with, none have ended up that way, at least to my knowledge.

But there is a common attitude among foster children that somehow society owes them a living. If they were part of a program and they later learn that they can get a couple million dollars by just claiming they were abused, of course, many of them would jump at the chance. (A lot of young men with more normal backgrounds would also jump at the chance—but with this population, that's particularly true.)

That gives some perspective on what Sandusky tried to do. "It was more challenging for everybody with teenage foster kids," he wrote. "I was always looking for teachable moments. . . . There was so much I felt they missed." He recalled a sixteen-year-old Second Miler who had played delightedly with little children's toys because he had never had them. "I tried to replace those years by studying with them, exercising them, correcting them, scolding them, caring about them, and hugging them." And it seemed to work. "They soaked up the caring. It didn't enter my mind there would be this kind of ending."

Gary Johnson, Sandusky's childhood friend, visited him many times at SCI Greene, which is relatively near Washington, PA, where Johnson still lives. He was amazed that Sandusky didn't appear to be angry and bitter. "I have never heard him say anything disparaging of these people who accused him. I have never heard him say ill of anyone. He would joke, but never in a mean-spirited way." That fit with the youth he knew long ago. "I have never once heard him curse or swear. It can get pretty coarse in a locker room. Jerry never once did. He just quietly accepted it and moved on. If I were in his situation, I would fill the air with blue language about the people who did what they did."

Johnson calls Sandusky childlike (not childish). "There is a naiveté to Jerry." He viewed the world as an essentially benign place.

"It was a very sobering experience for him when all this broke. I think Jerry thought, 'It will all come out OK because I'm telling the truth.'"[16]

That's the same impression I got when I visited Sandusky in prison. He remained amazingly upbeat, hoping that he would get a new trial. He frequently laughed ruefully, in a way that has gotten him in trouble when people think he is mocking alleged victims. I was reminded of this passage in *Touched*, his 2000 autobiography: "Sometimes, when I'm uncomfortable, I laugh. . . . Sometimes, my laughing is misinterpreted. It appears that I have no feelings for people or their problems. But that is not the case. Laughing is just my way of tending to what might or might not develop into a touchy situation."[17]

In his prison writings, Sandusky retained some level of compassion towards his accusers. "These are people I cared about, still do." He had tried to make them feel better about themselves and to show them that they were valued and loved. But he recognized, "My world was foreign to many. People misunderstood my passion to make a difference. My belief in the importance of love and connection was misrepresented and twisted."

In prison, he strove to maintain a positive attitude, even attempting to empathize with the people who put him there. "I'll move on and try to become better, not bitter. I can put myself in their shoes (the media, the judge, the system, the accusers, etc.), but I wouldn't want to walk in them."*

He was determined to persevere. "Will I quit? I don't believe I will, not until my last breath. Why? I will endure for those who bring me light. I will endure for what I believe to be right."

He prays for a new trial. "I've given second chances all my life. Now, I'm asking for one."

---

* It would be nice if Sandusky could literally walk in tennis shoes, which he has repeatedly requested, to no avail, to help his lower back pain. Instead, he wears standard-issue flimsy prison slippers.

— CHAPTER 23 —

What's the Verdict?

S O, IS Jerry Sandusky a justly convicted serial child molester or an innocent man who really tried to help troubled children? I've presented the facts as I have been able to uncover them, but readers will of course make up their own minds, and there's certainly much that we don't know. I personally think Sandusky is innocent, for a number of reasons already enumerated. The case developed an unstoppable momentum as a moral panic in which he was judged guilty before the jurors were ever chosen. As we have seen, the trial was a travesty, with inconsistent or hearsay testimony tainted by leading police interviews, civil attorneys who smelled money, recovered "repressed memories," and ineffective, unprepared defense attorneys. In the eighteenth century, Charles de Montesquieu observed, "There is no crueler tyranny than that which is perpetrated under the shield of law and in the name of justice." If I am correct, the Sandusky case provides ample evidence.

Other than Matt Sandusky, who defended his father under oath before "flipping" under the influence of repressed memory therapy, Jerry Sandusky's five other children insist that their father never molested them. Since all were adopted and therefore not biologically related, and four were boys, it would seem likely that he would have tried something with one of them. If Sandusky were a pedophile, he was probably sexually attracted to children by the time he was seventeen, yet no hint of an allegation arose until 1998, when he was fifty-four.

After Penn State began paying out millions to virtually anyone who claimed abuse by Sandusky, dozens of alleged victims came forward, dating back as far as 1966, when Sandusky was twenty-two years old. Most remain anonymous, and the known stories are outlandish and stereotypical, as we have seen. Also, research indicates that most adolescents who suffer from sexual abuse reveal it to *someone*. In one 1995 study, for instance, 85% of young adults had disclosed to someone in the past. In a 2003 random national study of adolescents, 68% of those who were molested as children revealed it soon after the abuse. Of those, 39% told a friend, 34% told their mothers, and the rest told someone else—usually a teacher, father, doctor, social worker, or police officer. More teenage girls than boys told anyone (74% vs 46%).[1] Nonetheless, the odds are extremely small that *none* of Sandusky's alleged victims ever told anyone, nor did their mothers suspect anything.

And it would have been outrageous for Sandusky to call Second Milers such as Allan Myers or Sabastian Paden to ask them to testify for him if he had, in fact, been molesting them. Why would he do that?

I also don't automatically accept the "nice guy" FBI profile that Jim Clemente espouses. I interviewed Fred Berlin, a Johns Hopkins psychiatrist who has worked with pedophiles for decades. "Be wary of stereotypes," he advised. Pedophiles, like normal heterosexuals, come in all varieties and personalities, from decent people to rapists. So yes, there are child-friendly men who are sexually attracted to children. But "you may be a nice guy who just has a genuine affection and concern for kids," Berlin cautioned. Yes, one of the signs of a pedophile can be someone who spends an inordinate amount of time with children. "But there are also people who want to do that for positive and wholesome reasons."

The "nice guy pedophile" stereotype created a kind of Catch-22 situation in Sandusky's case. Evidence of his good character just meant he was really guilty, so that every character witness introduced by the defense just added another shovel of dirt, whereas the bad character of the alleged victims (which included drug-taking, crime, a history of lying) was interpreted as evidence that they were really abused and therefore proved the allegations.

Berlin said that in his experience, it is unusual for a serial child molester to maintain his innocence. Such perpetrators often rationalize what they have done, but they usually admit it. "When I was working as a prison consultant," he said, "one of the few men who insisted that he was innocent when speaking with me had been convicted of molesting and murdering a child. He was eventually exonerated by DNA evidence."[2]

Shortly before the trial, Joe Amendola asked Fred Berlin to serve as a defense expert witness, but the psychiatrist declined because there was not enough time for him to read all the background material and conduct a thorough clinical assessment of Sandusky. That's why Amendola opted for the ill-prepared, ill-informed psychologist who disastrously insisted that Sandusky had "histrionic personality disorder."

Former federal investigator John Snedden, who interviewed players in the Penn State drama soon after the trial, concluded that there was no cover-up because there was nothing to cover up. Mike McQueary had only heard slapping sounds in the shower. If McQueary really thought he was witnessing a sexual assault on a child, Snedden said, wouldn't he have intervened to stop a "wet, defenseless naked 57-year-old guy in the shower?" Snedden's boss told him, as a rookie agent, that the first question to ask in an investigation is, "Where is the crime?" In this case, there didn't appear to be one. "I've never had a rape case successfully prosecuted based only on sounds, and without credible victims and witnesses."

Snedden concluded that then-Governor Tom Corbett orchestrated the Sandusky investigation because Graham Spanier had defeated his attempt to slash the Penn State budget. "It's a political vendetta by somebody who had an epic degree of vindictiveness and would apparently stop at nothing." Then mass hysteria took over. "Ninety-nine percent of what happened at Penn State boiled down to people running around yelling, 'Oh my God, we've got to do something immediately.' There was no investigation, no determination of the facts. Instead, the officials running the show at Penn State wanted to move on as fast as possible from the scandal by sacrificing a few scapegoats," Snedden said. The media immediately jumped on board the abuse narrative train. "Sadly," he concluded, "I think they've demonstrated that investigative journalism is dead."[3]

* * *

I hope that this book demonstrates that deep dives by investigative writers are not, in fact, dead. Like all of my nonfiction work, this book is thoroughly researched and well-documented, yet I suspect that I may be harassed and vilified for writing it. Some people may judge me harshly without bothering to read the book. *How dare he say he thinks the evil Jerry Sandusky is innocent?* In 2012, a few months after the trial and its guilty verdict, a State College resident, who insists on anonymity, wrote the following:

> The venom that the nation had for Jerry Sandusky was at incredible levels, but the interesting thing was that nobody really knew

the facts surrounding the case. And what was strange was that nobody wanted to know the facts of the case. I quickly learned that this was not something that you discuss in public. Ever. Under any circumstances. I remember being out with my girlfriend at a dinner last year with her friends. I stupidly brought up the Sandusky case, and I remember the waitress turned around while waiting on another table and said, "He should rot in hell." My girlfriend's friends then went on to get angry at me because I had the audacity to suggest that there "might" be something amiss here. I was basically no better than a child molester for the rest of the night. That was the last time I brought it up in public and why I would never want my name used in any type of public forum when it came to this. It's fruitless. Completely fruitless. The public's mind is made up.[4]

I fear that not much has changed since then. The venom continues to flow. In July 2016, for instance, *New York Daily News* reporter Evan Grossman dismissed "the group that covers their ears and pounds their feet denouncing any and all ideas that former Penn State football coach Joe Paterno knew Jerry Sandusky was up to no good." Grossman accepted the unsubstantiated, anonymous 1976 accuser without question. "Rape victims sometimes take decades to come forward because of the very treatment they are now enduring from Paterno apologists."[5]

A few months later, in a fawning profile of Detroit Lions linebacker DeAndre Levy in *Men's Journal,* Levy said that his "proudest moment in college" at the University of Wisconsin came during a 2006 game against Penn State, when Levy accidentally broke Joe Paterno's leg during a sideline tackle. At the time, the coach was seventy-nine years old. Levy called Paterno a "dirtbag." The reporter asked admiringly, "Why aren't more football players like DeAndre Levy?"[6]

In April 2017, *Pittsburgh Post-Gazette* writer Ron Cook continued to heap hatred on Jerry Sandusky, whose presumed serial molestations caused "the most tragic scandal in the history of college sports." Cook also had plenty of ill-informed, self-righteous wrath to spare for Joe Paterno, Graham Spanier, Gary Schultz, and Tim Curley. "Penn State will never get past Sandusky," he concluded.[7]

In June 2017, Pennsylvania's auditor general, Eugene De-Pasquale, issued a report that was harshly critical of the Penn State leadership and board, the NCAA, and the Freeh Report, in the wake of the scandal. In a press conference, he noted, "When you panic, you make mistakes." Nonetheless, he felt the need to clarify his

hatred for the evil convicted molester: "Put cement loafers on Sandusky and dump him in the ocean for all I care."[8]

And now Al Pacino will be taking a star turn as a villainous Joe
Paterno in a movie version endorsing the abuse narrative.

WHAT ABOUT ALL THOSE ACCUSERS?

I am sure that many readers are still asking: "But what about all
those claims? Nearly three dozen alleged Sandusky victims came
forth. Maybe some of them were misled by repressed memories or
suggestive police interviews or were consciously lying, but surely not
all of them." Yet there is ample evidence that in a moral panic, multiple false accusers can come forward, as in the Salem Witch Trials.
Group delusions are not new, as proven by the cases reviewed in the
classic 1852 book, *Extraordinary Popular Delusions and the Madness of Crowds*, by Charles Mackay. "We find that whole communities suddenly fix their minds upon one object, and go mad in its
pursuit; that millions of people become simultaneously impressed
with one delusion, and run after it, till their attention is caught
by some new folly more captivating than the first," wrote Mackay.
"Men, it has been well said, think in herds; it will be seen that they
go mad in herds, while they only recover their senses slowly, and
one by one."

Among other things, Mackay wrote about the Great Witch Craze,
but his main focus was on financial scams such as the South-Sea
Bubble and Tulipomania, examples of mass gullibility and greed
rather than false allegations. Nonetheless, there was greed galore
in the Sandusky case, too.[9]

Because humans are social creatures, we are influenced by the
opinions and recall of those around us. False memories and accusations can spread like a virus in a process experimental psychologist Henry Roediger called the "social contagion of memory."[10]

In researching *Memory Warp* (2017), my book about the disastrous repressed memory epidemic, I encountered families in which
multiple children recovered abuse memories and cut off all contact
with their parents, as I wrote in this passage:

> In many cases, there was a sibling domino effect. Many families
> lost first one, then several children to recovered-memory therapy.
> One father I interviewed had lost four of his five daughters. . . .
> Another couple told me they had lost seven of their eight children.
> These cases were particularly devastating because so many people

assumed that if multiple children made the accusations, they must be true. They did not stop to consider the improbability of several children completely forgetting abuse for years, let alone one.[11]

Similarly, what were the odds of thirty-three people failing to tell *anyone* that Jerry Sandusky was abusing them until Aaron Fisher and his therapist Mike Gillum started the ball rolling? Yes, some sex abuse victims may keep mum about their abuse for many years out of shame or embarrassment. But surely some of them would have told their friends, parents, teachers, coaches, counselors, or diaries.

In *The Secret of Bryn Estyn: The Making of a Modern Witch Hunt* (2005), Richard Webster documented a startlingly similar case of false convictions of teachers and caregivers in Welsh homes for troubled boys, in which a crusading reporter and police trawling led young men to make multiple false allegations. Webster's description should sound familiar:

> Instead of waiting for allegations to be made spontaneously, the police began actively to look for them. They did so through massive trawling operations in which they deliberately sought out former residents of care homes and invited them to make complaints. . . . Many of them were damaged and highly suggestible, and a significant proportion had criminal records which included offences of dishonesty and deception.

Welsh Detective Chief Inspector Lorraine Johnson assumed that witnesses might be "blocking out memories," so that repeated interviews were necessary. "When I have spoken to psychiatrists and psychologists, [they say] it's very unlikely that the unblocking will occur at the first meeting," said Johnson, "and it's very important that the door is left open for them to make contact at a later stage."

Webster went beyond such repressed memory involvement to explain how attractive the victim role could be for adults with hard lives:

> An allegation of abuse may also furnish a beguiling explanation for aspects of their lives which may previously have induced feelings of guilt. Broken relationships, sexual confusion, emotional difficulties, alcoholism, drug addiction and criminality can all be "explained" by invoking a history of abuse. Whether or not that history is true may be all but irrelevant to its explanatory power and psychological potency. When all this is placed alongside the

possibility of gaining thousands of pounds in compensation . . .
the temptation to make an allegation may be difficult to resist.

In 1995, during an investigation into abuse claims at Shelburne
Youth Centre in Nova Scotia, the province announced that it had
set aside $56 million to pay alleged victims. Within two years, 1,457
people had come forward with complaints. In this case (unlike in
the United Kingdom's "Great Children's Home Panic") a police panel
concluded that the allegations contained "blatant falsehoods and
gross exaggerations," and the case collapsed.[12]

Because of some documented abuses in fraternity houses and
criminal acts by various athletes, it seems that allegations of sexual
abuse on college campuses involving sports figures may be particularly susceptible to a rush to judgment. Other recent scandals have
involved false allegations and credulous, overeager media, though
none can compare to the Sandusky juggernaut. For instance, in
2014 *Rolling Stone* published the chilling story of "Jackie," a college
freshman at the University of Virginia who was raped by seven men
at a fraternity party, while her date and another man gave instruction and encouragement. Only it didn't happen. Because the story
fit the prevailing "rape-epidemic-on-college-campuses" narrative,
most horrified readers initially accepted that it must be true, just
as the *Rolling Stone* editors did.[13]

In 2006, a stripper accused three Duke University lacrosse
players of raping her. The police and prosecutor Mike Nifong pursued the case in a flawed investigation that provided an excellent
example of "confirmation bias," in which people select and mis-
interpret information that confirms a pre-existing belief. Because
he was sure that the young men were guilty, Nifong ignored DNA
evidence and did not closely question the accuser or worry about
her inconsistent statements. Eventually, the lacrosse players were
exonerated and Nifong was disbarred.

There are four books about the Duke lacrosse case, with titles
such as *Until Proven Innocent, A Rush to Injustice,* and *It's Not About
the Truth,* but no books (until this one) have taken a hard look at
the Sandusky case.[14] Why? Because Sandusky was convicted, and
because the accepted abuse narrative has been impenetrable. The
case has been considered too toxic to re-examine. Despite my stature
as a science writer and author of many critically acclaimed books,
I could not find a major trade publisher to accept *The Most Hated
Man in America.* Publishers usually jump all over revelatory books
about famous cases. But not this one. And none of the journalists

covering the case were interested in writing about the evidence of repressed memory involvement or the fact that the janitor said on tape that Sandusky was *not* the abuser he saw in a shower. In any other high-profile case, these would be explosive news items.

MISTAKES WERE MADE

Part of the problem is that such reporters might have to admit that they got something wrong. In the landmark 2015 book, *Mistakes Were Made (But Not by Me)*, social psychologists Carol Tavris and Elliot Aronson document the impact of "cognitive dissonance" on humans, explaining that it causes enormous stress for us to hold two contrary ideas in our heads, so we must come down firmly on one side—and once we do, we are extremely resistant to changing our minds, even in the face of strong evidence to the contrary.

In one chapter, Tavris and Aronson review the disastrous repressed memory epidemic. In another, "Law and Disorder," they discuss false convictions, using the 1989 Central Park jogger rape case as an example. The police got five black and Hispanic teenagers to confess to the crime, though none of their DNA matched that at the crime scene. Thirteen years later, Matias Reyes, in prison for other rapes and a murder, confessed to the crime, and his DNA was a match. Nonetheless, prosecutor Linda Fairstein still refused to admit she had convicted and imprisoned innocent men.

It is, therefore, highly unlikely that anyone involved in the investigation, prosecution, and conviction of Jerry Sandusky will admit that they made mistakes. As with many other cases of alleged child sexual abuse, there was no DNA to exonerate him, because there was no physical evidence and, indeed, quite possibly no crime.

But what about those detailed false confessions of the Central Park Five? The teenagers had been questioned, without lawyers, for fourteen to thirty hours. Each was told that the others had confessed and identified them. They were told that they must have blocked out the memory of the assault. If only they would confess, they could go home. False confessions are far more common, and easier to elicit, than most people realize. *Criminal Interrogation and Confessions*, now in its fifth edition, provides a template for how to secure confessions, including lying to the subject. As Tavris and Aronson note, "The interrogator's presumption of guilt creates a self-fulfilling prophecy."[15]

As we have seen, Pennsylvania police investigators Joseph Leiter and Scott Rossman used grossly leading methods in their taped interview with Brett Houtz. Neither had any training in acceptable sex abuse investigation methodology. They contaminated the interview by allowing the civil attorney to be present and colluding with him, by telling Houtz that many others had accused Sandusky of sexual abuse (not true at the time), and by praising him for his cooperation. They told him that he should try to remember more and tell them in another session. In their testimony, they admitted that they had conducted other interviews in a similar fashion. Such tactics can influence recall in a similar manner to recovered memory therapy. "Exposure to misinformation provided by interviewers can lead to major distortions in memory," concluded experimental psychologist Julia Shaw and a colleague in a 2015 article.[16] Because Leiter and Rossman were convinced that Sandusky was guilty, they ignored any contrary evidence, such as Second Milers who said their mentor never molested them.

"Because no one, no matter how well trained or well intentioned, is completely immune to the confirmation bias and his or her own cognitive blind spots," wrote Tavris and Aronson, "the leading social scientists who have studied wrongful convictions are unanimous in recommending . . . videotaping of all interviews."[17] Yet no other interviews were recorded during the Sandusky investigation. Indeed, one policeman in the case specifically banned video because it might help the defense.

In a summary article, "Suggestibility, Reliability, and the Legal Process," lawyer Robert Rosenthal wrote that "well-established legal principles demand the exclusion of suggestion-induced accusations in child abuse cases." Although he focused on leading interviews with younger children, many of his observations were equally applicable to the way young adult Second Milers were interviewed, as well as the way their memories were influenced and revised through suggestive psychotherapy. "Just as a conclusion based on bad data cannot be supported," Rosenthal wrote, "a jury verdict based on bad information, such as tainted or adulterated evidence, cannot be supported." That is why hypnotically-enhanced testimony is inadmissible, and why "repressed memories" of abuse are banned by most courts.

Rosenthal listed characteristics of suggestive interviews, including interviewer bias, interviews by adults with high status (such as policemen or therapists), repeated questions, leading/misleading questions, repeated interviews, stereotype induction, and peer pressure—all of which occurred during the Sandusky investigation. "Stereotype induction is the process of conveying negative characteristics of a suspect"—i.e., the police telling Second Milers that they knew Sandusky was a pedophile, or Mike Gillum telling his client that Sandusky fit "the exact profile of a predator." Peer pressure (also called "co-witness information") is the strategy of saying that others have said they were abused, so how about you?*

"These same tactics can also influence the accuracy of reports provided by older children and adults," Rosenthal observed. Thus, much of the testimony in the Sandusky trial should have been excluded because it was obtained by suggestive means. Judges have a responsibility to ensure that testimony is sufficiently reliable, not tainted before the witnesses take the stand.[18]

Nor should we underestimate the influence of the media on sensational cases. In his 2011 book, *Convicting the Innocent*, Brandon Garrett examined the first 250 cases of men exonerated by DNA evidence. "The press . . . played a role leading up to these trials," he wrote. "Eyewitnesses sometimes saw news reports about a crime . . . and seeing these . . . may have contaminated their memory and increased their certainty. Likewise, studies have shown that jurors are far more likely to convict in cases in which there is pretrial publicity."[19]

As we have seen, *memory* was a crucial issue in the Sandusky trial, so it is worth emphasizing that numerous cognitive studies have demonstrated how malleable memory and attitudes can be, even without overt influence. But there was in fact a great deal of blatant suggestion in the Sandusky case. Psychological experiments have demonstrated that "confirmatory feedback increased false memory for forcibly confabulated events, increased confidence in those false memories, and increased the likelihood that participants would freely report the confabulated events 1 to 2 months later," concluded one experimental report in 2001. "The results illustrate the powerful role of social-motivational factors in promoting the development of false memories."[20]

In *The Invisible Gorilla and Other Ways Our Intuitions Deceive Us* (2010), cognitive psychologists Christopher Chabris and Daniel Simons document that memory is not like a video recording but is rather a reconstructed best guess. They write about a 2008 study in

---

* In a series of experiments, psychologist John Shaw and colleagues documented the impact of co-witness information and suggestive questioning, giving as an example: "Don't be afraid to tell us what happened. Your sister Alice has already told us that. . . ." The authors concluded: "In situations involving multiple witnesses, both informational and normative influences could exert pressure on a witness to have his or her memory report conform to the reports of other witnesses."

which people were asked what life-sustaining treatments they would want if they were seriously ill. A year later, when the same subjects answered the questions again, nearly a quarter of them changed their minds about this life-and-death issue. What is most astonishing, though, is that most of them didn't think they *had* changed their minds. They were sure they had answered the same way![21]

In 2016, psychologist Julia Shaw published *The Memory Illusion,* a summary of her own and others' work. "[My colleagues and] I have convinced people they have committed crimes that never occurred, suffered from a physical injury they never had, or were attacked by a dog when no such attack ever took place," she wrote. *The Memory Hackers* (2016), a Nova public television program, featured one of Shaw's subjects recalling an illusory crime in three sessions. In that study, over 70% of her subjects developed false memories.* "What could have been turns into what would have been turns into what was," the experimental psychologist explained. Her conclusion? "Any event, no matter how important, emotional or traumatic it may seem, can be . . . misremembered, or even be entirely fictitious. . . . All of us can come to confidently and vividly remember entire events that never actually took place."[22]

Experimental psychologist Frederic Bartlett made similar observations in his classic 1932 text, *Remembering: A Study in Experimental and Social Psychology.* Our memories, he noted, "live with our interests and with them they change." We tend to incorporate details of what really happened, along with other inserted elements, perhaps from a movie we saw or a book we read, or a story someone else told us. This kind of "source amnesia" is amazingly common. In fact, many of us are sure something happened to us, when it was our sibling who actually experienced it.[23]

That is how Mike McQueary's memory of the infamous 2000 shower changed. The night of the shower, he said he had heard slapping sounds but had not seen anything incriminating. Ten years later, his retrospective bias led him to have questionable memories of seeing Sandusky moving his hips behind a boy in the shower. With rehearsal, his new memories were solidified, and he became quite confident in them. That phenomenon, called "the illusion of confidence" by *The Invisible Gorilla* authors, is not unusual, either.

---

* A critique of this study recoded the data to distinguish between false memory and false belief, thereby reducing the false memory incidence to 26-30%. Either way, the critique concluded, the findings "show that suggestive techniques . . . fused with a heavy dose of social demand, can lead people to generate personal [false] memories of stealing or assaulting another person."

SANDUSKY'S THOUGHTS

In his prison writings, Jerry Sandusky pondered many of these issues himself. "Why were their [Second Mile accusers'] memories just unlocked now? Why didn't they accuse me when these events supposedly occurred? . . . You heard some say they broke away from me. Why didn't they accuse me then?"

He pointed out that the Second Mile program began as a foster home. "Why would I have started a foster home for kids and had so little contact with them, if my purpose was to recruit children? Why would I have initiated an effort for young men and women from inner cities involved in A Better Chance program to be nurtured in our foster home?" He was particularly disgusted with the idea that he had been "grooming" children for abuse. "If I had wanted to groom kids, there would have been many other ways to do it with less effort."

He also pointed out that he would have been insane to parade his relationship with troubled teens if he had been molesting them. "Would a sneaky pedophile advertise and promote his victims—put their pictures in books, take them to many public events, have his so-called victims attend, speak at, and participate in fund-raising and other events?" After prolonged, unwanted sexual abuse, would these alleged victims have continued to be friendly? "The long-term relationships and continued contact don't seem to fit. I didn't sense embarrassment. They enjoyed being seen with me in public."

Sandusky also complained that the frequency and timing of abuse claims made them implausible. "I must not have had anything else to do, no commitments, no speaking engagements, no visits with family. Why would he come back over and over for such horrific acts? Nobody forced him! This doesn't make sense!" He was writing about Aaron Fisher, but the same could be said of many accusers.

Sandusky also pointed out that his low testosterone meant that he was unlikely to be a perpetually priapic sexual predator. "In 1967 I was told I was sterile. I brought the issue of testosterone up in relation to the idea I would not have had the kind of sex drive to do all that was alleged. In addition to feeling it wouldn't have been right, I didn't have the interest."*[24] Nor did he obsess over sex the

---

* In fact, the treatment of pedophiles often involves intentionally lowering testosterone levels with drugs such as depo-leuprolide.

way the young men did. "The accusers and I came from different worlds. . . . Their world was much more sexually-oriented than mine." Sandusky didn't own or watch pornography. "Usually, child molesters are found with pornography, videos, internet correspondence, text messages, etc.," he wrote. There was none of that in his case, just innocuous pictures of Second Mile kids, many sent by the boys themselves. "Were they grooming me?" Sandusky asked facetiously.

His heart-felt letters to Brett Houtz and other Second Milers were portrayed by prosecutors as nefarious love letters, but Sandusky said that they were nothing of the sort. "When they hear the word love, they seem to equate sex with it."

In prison, he had educated himself about proper interviewing protocol and issues such as confirmation bias. "People were interviewed multiple times. If they gave what was requested, they were applauded as heroes. If they didn't give what was wanted, they were accused of lying."

Sandusky was enormously frustrated that nothing he said made any difference. No one would listen to him. "Why can others talk about what they say happened to them, and I can't say something without being an insensitive human being?" But it didn't matter whether he remained silent or spoke his mind. "If you don't say something, you're guilty. If you say you're not guilty, you're in denial."

FINAL QUESTIONS

I began to look into the Sandusky case in 2013, after I realized that some of the accusations stemmed from highly questionable recovered memories. Over the next four years, I kept looking for convincing evidence that Sandusky was guilty, or at least that he was sexually attracted to boys. Wasn't it weird that he took showers with boys? And sometimes cracked their backs and blew raspberries on their stomachs?

I was disturbed by the image of him grabbing Zachary Konstas from behind during the 1998 shower, while saying, "I'll squeeze your guts out." During a prison visit, I asked him about it. "Jerry, why would you, a naked adult, hug a naked boy in a shower like that?" He answered that he was just trying to show "enthusiasm," a word he used frequently when he wrote or spoke about his efforts to help troubled youth or others. What he apparently meant was that he wanted to be upbeat, energetic, and playful.

About his approach to coaching, for instance, he wrote: "If I expected them to play enthusiastically, I would have enthusiasm. If I expected them to work long hours, I would work long hours." Similarly, Sandusky repeatedly expressed his love for Bo, his Saint Bernard. "Dogs remind me to be kind, to love, to show appreciation, and to be enthusiastic. Bo's love is unconditional. . . . He has greeted me with a waggle and run in circles to our laughter. He did and would do the same to the accusers." That's the kind of enthusiasm he tried to convey in a song he made up for Second Mile camp: "Care for a friend! Stay to the end! Greet with a smile! Go the Second Mile!"

"But Jerry," I said, "most people would think that hugging a boy in the shower was really strange." He basically just shrugged and repeated once again that this was the way he had grown up in what he called his "Mayberry World" at his parents' recreation center. At the YMCA and the rec center, "males shared the same shower. After practice, the shower was a place for relaxation and horseplay."

I pressed him again about why he continued to shower with boys, even after the 1998 investigation. Once again, he said that it hadn't seemed like a big deal to him. It was Zach's mother who was upset, not the boy, who had continued to want to spend time with him. After his brief interview with child protective services and campus policeman Ron Schreffler, he was cleared almost immediately. He didn't recall Schreffler advising him to stop showering with *all* boys. The message he got was not to shower again with Zach Konstas, and he didn't. Despite Konstas wanting to work out together again, Sandusky wouldn't do that, either.

I asked about the 2000 shower with Allan Myers, which Mike McQueary overheard, and about Sandusky's subsequent meeting with athletic director Tim Curley. What about the email in which Curley said that he planned to tell Sandusky that "we feel there is a problem," and that he would suggest he seek "professional help"? Sandusky answered: "I don't think Tim had anybody in mind as a therapist, and he didn't come across ever in a way to make me think I had any sexual problem." But that second shower incident *did* get Sandusky's attention. "I didn't shower with kids after the 2001 meeting with Tim Curley. It was clear to me at that point that it wasn't a good idea."

But even then, he didn't think much about it. He had no idea that Mike McQueary had been the one who reported the shower incident. "Mike participated in fund-raising events with me and played in Second Mile golf outings. I remember him talking to me about some football players I knew as walk-on candidates." Penn State continued to recognize Sandusky as an Alumni Fellow and to support the Second Mile. "I spoke at the College of Human Development commencement and a Smeal College of Business graduation ceremony. Tim Curley's son attended my football camp."

As I became familiar with the case, I began to discern a pattern. Sandusky was an important mentor and father figure to many Second Mile kids when they were ten to thirteen or so, but as they got into their mid-teen years, some began to rebel and pull away. Sandusky saw this as a dangerous thing, since they sometimes became juvenile delinquents, got into drugs, and sought promiscuous sex. He feared they might end up dropping out of school and perhaps landing in prison (which some of them did). So out of concern, he pursued them, having them sign contracts to earn small amounts of money through good study habits and participation on sports teams. But some were too old to want to submit to such blandishments, accompanied by sermonizing letters.

When I asked Sandusky whether he thought that this was indeed a pattern, he agreed. "What was my reaction to kids pulling away as they grew older?" he wrote. "Even though I recognized this as a stage, it bothered me because so many drifted into problems and trouble. I didn't want it to happen (legal, otherwise). I never wanted to give up on them reaching their potential (like my Dad). Never quit!"

Probing for more insight into his marriage, I asked about marital conflict. "Dottie and I were too busy to argue about much." But he added that he wasn't useful fixing anything around the house. "It bothered her when I would invite family, friends, or others without asking her, and when I didn't want to do some of the activities she hoped I would, especially after retirement. Our worst arguments occurred when she would hold everything inside until later at night. She wanted to discuss, and I didn't."

Nonetheless, he emphasized that they had a solid marriage. "Dottie and I shared many common beliefs and feelings, including a belief in a creator, love, enthusiasm, the importance of family, and respect for one another. We tried to instill these values in our children."

With some trepidation, I asked both Jerry and Dottie Sandusky about their sex life, explaining that, under the circumstances, I really *had* to ask, even though it clearly was not something either one of them was comfortable talking about. "I would like to think our sex life was normal," Jerry wrote. "Dottie probably wanted more spontaneity, and I tended to plan. It wasn't a source of contention. I think both of us felt loved. The number of instances varied with my schedule. My guess would be an average of 2-3 times per week."

I asked if he felt they were both happy with their intimate life. "Yes, we felt as though we had been sexually satisfying to one another. It was not a major focus. Love was a focus, not lust. It was based on a normal respect and attraction for two people in love (beyond sex). I didn't fantasize about sex or look at pornography. I noticed attractive women on occasions." In another letter, he added, "Dottie has been my only sex partner, and that was after marriage. I have not had oral or anal sex with anybody, including her."

In a 2013 phone interview, Dottie confirmed much of what her husband said. "We had a really good sexual relationship until about two years ago, around the time when this all happened. He started having trouble with an enlarged prostate, and he had a hard time having sex." Before that, she said they had intercourse three or four times a week, a bit higher than her husband's estimate. "Yes, we enjoyed each other sexually, as far as I am concerned. I would be very surprised if he had an affair."

She emphasized that he invariably told the truth, which was part of the problem with his hesitancy during the Costas interview. "That's just how he talks. He thinks through things before he answers. I am positive he isn't sexually attracted to boys. He would goof around with girls, too, in the pool, and he was supportive of them as well." In general, he loved people, dogs, and kids. "A mouse came into the house, and he wouldn't kill it. He took it across the street and it came back the next day, and he still didn't kill it." It was ironic, she said, that her husband was supposed to be a perverted sex offender. "We are both prudes. One Friday night a Second Mile kid came over and wanted to watch TV, and after five minutes, Jerry said, 'That's not appropriate to watch.' That's just us. Did I ever doubt him? No. I knew he took showers with kids, he goofs around. I know who he is."

In a letter to Judge John Cleland before the sentencing hearing, she said much the same thing: "I have known Jerry for 47 years, and he has always been truthful with me, even if it hurt. He is a very up-front man and a man of very high morals. Jerry always put others before himself and always wanted to make each person feel special, no matter who they were." A Second Miler now in his forties had recently stopped by, she wrote, and said that Sandusky had helped make him a better husband and father. "Our house was a fun house with lots of games, picnics, laughs and caring.

There were always lots of people around, whether it was friends of our kids, Second Mile kids, or neighbors. I never saw him doing anything inappropriate to any child. If I had, as a Mother and Grandmother I would have taken action. Jerry is not the monster everyone is making him out to be."

She added that, as Sandusky had told me, he had not bought most of the gifts he gave to troubled kids. "One of the accusers called Jerry and said he could not do his school work because his computer broke, so Jerry found a used computer that someone was not using and gave it to him. Fact is, most of the things he gave to the accusers were used or given to him by people who wanted to help these young men."

Her heartfelt letter to the judge made no difference.

I have met Dottie only once, when she made me an ample dinner at her home during my research trip to Pennsylvania in 2014, but I've exchanged many emails, and I have gotten to know her as a reliable but relatively succinct, efficient correspondent. She usually signs off with "Blessings, Dottie," and an inspirational quote, typical of the somewhat corny positive thinking that keeps both her and her imprisoned husband going:

"If you're alive, there's a purpose for your life." —Rick Warren

"When everything seems to be going against you, remember that the airplane takes off against the wind, not with it." —Henry Ford

"Most of the important things in the world have been accomplished by people who have kept on trying when there seemed to be no hope at all." —Dale Carnegie

"Reflect upon your present blessings—of which every man has many—not on your past misfortunes, of which all men have some." —Charles Dickens

If I were in Jerry or Dottie Sandusky's position, I am not sure such platitudes would make me feel much better, but I am glad that such sentiments help them. Let me end with a poem by Kara Sandusky, who obviously wrote it one night when missing her father:

Got ready for bed just like any other night.
Did I brush my teeth? I can't remember because I was missing
One very important person . . .

Life will go on by the grace of God,
But it will never be the same without the loving, strong, encour-
    aging presence of
One very important person.

A monster he is not,
For to hundreds of thousands of loving, compassionate, under-
    standing people,
He was one very important person.

— ACKNOWLEDGMENTS —

GLENNA KERKER of Oregon first called my attention to the involvement of repressed memories in the Sandusky case, and she continued to help with research and thoughtful observations during my four years of research and writing. She had no personal stake in the case. She's just smart.

Before I delved into the Penn State scandal, John Ziegler, the subject of Chapter 19, took on the Sandusky case and its alleged victims like a dog with a bone, despite its adverse impact on his career. He and I are opposites in many ways in terms of political views and approaches, but we are similar in our determination to find the truth in this case. I owe him a huge debt for his dedicated work, which helped to inform my own.

Robert Long's critique of the Freeh Report at www.robertlong1. tripod.com was useful to me, as was material from Ray Blehar's www.notpsu.blogspot.com, although Blehar and I disagree about Sandusky's culpability.

Thanks to Elaine Steinbacher, herself a long-time friend of Dottie and Jerry Sandusky, for conducting some of the interviews with Second Mile alums and Sandusky colleagues.

Anthropologist David Stoll, a hiking buddy and friend, read portions of the book and helped with preliminary edits and observations.

Independent researcher John Risse gathered journalist Sara Ganim's articles on the Sandusky case for me, despite his distaste for the case.

Defense lawyer Harvey Silverglate read an early version of the manuscript and provided helpful suggestions and encouragement.

Speaking of lawyers, Al Lindsay and Andrew Salemme graciously allowed me to look through police reports and other discovery materials for the Sandusky case (excluding any grand jury material), and Salemme was particularly helpful as I completed the research for this book. Lindsay's investigator, Jim Smith, accompanied me on a memorable 2014 expedition to Allan Myers's

("Victim 2") driveway, where we were scared off by harshly worded no trespassing signs.

Investigative journalist Ralph Cipriano took on the "Billy Doe" case of false allegations in Pennsylvania and put pre-publication excerpts from this book on his website, BigTrial.net. Former federal investigator John Snedden shared insights and encouragement and assisted with the online petition for Sandusky to get a new trial: www.bit.ly/2r9KjvI.

I wish to thank literary agent Susan Lee Cohen for helping me to fine-tune my book proposal and for submitting it to numerous major publishers, although it was to no avail.

Finally, my gratitude to publisher Lawrence Knorr of Sunbury Press Books for taking on this project, when the "big guys" were all too timid. Editor Janice Rhayem not only made the book read better but played the role of devil's advocate, asking hard, clarifying questions.

— ENDNOTES —

(Abbreviated citations refer to full information in the bibliography.)

INTRODUCTION

1. Rushdie, *Joseph Anton.*
2. Fisher, *Silent No More.*
3. Ganim, "Grand Jury Is Used."
4. Menzie, "President Obama Speaks Out."
5. See Luciew, *Hear No Evil*, for a good overall summary.
6. Ganim, "Gov. Corbett Plays Unique."
7. NBC News, "Penn State to Pay $59.7 Million."
8. Bella, "Jerry Sandusky More Than a Monster."
9. Moulton Report, Appendix N.
10. Sokolove, "Trials of Graham Spanier."
11. Moushey, *Game Over*, p. 156; Sandusky, Touched, p. 210-211.
12. Sandusky, *Touched*, p. 12, 211.
13. Sandusky, *Touched*, p. 33, 100, 209.

CHAPTER 1

1. Grand Jury Presentment, p. 6-7.
2. https://soundcloud.com/freespeechbroadcasting/2017-11-19-3-tom-frederick; https://soundcloud.com/freespeechbroadcasting/2017-11-26-3-penn-state-update.
3. Trial Transcript, Day 2, p. 192.
4. Van Natta, "Whistleblower's Last Stand."
5. Trial Transcript, Day 7, p. 9-16.
6. Trial Transcript, Day 2, p. 208-211.
7. Ganim, "Mike McQueary Attended"; Van Natta, "Whistleblower's Last Stand."
8. Sandusky prison interview with John Ziegler; Sandusky, *Can We Endure?*
9. *Ibid.*
10. Curtis Everhart interview with Allan Myers.
11. Van Natta, "The Whistleblower's Last Stand."
12. Curtis Everhart interview with Allan Myers.
13. *The Express*, Lock Haven PA, a letter to the editor published 05/06/2011; http://framingpaterno.com/sites/default/files/LtAG_redacted_web.pdf
14. Ziegler, "Real Story."
15. Van Natta, "Whistleblower's Last Stand."

CHAPTER 2

1. Trial Transcript, Day 4, p. 18; Ganim, "Mothers of Two"; Alicia A. Chambers clinical notes, May 4, 1998, FREEHdom Fighters website.
2. Trial Transcript, Day 4, Page 53-54.
3. State of Michigan Task Force, *Forensic Interviewing Protocol.*
4. Trial Transcript, Day 4, p. 71-76.
5. Framingpaterno.com, page 13 of transcript of prison interview of March 2013

6.   Sandusky interview with John Ziegler, Framing Paterno website.
7.   Redacted 1998 police report, on Freehdom Fighters website; Penn Law Fumble.
8.   Trial Transcript, Day 4, p. 66-67; Jerry Sandusky interview, Oct. 2014.
9.   Penn Law Fumble website, http://www.pennlawfumble.info/,
10. Pennsylvania State Police Interview, 09/20/11 (Leiter & Ellis; PSP p. 154)
11. Trial Transcript, Day 4, p. 48.
12. Sentencing Transcript, Day 4, p. 28.
13. Trial Transcript, Day 4, p. 72.
14. Youtube Video of Howard Janet on CNN: https://www.youtube.com/watch?v=71ZbFZAyk60, June 15, 2012.

CHAPTER 3

1.   http://markpendergrast.com/victims-of-memory.html
2.   Loftus, *Myth of Repressed Memory*; Shaw, *Memory Illusion;* Crews, *Memory Wars*; Crews, *Freud*; McNally, *Remembering Trauma*; Pope, *Psychology Astray*; Simpson, *Second Thoughts*; McHugh, *Try to Remember.* Ofshe, *Making Monsters.*
3.   Pendergrast, *Memory Warp;* Pendergrast, *Repressed Memory Epidemic*; Pendergrast, *Victims of Memory*; Acocella, *Creating Hysteria*; Piper, *Hoax and Reality*;
4.   PCRA Brief, July 11, 2017, p. 77.
5.   Shaw, "Constructing Rich False Memories"; for a good review of repressed memories in reference to the Sandusky case, see PCRA Brief, July 11, 2017, p. 72-96.
6.   Bartlett, *Remembering*, p. 212, 227.
7.   Bartlett, *Remembering*, p. 205.
8.   Pendergrast, *Memory Warp*, p. 66-74.
9.   Bartlett, *Remembering*, p. 209.
10. Loftus, *Witness for the Defense*, p. 13.
11. Shaw, *Memory Illusion*, p. xiv-xv; *Memory Hackers.*
12. Freud, *Standard Edition*, v. 2, p. 279, 281; v. 3, p. 269.
13. Freud, *Standard Edition,* v. 3, p. 153.
14. Pendergrast, *Memory Warp*, p. 255-267, for all Freud quotes and coverage.
15. Pendergrast, *Memory Warp*, p. 25-44; Bass and Davis, *Courage to Heal*, p. 22-39.
16. Fredrickson, *Repressed Memories*; Blume, *Secret Survivors.*
17. Petersen, *Dancing With Daddy*, p. 62-75.
18. Bartlett, *Remembering*, p. 217-220.
19. Hunter, *Abused Boys*, p. 149-196; Pendergrast, *Victims of Memory*, p. 55.
20. *Ibid*, p. 119-149, for methods of illusory memory retrieval.
21. Pendergrast, *Memory Warp*, p. 116-124.
22. Pendergrast, *Memory Warp*, p. 86-89; http://blogs.brown.edu/recoveredmemory/case-archive/legal-cases/
23. Loftus, *Myth of Repressed Memory*, p. 219; PCRA Brief, July 11, 2017, p. 78.
24. McNally, *Remembering Trauma*, p. 275; Brainerd, *Science of False Memory.*
25. McHugh, *Try to Remember,* p. 46, 66.
26. "Distinguishing True from False Memories."
27. Patihis, "Are the 'Memory Wars' Over?"; Pendergrast, *Memory Warp*, p. 19.
28. Pendergrast, *Memory Warp*, p. 20, 357-359.
29. Commonwealth of PA vs T.J.W. Jr, Superior Ct of PA, No. 1351 EDA 2014; PCRA Brief, June 11, 2017, p. 68-71.
30. Yoffe, "Bad Science."

CHAPTER 4

1.   For most of the material about Fisher, see Fisher, *Silent No More.*
2.   Fisher, *Silent No More*, p. 8; Stevens, "Pair Charged."

3.   Dawn Daniels' My Space 2008 printouts, courtesy Dottie Sandusky; Fravel interview.
4.   Fisher, *Silent No More*, p. 14-15, 38.
5.   *Ibid*, p. 22.
6.   Sandusky, *Can We Endure?*
7.   *Ibid*, p. 19-21; Moushey, *Game Over*, p. 22-23.
8.   Sandusky, *Touched*.
9.   Fisher, *Silent No More*, p. 48.
10.   *Ibid*, p. 49.
11.   *Ibid*, p. 50.
12.   *Ibid*, p. 51.
13.   *Ibid*, p. 52-53.
14.   Josh Fravel interview with private investigator Greg Auld; Trial Testimony, Day 6, p. 151-152.
15.   *Ibid*, p. 58.
16.   Moulton, *Report*, p. 32-33.
17.   Jerry Sandusky correspondence with Mark Pendergrast.
18.   Fisher, *Silent No More*, p. 54-55.
19.   Buell, "Penn State Scandal."
20.   Fisher, *Silent No More*, p. 55, 82.
21.   Moulton, *Report*, p. 33-34.
22.   Moulton, *Report*, p. 35.
23.   Sandusky to Pendergrast.
24.   11/20/08 audio interview CYS (Dershem Report)
25.   Fisher, *Silent No More*, p. 62; Steele, "Clinton County Caseworker."
26.   Johnson, "Sandusky 'Victim 1' Psychologist Loses County Job."
27.   Fisher, *Silent No More*, p. 63.
28.   Fisher, *Silent No More*, p. 70.
29.   Trial Transcript, Day 2, Page 128, 129; Fisher, *Silent No More*, p. 83-84; Penn Law Fumble.
30.   Dershem Report, p. 5.
31.   Dershem Report p. 4, dated 11/25,12/02, & 12/12/08 p. 4.
32.   *Ibid*, p. 57.
33.   *Ibid,* p. 64-65.
34.   Fisher, *Silent No More*, p. 26, 217.
35.   Johnson, "The Tortuous Winding Path of Victim One", Mike Gillum featured in video included in the online article.
36.   Mike Gillum interview.
37.   Fisher and Gillum, *Silent No More*, p. 127.
38.   *Ibid,* p. 22.
39.   *Ibid,* p. 65.
40.   Ganim, "Mothers of Two."
41.   *Ibid,* p. 66.
42.   *Ibid,* p. 67; Mike Gillum interview.
43.   Fisher and Gillum, *Silent No More*, p. 81.
44.   Fisher, *Silent No More*, p. 25, 71-72.
45.   Ofshe, *Making Monsters*.
46.   Let Go Let Peace In website; Mike Gillum interview.
47.   Fisher, *Silent No More,* 28-29.
48.   Amendola, "Aaron Fisher notes."
49.   Fravel, Joshua interview.
50.   Vestal, "Jerry Sandusky Victim Says Reporting Crimes Was Harder."
51.   Fisher, *Silent No More,* p. 69, 73.
52.   *Ibid*, p. 87.
53.   *Ibid*, p. 89.
54.   *Ibid*, p. 90.

55. Moulton, *Report*, p. 38.
56. Steele, "Clinton County Caseworker."
57. Penn Law Fumble; Moulton Report, p. 37.
58. Fisher, *Silent No More*, p. 93-94.
59. Fisher, *Silent No More*, p. 96.
60. *Ibid*, p. 71.
61. Penn Law Fumble.
62. Moulton, *Report*, p. 38-40.
63. Moulton, *Report*, p. 41; Ganim, "State Trooper Lear Charged."
64. Fisher, *Silent No More*, p. 97.
65. *Ibid*, p. 99.
66. See Pendergrast, *Memory Warp*, and Victor, *Satanic Panic.*
67. Fisher, *Silent No More*, p. 97
68. *Ibid*, p. 68-69
69. *Ibid*, p. 101-102.
70. Pendergrast, *Memory Warp*; Loftus, *Myth of Repressed Memory.*
71. Fisher, *Silent No More*, p. 103.
72. Pendergrast, *Memory Warp.*
73. Fisher, *Silent No More*, p. 104.
74. *Ibid*, p. 137; Mike Gillum interview.
75. *Ibid*, p. 157; Mike Gillum interview.
76. *Ibid*, p. 68, 124.
77. Trial Transcript, Day 2, p. 66.-67.
78. Trial Transcript, Day 2, p. 67.
79. Fisher, *Silent No More*, p. 146
80. Coffey, "Aaron Fisher, Victim No. 1."
81. Fisher, *Silent No More*, p. 107-108.
82. *Ibid*, p. 22
83. *Ibid*, p. 111.
84. Scott Rossman, Penn State Police report, July 10, 2009.
85. *Ibid*, p. 112.
86. Sandusky PCRA hearing, March 24, 2017, p. 180.
87. "Penn State Child Sex Abuse Scandal."
88. Fisher, *Silent No More*, p. 113-119.
89. *Ibid*, p. 122.
90. *Ibid*, p. 129.
91. *Ibid*, p. 130.
92. *Ibid*, p. 130.
93. *Ibid*, p. 135-138.
94. Bass, *Courage to Heal*, p. 62-66; Pendergrast, *Memory Warp, p. 37-38.*
95. Fredrickson, *Repressed Memories*, p. 27-28, 104; Pendergrast, *Memory Warp*, p. 52.
96. Moulton, *Report*, p. 72.
97. Fisher, *Silent No More*, p. 154.
98. Mike Gillum interview.
99. *Ibid*, p. 155.
100. *Ibid*, p. 158-159.
101. *Ibid*, p. 162.
102. Trial Transcript, Day 2, p. 76.
103. Trial Transcript, Day 2, p. 75.
104. Trial Transcript, Day 2, p. 75.
105. Trial Transcript, Day 2, p. 76.
106. Trial Transcript, Day 2, p. 76.
107. Joe Amendola notes on Grand Jury testimony (p. 4:10-20) 11/16/09
108. Trial Transcript, Day 2, p. 98.
109. Trial Transcript, Day 2, p. 29.

110. Ziegler, Framing Paterno website.
111. Wetzel, "Jerry Sandusky Engaged in Repeated Acts"; Trial Transcript, Day 2, p. 23.
112. Yoffe, "Bad Science."
113. Trial Transcript, Day 2, p. 23.
114. Trial Transcript, Day 2, p. 12-15.
115. Trial Transcript, Day 2, p. 27.

CHAPTER 5

1.   Moulton, *Report to the Attorney General*, p. 42.
2.   *Ibid*, p. 43.
3.   PCRA "Brief Re: Subject Matter Jurisdiction Claim," May 19, 2016.
4.   Hopper, "Jerry Sandusky 'Clingy.'"
5.   *Ibid*, p. 45-48.
6.   *Ibid*, Appendix D.
7.   *Ibid*, Appendix E.
8.   Freeh Report, p. ___.
9.   Moulton, *Report*, Appendix F.
10.   *Ibid*, Appendix G.
11.   *Ibid*, Appendix G.
12.   *Ibid*, p. 61-62, Appendix I.
13.   *Ibid*, Appendix J.
14.   Van Natta, "Whistleblower's Last Stand."
15.   Moulton, *Report*, p. 63.
16.   *Ibid*, p. 63-66.
17.   Trial Transcript, Day 6, p. 309-310.
18.   Sandusky, *Touched*, photo insert.
19.   Moulton, *Report*, p. 68-69.
20.   Ganim, "Grand Jury Is Used."
21.   Ganim, "Grand Jury Is Used"; Ganim, "Jerry Sandusky, Former Penn State Football Staffer."
22.   Moulton, *Report*, Appendix N.
23.   Grand Jury Presentment, p. 1.
24.   Joseph Leiter report, May 23, 2011, Penn State Police.
25.   Joseph Leiter, Penn State Police report, Dec. 8, 2011.
26.   Moulton, *Report,* p. 78-79; Trooper Scott Rossman report, June 7, 2011, Penn State Police.
27.   Moulton, *Report,* p. 80; Sandusky to Pendergrast email, June 20, 2017.
28.   *Ibid*, p. 81.
29.   *Ibid*, p. 84.
30.   *Ibid*, p. 84-87.

CHAPTER 6

1.   Struble interview with Pendergrast, Oct. 2014.
2.   Joseph Leiter, Penn State Police report, Feb. 4, 2011.
3.   Trial Transcript, Day 3, p. 154.
4.   Trial Transcript, Day 3, p. 143.
5.   http://thompsonhall.com/contingency-fees/.
6.   Lindsay lawfirm files, "Interview of Todd Reed," May 4, 2012.
7.   Sandusky trial transcript, Day 3, p. 143.
8.   Trial Transcript, Day 3, p. 146.
9.   Trial Transcript, Day 3, p. 152.
10.   Trial Transcript, Day 3, p. 154.
11.   Trial Transcript, Day 3, p. 119.
12.   Dustin Struble interview; Struble email, Oct. 15, 2014.

13. Struble email, Oct. 16, 2014.
14. Pendergrast, *Memory Warp*, p. 39, 55, 110, 264. 382; Bass, *Courage to Heal*, p. 72.
15. Struble interview.
16. Dustin Struble interview.
17. Jerry Sandusk to Mark Pendergrast, Sept. 25, 2013.
18. Scott Rossman interview with Michal Kajak, June 7, 2011, Penn State Police.
19. *Ibid.*
20. "#5, Michael Kajak Matrix Notes," from Joe Amendola.
21. Joseph Leiter, Penn State Police report, Nov. 10, 2011.
22. Trial Transcript, Day 3, p. 177.
23. Trial Transcript, Day 3, p. 174.
24. Trial Transcript, Day 5, p. 10-11.
25. Moulton Report, p. 20-21, 83.
26. Mark Yakicic interview with Jason Simcisko, July 19, 2011, Penn State Police; Moulton, *Report*, p. 81.
27. Moulton, *Report*, p. 82-83; Scott Rossman, Penn State Police report, Aug. 19, 2011.
28. Trial Transcript, Day 4, p. 122.
29. Trial Transcript, Day 4, p. 117.
30. Trial Transcript, Day 4, p. 105.
31. Trial Transcript, Day 4, p. 107.
32. Trial Transcript, Day 4, p. 108-109.
33. Jerry Sandusky to Mark Pendergrast, June 13, 2017.

CHAPTER 7

1. Trial Transcript, Day 1, p. 213-216.
2. Trial Transcript, Day 1, p. 42, 143-144.
3. Sandusky, *Can We Endure?*
4. Trial Transcript, Day 1, p. 189-190.
5. Sandusky, *Can We Endure?*
6. Trial Transcript, Day 1, p. 122-123.
7. Trial Transcript, Day 1, p. 120-121, 202.
8. Trial Transcript, Day 1, p. 203.
9. Trial Transcript, Day 1, p. 89.
10. Trial Transcript, Day 1, p. 116.
11. Trial Transcript, Day 1, p . 117-118, 192-193.
12. Trial Transcript, Day 1, p. 118-119.
13. Sandusky letter to Brett Houtz, discovery material.
14. *Ibid.*
15. *Ibid.*
16. Trial Transcript, Day 1, p. 95.
17. Sandusky, *Can We Endure?*
18. Sandusky letter to Brett Houtz, discovery material.
19. Trial Transcript, Day 1, p. 187-188.
20. Trial Transcript. Day 1, p. 201.
21. Sandusky, *Can We Endure?*
22. Trial Transcript, Day 1, p. 144.
23. Trial Transcript, Day 6, p. 13.
24. Megan Rash interview with Rance Morey.
25. Trial Transcript, Day 1, p. 137.
26. Elaine Steinbacher testimony; Trial Transcript, Day 1, p. 139, 218-220; Sandusky, *Can We Endure?*
27. Defense investigator Joe Amendola's notes.
28. Trial Transcript, Day 1, p. 164-166.
29. David McNitt interview with Glenna Kerker.

30. Moulton, *Report*, p. 19, 71.
31. Trial Transcript, Day 1, p. 164-166.
32. Benjamin Andreozzi interview; Trial Transcript, Day 1, p. 166.
33. Moulton, *Report*, p. 72.
34. Trial Transcript, Day 1, p. 166.
35. Rossman, Leiter, and Andreozzi interview with Brett Houtz, April 21, 2011, Penn State Police.
36. Trial Transcript, Day 6, p. 76-77.
37. Trial Transcript, Day 6, p. 78; Rossman, Leiter & Andreozzi interview with Brett Houtz, April 21, 2011, Penn State Police.
38. Trial Transcript, Day 6, p. 80-83.
39. Trial Transcript, Day 6, p. 81; Rossman, Leiter & Andreozzi interview with Brett Houtz, April 21, 2011, Penn State Police.
40. Rossman, Leiter & Andreozzi interview with Brett Houtz, April 21, 2011, Penn State Police.
41. Trial Transcript, Day 6, p. 110, p. 106.
42. Trial Transcript, Day 6, p. 102.
43. Trial Transcript, Day 6, p. 103.
44. Trial Transcript, Day 6, p. 32-33.
45. Trial Transcript, Day 6, p. 32-33.
46. Trial Transcript, Day 6, p. 91.
47. 33rd Grand Jury Presentment, November 5, 2011, p. 16.
48. Trial Transcript, Day 1, p. 84; Day 6, p. 84.
49. Trial Transcript, Day 1, p. 216.
50. Trial Transcript, Day 1, p. 208.
51. Ganim, "Penn State Board of Trustees."
52. "Victim #4's Motion."
53. Trial Transcript, Day 1, p. 63.
54. Centre County Probation, Pennsylvania State Police, p. 53, 81.
55. Trial Transcript, Day 1, p. 64.
56. Trial Transcript, Day 1, p. 64-66.
57. Trial Transcript, Day 1, p. 68-71.
58. Trial Transcript, Day 1, p. 133.
59. Trial Transcript, Day 1, p. 133.
60. Trial Transcript, Day 1, p. 135.
61. Trial Transcript, Day 1, page 156-157.
62. Trial Transcript, Day 1, page 162-163.
63. Dottie Sandusky and Sandusky children interviews; Sandusky, *Can We Endure?*
64. Sandusky, *Can We Endure?*; Jerry Sandusky interview, Oct. 16, 2014.
65. Trial Transcript, Day 1, p. 174-182.
66. Sandusky, *Can We Endure?*

CHAPTER 8

1. Trial Transcript, Day 4, p. 248. Sabastian Paden testified that this was a game on Oct. 29 in Illinois, but it was probably an earlier home game.
2. Trial Transcript, Day 5, p. 41.
3. Dottie Sandusky interview.
4. PCRA Petition, May 6, 2015, p. 73.
5. Sandusky, *Can We Endure?*
6. Trial Transcript, Day 4, p. 218.
7. Jerry Sandusky to Mark Pendergrast, June 13, 2017.
8. Trial Transcript, Day 4, p. 230.
9. Trial Transcript, Day 4, p. 214.
10. Trial Transcript,, Day 4, p. 214.
11. Trial Transcript, Day 4, p. 215.
12. Trial Transcript, Day 4, p. 235.

13. Trial Transcript, Day 4, p. 235.
14. Trial Transcript, Day 4, p. 216-217.
15. Trial Transcript, Day 4, p. 208, 230, 236.
16. Trial Transcript, Day 4, p. 216-217, 231.
17. Trial Transcript, Day 5, p. 45.
18. Trial Transcript, Day 4, p. 233-234.
19. Trial Transcript, Day 5, p. 45, 54.
20. Trial Transcript, Day 5, p. 55.
21. Trial Transcript, Day 5, p. 44-45.
22. Trial Transcript, Day 5, p. 51-52.
23. Sandusky, *Can We Endure?*
24. Trial Transcript, Day 5, p. 57.
25. "Victim 9 Files Abuse Claim."
26. Ziegler interview with Sandusky, on Framing Paterno website.
27. Scolford, "Sandusky Abuse Victim Sues Ex-Coach."
28. Michael Cranga interview with Ryan Rittmeyer, report dated Nov. 29, 2011, Penn State Police.
29. Trial Transcript, Day 3, p. 65.
30. Trial Transcript, Day 3, p. 66.
31. Trial Transcript, Day 3, p. 64.
32. See interviews with Sandusky children other than Matt.
33. Interviews with Dottie and Jerry Sandusky.

CHAPTER 9

1. Trial Transcript, Day 3, p. 235-241.
2. http://www.sports-reference.com/cfb/schools/penn-state/2000-schedule.html
3. Trial Transcript, Day 3, p. 222-228.
4. Trial Transcript, Day 3, p. 227-228.
5. Trial Transcript, Day 3, p. 229-230.
6. Trial Transcript, Day 3, p. 230-231.
7. Trial Transcript, Day 3, page 232.
8. Trial Transcript, Day 3, p. 233.
9. Trial Transcript, Day 3, p. 244.
10. Trial Transcript, Day, 3, p. 225.
11. Trial Transcript, Day 3, p. 200-221,
12. Trial Transcript, Day 3, p. 199.
13. Trial Transcript, Day 3, p. 215-216.
14. Trial Transcript, Day 3, p. 217.
15. Trial Transcript, Day 3, p. 217.
16. Grand Jury Presentment.
17. Grand Jury Presentment.
18. Trial Transcript, Day 3, p. 235.
19. Trial Transcript, Day 3, p. 248.
20. Moulton, *Report*, p. 76, 155, Appendix M.
21. *Second Amended Petition*, p. 116; Taped interview and transcript of interview with James Calhoun, May 15, 2011, courtesy Office of Al Lindsay.
22. Al Lindsay interview; Sandusky PCRA hearing, March 24, 2017, p. 70-77.

CHAPTER 10

1. Scott Rossman, Penn State Police report, Nov. 10, 2009; Interview with anonymous Sandusky son.
2. "Matt Sandusky on Hearing Victim Testimony."
3. Dottie Sandusky interview.
4. Sandusky, *Touched*, p. 100.
5. *Ibid.*

6.   Ganim, "Jerry Sandusky, Adopted Son Had 'Rocky' Relationship."
7.   Sandusky, *Touched*, p. 101-102; Dottie Sandusky interview.
8.   Pennsylvania Children & Youth Services report, Dec. 1994, courtesy Dottie Sandusky.
9.   Kara Sandusky interview.
10. "Anne" letter.
11. Isikoff, "Matt Sandusky Claims Abuse"; Winfrey, "Televised Interview."
12. "Anne" letter.
13. Sandusky, *Touched*, p. 102.
14. Ganim, "Jerry Sandusky, Adopted Son."
15. Sandusky, *Touched*, p. 102; Dottie Sandusky interview.
16. Dottie Sandusky interview.
17. Sandusky, *Touched*, p. 103.
18. *Ibid*; Dottie Sandusky interview.
19. McCallum, "Last Call," p. 88.
20. Sandusky, *Touched*, p. 103-104.
21. Dottie Sandusky interview.
22. Dottie Sandusky interview.
23. Kotz, "Mirinda Boob Conspired."
24. "Superior Court Affirms Heichel Sentences"; Ganim, "Victim's Wife, Man Charged."
25. Sandusky, *Can We Endure?*
26. Dottie Sandusky interview; Jerry Sandusky interview.
27. Dottie Sandusky interview.
28. Dottie Sandusky interview.
29. Jerry Sandusky interview, Oct. 16, 2014; Sandusky email, June 27, 2017.
30. Trial Transcript, Day 1, p. 86-87.
31. Anonymous Sandusky child interview.
32. Trial Transcript, Day 1, p. 57.
33. Trial Transcript. Day 4, p. 187-189.
34. Kara Sandusky interview.
35. Simpson, "Matt Sandusky, Silent No More."
36. Kara Sandusky interview; Dottie Sandusky interview.
37. Jerry Sandusky interview, Oct. 16, 2014.
38. Isikoff, "Matt Sandusky Claims Abuse."
39. Ganim, "Jerry Sandusky Interview Prompts Long-Ago Victims."
40. "Anne" letter.
41. Winfrey, "Televised Interview"; Winfrey, "Matt Sandusky on Hearing Victim Testimony."
42. Pendergrast, *Memory Warp*, p. 41, 46, 59, 139, 166, 280, 308, 367, 384, 389.
43. Peaceful Hearts Foundation website.
44. Winfrey, "Televised Interview."
45. Sandusky, *Undaunted*, p. p. 20, 63, 122, 142, 146-155, 164, 192-193.

CHAPTER 11

1.   Cohen, *Folk Devils and Moral Panics,* p.9.
2.   Jenkins, *Moral Panic*, p. 2.
3.   Jenkins, "Penn State's Catholic Problem."
4.   Begos, "Sandusky Had Access."
5.   Ganim, "Inside the Jerry Sandusky Investigation"; Ganim, "Former Tom Corbett Agent."
6.   Let Go Let Peace website.
7.   Mike Gillum interview.
8.   Trial Transcript, Day 6, p. 76-77.
9.   Trial Transcript, Day 6, p. 78.
10. Sandusky PCDA hearing, March 24, 2017, p. 186.

11. Joseph Leiter report on Dustin Struble interview, 2/4/11, Penn State Police.
12. Moulton, *Report*, p. 152.
13. Moulton, *Report*, p. 153.
14. Moulton, *Report*, p. 156.
15. Grand Jury Presentment.
16. Van Natta, "The Whistleblower's Last Stand;" Cipriano, "Prosector Told McQueary to Clam Up."
17. Grand Jury Presentment.
18. Trial Transcript, Day 2, p. 308-309, 319; Sandusky interview.
19. Grand Jury Presentment, p. 21.
20. Grand Jury Presentment, p. 22.

CHAPTER 12

1. Ganim, "Former Penn State Coach Indicted on Felony Charges of Sex Crimes Against Minors"; Ganim, "Charges against former Penn State coach Jerry Sandusky removed from court website"; Ganim, "Jerry Sandusky, a Penn State University Football Legend and Founder of the Second Mile, Faces Charges of Sex Crimes."
2. Ganim, "Pedophiles Exploit the Influence."
3. Ganim, "Former Coach Sandusky."
4. Ganim, "Penn State Coach Joe Paterno"; Posnanski, *Paterno*, p. 247.
5. Ganim, "Penn State Trustees Discuss Sandusky Case, Alleged Cover-up."
6. Ganim, "Commentators, Students Express Anger."
7. Ibid.
8. Scott Rossman, Penn State Police report, Jan. 10, 2011.
9. Gray, "Story Fit For the Tabloids" letter, March 31, 2011.
10. Gray, *My Last Visit with Coach Paterno*, p. 47-57.
11. Kelly & Noonan, "Statements Regarding Jerry Sandusky."
12. Joseph Leiter report of interview with Allan Myers, Sept. 22, 2011, Penn State Police.
13. Curtis Everhart interview with Allan Myers, Nov. 9, 2011.
14. Pendergrast, *Memory Warp*, p. 408-412; Rind, "Meta-Analytic Examination."
15. Kelly & Noonan, "Statements."
16. Ganim, "Penn State Football Press Conference Cancelled"; Ziegler, *Betrayal of Joe Paterno*, Chapter 4.
17. Ganim, "Penn State's Joe Paterno Retires."
18. Ganim, "Gov. Corbett Plays Unique."
19. Ganim, "Paterno to Fans"; Ganim, "Penn State Interim Coach"; Ganim, "Penn State Student Riot"; Ganim, "State College Police."
20. "No. 19 Nebraska"; Ganim, "Joe Paterno's Lung Cancer"; Flounders, "Joe Paterno Is Dead."
21. McCallum, "Last Call."
22. Ganim, "Penn State Student Riots."
23. Watson, "Alma Mater's Meltdown."
24. Ganim, "Who Knew What About Jerry Sandusky?" Ganim, "PSU assistant coach, grand jury witness Mike McQueary placed on paid administrative leave."
25. Van Natta, "Whistleblower's Last Stand."
26. Reiber, *Science of Perception and Memory*, p. 62-69.
27. Jim Clemente interview; Don Van Natta and John Ziegler conversation, https://www.youtube.com/watch?v=xXWodkR0LxM; 2017 McQueary penis shot, http://www.framingpaterno.com/exclusive-mike-mcqueary-sent-pictures-his-penis-joe-amendolas-former-fiance-nsfw.
28. Van Natta, "Whistleblower's Last Stand."
29. Gary Gray letter to Penn State President, Aug. 9, 2012.
30. Posnanski, *Paterno*, p. 272.
31. Posnanski, *Paterno*, p. 247-259.

32. Trial Transcript, Day 2, p. 212.
33. Ibid; Ganim, "Mike McQueary, Key Witness"; Ganim, "Mike McQueary's Statement to Police"; Ganim, "Questions Mount."
34. Trial Transcript, Day 2, p. 195-197, 240-241.
35. Benjamin Andreozzi interview.
36. Ganim, "Who Knew What about Jerry Sandusky?"
37. Ibid.
38. James P. Ellis, Nov. 30, 2011, Penn State Police.
39. Joseph Leiter, Penn State Police report, Nov. 10, 2011.
40. Sandusky hearings, Aug. 23, 2016, p. 34-35.
41. Pelullo, *Betrayal and the Beast*, p. 141-142.
42. Pendergrast, *Memory Warp*, p. 55-58.
43. Let Go Let Peace In website.
44. Pendergrast, *Memory Warp*, p. 145-147.
45. Pelullo, *Betrayal and the Beast*, p. 301.
46. Ganim, "Penn State Board of Trustees Got It Wrong"; "Victim #4's Motion."
47. Moushey, *Game Over*, p. 200-201.
48. Storm, *Echoes of Penn State*, Kindle edition, 21%-22%.
49. Jennifer Storm interview, Oct. 8, 2014.
50. Moushey, *Game Over*, p. 204-205.

CHAPTER 13

1. Ganim, "For Jerry Sandusky's State College Neighbors."
2. "Amendola: Jerry Sandusky 'Devastate.'"
3. "Supplement to Mr. Sandusky's Ineffectiveness Claim," Feb. 6, 2017; Sandusky case hearings, Aug. 12, 2016, p. 16, 105-117; March 24, 2017, p. 17-43.
4. Costas, "Interview."
5. Ganim, "Former Penn State coach Jerry Sandusky tells Bob Costas: 'I shouldn't have showered with those kids'"; Sandusky writing to Mark Pendergrast.
6. Ganim, "Man, 19, Says."
7. Ganim, Penn State pines for normalcy."
8. Ganim, "Jerry Sandusky interview prompts."
9. Ganim, "Jerry Sandusky's attorney says one alleged victim."
10. Sandusky interview, March 1, 2017; Fisher and Gillum, *Silent No More*, p. 108.
11. Curtis Everhart Interview with Allan Myers.
12. Sandusky hearing transcripts, Aug. 12, 2016, p. 145-146.
13. Leiter report on interview with Allan Myers, Sept. 22, 2011, Penn State Police.
14. Ganim, "Jerry Sandusky's Bail Set"; Ganim, "Jerry Sandusky placed under house arrest."
15. Ganim, "Jerry Sandusky placed under house arrest."
16. Ganim, "Victim rights lawyers respond."
17. Ganim, "Jerry Sandusky's neighbors."
18. Ganim, "Jerry Sandusky's speech to the press."
19. Ganim, "As Jerry Sandusky's preliminary hearing nears."
20. Sandusky hearings, Aug. 12, 2016, p. 18-22, 86-97, 120-141.
21. Joe Amendola press conference, Dec. 13, 2011, https://www.youtube.com/watch?v=DGjSRD62O54.
22. Sandusky hearings transcripts, Aug. 22, 2016, p. 105-110, Aug. 22, 2016, p. 23-61; Anthony Sassano Supplemental Report on Allan Myers, 4/11/12, Penn State Police.
23. Sandusky hearings, Aug. 12, 2016, p. 69-71.
24. Ganim, "Penn State Names Former FBI Director."
25. Eichelberger, "Joe Paterno Is Stripped."
26. "NCAA Had Doubts."
27. Bonner, "409 Again."
28. Ganim, "The Second Mile, Jerry Sandusky's charity."

29. Ganim, "Second Mile Weighs Options"; Ganim, "Second Mile and Penn State."
30. Ganim, "Victim Preparing to Testify."
31. Ganim, "Alleged Victim's Dinner."
32. Ganim, "Jerry Sandusky trial: Accuser testifies he denied abuse."
33. Ganim, "Man, 19, Says"; Moushey, *Game Over*, p. 191-196.
34. Moushey, *Game Over*, p. 196.
35. Ganim, "Penn State Pines for Normalcy."
36. RAINN website; Pendergrast, *Memory Warp*, p. 142-147.
37. "Report of the Board of Trustees."
38. Ganim, "Penn State hasn't yet helped."
39. Ganim, "Penn State's Scandal Tab."

CHAPTER 14

1. Ganim, "Inside the Jerry Sandusky Investigation: Why Did It Take So Long?"
2. "Judge Sets May Trial Date."
3. Ganim, "Jerry Sandusky Requests"; "Start of Sandusky Trial Delayed."
4. Ganim, "Jerry Sandusky Requests."
5. Thompson, "Court Bars Release of Sexually Explicit Emails."
6. Ganim, "Jerry Sandusky's Next Court Date"; Ganim, "Jerry Sandusky's attorney says prosecutors didn't share all evidence"; Ganim, "Jerry Sandusky's lawyer wants info from his client's computer"; Sandusky PCRA hearing, March 24, 2017, p. 50, 77.
7. Ganim, "Judge in Jerry Sandusky case won't order prosecutors to give more details"; Ganim, "Jerry Sandusky's lawyer asks for more details"; Ganim, "Jerry Sandusky's lawyer threatens."
8. Trial Transcript, Jury Selection, Day 1, p. 132-133.
9. Ganim, "Private Meeting."
10. Sandusky PCRA hearing, March 24, 2017.
11. Ganim, "Judge in Jerry Sandusky case to rule."
12. Trial Transcript, "Motion to Withdraw," June 5, 2012.
13. Ganim, "Judge Tells Potential Jurors."
14. Trial Transcript, Jury Selection, Day 1, June 5, 2012, p. 3-12.
15. Ganim, "Is This the Real Jerry Sandusky?"
16. Trial Transcript, Jury Selection, Day 1, p. 25-30.
17. Trial Transcript, Jury Selection, Day 1, p. 80.
18. Trial Transcript, Jury Selection, Day 1, p. 92-100.
19. Trial Transcript, Jury Selection, Day 1, p. 121-133.
20. Trial Transcript, Jury Selection, Day 1, p. 135.
21. Trial Transcript, Jury Selection, Day, 1, p. 173-176.
22. Trial Transcript, Jury Selection, Day 1, p. 248-263.
23. Trial Transcript, Jury Selection, Day 1, p. 291-299.
24. Trial Transcript, Jury Selection, Day 1, p. 281-290.
25. Trial Transcript, Jury Selection, Day 1, p. 315.
26. Trial Transcript, Day 1, p. 5.
27. Goldman, "Meet Sandusky's Prosecutor"; Ganim, "Jerry Sandusky Trial: Prosecutor Is Used to the Spotlight."
28. Trial Transcript, McGettigan opening statement, Day 1, June 11, 2012, p. 3-45; Ganim, "Sandusky Trial: Prosecutor's Opening Statements."
29. Karl Rominger Affidavit, in *Second Amended Petition for Post Conviction Relief*.
30. Trial Transcript, Day 1, p. 22-29.
31. Ganim, "Joe Amendola Ponders His Life"; Ganim, "Jerry Sandusky Trial: Defense attorney is repected"; Dawson, "Jerry Sandusky's lawyer Joe Amendola."
32. Trial Transcript, Amendola Opening Statement, June 11, 2012, p. 3-29; Karl Rominger affidavit, in *Second Amended Petition for Post Conviction Relief*.

CHAPTER 15

1.   Sandusky interview with Pendergrast, Oct. 2014.
2.   Jerry Sandusky to Mark Pendergrast, June 13, 2017.
3.   Trial Transcript, Day 1, p. 41-141.
4.   Trial Transcript, Day, 1, p. 142-226.
5.   Trial Transcript, Day 2, p. 4-104.
6.   Trial Transcript, Day 2, p. 104-123.
7.   Trial Transcript, Day 2, p. 123-185.
8.   Steele, "Clinton County Caseworker."
9.   Trial Transcript, Day 2, p. 186-300; Karl Rominger affidavit, in *Second Amended Petition for Post Conviction Relief.*
10. Trial Transcript, Day 2, p. 300-321.
11. Trial Transcript, Day 3, p. 4-27.
12. Trial Transcript, Day 3, p. 27-69.
13. Trial Transcript, Day 3, p. 69-80.
14. PCRA Brief, July 11, 2017, p 59-71.
15. Trial Transcript, Day 3, p. 85-123, 126-163.
16. Trial Transcript, Day 3, p. 165-195.
17. Trial Transcript, Day 3, p. 196.
18. Trial Transcript, Day 3, p. 197-221.
19. Trial Transcript, Day 3, p. 222-252.
20. Trial Transcript, Day 4, p. 3-49.
21. Trial Transcript, Day 4, p. 50-81.
22. Trial Transcript, Day 4, p. 82-127.
23. Trial Transcript, Day 4, p. 130-132.
24. Trial Transcript, Day 4, p. 201-249.
25. Trial Transcript, Day 5, p. 32-59.
26. Trial Transcript, Day 4, p. 195-198.

CHAPTER 16

1.   Sandusky hearings, Aug. 12, 2016, p. 24-35, 53-55; March 24, 2017, p. 84-85; Sandusky interview, Oct. 16, 2014.
2.   Trial Transcript, Day 5, p. 3-32.
3.   Trial Transcript, Day 5, p. 61-109.
4.   Trial Transcript, Day 5, p. 110-114.
5.   Trial Transcript, Day 5, p. 120-129.
6.   Trial Transcript, Day 5, p. 130-143.
7.   Trial Transcript, Day 5, p. 144-152.
8.   Trial Transcript, Day 6, p. 4-6.
9.   Trial Transcript, Day 6, p. 10-15.
10. Trial Transcript, Day 6, p. 66-68.
11. Trial Transcript, Day 6, p. 7-10.
12. Trial Transcript, Day 7, p. 36-48.
13. Trial Transcript, Day 7, p. 48-63.
14. Trial Transcript, Day 6, p. 15-19.
15. Trial Transcript, Day 6, p. 20-22.
16. Trial Transcript, Day 6, p. 23-28.
17. Trial Transcript, Day 6, p. 59-62.
18. Trial Transcript, Day 6, p. 62-66.
19. Trial Transcript, Day 6, p. 117-129.
20. Trial Transcript, Day 6, p. 129-141.
21. Trial Transcript, Day 6, p. 69-97.
22. Trial Transcript, Day 6, p. 98-111.
23. Trial Transcript, Day 6, p. 148-159.
24. Trial Transcript, Day 7, p. 9-13.

25. Trial Transcript, Day 8, p. 17-24.
26. Whitbourne, "What's New (And Old) in the DSM 5 Personality Disorders."
27. Pendergrast, *Memory Warp*, p. 279, 361-362, 370; http://www.zurinstitute.com/dsmcritique.html.
28. Sandusky hearings, Aug. 12, 2016, p. 29-35; 160-170, 185-187.
29. Trial Transcript, Day 6, p. 164-225.
30. Trial Transcript, Day 6, p. 226-272.
31. Trial Transcript, Day 6, p. 273-303.
32. Trial Transcript, Day 7, p. 64-84.

CHAPTER 17

1. Trial Transcript, Day 8, p. 35-91.
2. Pendergrast, *Memory Warp*, p. 154, 354, 360-361, 369,
3. Trial Transcript, Day 8, p. 97-156.
4. Cleland opinion, Jan. 30, 2013, p. 7, Centre County website.
5. Trial Transcript, Day 8, p. 4, 22; PCRA Brief, July 11 2017, p. 133.
6. Sandusky PCRA hearing, March 24, 2017, p. 44-46.
7. Trial Transcript, Day 8, p. 22-33, 158-176; Day 9, p. 3-37; Sandusky hearings, Aug. 22, 2016, p. 87-89.
8. Hockensmith, "Jerry Sandusky Verdict"; Linda Kelly speech video, https://www.youtube.com/watch?v=B0Rw8aEQe8Y.
9. "Defense attorney Joe Amendola reacts to Sandusky verdict"; "Anderson Cooper Interviews Joe Amendola"; Ganim, "Joe Amendola Ponders."
10. Jurors on CNN, June 25, 2012, with Soledad O'Brien, https://www.youtube.com/watch?v=L2C7uurdZiE
11. "Jerry Sandusky Proclaims His Innocence."
12. Sandusky Sentencing hearing, Oct. 9, 2012.
13. Warner, "Convicted Child Abuser Jerry Sandusky Loses $59,000 Annual Pension."

CHAPTER 18

1. Thompson, "Law Allows Experts to Testify."
2. Otterson, "Al Pacino to Star."
3. The Freeh Report is the source of most quotes in this section.
4. Spanier trial transcript, March 22, 2017, Curley testimony, p. 47.
5. Hartley, "McQueary, Others Testify"; Spanier trial transcript, March 21, 2017, Raykovitz, p. 204.
6. Jerry Sandusky letter, April 22, 2017.
7. Curley-Schultz Preliminary Hearing, p. 173-178.
8. Cipriano, "Penn State Confidential."
9. Cipriano, "No Sex Scandal at Penn State"; Ziegler interview with John Snedden, March 26, 2017, https://soundcloud.com/freespeechbroadcasting; Ziegler, "There Was No Cover-up"; Battaglia, "Spanier Vows to Fight Budget Cuts"; Snedden Report; John Snedden interview.
10. Scolforo, "Lawyer Cynthia Baldwin."
11. Posnanski, *Paterno*, p. 15, 273.
12. Curley-Schultz Preliminary Hearing, p. 179-204.
13. Curley-Schultz Preliminary Hearing, p. 204-236.
14. Spanier trial transcript, March 22, 2017, Curley testimony, p. 63.
15. Kelley, "Penn State Investigator Louis Freeh Accused."
16. Ganim, "Joe Paterno's Family."
17. Ganim, "Penn State Trustees Must Decide"; Ganim, "Joe Paterno's Family Says Statue Removal."
18. Ganim, "Penn State Sanctions"; Ganim, "Penn State President Rodney Erickson Signe Consent Agreement."

19. Ganim, "Joe Paterno Family Says NCAA Sanction."
20. "Joe Paterno Is Now Winningest Coach"; http://co.centre.pa.us/centreco/media/upload/PATERNO%20VS%20NCAA%20COMPLAINT.pdf; Bonesteel, "Paterno Family Very Quietly Drops Lawsuit."
21. Freeh Report, p. 78.
22. Gladwell, "In Plain View."
23. Ganim, "Jerry Sandusky's Crimes Put an End to Second Mile Charity"; http://co.centre.pa.us/centreco/media/upload/Second%20Mile%20Petition%20for%20Distribution%20of%20Assets.pdf
24. http://centrecountypa.gov/index.aspx?NID=506
25. Ganim, "Jerry's Sandusky's Charity."
26. Wetzel, "Mike McQueary, Broken Down and Estranged."
27. Ganim, "Graham Spanier's Lawyers Refute Freeh Report"; Ganim, "Ex-Penn State President."
28. Graham Spanier interview by Josh Elliott.
29. Ganim, "Ex-PSU President Graham Spanier Charged"; Ganim, "Penn State Officials Conspired"; Ganim, "Graham Spanier, Other Penn State Officials."
30. Ganim, "Jerry Sandusky Scandal One Year Later"; DeJesus, "Sara Ganim, Who Won Pulitzer Prize."
31. Griffin, "Man Claims Sandusky Sexually Assaulted Him."
32. Sandusky, *Can We Endure?*
33. http://www.drphil.com/shows/1880/
34. http://www.philly.com/philly/news/Victim_1_finds_his_voice.html
35. "Penn State Approved $60 Million"; Dawson, "Victim 2, Matt Sandusky Settlements"; Snyder, "Penn State Reaches Settlement."
36. Cipriano, "Federal Agent"; https://soundcloud.com/glennbeck/31617-full-show.
37. https://www.courts.phila.gov/common-pleas/, Pennsylvania Manufacturers' Association Insurance Company v Pennsylvania State University, Civil case 131103197.; https://fjdefile.phila.gov/efs/temp/3V_UcI2N.pdf' ;Snyder, "How Penn State Decided to Pay $93 Million."
38. Falce, "Sandusky Accuser Wants"; Garcia, "Exclusive: New Sandusky"; Semon, "Anthony Spinelli"; Murray, "Former Athlete Pleads Guilty."
39. Jackson, "Local Survivor"; Loop 21, "Curious Case of Ed Manigo"; John Zieger podcast, https://soundcloud.com/freespeechbroadcasting, Feb. 19, 2017, Hour 3.

CHAPTER 19

1. Dent, "Franco Harris' Crusade."
2. Wallace, "Host"; John Ziegler interview with Mark Pendergrast; "John Ziegler," Wikipedia.
3. Ziegler, "ESPN's Coverage of Joe Paterno"; Ziegler, "Penn State Scandal."
4. Posnanski, *Paterno*, p. 264.
5. Ziegler, *The Framing of Joe Paterno.*
6. Ziegler, *Betrayal of Joe Paterno*, Chapter 9.
7. Berlin, *Re: Paterno.*
8. Clemente, *Analysis of the Special Investigative Counsel Report.*
9. John Ziegler interview with Jerry Sandusky, www.framingpaterno.com
10. John Ziegler interviews with Jerry Sandusky; https://www.youtube.com/watch?v=c9ytgza2mDw
11. Stump, "Sandusky: Paterno Would Not Have"; John Ziegler interview; https://youtu.be/GmjfXAI3iwo
12. Ziegler on CNN, March 25, 2013, https://www.youtube.com/watch?v=jwsAqaRKLDA
13. Ziegler, *Betrayal of Joe Paterno.*
14. https://www.youtube.com/watch?v=fxH8d6smRbg&sns=tw
15. http://www.today.com/news/jerry-sanduskys-wife-victims-were-manipulated-they-saw-money-2D79356845; http://www.today.com/video/today/54648895

16. Wetzel, "TV interview with Jerry Sandusky's wife an insult to his victims."
17. Roebuck, "Journey of Sandusky's 'Victim 1' involves advocacy.
18. Gibb, "Doctor Facing Teen-Age Sex Charges"; Barry Bender Appellate Decision.
19. http://www.framingpaterno.com/huge-release-new-interviews-documents-my-trip-state-college-leave-little-doubt-jerry-sandusky-innoce; Thomas Dickey interview.
20. Falce, "Watchdogs Ask."
21. https://ml-law.net/
22. Erdely, "Catholic Church's Secret"; Erdely, "A Rape on Campus"; Shapiro, "Jury Finds Reporter."
23. Cipriano, "Another Rolling Stone Rape Article"; Cipriano, "Billy Doe's Fantasy"; Cipriano, "Catholic Guilt"; Cipriano, "Star Witness' Story"; https://soundcloud.com/freespeechbroadcasting/hour-2-011517
24. Gambacorta, "Great Pennsylvania Government Porn Caper"; Lavelle, "Pennsylvania Gets F Grade."
25. Moulton, *Report to the Attorney General;* Gambacorta, "Great Pennsylvania Government Porn Caper"; Mathis, "Porn Scandal"; Brenna, "Corbett Stands By One of His Appointees."
26. http://www.framingpaterno.com/video-documentary-evidence-shows-john-zieglers-arrest-matt-sandusky-event-was-farce-likely-criminal; John Ziegler interview.
27. Mantila, "Glenn Beck Gives Guest Two Hours"; https://soundcloud.com/glennbeck/31617-full-show; John Ziegler interview.

CHAPTER 20

1. All legal material related to Commonwealth vs Sandusky can be found at http://centrecountypa.gov/index.aspx?NID=506. Cleland's decision was posted 1/30/2013; Muskal, "Jerry Sandusky Loses Bid."
2. Thompson, "Jerry Sandusky Loses Appeal."
3. Balser, "Buffalo Township Attorney."
4. PCRA Petition, May 6, 2015; "Jerry Sandusky Appeal Seeks."
5. "Commonwealth of Pennsylvania's Response"; https://www.courtlistener.com/opinion/1908567/com-v-crawford/?.
6. All documents pertaining to the Sandusky case are online at http://centrecountypa.gov/index.aspx?NID=506 by date.
7. Scolforo, "Sandusky Wants Subpoena Power."
8. http://law.justia.com/cases/pennsylvania/supreme-court/1981/496-pa-97-0.html
9. *Second Amended Petition.*
10. Thompson, "Child Told Paterno"; Pynes, "Penn State Settlements Covered 1971"; Glazer order, Penn State Univ v. Pennsylvania Manufactureres' Association Insurance, May 4, 2016; Ganim, "Sandusky Victim: Joe Paterno Told Me."
11. Hobson, "New Court Documents."
12. Paterno, "Open Letter."
13. Scolforo, "Jerry Sandusky Presses Appeal."
14. Miller, "Ex-Sandusky Lawyer Karl Rominger."
15. For all hearings transcripts, see Sandusky case documents on Centre County website; Deppen, "Sandusky Lawyer on Divided Defense."
16. Falce, "Victim 2 Attorney."
17. All documents pertaining to the Sandusky case are online at http://centrecountypa.gov/index.aspx?NID=506 by date; "Judge Handling Jerry Sandusky's Appeal Removes Himself"; Roebuck, "Exasperated Sandusky Judge."
18. Al Lindsay interview.
19. Court documents in McQueary case at http://centrecountypa.gov/index.aspx?NID=506; Falce, "McQueary Verdict Dwarfs"; "Judge Adds $5M-plus"; Scolforo, "Former Penn State Assistant Gets $1.7M."

20.   Hill, "Department of Education Releases Investigation Results."
21.   Coppinger, "Jerry Sandusky's Son Arrested"; Smith, "Jerry Sandusky's Son Charged"; Falce, "Jerry Sandusky's Son Arrested"; Lance Marshall interview; Dottie Sandusky email.
22.   "Jeffrey Sandusky, Son of Jerry, Pleads Guilty"; Connor, "Anthony Weiner Sentenced"; Sandusky, *Enduring Prison.*
23.   "Penn State Ex-Athletic Director Pleads Guilty";
24.   Spanier trial transcript, March 21, 2017, p. 17-29.
25.   Spanier trial transcript, March 21, 2017, p. 126.
26.   Miller, "Graham Spanier Illegally"; Thompson, "A Look at the Strengths"; "Spanier's Defense Rests"; Cipriano, "Showers and Leaks"; Thompson, "Jury Reaches Split Verdict"; Armstrong, "Ex-Penn State Prez"; Falce, "Judge Denies Motions"; Thompson, "Penn State to Graham Spanier"; Thompson, "Spanier Punches Back"; "5 Years After Sandusky Conviction"; Miller, "Ex-Penn State Athletic Director."
27.   "Penn State Files Paperwork."
28.   Michlowski, "New Judge Appointed"; https://ballotpedia.org/John_H._Foradora.
29.   Sandusky PCRA hearing, March 24, 2017, p. 17-139.
30.   Fisher, *Silent No More,* p. 107-108.
31.   Fisher and Gillum, *Silent No More,* p. 64-69, 158-159.
32.   Sandusky PCRA hearing, March 24, 2017, p. 140-165.
33.   Sandusky PCRA hearing, March 24, 2017, p. 166-199.
34.   Brothman, "Jerry Sandusky Returns to Court"; Procyk, "Former Defense Attorney"; Sandusky PCRA heating, March 24, 2017, p. 204-215.
35.   Sandusky PCRA hearing, May 11, 2017, p. 45-46.
36.   http://www.teagandarnelltherapy.com/emdr/
37.   Sandusky PCRA Hearing, May 11, 2017, p. 3-25.
38.   Sandusky PCRA hearing, May 11, 2017, p. 25-44.
39.   Sandusky PCRA hearing, May 11, 2017, p. 55-100; Loftus, "Planting Misinformation."
40.   Foradora, "Opinion."

CHAPTER 21

1.   Unless otherwise noted, the information in this section comes from Sandusky, *Touched.*
2.   http://www.webmd.com/men/features/low-testosterone-explained-how-do-you-know-when-levels-are-too-low#1
3.   Dottie Sandusky interview.
4.   Kara Sandusky, "Inside Perspective."
5.   Sandusky, *Touched,* p. 109.
6.   Sandusky, *Coaching Linebackers,* p. 5-7.
7.   Posnanski, *Paterno,* p. 192-202, 211-217, 228, 247-261.
8.   Sandusky, *Can We Endure?;* Jerry Sandusky interview, Oct. 16, 2014; Sandusky to Pendergrast, June 13, 2017.
9.   Sandusky, *Touched,* p. 182-206.
10.   Posnanski, *Paterno,* p. 228, 251-261.
11.   Free Report, p. 56-59.
12.   Posnanski, *Paterno,* p. 280-281.
13.   Ziegler, *Betrayal of Joe Paterno.*
14.   Heim, "Shedding Light."
15.   Buddy Tesner interview, May 27, 2014.
16.   Chad Rexrode interview with Elaine Steinbacher, Oct. 14, 2013. Steinbacher interviewed many of the Second Milers quoted in this section.
17.   David Hilton interview, Aug. 24, 2013.
18.   Trial Transcript, Day 6, p. 184.

CHAPTER 22

1. Sandusky, *Can We Endure?* Unless otherwise noted, material in this chapter is from this manuscript.
2. Jerry Sandusky to Mark Pendergrast, Jan. 5, 2017.
3. Arif Shaikh interview with Elaine Steinbacher; Shaikh, *Healing Tips.*
4. US Court of Appeals for the Third Circuit, Craig Williams case, p. 9.
5. Jerry Sandusky to Mark Pendergrast, July 11, 2016.
6. Fenno, "Trace McSorley Tries"; Collins, "USC Fans (Rightfully)."
7. Alexandersen, "Jerry Sandusky Placed in 'Restrictive Housing.'"
8. Murphy, "Life on Death Row Inside Greene Prison."
9. *Investigation of the State Correctional Institution at Cresson.*
10. US Court of Appeals for the Third Circuit Craig Williams decision; Reiter, *23/7,* p. 204.
11. *Hell Is a Very Small Place.*
12. US Court of Appeals for the Third Circuit Craig Williams decision; http://solitarywatch.com/facts/faq/
13. Wiesel, *Night*; Ilibagiza, *Left to Tell.*
14. Yoder, *Small Price to Pay.*
15. Sandusky to Pendergrast, May 21, 2016; Stevenson, *Just Mercy.*
16. Gary Johnson interview.
17. Sandusky, *Touched*, p. 27.

CHAPTER 23

1. Kellogg, "Unwanted Sexual Experiences in Adolescents"; Hanson, "Correlates of Adolescent Reports."
2. Fred Berlin interview; Berlin, "Pedophilia: Criminal Mind-set or Mental Disorder?"; Berlin, "Pedophilia: When Is a Difference a Disorder?"
3. John Snedden interview; Cipriano, "Federal Agent: No Sex Scandal."
4. Anonymous quote courtey of Glenna Kerker.
5. Grossman, "Joe Paterno Apologists."
6. Rubin, "DeAndre Levy."
7. Cook, "Penn State's Sandusky Nightmare."
8. Falce, "Auditor General Delivers."
9. Mackay, *Extraordinary Popular Delusions.*
10. Roediger et al, "Social Contagion of Memory."
11. Pendergrast, *Memory Warp*, p. 352.
12. Webster, *Secret of Bryn Estyn*, p. 3-8, 133, 225-228.
13. Erdely, "Rape on Campus"; Schonfeld, "After Gang Rape Article."
14. Badoun, *Rush to Injustice;* Cohan, *Price of Silence*; Taylor, *Until Proven Innocent*; Yaeger, *It's Not About the Truth.*
15. Tavris, *Mistakes Were Made*, p. 164-205; Inbau, *Criminal Interrogation and Confessions*; Gudjonsson, *Psychology of Interrogations and Confessions.*
16. Shaw, "Constructing Rich False Memories.," P. 298.
17. Tavris, *Mistakes Were Made*, p. 200.
18. Rosenthal, "Suggestibility, Reliability, and the Legal Process"; Shaw, "Co-witness Information."
19. Garrett, *Convicting the Innocent*, p. 149-150.
20. Zaragoza, "Interviewing Witnesses."
21. Chabris, *Invisible Gorilla*, p. 65-66.
22. Shaw, *Memory Illusion*, p. xiv-xv; *Memory Hackers*; Pendergrast, *Memory Warp*, p. 96; Wade, "De-constructing Rich False Memories."
23. Bartlett, Remembering, p. 212, 227; Pendergrast, *Memory Warp*, p. 70.
24. Berlin, "Pedophilia: Criminal Mindset or Mental Disorder?"

— BIBLIOGRAPHY —

Acocella, Joan. *Creating Hysteria: Women and Multiple Personality Disorder.* San Francisco, CA: Jossey-Bass, 1999.

Alexandersen, Christian. "Jerry Sandusky Placed in 'Restrictive Housing' to Avoid Prison Assaults, Murder Attempts, Official Says." PennLive.com, Oct. 30, 2015.

"Amendola: Jerry Sandusky 'Devastated.'" *CNN*, Sept. 14, 2011.

Amendola, Joe. "Aaron Fisher Notes." preparation for trial, courtesy Joe Amendola.

An American Voice. *The Last Monster: Jerry (Disgusting) Sandusky.* Kindle edition. Baltimore, MD: Baltimore Publishing, 2011.

"Anderson Cooper Interviews Joe Amendola, Jerry Sandusky's Lawyer." *CNN*, June 22, 2012, https://www.youtube.com/watch?v=SfrY1JUwwv8.

Andreozzi, Benjamin. "Ben Andreozzi Represents Victims of Penn State Sexual Abuse Scandal." YouTube posting from NBC Today appearance. https://www.youtube.com/watch?v=QQn3okatWj0.

"Anne" letter to John Ziegler. Courtesy of Dottie Sandusky, April 25, 2014.

Armstrong, Kevin. "Ex-Penn State Prez Graham Spanier, Two Others Get Jail Time for Failing to Report Jerry Sandusky." *New York Daily News*, June 3, 2017.

Badoun, Nader and R. Stephanie Good. *A Rush to Injustice: How Power, Prejudice, Racism, and Political Correctness Overshadowed Truth and Justice in the Duke Lacrosse Rape Case.* NY: Thomas Nelson, 2007.

Balser, Emily. "Buffalo Township Attorney Joins Jerry Sandusky Legal Fight." *TribLive.com*, July 6, 2014.

[Barry Bender Appellate Decision]. Commonwealth of Pennsylvania v. Dr. Barry L. Bender, no. 674 WDA 2013.

Bartlett, Frederic C. *Remembering: A Study in Experimental and Social Psychology.* Cambridge: Cambridge U. Pr., 1932, 1977.

Bass, Ellen and Laura Davis. *The Courage to Heal: A Guide for Women Survivors of Child Sexual Abuse.* 2d ed. NY: HarperPerennial, 1988, 1992.

Battaglia, Emily. "Spanier Vows to Fight Budget Cuts." *Daily Collegian,* March 9, 2011.

Becker, Jo. Interview with Jerry Sandusky. *New York Times,* Dec. 3, 2011, http://www.nytimes.com/2011/12/03/sports/ncaafootball/at-center-of-penn-state-scandal-sandusky-tells-his-own-story.html.

Bella, Peter. "Jerry Sandusky More Than a Monster." *Washington Times,* June 23, 2012.

Berlin, Fred S. "Pedophilia: Criminal Mindset or Mental Disorder, A Conceptual Review." *American Journal of Forensic Psychiatry,* 2011, vol. 32, no. 2, p. 3-26.

Berlin, Fred S., "Pedophilia: When Is a Difference a Disorder?" *Archives of Sexual Behavior*, Dec. 2002, vol. 31, no. 6, p. 479-480.

———. *Re: Joseph Paterno*, to J. Sedwick Sollers, III, King & Spalding, Washington, DC, Feb. 6, 2013. http://www.paterno.com/Expert-Reports/Dr-Fred-S-Berlin.aspx#.WNQhk2e1vIU.

Begos, Kevin and Mark Scolforo. "Sandusky Had Access to Vulnerable Kids Via Charity." Associated Press, Nov. 12, 2011.

Blume, E. Sue. *Secret Survivors: Uncovering Incestand Its Aftereffects in Women.* NH: Ballantine, 1990.

Bonesteel, Matt. "Paterno Family Very Quietly Drops Lawsuit against NCAA." *Washington Post,* July 1, 2017.

Bonner, Teresa. "408 Again: Penn State Football Wins Restored Under Settlement," *PennLive*, Jan. 16, 2015.

Brainerd, Charles J. and Valerie F. Reyna. *The Science of False Memory*. NY: Oxford U. Pr., 2005.

Brennan, Chris. "Corbett Stands by One of his Appointees in Porn Scandal, Wants Another to Resign." *Philadelphia Daily News*, Oct. 6, 2014.

Brothman, Amanda. "Jerry Sandusky Returns to Court for Appeals Hearing." WHTM-TV, March 24, 2017.

Buell, Ryan D. "Penn State Scandal: Mother Of Alleged Jerry Sandusky Victim Claims Mistreatment By Son's School." *Huffington Post*, Nov. 22, 2011.

Cara, Ed. "The Most Dangerous Idea in Mental Health." *Pacific Standard*, Nov. 3, 2014.

Chabris, Christopher and Daniel Simons. *The Invisible Gorilla and Other Ways Our Intuitions Deceive Us*. NY: Crown, 2010.

Cipriano, Ralph. "Another *Rolling Stone* Rape Article Has Major Holes." *Newsweek*, Nov. 11, 2014.

———. "Billy Doe's 'Fantasy of Sexual Abuse.'" *BigTrial.net*, April 4, 2014.

———. "Catholic Guilt? The Lying, Scheming Altar Boy Behind a Lurid Rape Case." *Newsweek*, Jan. 20, 2016.

———. "No Sex Scandal at Penn State, Just a 'Political Hit Job.'" *BigTrial.Net*, April 10, 2017.

———. "Penn State Confidential: U.S. Attorney, FBI Investigated Second Mile Charity And Came Up With A Big 'Nothing Burger.'" *BigTrial.Net*, July 20, 2017.

———. "Prosecutor Told McQueary to Clam Up." *BigTrial.net*. Oct. 10, 2017.

———. "Showers And Leaks: Mike McQueary Blows The Whistle On AG's Office." *BigTrial.net*, April 4, 2017.

———. "Star witness' Story in Philadelphia Sex Abuse Trials Doesn't Add Up." *National Catholic Reporter*, April 29, 2013.

Clemente, James T. *Analysis of the Special Investigative Counsel Report and the Crimes of Gerald A. Sandusky and Education Guide to the Identification and Prevention of Child Sexual Victimization*. Feb. 6, 2013. http://paterno.com/Resources/Docs/CLEMENTE_FINAL_REPORT_2-7-2013.pdf.

Cohen, Stanley. *Folk Devils and Moral Panics: The Creation of the Mods and the Rockers*. London: MacGibbon and Kee, 1972.

Coffey, Wayne. "Aaron Fisher, Victim No. 1 in the Jerry Sandusky Case, Sits Down with the Daily News To Tell His Story of Sexual Abuse from The Monster." *New York Daily News*, Dec. 8, 2012.

Cohan, William D. *The Price of Silence: The Duke Lacrosse Scandal, the Power of the Elite, and the Corruption of Our Great Universities*. NY: Scribner, 2014.

Collins, Penn. "USC Fans (Rightfully) Brought Joe Paterno and Jerry Sandusky Piñatas to the Rose Bowl." TotalProSports.com, Jan. 4, 2017.

"Commonwealth of Pennsylvania's Response to Petition for Post-Conviction Relief." Sept. 1, 2015. http://co.centre.pa.us/centreco/media/upload/SANDUSKY%20ANSWER%20TO%20PETITION%20FOR%20POST%20CONVICTION%20RELIEF.pdf.

Connor, Tracy. "Anthony Weiner Sentenced to Nearly Two Years in Prison for Sexting Scandal." *NBC News*. Sept. 25, 2017.

Cook, Ron. "Penn State's Sandusky Nightmare Just Gets Worse." *Pittsburgh Post-Gazette*, April 4, 2017.

Coppinger, Mike. "Jerry Sandusky's Son Arrested, Charged with Child Sexual Abuse." *USA Today*, Feb. 13, 2017. (Contains redacted police affidavit.)

Costas, Bob. Interview with Jerry Sandusky on NBC's "Rock Center." Nov. 14, 2011. http://www.newsday.com/sports/media/transcript-jerry-sandusky-s-interview-with-bob-costas-1.3322457.

Crews, Frederick. *Freud: The Making of an Illusion*. NY: Metropolitan Books, 2017.

———. *The Memory Wars: Freud's Legacy in Dispute*. NY: New York Review of Books, 1995.

Curley-Schultz Preliminary Hearing. Dec. 16, 2011, Commonwealth of Pennsylvania v. Timothy Mark Curley and Gary Charles Schultz, In the Court of Common Pleas of Dauphin County, Pennsylvania, No. CP-22-MD-1374-2011, No. CP-22-

MD-1375-2011, www.dauphincounty.org/government/Court-Departments/Curley-Schultz-Spanier/Pages/default.aspx.

Curtis Everhart Interview with Allan Myers, Nov. 9, 2011, http://www.framingpaterno.com/sites/default/files/Interview_Vic_2_Redacted.pdf.

Dawson, Mike. "Jerry Sandusky's Lawyer Joe Amendola in Spotlight as Trial Nears." *Centre Daily Times*, June 4, 2012.

———. "Lawyer: Victim 2, Matt Sandusky Settlements Against Penn State in 'Final Stages.'" *Centre Daily Times*, Aug. 19, 2013.

"Defense Attorney Joe Amendola Reacts to Sandusky Verdict." WTAE-TV Pittsburgh, June 22, 2012.

DeJesus, Ivey. "Sara Ganim, Who Won Pulitzer Prize for Sandusky Coverage, Accepts Job with CNN." *PennLive*, Nov. 13, 2012.

Dent, Mark. "Franco Harris' Crusade is Defending Late Penn State Coach Joe Paterno." *Pittsburgh Post-Gazette*, July 7, 2013.

Deppen, Colin. "Sandusky Lawyer on Divided Defense: 'I Can't Explain Why I Wouldn't Have Asked for a Mistrial.'" *PennLive*, Aug. 12, 2016.

"Distinguishing True From False Memories: Need for Corroboration." http://www.fmsonline.org/links/fmsfrecoveredmemories.html.

Eichelberger, Curtis. "Joe Paterno Is Stripped of 111 Wins as Bowden Climbs to No. 1." *Bloomberg News*, July 24, 2012.

Erdely, Sabrina Rubin. "The Catholic Church's Secret Sex Crime Files," *Rolling Stone*, Sept. 6, 2011.

———. "A Rape on Campus: A Brutal Assault and Struggle for Justice at UVA." *Rolling Stone*, Nov. 19, 2014.

Esposito, Frank. "Lawyer Al Lindsay Says Sandusky Is 'An Innocent Man' in Unlisted YouTube Video 'Why I'm Defending Jerry Sandusky.'" *Daily Collegian*, Nov. 4, 2016.

Essany, Michael. *Joe Paterno: Sandusky Scandal Ends a Coaching Legend's Career.* Hyperink, 2012.

Falce, Lori and Jeremy Hartley. "Jerry Sandusky's Son Arrested on Child Sex Assault, Porn Charges." *Centre Daily Times*, Feb. 13, 2017.

Falce, Lori. "Auditor General Delivers Harsh Critique of Penn State, Sandusky, Freeh, Erickson." *Centre Daily Times*, June 22, 2017.

———. "Judge Denies Motions for Schultz and Spanier, Grants Work Release." *Centre Daily Times,* July 5, 2017.

———. "McQueary Verdict Dwarfs Average Sandusky Abuse Settlement." *Centre Daily Times*, Oct. 28, 2016.

———. "Sandusky Accuser Wants to be 'Voice of the Voiceless.'" *Centre Daily Times*, June 3, 2015.

———. "Victim 2 Attorney, Investigators Testify in Sandusky Hearing." *Centre Daily Times*, Aug. 22, 2016.

———. "Watchdogs Ask New AG to Investigate Parks Miller, Castor." *Centre Daily Times*, Jan. 17, 2017.

Fenno, Nathan. "Trace McSorley Tries to Make Sense of Penn State's Loss in Rose Bowl." *Los Angeles Times*, Jan. 2, 2017.

Fisher, Aaron and Michael Gillum, with Dawn Daniels [actually written by Stephanie Gertler]. *Silent No More: Victim 1's Fight for Justice Against Jerry Sandusky.* NY: Ballantine Books, 2012.

"5 Years after Sandusky Conviction, Many Unresolved Issues." Associated Press, June 23, 2017.

Flounders, Bob. "Joe Paterno Is Dead." *PennLive.com*, Jan. 22, 2012.

Foradora, John, "Opinion on Defendant's PCRA Petition," Commonwealth v. Gerald A. Sandusky, Oct. 18, 2017.

Frank, Jerome D. *Persuasion and Healing: A Comparative Study of Psychotherapy.* Baltimore, MD: Johns Hopkins University Press, 1961, 1973.

Fravel, Joshua. interview by Greg Ault, June 10, 2012.

Fredrickson, Renee. *Repressed Memories: A Journey to Recovery from Sexual Abuse.* NY: Fireside/Parkside, S&S, 1992.

[Freeh Report] Freeh Sporkin & Sullivan, LLP. *Report of the Special Investigative Counsel Regarding the Actions of The Pennsylvania State University Related to the Child Sexual Abuse Committed by Gerald A. Sandusky.* July 12, 2012. http://progress.psu.edu/the-freeh-report.

FREEHdom Fighters website. http://notpsu.blogspot.com/2012/11/freehdom-fighters-answer-daily.html.

Freud, Sigmund. *Standard Edition of the Complete Psychological Works of Sigmund Freud,* trans. By James Strachey. 24 volumes. London: Hogarth Pr., 1953-1974.

Gallini, Brian. "Bringing Down a Legend: How Pennsylvania's Investigating Grand Jury Ended Joe Paterno's Career," *Tennessee Law Review,* vol. 80, Feb. 20, 2013.

Gambacorta, David. "The Great Pennsylvania Government Porn Caper." *Esquire,* Feb. 24, 2016.

Ganim, Sara. "Alleged Victim's Dinner with Jerry Sandusky Was OK'd by Police, Attorney Says." *Patriot-News,* Dec. 2, 2011.

———. "As Jerry Sandusky's Preliminary Hearing Nears, the ex-PSU Coach has Supporters in Happy Valley." *Patriot-News,* Dec. 13, 2011.

———. "Charges Against Former Penn State Coach Jerry Sandusky Removed from Court Website, But You Can Read Them Here." *Patriot-News,* Nov. 4, 2011.

———. "Commentators, Students Express Anger At Allegations of Cover-up at Penn State University." *Patriot-News,* Nov. 6, 2011.

———. "Ex-PSU President Graham Spanier Charged with Obstruction, Endangerment and Perjury; More Charges Filed Against Other Administrators." *Patriot-News,* Nov. 1, 2012.

———. "Ex-Penn State President Graham Spanier Says It Was His Choice to Resign, Not the Board of Trustees." *Patriot-News,* Aug. 23, 2012.

———. "For Jerry Sandusky's State College Neighbors, the Case Is 'Hard to Handle.'" *Patriot-News,* Nov. 21, 2011.

———. "Former Centre County DA Ray Gricar's Reasons for Not Pursuing Case Against Jerry Sandusky Are Unknown." *Patriot-News,* Nov. 6, 2011.

———. "Former Penn State Coach Jerry Sandusky Tells Bob Costas: 'I Shouldn't Have Showered with Those Kids.'" *Patriot-News,* Nov. 14, 2011.

———. "Former Coach Jerry Sandusky Used Charity to Molest Kids." *Patriot-News,* Nov. 6, 2011.

———. "Former Penn State Coach Indicted on Felony Charges of Sex Crimes Against Minors." *Patriot-News,* March 31, 2011.

———. "Former PSU President Graham Spanier Keeps National Security Clearance Amid Sandusky Scandal." *Patriot-News,* July 16, 2012.

———. "Former Tom Corbett Agent Defends Jerry Sandusky Investigation." *Patriot-News,* Nov. 1, 2012.

———. "Gov. Corbett Plays Unique Role on Penn State's Board of Trustees." *Patriot-News,* Jan. 21, 2012.

———. "Graham Spanier, Other Penn State Officials Showed 'Total Disregard to the Suffering of Children,' AG Says." *Patriot-News,* Nov. 1, 2012.

———. "Graham Spanier's Attorneys Refute Freeh Report, but Answer Few Questions." *Patriot-News,* Aug. 22, 2012.

———. "Grand Jury Is Used to Investigate Potential Crimes; No Charges Have Been Filed Against Jerry Sandusky." *Patriot-News,* March 31, 2011.

———. "Inside the Jerry Sandusky Investigation: Why Did It Take So Long?" *Patriot-News,* Nov. 13, 2011.

———. "Is This the Real Jerry Sandusky?" *Patriot-News,* Feb. 20, 2012.

———. "Jerry Sandusky, a Penn State University Football Legend and Founder of the Second Mile, Faces Charges of Sex Crimes." *Patriot-News,* Nov. 4, 2011.

———. "Jerry Sandusky, Adopted Son Had a 'Rocky' Relationship." *Patriot-News,* March 25, 2012.

———. "Jerry Sandusky Case: Lawyers Say They've Found Victim 2, the Boy Mike McQueary Saw Being Molested." *Patriot-News,* July 26, 2012.

———. "Jerry Sandusky Case: Penn State President Rodney Erickson Says There's More Openness Now." *Patriot-News,* July 18, 2012.

————. "Jerry Sandusky Case: Three Men Say They Were Abused in '70s or '80s." *Patriot-News*, July 16, 2012.

———— "Jerry Sandusky, Former Penn State Football Coach, Maintains Innocence." *Patriot-News*, March 31, 2011.

————. "Jerry Sandusky, Former Penn State Football Staffer, Subject of Grand Jury Investigation." *Patriot-News*, March 31, 2011.

————. "Jerry Sandusky interview prompts long-ago victims to contact lawyer." *Patriot-News,* Nov. 17, 2011.

————. "Jerry Sandusky Placed Under House Arrest in College Township." *Patriot-News,* Dec. 9, 2011.

————. "Jerry Sandusky Requests Copies of Grand Jury Testimony." *Patriot-News*, Feb. 7, 2012.

————. "Jerry Sandusky Says He's Saddened by Joe Paterno's Retirement." *Patriot-News*, Nov. 9, 2011.

————. "Jerry Sandusky Scandal One Year Later: A Lot Has Happened in a Year, and There's More to Come." *Patriot-News*, Nov. 4, 2012.

————. "Jerry Sandusky Trial: Accuser Testifies He Denied Abuse Even Though Many Suspected It Was Happening." *Patriot-News*, June 11, 2012.

————. "Jerry Sandusky Trial: Defense Attorney is Respected and Unconventional." *Patriot-News*, June 10, 2012.

————. "Jerry Sandusky Trial: Judge Has Been Anything But Predictable." *Patriot-News*, June 10, 2012.

————. "Jerry Sandusky Trial: Prosecutor Is Used to the Spotlight." *Patriot-News*, June 10, 2012.

————. "Jerry Sandusky Trial: Prosecutor's Opening Statements Portray Ex-coach as 'Predatory Pedophile.'" *Patriot-News*, June 11, 2012.

————. "Jerry Sandusky's Attorney Says One Alleged Victim May Come to His Defense." *Patriot-News*, Nov. 30, 2011.

————. "Jerry Sandusky's attorney says prosecutors didn't share all evidence." *Patriot-News*, Feb. 7, 2012.

————. "Jerry Sandusky's Bail Set at $250,000 After 2 New Alleged Victims Come Forward." *Patriot-News*, Dec. 7, 2011.

————. "Jerry Sandusky's Charity, The Second Mile, Puts Money Transfer to Texas Charity on Hold While Victims' Suits Are Settled." *Patriot-News*, Aug. 27, 2012.

————. "Jerry Sandusky's Crimes Put an End to Second Mile Charity." parts 1-5, *Patriot-News*, Aug. 12, 2012.

————. "Jerry Sandusky's Hearing on Child Sex Charges Moved to December." *Patriot-News,* Nov. 8, 2011.

————. "Jerry Sandusky's lawyer Asks for More Details from Alleged Victims." *Patriot-News*, March 12, 2012.

————. "Jerry Sandusky's Lawyer Threatens to File for Dismissal of Charges." *Patriot-News*, March 12, 2012.

————. "Jerry Sandusky's Lawyer Wants Info from His Client's Computer." *Patriot-News*, May 8, 2012.

————. "Jerry Sandusky's Neighbors, School Employee Complained about Him Sitting Outside Near School, Prosecutors Say." *Patriot-News*, Feb. 7, 2012.

————. "Jerry Sandusky's Next Court Date Is No Longer March 22; Attorney Files 21-page Motion for Evidence." *Patriot-News*, Jan. 19, 2012.

————. "Jerry Sandusky's Speech to the Press Following His Hearing in Bellefonte." *Patriot-News*, Feb. 10, 2012.

————. "Joe Amendola Ponders His Life After Jerry Sandusky." *Patriot-News*, Sept. 5, 2012.

————. "Joe Paterno Family Says NCAA Sanctions 'Defame' Coach." *Patriot-News*, July 23, 2012.

————. "2012-July 12-Joe Paterno's Family: Coach 'Did Not Suspect (Sandusky) Was a Pedophile.'" *Patriot-News*, July 12, 2012.

————. "Joe Paterno's Family Says Statue Removal 'Does Not Serve Victims' of Jerry Sandusky." *Patriot-News*, July 22, 2012.

———. "Joe Paterno's Lung Cancer Stuns Shell-shocked Penn State Fans." *Patriot-News*, Nov. 19, 2011.

———. "Judge in Jerry Sandusky Case to Rule about Whether to Prevent Jury from Hearing about 3 Cases." *Patriot-News*, May 30, 2012.

———. "Judge in Jerry Sandusky Case Won't Order Prosecutors to Give More Details about Sex Abuse Charges." *Patriot-News*, March 13, 2012.

———. "Judge Tells Potential Jurors in Jerry Sandusky: 'I Need You to All Have an Open Mind.'" *Patriot-News*, June 5, 2012.

———. "Man, 19, Says Sandusky Gave Him Whiskey and Assaulted Him Inside a PSU Football Office." *Patriot-News*, Dec. 6, 2011.

———. "Mike McQueary Attended Jerry Sandusky Fundraiser One Year After Making Sexual Assault Allegations." *Patriot-News*, Nov. 16, 2011.

———. "Mike McQueary, Key Witness in Jerry Sandusky Sex Abuse Case, Changes Story About Shower Incident." *Patriot-News*, Nov. 16, 2011.

———. "Mike McQueary's Statement to Police Doesn't Say He Stopped Attack or Notified Police about Sandusky Allegations." *Patriot-News*, Nov. 16, 2011.

———. "Mothers of Two of Jerry Sandusky's Alleged Victims Lash Out at Penn State Officials' Handling of Scandal." *Patriot-News*, Nov. 7, 2011.

———. "Paterno to Fans after Board of Trustees Announced Firing: 'I love you guys.'" *Patriot-News*, Nov. 9, 2014.

———. "Pedophiles 'Exploit the Influence They Have on Children,' Clinical Psychologist Says." *Patriot-News*, Nov. 5, 2011.

———. "Penn State Board of Trustees Trustees 'Got It Wrong,' Says Attorney Advising Jerry Sandusky's Alleged Victims." *Patriot-News*, Nov. 10, 2011.

———. "Penn State Coach Joe Paterno Says He Was Only Told Witness Had Seen Jerry Sandusky Doing 'Something Inappropriate' in the Shower." *Patriot-News*, Nov. 6, 2011.

———. "Penn State Football Press Conference Cancelled by University President." *Patriot-News*, Nov. 8, 2011.

———. "Penn State Hasn't Yet Helped Alleged Sandusky Victims as Promised, Lawyer Says." *Patriot-News*, March 21, 2012.

———. "Penn State Interim Head Coach Coach Tom Bradley to Hold Press Conference Today at 11 a.m." *Patriot-News*, Nov. 10, 2011.

———. "Penn State Names Former FBI Director Louis Freeh to Investigate Sex Abuse Scandal." *Patriot-News*, Nov. 21, 2011.

———. "Penn State Officials Conspired to Protect Themselves and Jerry Sandusky, AG Says." *Patriot-News*, Nov. 1, 2012.

———. "Penn State Pines for Normalcy Amid Sex Abuse Scandal." *Patriot-News*, Nov. 29, 2011.

———. "Penn State President Rodney Erickson Signed Consent Agreement to NCAA Sanctions." *Patriot-News*, July 23, 2012.

———. "Penn State Sanctions: What They Mean for Fans, Players, Coaches and Your Tax Dollars." *Patriot-News*, July 23, 2012.

———. "Penn State Student Riots Were Another Blow to School's Pride, Sister of Sandusky Victim Says." *Patriot-News*, Nov. 10, 2011.

———. "Penn State Trustees Discuss Sandusky Case, Alleged Cover-up." *Patriot-News*, Nov. 6, 2011.

———. "Penn State Trustees Must Decide Individually if They Should Remain on the Board, President Rodney Erickson Says." *Patriot-News*, July 17, 2012.

———. "Penn State's Joe Paterno Retires." *Patriot-News*, Nov. 9, 2011.

———. "Penn State's Scandal Tab Tops $7.5 Million." *Patriot-News*, April 17, 2012.

———. "Private Meeting among Jerry Sandusky, Prosecutors and Judge Was to Ask Again for Trial Delay." *Patriot-News*, May 30, 2012.

———. "PSU Assistant Coach, Grand Jury Witness Mike McQueary Placed on Paid Administrative Leave." *Patriot-News*, Nov. 11, 2011.

———. "Questions Mount about Mike McQueary's Account of the Locker Room Sexual Assault." *Patriot-News*, Nov. 17, 2011.

———. "Sandusky Victim: Joe Paterno Told Me to Drop Abuse Accusation." CNN, May 8, 2016.

———. "Second Mile Weighs Options as 2 of 3 Charities Step Away from Taking Over Programs." *Patriot-News*, Jan. 4, 2012.

———. "Sister of Sandusky Victim Talks about the Pain of Life at Penn State Where Students Are Joking About Being 'Sanduskied.'" *Patriot-News*, Nov. 9, 2011.

———. "State College Police to Make Arrests in Post-Paterno-firing Riot." *Patriot-News*, Nov. 10, 2011.

———. "State Trooper Lear Charged with Assault, Burglary, False Imprisonment of Ex-Girlfriend." *Centre Daily Times*, Aug. 14, 2009.

———. "The Second Mile and Penn State: Charity and University's Fates Were Tied Together." *Patriot-News*, Nov. 17, 2011.

———. "The Second Mile, Jerry Sandusky's Charity, Still Evaluating its Future as 2012 Begins." *Patriot-News*, Jan. 3, 2012.

———. "Victim Preparing to Testify at Jerry Sandusky Hearing, Attorney Says." *Patriot-News*, Nov. 29, 2011.

———. "Victim Rights Lawyers Respond to Claims by Jerry Sandusky's Attorney about Victim Two." *Patriot-News*, Nov. 30, 2011.

———. "Victim 2 Wasn't a Participant in Jerry Sandusky's Trial, but May Be Key in Penn State Cover-up Allegations." *Patriot-News*, July 26, 2012.

———. "Victim's Wife, Man Charged." *Centre Daily Times*, Aug. 29, 2009.

———. "Who Knew What About Jerry Sandusky?" *Patriot-News*, Nov. 11, 2011.

Garcia, Ana. "Exclusive: New Sandusky Child-abuse Accuser Steps Forward." *Crime Watch Daily*, Nov. 11, 2015.

Garrett, Brandon L. *Convicting the Innocent: Where Criminal Prosecutions Go Wrong*. Cambridge. MA: Harvard U. Pr. 2012.

Gibb, Tom. "Doctor Facing Teen-sex Charges." *Pittsburgh Post-Gazette*, Nov. 10, 2001.

Gladwell, Malcolm. "In Plain View." *New Yorker*, Sept. 24, 2012.

Goldman, Laura. "Meet Sandusky's Prosecutor: Joe 'Hollywood' McGettigan." *Naked Philadelphian*, June 11, 2012.

Graham Spanier interview by Josh Elliott. *ABC News*, Aug. 22, 2012, http://abcnews.go.com/Nightline/video/graham-spanier-interview-17290926.

[Grand Jury Presentment]. Thirty-Third Statewide [Pennsylvania] Grand Jury Presentment, Nov. 5, 2011.
http://www.attorneygeneral.gov/uploadedfiles/press/sandusky-grand-jury-presentment.pdf.

Gray, Gary and Ronald A. Smith. *My Last Visit with Coach Paterno: The Sandusky Scandal and the Fallout at Penn State*. Book proposal, courtesy of Gary Gray.

Gray, Gary. Letter to Penn State President Rodney Erickson and Members of the Board of Trustees, Aug. 9, 2012. ABC news website. http://abcnews.go.com/US/page/penn-state-football-player-gary-gray-letter-joe-17057945.

———. "A Story Fit For the Tabloids." Letter to the Editor, Harrisburg *Patriot-News*, March 31, 2011.

Griffin, Marty. "Man Claims Sandusky Sexually Assaulted Him Over 40 Years Ago." KDKA-TV, Oct. 29, 2012.

Grossman, Evan. "Joe Paterno Apologists Are Blind to Reality, Unwilling to Face Facts about Ex-Penn State Coach." *New York Daily News*, July 17, 2016.

Gudjonsson, Gisli H. *The Psychology of Interrogations and Confessions: A Handbook*. NY: Wiley, 2003.

Hanson, Rochelle F. et al. "Correlates of Adolescent Reports of Sexual Assault: Findings from the National Survey of Adolescents." *Child Maltreatment*. vol. 8, no. 4, Nov. 2003. p. 261-272.

Hartley, Jeremy. "McQueary, Others Testify in Opening Day of Spanier Trial." *Centre Daily Times*, March 21, 2017.

Heim, Bruce. "Shedding Light on the Second Mile's Decision Making." *StateCollege.com*, Oct. 7, 2015.

Hell Is a Very Small Place: Voices from Solitary Confinement. ed. Jean Casella et al. NY: New Press, 2016.

Henneberger, Melinda. "Does Dottie Sandusky Deserve a Jail Cell of Her Own?" *Washington Post*, June 26, 2012.

Hill, Elissa. "Department Of Education Releases Investigation Results On Penn State Clery Reporting, Fines University Record $2.4 Million For Violations." *Onward State*, Nov. 3, 2016.

Hobson, Will and Cindy Boren. "New Court Documents Suggest Others at Penn State Knew of Jerry Sandusky Abuse." *Washington Post*, July 12, 2016.

Hockensmith, Dustin. "Jerry Sandusky Verdict: Attorney General Linda Kelly Praises Courage of Victims Who Testified." PennLive.com, June 22, 2012. http://www.pennlive.com/midstate/index.ssf/2012/06/jerry_sandusky_verdict_attorne.html.

Hopper, Jessica et al. "Jerry Sandusky 'Clingy,' Says Man Mentored by Former Penn State Asst. Coach." *Rock Center*, Nov. 21, 2011.

Hunter, Mic. *Abused Boys: The Neglected Victims of Sexual Abuse.* Lexington, MA: Lexington Books, 1990.

Ilibagiza, Immaculée. *Left to Tell: Discovering God Amidst the Rwandan Holocaust.* Hay House, 2014.

Inbau, Fred E. et al. *Criminal Interrogations and Confessions.* 5th ed. Burlington, MA: Jones & Bartlett Learning, 2011.

Investigation of the State Correctional Institution at Cresson and Notice of Expanded Investigation. by Thomas E. Perez and David J. Hickton. https://www.justice.gov/sites/default/files/crt/legacy/2013/06/03/cresson_findings_5-31-13.pdf. Civil Rights Division, US Dept of Justice, May 31, 2013.

Isikoff, Michael. ["Matt Sandusky Claims Abuse,"] June 26, 2012. http://usnews.nbcnews.com/_news/2012/06/26/12417694-nbc-exclusive-matt-sandusky-details-alleged-sex-abuse-by-his-father?lite.

Jackson, Mike. "Local Survivor of Jerry Sandusky's Abuse Speaks Out about Life after Being Abused," WCMH-TV, Feb. 17, 2017.

Jenkins, Philip. *Moral Panic: Changing Concepts of the Child Molester in Modern America.* New Haven, CT: Yale U. Press, 1998.

———. "Penn State's Catholic Problem," *Real Clear Religion,* July 3, 2012, http://www.realclearreligion.org/articles/2012/07/03/penn_states_catholic_problem.html.

"Jerry Sandusky Appeal Seeks to Have Molestation Case Thrown Out." *Associated Press*, May 6, 2015.

"Jerry Sandusky Proclaims His Innocence in Jailhouse Audio Recording." *CNN*, Oct. 8, 2012. http://www.cnn.com/2012/10/08/justice/pennsylvania-jerry-sandusky-sentencing/.

"Jeffrey Sandusky, Son of Jerry, Pleads Guilty to Child Sex Abuse Allegations." *Associated Press.* Sept. 16, 2017.

"Jerry Sandusky Trial: Accuser Tearfully Recounts How He 'Froze' During Abuse." *Associated Press*, June 12, 2012. http://www.lehighvalleylive.com/breaking-news/index.ssf/2012/06/jerry_sandusky_trial_day_2_vic.html.

"Joe Paterno Is Now Winningest Coach." *ESPN*, Jan. 16, 2015.

Johnson, Kevin. "Sandusky 'Victim 1' psychologist loses county job." *USA Today*, Oct. 8, 2013.

———. "The Tortuous Winding Path of Victim One." *USA Today*, July 18, 2012, Mike Gillum featured in video included in the online article. http://usatoday30.usatoday.com/news/nation/story/2012-07-09/victim-1-sandusky-witness/56278226/1.

"Judge Adds $5M-plus to McQueary's $7M Verdict vs. Penn State." *Associated Press*, Nov. 30, 2016.

"Judge Handling Jerry Sandusky's Appeal Removes Himself from Case." *Associated Press*, Nov. 18, 2016.

"Judge Sets May Trial Date for Sandusky Abuse Case." *Associated Press*, Feb. 10, 2012.

Kelley, Michael B. "Penn State Investigator Louis Freeh Accused Of Heading A Massive Cover-Up As Director Of FBI." *Business Insider*, July 16, 2012, http://www.businessinsider.com/penn-state-investigator-louis-freeh-accused-of-heading-a-massive-cover-up-as-director-of-fbi-2012-7.

Kellogg, N. D. and R. H. Huston. "Unwanted Sexual Experiences in Adolescents: Patterns of Disclosure." *Clinical Pediatrics*. vol. 34, p. 306-312, 1995.

Kelly, Linda and Frank Noonan. "Statements Regarding Jerry Sandusky Sex Crimes Investigation." Nov. 7, 2011.

Kotz, Pete. "Mirinda Boob Conspired with Boyfriend Ron Heichel to Kill Her Husband." *True Crime Report*, Sept. 2, 2010. http://www.truecrimereport.com/2010/09/mirinda_boob_conspired_with_bo.php.

Kurtz, Sylvia L. *To Believe a Kid: Understanding the Jerry Sandusky Case and Child Sexual Abuse*. XLibris, 2014.

Lanning, Kenneth V. *Child Molesters: A Behavioral Analysis*. 5th ed. Washington, DC: National Center for Missing and Exploited Children, 2010.

Lavelle, Marianne. "Pennsylvania Gets F Grade in 2015 State Integrity Investigation," Center for Public Integrity, Nov. 20, 2015, https://www.publicintegrity.org/2015/11/09/18507/pennsylvania-gets-f-grade-2015-state-integrity-investigation.

Let Go Let Peace Come In website. http://www.letgoletpeacecomein.org/

Loftus, Elizabeth and Katherine Ketcham. *The Myth of Repressed Memory: False Memories and Allegations of Sexual Abuse*. NY: St. Martin's, 1996.

Loftus, Elizabeth F. "Planting Misinformation in the Human Mind: A 30-year Investigation of the Malleability of Memory." *Learning and Memory*, 2005, vol. 12, p. 361-366.

Loftus, Elizabeth and Katharine Ketcham. *Witness for the Witness: The Accused, the Eyewitness, and the Expert Who Puts Memory on Trial*. NY: St. Martin's Griffin, 1992.

Long, Robert. *Analysis of the Freeh Report*, 2013. http://robertlong1.tripod.com/.

Loop 21. "The Curious Case of Ed Manigo." *Ebony*, June 6, 2012.

Luciew, John and *Patriot-News* Staff. *Hear No Evil: How the Sandusky Sex Abuse Scandal Rocked Penn State, Toppled Joe Paterno, and Stunned a Nation*. Kindle ebook, 2011.

Mackay, Charles. *Extraordinary Popular Delusions and the Madness of Crowds*. Philadelphia: Templeton Foundation Press, [1841, 1852], 1999.

Mantila, Kyle. "Glenn Beck Gives Guest Two Hours To Lay Out His Theory That Jerry Sandusky Sex Abuse Case Was 'Fake News.'" *Right Wing Watch*, March 16, 2017.

Mathis, Joel. "Porn Scandal Missed Its Target: The Latest Battle between Kathleen Kane and Frank Fina." *Philadelphia Magazine*, Oct. 13, 2014.

McCallum, Jack. "Last Call." *Sports Illustrated*, Dec. 20, 1999.

McHugh, Paul R. *Try to Remember: Psychiatry's Clash Over Meaning, Memory, and Mind*. NY: Dana Press, 2008.

McKelvey, Wallace. "Kathleen Kane's Feud with Barry Feudale: 7 Takeaways." *PennLive*, Nov. 5, 2015.

McNally, Richard J. *Remembering Trauma*. Cambridge, MA: Belknap, 2003.

The Memory Hackers. Nova TV program. PBS, May 5, 2016, https://www.youtube.com/watch?v=mIsIPqYvwUM.

Menzie, Nicola. "President Obama Speaks Out on Jerry Sandusky Scandal at Penn State University." *Christian Post*, Nov. 13, 2011.

Michlowski, Bill. "New Judge Appointed to Oversee Jerry Sandusky Appeal." WNEP-TV, Feb. 13, 2017.

Miller, Matt. "Ex-Penn State Athletic Director Tim Curley Freed from Prison, under House Arrest." *PennLive*. Oct. 9, 2017.

———. "Ex-Sandusky Lawyer Karl Rominger Gets State Prison for Stealing $767K." *PennLive*, Aug. 17, 2016.

———. "Graham Spanier Illegally and Badly Fumbled 'Penn State's Jerry Sandusky Problem,' Prosecutor Says." *PennLive*, March 21, 2017.

Moulton, H. Geoffrey, Jr. *Report to the Attorney General on the Investigation of Gerald A. Sandusky*. Harrisburg, PA: PA Office of Attorney General, 2014.

Moushey, Bill and Robert Dvorchak. *Game Over: Jerry Sandusky, Penn State, and the Culture of Silence*. NY: William Morrow, 2012.

Murphy, Jan. "Life on Death Row inside Greene Prison Unlike Scenes from Movies." *PennLive.com*, Jan. 8, 2015.

Murray, Gary V. "Former Athlete Pleads Guilty; Leominster Star Sent to Prison." *Telegram & Gazette*, Dec. 17, 2002.

Muskal, Michael. "Jerry Sandusky Loses Bid for New Sex-abuse Trial." *Los Angeles Times*, Jan. 30, 2013.

Newhouse, David. "Jerry Sandusky Patriot-News Report Deals in Facts." *Patriot-News*, March 31, 2011.

NBC News. "Penn State to Pay $59.7 Million to Settle Sandusky Sex Abuse Claims." Feb. 3, 2014. http://www.nbcnews.com/news/us-news/penn-state-pay-59-7-million-settle-sandusky-sex-abuse-v21213413.

"NCAA Had Doubts On Its Authority in Penn State Case." *Inside Higher Ed*, Nov. 6, 2014. https://www.insidehighered.com/quicktakes/2014/11/06/ncaa-had-doubts-its-authority-penn-state-case.

"No. 19 Nebraska Hangs on to Beat Somber Penn State." *Associated Press*, Nov. 12, 2011.

Ofshe, Richard and Ethan Watters. *Making Monsters: False Memories, Psychotherapy, and Sexual Hysteria*. NY: Scribner, 1994.

Otterson, Joe. "Al Pacino to Star as Penn State Coach Joe Paterno in New HBO Movie From Barry Levinson." *Variety*, June 5, 2017.

Paterno, Jay. "An Open Letter to Sally Jenkins." *StateCollege.com*, July 14, 2016.

———. *Paterno Legacy: Enduring Lessons from the Life and Death of My Father*. Chicago, IL: Triumph Books, 2014.

Patihis, Lawrence et al. "Are the 'Memory Wars' Over? A Scientist-Practitioner Gap in Beliefs about Repressed Memory." *Psychological Science*, 2013, v. 20, p. 1-12.

Patriot-News Staff. "Read the Grand Jury Presentment on the Jerry Sandusky Case Here." *Patriot-News*, Nov. 5, 2011.

[PCRA Brief, July 11, 2017], Commonwealth v. Gerald A. Sandusky. http://co.centre.pa.us/centreco/media/upload/SANDUSKY%20DEFENDANTS%20POST%20HEARING%20BRIEF%20AN%20DPROPOSED%20FINDINGS%20OF%20FACT%20AND%20CONCLUSION%20OF%20LAW.pdf.

[PCRA Petition, May 6, 2015]. Commonwealth v. Gerald A. Sandusky. Amended Petition for Post Conviction Relief. http://co.centre.pa.us/centreco/media/upload/Sandusky%20Amended%20Petition%20for%20Post%20Conviction%20Relief.pdf.

Peaceful Hearts Foundation website. http://www.peacefulheartsfoundation.org/.

Pelullo, Peter S. *Betrayal and the Beast*. Plymouth Meeting, PA: Only Serenity LLC, 2012.

Penn Law Fumble website. http://www.pennlawfumble.info/. Sept. 21, 2015.

"Penn State Approved $60 Million in Sandusky Settlement Claims." *Associated Press*, July 17, 2013.

"Penn State Child Sex Abuse Scandal." Wikipedia. http://en.wikipedia.org/wiki/Penn_State_child_sex_abuse_scandal#Grand_Jury_Investigation.

"Penn State Ex-athletic Director Pleads Guilty in Jerry Sandusky Case." *Associated Press*, March 13, 2017.

"Penn State Files Paperwork to Sue 'Second Mile' Charity Jerry Sandusky Founded," *Associated Press*, Sept. 5, 2017.

Pendergrast, Mark. *Memory Warp: How the Myth of Repressed Memory Arose and Refuses to Die*. Hinesburg, VT: Upper Access, 2017.

———. *The Repressed Memory Epidemic: How It Happened and What We Need to Learn from It*. NY: Springer, 2017.

———. *Victims of Memory: Sex Abuse Accusations and Shattered Lives*. Hinesburg, VT: Upper Access, 2d ed, 1996.

Petersen, Betsy. *Dancing With Daddy: A Childhood Lost and Life Regained*. NY: Bantam, 1991.

Piper, August, Jr. *Hoax and Reality: The Bizarre World of Multiple Personality Disorder*. Northvale, NJ: Jason Aronson, 1997.

Pope, Harrison G. *Psychology Astray: Fallacies in Studies of "Repressed Memory" and Childhood Trauma.* Boca Raton, FL: Upton Books, 1997.

Pope H.G., Hudson J.I., "Repressed Memories: Scientific Status," in *Modern Scientific Evidence: The Law and Science of Expert Testimony* (2011-2012 edition). Edited by Faigman DL et al. Eagen, MN, West Group, 2012, pp 828-913.

Posnanski, Joe. *Paterno.* NY: Simon & Schuster, 2012.

Procyk, Kat. "Former Defense Attorney, Psychologist and other Witnesses Take the Stand in Jerry Sandusky's Appeal Hearing." *Daily Collegian,* March 24, 2017.

Pynes, Mark. "Penn State Settlements Covered 1971 Sandusky Abuse Claim." *PennLive,* May 9, 2016.

RAINN website. https://www.rainn.org/.

Reisberg, Daniel. *The Science of Perception and Memory: A Pragmatic Guide for the Justice System.* NY: Oxford U. Pr., 2014.

Reiter, Keramet. *23/7: Pelican Bay Prison and the Rise of Long-Term Solitary.* New Haven, CT: Yale U. Pr., 2016.

"Report of the Board of Trustees Concerning Nov. 9 Decisions." *Patriot-News,* March 12, 2012.

Rind, Bruce et al. "A Meta-Analytic Examination of Assumed Properties of Child Sexual Abuse Using College Samples." *Psychological Bulletin.* vol. 124, no. 1, p. 22–53, 1998.

Robbins, Don. *He is Innocent: Blog Posts by NewC Blog.* Amazon Digital Service, 2016.

Roebuck, Jeremy. "Exasperated Sandusky Judge Withdraws from Case, Urges Probe of Lawyers." *Philadelphia Inquirer,* Nov. 19, 2016.

———. "Journey of Sandusky's 'Victim 1' Involves Advocacy." *Philadelphia Inquirer,* May 3, 2015.

Roediger, Henry L. et al. "Social Contagion of Memory." *Psychonomic Bulletin and Review,* 2001, vol. 8(2), p. 365-371.

Rosenthal, Robert. "Suggestibility, Reliability, and the Legal Process." *Developmental Review,* 2002, v. 22, p. 334-369.

Rubin, David C. and Dorthe Berntsen. "People Believe It Is Plausible to Have Forgotten Memories of Childhood Sexual Abuse." *Psychological Bulletin Review,* Aug. 2007, vol. 14, no. 4, p. 776-778.

Rubin, Mike. "DeAndre Levy: The Most Interesting Man in the NFL." *Men's Journal,* Nov. 2016.

Rushdie, Salman. *Joseph Anton: A Memoir.* NY: Random House, 2012.

Salemme, J. Andrew. *Guilty Until Proven Innocent: A Practitioner's and Judge's Guide to the Pennsylvania Post-Conviction Relief Act.* rev. ed. CreateSpace, 2016.

[Sandusky case documents]. Commonwealth vs. Gerald A. Sandusky, on Centre County website. http://centrecountypa.gov/index.aspx?NID=506. various dates.

Sandusky, Jerry. *Can We Endure?* manuscript sent to Mark Pendergrast, courtesy of the author.

Sandusky, Jerry and Cedric X. Bryant. *Coaching Linebackers.* Monterey, CA: Coaches Choice, 1995.

———. *Coaching Linebackers.* Monterey, CA: Coaches Choice Books, 1995.

———. *101 Linebacker Drills.* Monterey, CA: Coaches Choice Books, 1997.

Sandusky, Jerry and Kip Richeal. *Touched: The Jerry Sandusky Story.* Champaign, IL: Sports Publishing, 2000.

Sandusky, Kara. "Inside Perspective." unpublished manuscript, courtesy of author.

Sandusky, Matthew. *Undaunted: Breaking My Silence to Overcome the Trauma of Child Sexual Abuse.* Rothco Press, 2015.

Schacter, Daniel L. *The Seven Sins of Memory: How the Mind Forgets and Remembers.* NY: Mariner Books, 2002.

Schonfeld, Zach. "After Gang Rape Article, *Rolling Stone* Settles with University of Virginia Fraternity," *Newsweek,* June 13, 2017.

Scolforo, Mark. "Former Penn State Assistant Gets $1.7M in Whistleblower Fees." *Associated Press,* March 31, 2017.

———. "Jerry Sandusky Presses Appeal, Wants to Question Witnesses." *Associated Press*, May 2, 2016.

———. "Lawyer Cynthia Baldwin Told Feds in 2012 Former Penn State President Graham Spanier Was Trustworthy." *Associated Press*, Dec. 22, 2013.

———. "Sandusky Abuse Victim Sues Ex-Coach, Penn State." *Associated Press*, Nov. 21, 2013.

———. "Sandusky Wants Subpoena Power to Look into 2011 Case Leaks." *Associated Press*, Sept. 30, 2015.

Second Amended Petition for Post Conviction Relief. Commonwealth v. Gerald A. Sandusky, Petitioner. March 9, 2016. http://co.centre.pa.us/centreco/media/upload/SANDUSKY%20SECOND%20AMENDED%20PCRA%20PETITION.pdf.

Semon, Craig S. "Anthony Spinelli, Charged in Boston Attack, Was One-time Leominster High Football Star." *Telegram & Gazette*, Dec. 22, 2016.

Shaikh, Arif M. *Healing Tips for the Mind, Body, & Soul, Part 1.* Mechanicsburg, PA: Sunbury Press Books Inc., 2015.

Shapiro, T. Reece. "Jury Finds Reporter, Rolling Stone Responsible for Defaming U-Va. Dean with Gang Rape Story." *Washington Post*, Nov. 4, 2016.

Shaw, John S. et al. "Co-witness Information Can Have Immediate Effects on Eyewitness Memory Reports," *Law and Human Behavior*, 1997, v. 21 (5), p. 503-520.

Shaw, Julia and Stephen Porter. "Constructing Rich False Memories of Committing Crime." *Psychological Science*, 2015, vol. 26(3),m p. 291-301.

Shaw, Julia. *The Memory Illusion: Remembering, Forgetting, and the Science of False Memory.* NY: Random House, 2016.

Simpson, Elizabeth. "Matt Sandusky, Silent No More, Works to Stop Abuse." *Virginian-Pilot*, Sept. 8, 2014.

Simpson, Paul. *Second Thoughts: Understanding the False Memory Crisis and How It Could Affect You.* Nashville, TN: Thomas Nelson, 1996.

Smith, Mitch. "Jerry Sandusky's Son Charged with Sexually Assaulting Children." *NYT*, Feb. 13, 2017.

Smith, Ronald A. *Wounded Lions: Joe Paterno, Jerry Sandusky, and the Crises in Penn State Athletics.* University of Illinois Press, 2016.

[Snedden Report] by John Snedden. "U.S. Office of Personnel Management Investigations Service." May 8, 2012. https://www.scribd.com/document/341764461/Spanier-High-Level-Clearance-FBI-Report-Redacted#from_embed.

Snyder, Susan and Jeremy Roebuck. "How Penn State Decided to Pay $93 Million to Sandusky Victims." *Philadelphia Inquirer*, July 16, 2016.

Snyder, Susan. "Penn State Reaches Settlement with Sandusky Victim." *Philadelphia Inquirer*, Aug. 19, 2013.

Sokolove, Michael. "The Trials of Graham Spanier, Penn State's Ousted President." *New York Times Magazine*, July 16, 2014.

"Spanier's Defense Rests Without Calling Any Witnesses." *Associated Press*, March 23, 2017.

"Start of Sandusky Trial Delayed until June 5." *Reuters*, March 29, 2012.

State of Michigan Governor's Task Force on Child Abuse and Neglect and Department of Human Services. *Forensic Interviewing Protocol*, 3d ed., DHS Pub 779. Lansing, Michigan: Dept of Human Services, 2011.

Steele, Allison. "The Clinton County Caseworker Who Broke Open the Sandusky Child Sex Scandal." *Philadelphia Inquirer*, Sept. 22, 2014.

Stevens, Alexis. "Pair Charged with 109 Counts of Sexual Exploitation of Children." *Atlanta Journal-Constitution*, Dec. 17, 2013.

Stevenson, Bryan. *Just Mercy: A Story of Justice and Redemption.* NY: Spiegel and Grau, 2015.

Stripling, Jack. "Behind an Ex-President, a Band of Loyalists." *Chronicle of Higher Education*, Aug. 11, 2014.

Storm, Jennifer. *Echoes of Penn State: Facing Sexual Trauma.* Ebook. Central Recovery Press, 2012.

Stump, Scott. "Sandusky: Paterno Would Not Have Let Me Coach If He Thought I Was a Pedophile." *Today* website, March 25, 2013. http://www.today.com/news/sandusky-paterno-would-not-have-let-me-coach-if-he-1B9051529.

"Superior Court Affirms Heichel Sentences for Murder." *The [Lock Haven] Express,* March 30, 2012. http://www.lockhaven.com/page/content.detail/id/537905/Superior-Court-affirms-Heichel-sentences-for-murder.html?nav=5009.

"Supplement to Mr. Sandusky's Ineffectiveness Claim Related to Bob Costas Interview and Request to Reopen the Record." Commonwealth v. Gerald A. Sandusky. http://co.centre.pa.us/centreco/media/upload/SANDUSKY%20SUPPLEMENT.pdf.

Taylor, Stuart and K. C. Johnson. *Until Proven Innocent: Political Correctness and the Shameful Injustices of the Duke Lacrosse Rape Case.* NY: St. Martin, 2008.

Thompson, Charles. "Child Told Paterno of Sex Abuse in 1976, Court Papers Allege." *PennLive,* May 5, 2016.

————. "Court bars Release of Sexually Explicit Emails Found During Kathleen Kane's Review of Jerry Sandusky Probe." *PennLive.com,* Aug. 30, 2014.

————. "Graham Spanier Punches Back against Penn State's Sandusky-related Refund Claim." *PennLive,* March 10, 2017.

————. "Jerry Sandusky Loses Appeal to Pennsylvania Superior Court." *PennLive.com,* Oct. 2, 2013.

————. "Jury Reaches Split Verdict in Trial of Ex-PSU President Graham Spanier." *PennLive,* March 25, 2017.

————. "Law Allows Experts to Testify on Sex Abuse." *PennLive,* June 29, 2012.

————. "A Llook at the Strengths, Holes of Prosecution Case Against Graham Spanier." *PennLive,* March 23, 2017.

————. "Penn State to Graham Spanier: Pay Us Back." *PennLive,* Dec. 20, 2016.

[Trial Transcript]. Commonwealth vs Gerald A. Sandusky, in the Court of Common Pleas, Centre County, Pennsylvania, Criminal Division, No. CP-14-CR-2421-2011, No. CP-14-CR-2422-2011. Transcript of Proceedings, June 11 -22, 2012.

U.S. Court of Appeals for the Third Circuit, "Craig Williams v. Secretary Penn DOC et al, No. 14-1469 [and] Shawn T. Walker v. Michael A. Farnan et al., No. 15-1390." http://www2.ca3.uscourts.gov/opinarch/141469p.pdf, Feb. 9, 2017.

Van Natta, Don, Jr. "The Whistleblower's Last Stand." *ESPN Magazine,* March 4, 2014. http://espn.go.com/espn/feature/story/_/id/10542793/the-whistleblower-last-stand.

Vestal, Shawn. "Jerry Sandusky Victims Says Reporting Crimes Was Harder Than Abuse," *Spokesman-Review.* Spokane, WA, May 15, 2014.

"Victim #4's Motion for Protective Order for the Use of Pseudonym." Commonwealth of Pennsylvania v. Gerald A. Sandusky, March 29, 2012.

"Victim 9 Files Abuse Claim." *Associated Press,* Nov. 21, 2013. http://espn.go.com/college-football/story/_/id/10011817/victim-9-files-abuse-claim-vs-jerry-sandusky-penn-state.

Victor, Jeffrey S. *Satanic Panic: The Creation of a Contemporary Legend.* Chicago, IL: Open Court Publishing, 1993.

Wade, Kimberley A. et al. "De-constructing Rich False Memories of Committing Crime: Commentary on Shaw and Porter (2015)." *Psychological Science,* 2017.

Warner, Dave. "Convicted Child Abuser Jerry Sandusky Loses $59,000 Annual Pension." *Reuters,* Oct. 10, 2012.

Watson, Graham. "Alma Mater's Meltdown Moves Matt Millen to On-Air Tears." *Yahoo Sports,* Nov. 8, 2011. http://sports.yahoo.com/ncaa/football/blog/dr_saturday/post/Former-Penn-State-LB-Matt-Millen-gets-emotional-?urn=ncaaf-wp9465.

Webster, Richard. *The Secret of Bryn Estyn: The Making of a Modern Witch Hunt.* Oxford: Orwell Press, 2005.

Wetzel, Dan. "Jerry Sandusky Engaged in Repeated Acts of Oral Sex, a Second Alleged Victim Testifies at Trial." *Yahoo Sports,* June 12, 2012. http://sports.yahoo.com/news/ncaaf--jerry-sandusky-trial-victim-no-1-joe-amendola-second-day-penn-state--.html.

———. "Mike McQueary, Broken Down and Estranged, Files $4 million Whistleblower Lawsuit." *Yahoo Sports*, Oct. 2, 2012.

———. "TV Interview with Jerry Sandusky's Wife an Insult to His Victims." *Yahoo Sports,* March 14, 2014. http://sports.yahoo.com/news/tv-interview-with-jerry-sandusky-s-wife-an-insult-to-his-victims-025526818.html.

Wiesel, Elie. *Night*. Hill and Wang, (1960), 2006.

Whitbourne, Susan Krauss. "What's New (and Old) in the DSM-5 Personality Disorders." *Psychology Today*, March 5, 2013.

Winfrey, Oprah. "Matt Sandusky on Hearing Victim Testimony: They Were Telling My Story." Oprah Prime website. http://www.oprah.com/own-oprahprime/Matthew-Sandusky-on-Hearing-Victim-Testimony-Video. (This segment was not aired on TV but was on website.)

———. Televised Interview with Matt Sandusky, transcript, Oprah Winfrey Network, July 17, 2014.

Yaeger, Don and Mike Pressler. *It's Not About the Truth: The Untold Story of the Duke Lacrosse Rape Case and the Lives It Shattered.* NY: Threshold/Simon & Schuster, 2007.

Yoder, Harvey. *A Small Price to Pay*. TGS International, 2006.

Yoffe, Emily, "The Bad Science Behind Campus Response to Sexual Assault," *Atlantic*, Sept. 8, 2017.

Zaragoza, M. S. "Interviewing Witnesses: Forced Confabulations and Confirmatory Feedback Increase False Memories." *Psychological Science*, Nov. 2001, vol. 12(6), p. 473-477.

Zaragoza, M. S. et al. "Misinformation Effects and the Suggestibility of Eyewitness Memory." In M. Garry & H. Hayne, (eds.). *Do Justice and Let the Sky Fall: Elizabeth F. Loftus and her Contributions to Science Law, and Academic Freedom* (p. 35-63). Mahwah, NJ Erlbaum, 2007.

Ziegler, John. *The Betrayal of Joe Paterno*. 2013, and subsequent updates online, www.framingpaterno.com.

———. *Dynasty at the Crossroads: A Story of Kids, Fans and Values*. Apollo, PA: Closson Press, 1994.

———. "ESPN's Coverage of Joe Paterno: One Disgrace Leads to Another." *Bleacher Report*, Nov. 10, 2011.

———. "Federal Report on Former Penn State President Concluded There Was No Cover-up." *LawNewz*, March 13, 2017.

———. *The Framing of Joe Paterno*. Nov. 7, 2012, https://www.youtube.com/watch?v=D3z-3CBfM8Q&t=13s.

———. *Framing Paterno* website. www.framingpaterno.com.

———. "The News Media Was Very Wrong to Make Jeffrey Sandusky's Arrest a Huge Story." *LawNewz*, Feb. 14, 2017.

———. Prison Interview with Jerry Sandusky, Feb. 28, 2013, http://www.framingpaterno.com/sites/default/files/Sandusky.prisonrevised.pdf.

———. "Penn State Scandal: A Plausible Scenario Where the Media Has It All Wrong." *Bleacher Report*, Nov. 16, 2011.

———. "The Real Story of 'The Ten Year Old Boy' in the Shower." March 26, 2013. http://www.framingpaterno.com/exclusive-evidence-real-story-ten-year-old-boy-shower.

———. "'There Was No Cover-up': Fed Agent Tasked with Investigation of Penn State Scandal Breaks Silence." *LawNewz*, March 27, 2017

— INDEX —

CPSIA information can be obtained
at www.ICGtesting.com
Printed in the USA
LVOW12s2321111217
559416LV00018B/920/P

9 781620 067659